BUGGRNER

1999→2001 THE PILOT EDITION

SAITOH 80

MISHIBA 80

NAKAJYO 80

← GAME START

Bus Gamer 1999-2001 The Pilot Edition
Created by Kazuya Minekura

Translation - Alethea Nibley
English Adaptation - Nathan Johnson
Copy Editor - Stephanie Duchin
Retouch and Lettering - Mike Estacio
Production Artist - John Lo
Cover Design - James Lee

Editor - Tim Beedle
Digital Imaging Manager - Chris Buford
Production Manager - Elisabeth Brizzi
Managing Editor - Vy Nguyen
VP of Production - Ron Klamert
Editor-in-Chief - Rob Tokar
Publisher - Mike Kiley
President and C.O.O. - John Parker
C.E.O. and Chief Creative Officer - Stuart Levy

A  Manga

TOKYOPOP Inc.
5900 Wilshire Blvd. Suite 2000
Los Angeles, CA 90036

E-mail: info@TOKYOPOP.com
Come visit us online at www.TOKYOPOP.com

ISBN: 1-59816-327-2

First TOKYOPOP printing: September 2006
10 9 8 7 6 5 4 3 2 1
Printed in the USA

BUS GAMER™

1999→2001 THE PILOT EDITION

**Kazuya
Minekura**

HAMBURG // LONDON // LOS ANGELES // TOKYO

CONTENTS

BUS

1999→20

THREE MONTHS AGO, THE MAN MADE THE PROPOSITION...

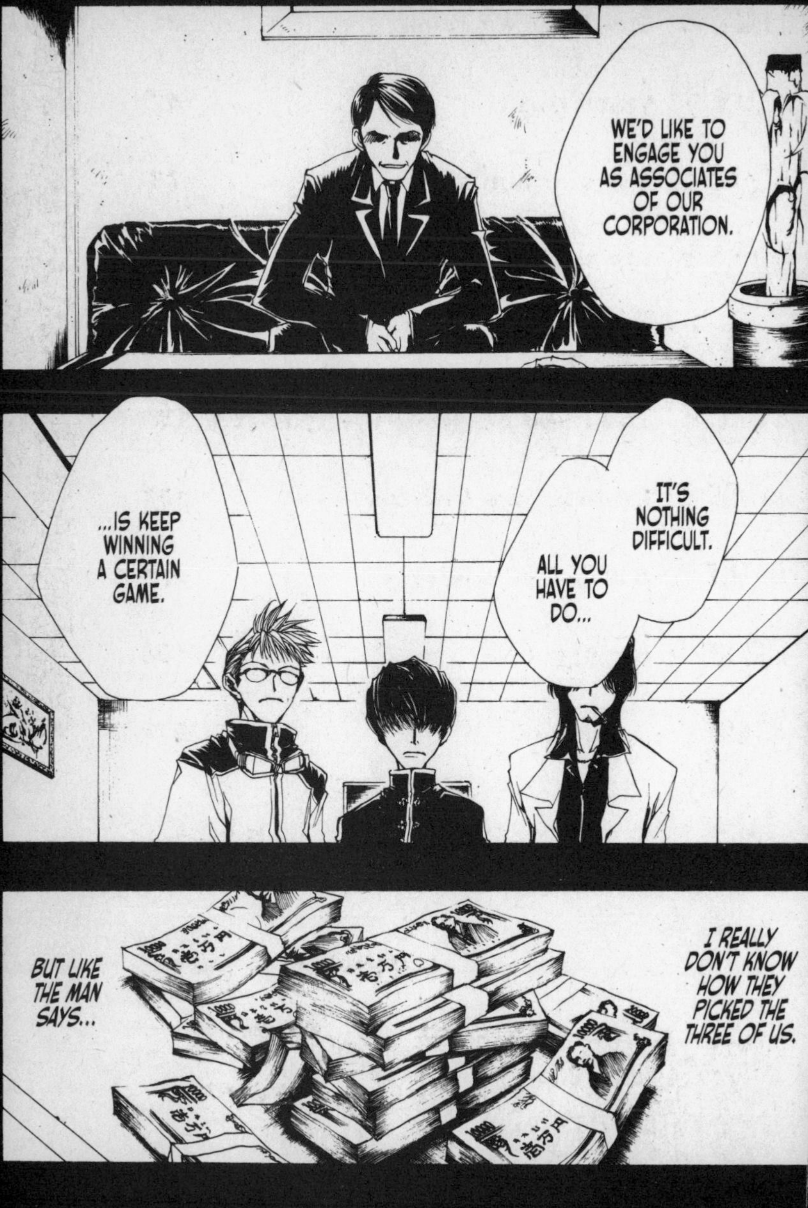
WE'D LIKE TO ENGAGE YOU AS ASSOCIATES OF OUR CORPORATION.
IT'S NOTHING DIFFICULT.
ALL YOU HAVE TO DO...
...IS KEEP WINNING A CERTAIN GAME.
I REALLY DON'T KNOW HOW THEY PICKED THE THREE OF US.
BUT LIKE THE MAN SAYS...

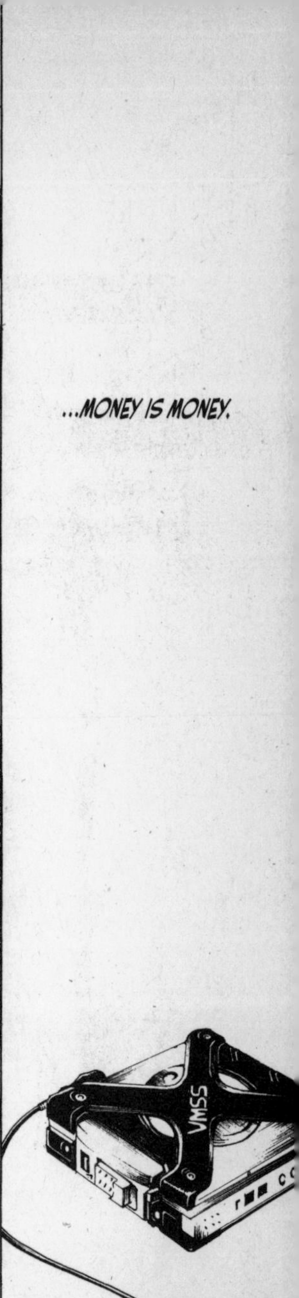
...MONEY IS MONEY.
VMSS
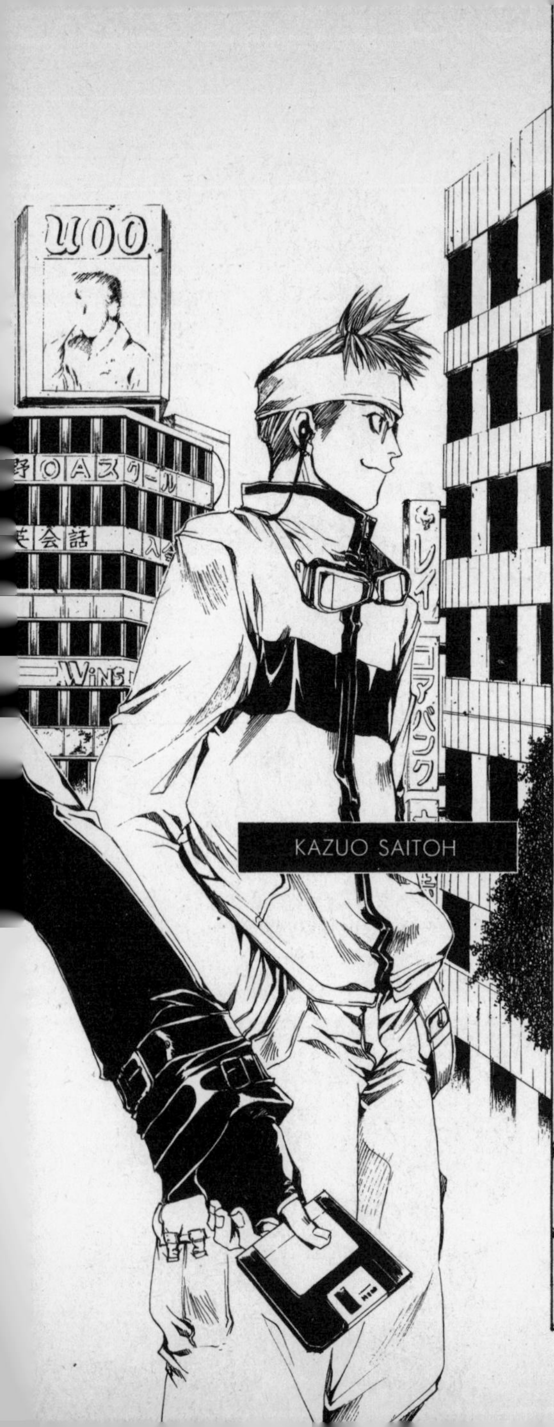
KAZUO SAITOH

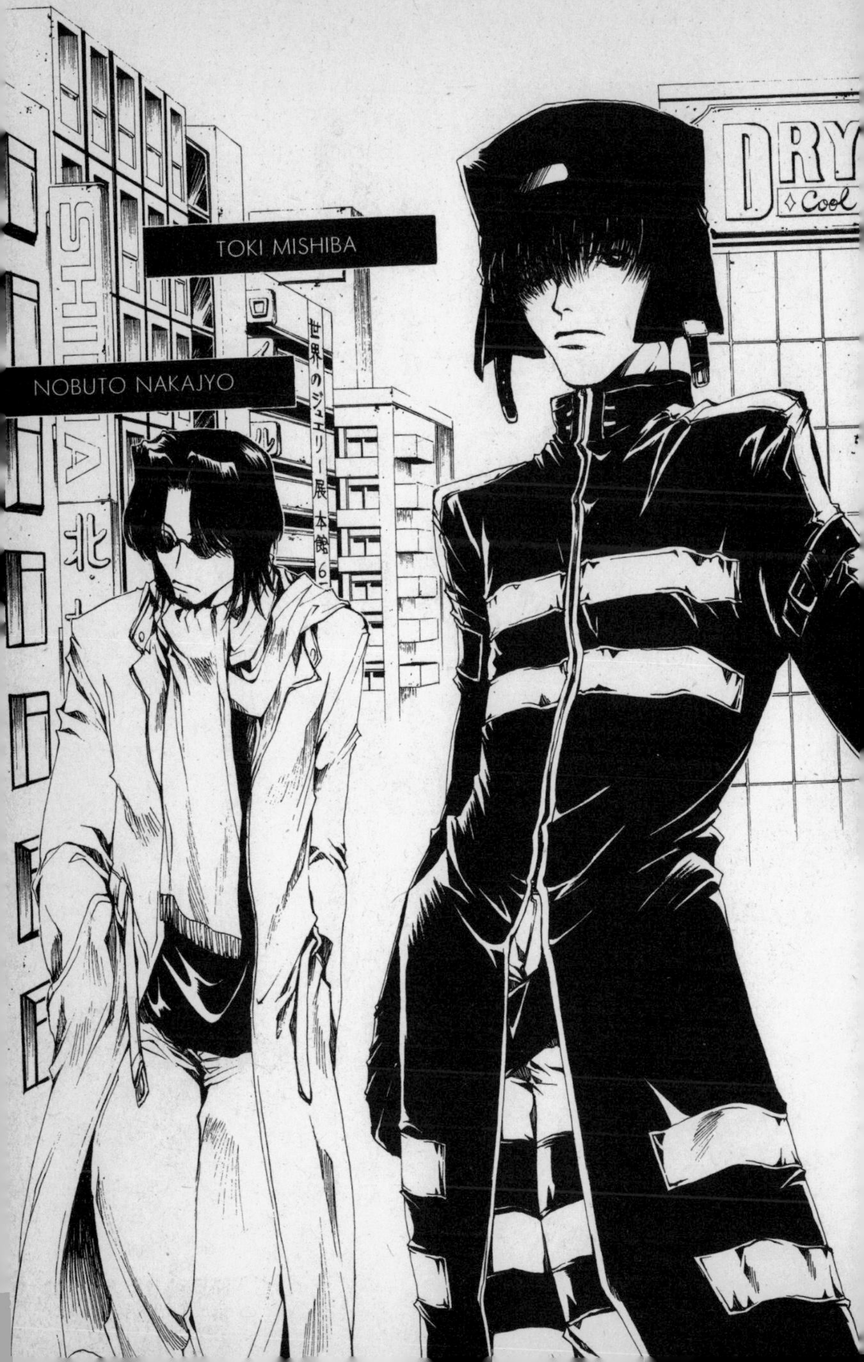
DRY
Cool
TOKI MISHIBA
世界のジュエリー展 本館6
NOBUTO NAKAJYO

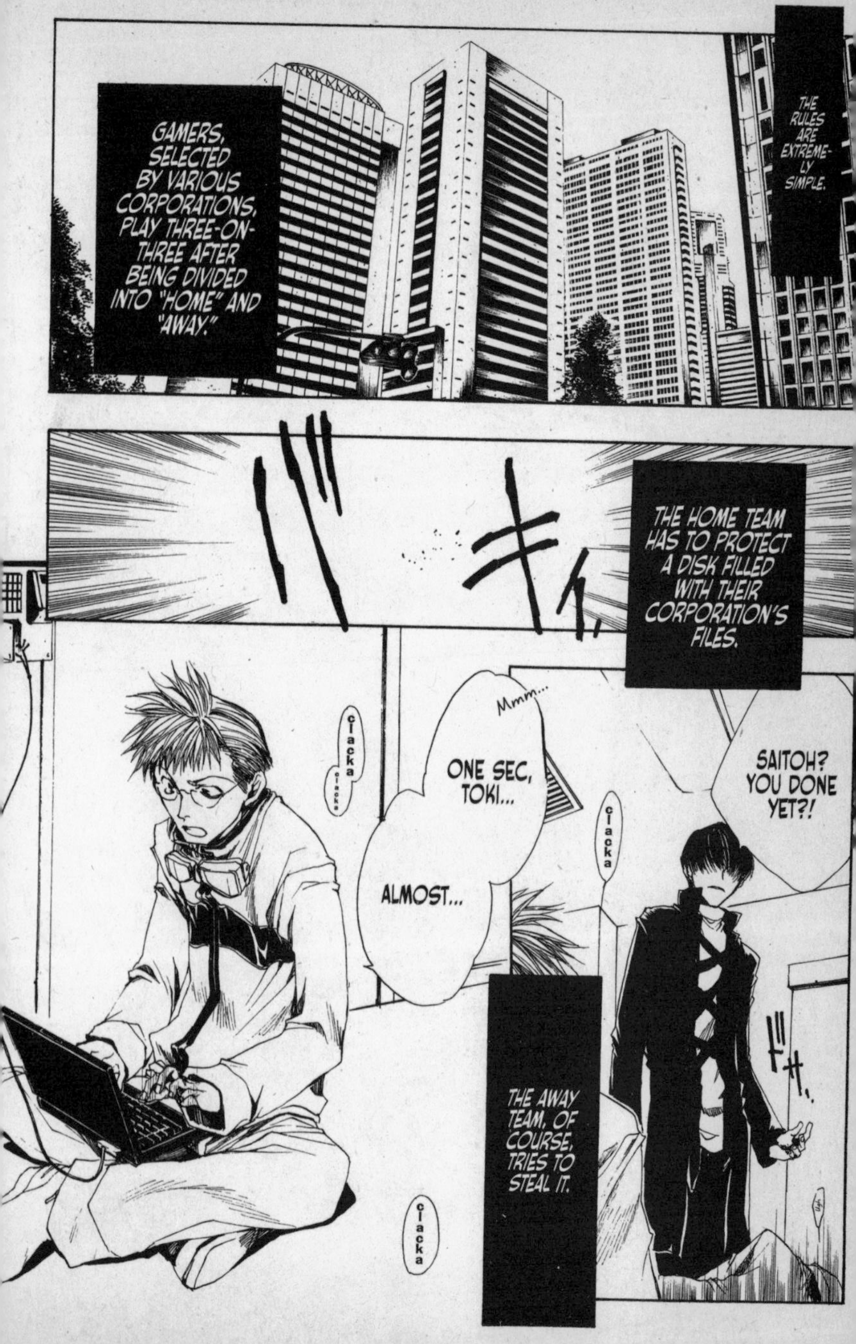
THE RULES ARE EXTREME-LY SIMPLE.
GAMERS, SELECTED BY VARIOUS CORPORATIONS, PLAY THREE-ON-THREE AFTER BEING DIVIDED INTO "HOME" AND "AWAY."
THE HOME TEAM HAS TO PROTECT A DISK FILLED WITH THEIR CORPORATION'S FILES.
バキィ
SAITOH? YOU DONE YET?!
ドサ
THE AWAY TEAM, OF COURSE, TRIES TO STEAL IT.
clacka
Mmm...
ONE SEC, TOKI...
ALMOST...
clacka
clacka
clacka

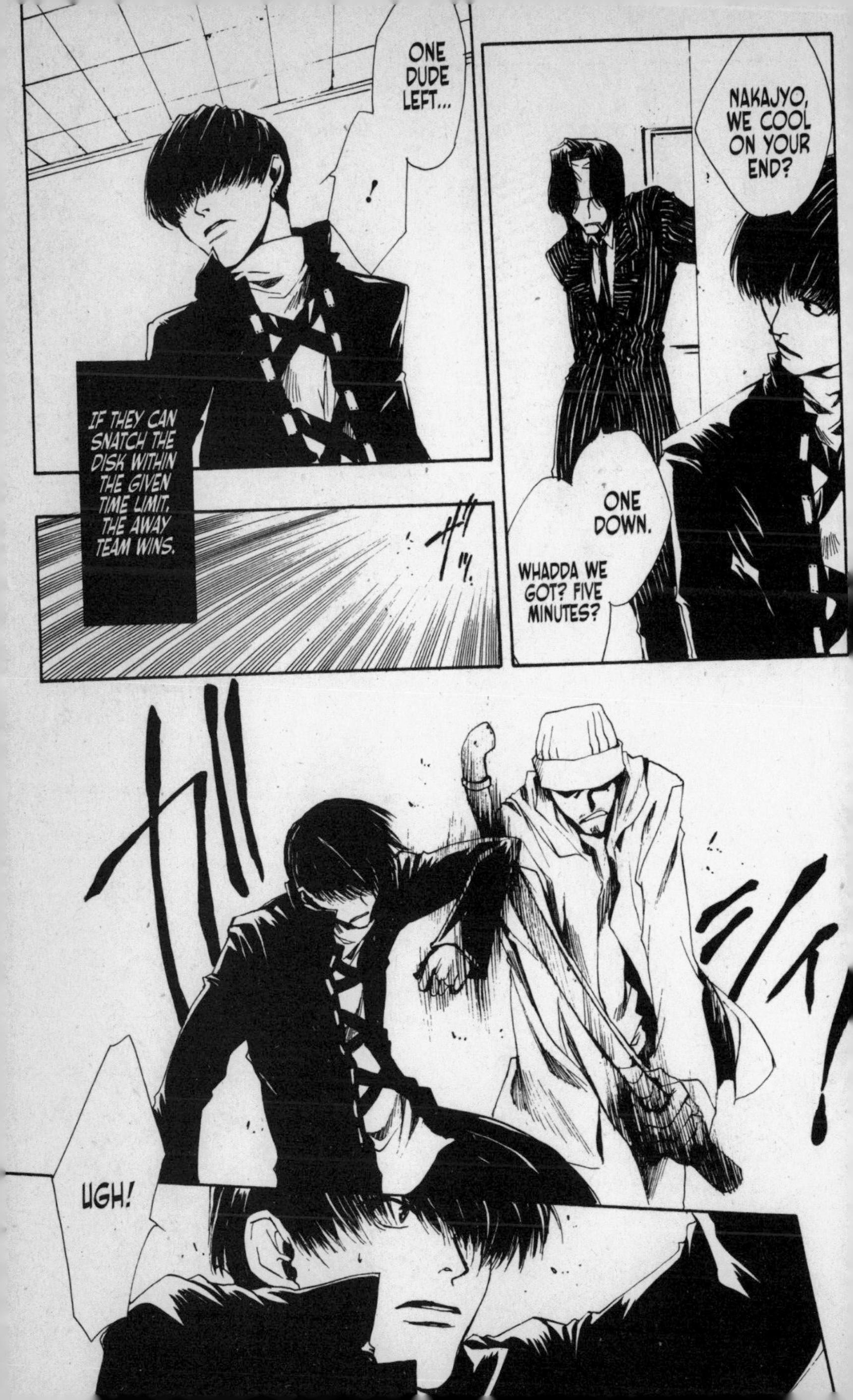
NAKAJYO, WE COOL ON YOUR END?
ONE DOWN.
WHADDA WE GOT? FIVE MINUTES?
ONE DUDE LEFT...
!
IF THEY CAN SNATCH THE DISK WITHIN THE GIVEN TIME LIMIT, THE AWAY TEAM WINS.
UGH!

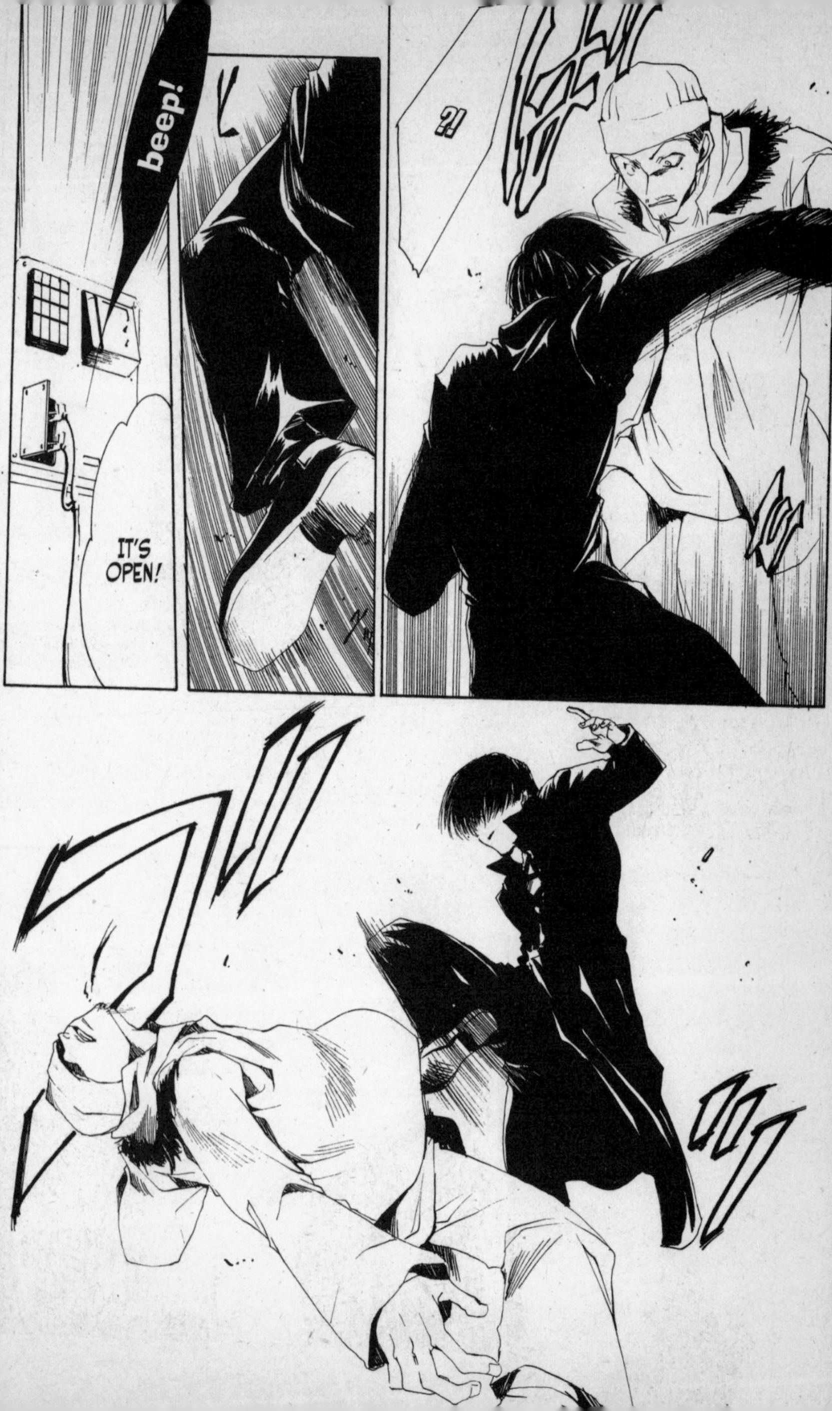
?!
beep!
IT'S OPEN!

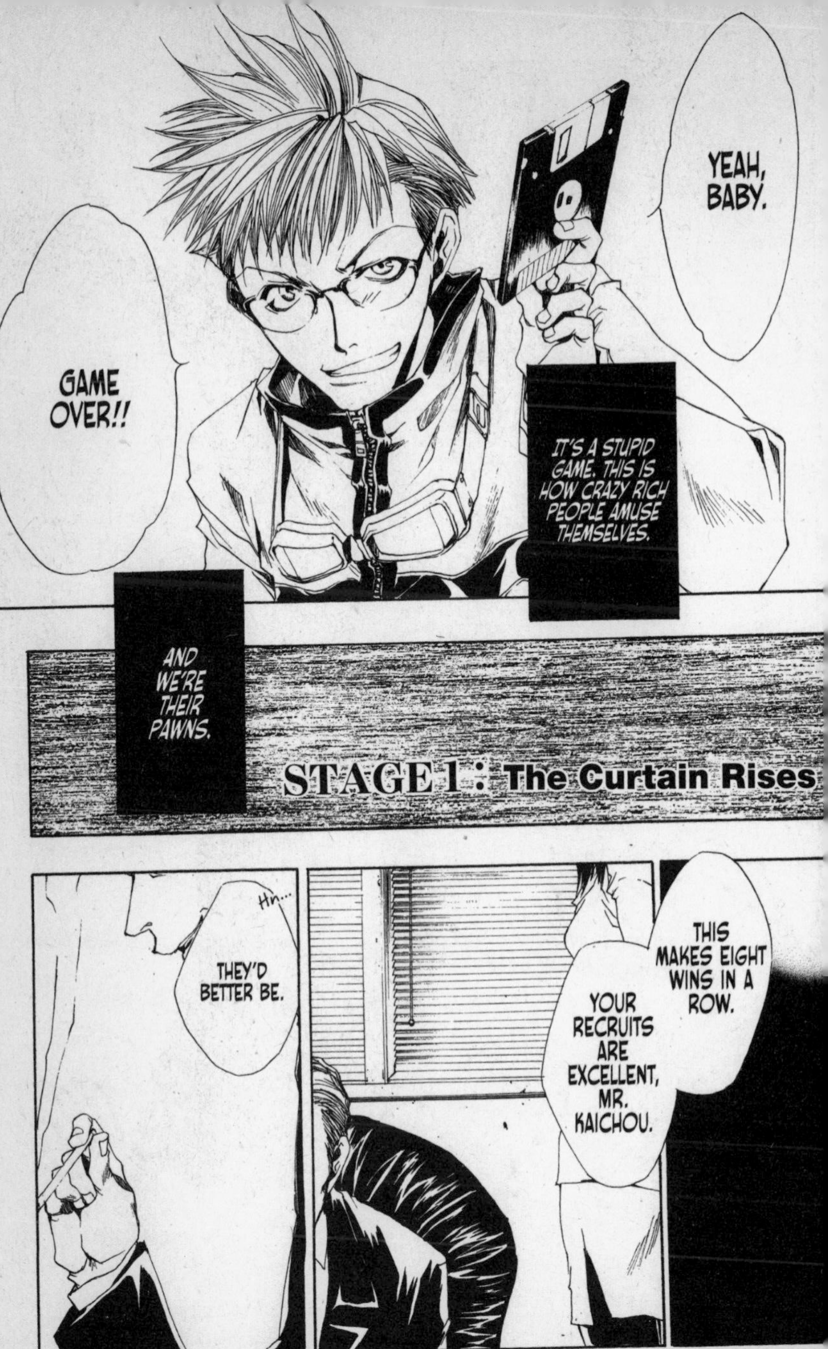
YEAH, BABY.
GAME OVER!!
IT'S A STUPID GAME. THIS IS HOW CRAZY RICH PEOPLE AMUSE THEMSELVES.
AND WE'RE THEIR PAWNS.
STAGE 1 : The Curtain Rises
THIS MAKES EIGHT WINS IN A ROW.
YOUR RECRUITS ARE EXCELLENT, MR. KAICHOU.
Hn...
THEY'D BETTER BE.

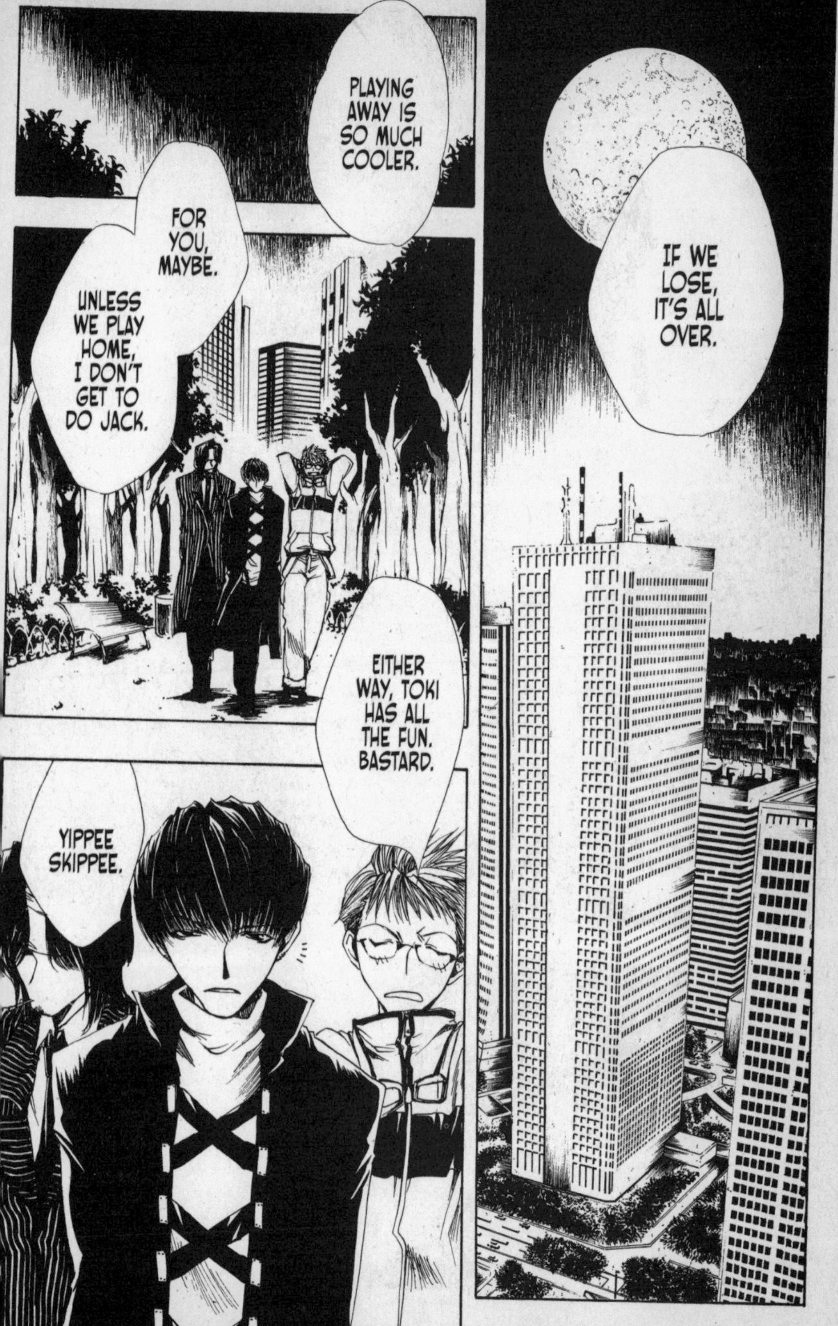
IF WE LOSE, IT'S ALL OVER.
PLAYING AWAY IS SO MUCH COOLER.
FOR YOU, MAYBE.
UNLESS WE PLAY HOME, I DON'T GET TO DO JACK.
EITHER WAY, TOKI HAS ALL THE FUN. BASTARD.
YIPPEE SKIPPEE.

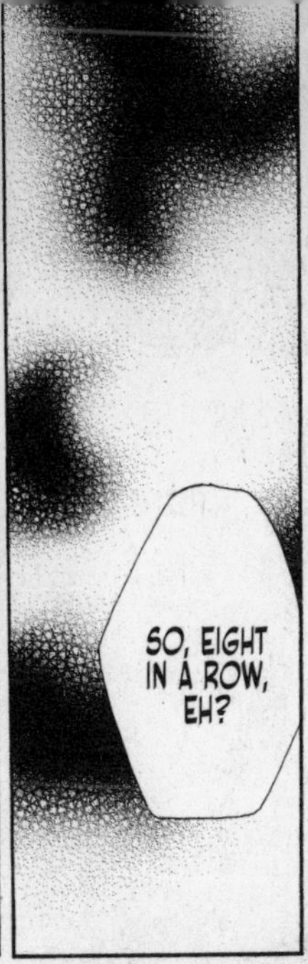
SO, EIGHT IN A ROW, EH?

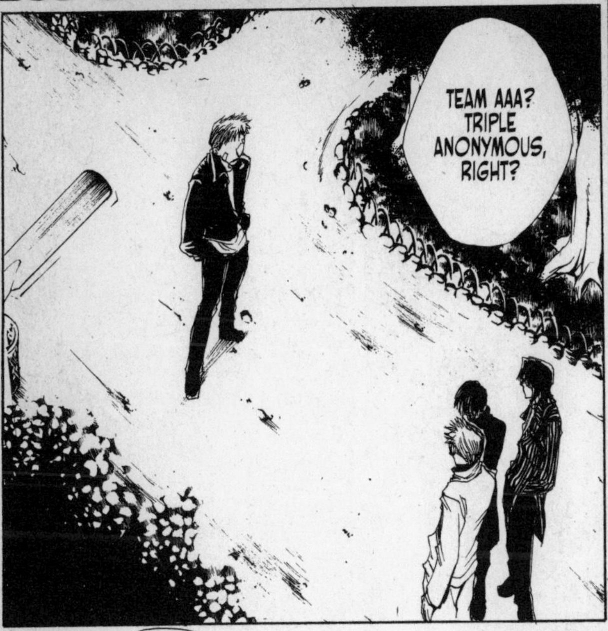
TEAM AAA? TRIPLE ANONYMOUS, RIGHT?

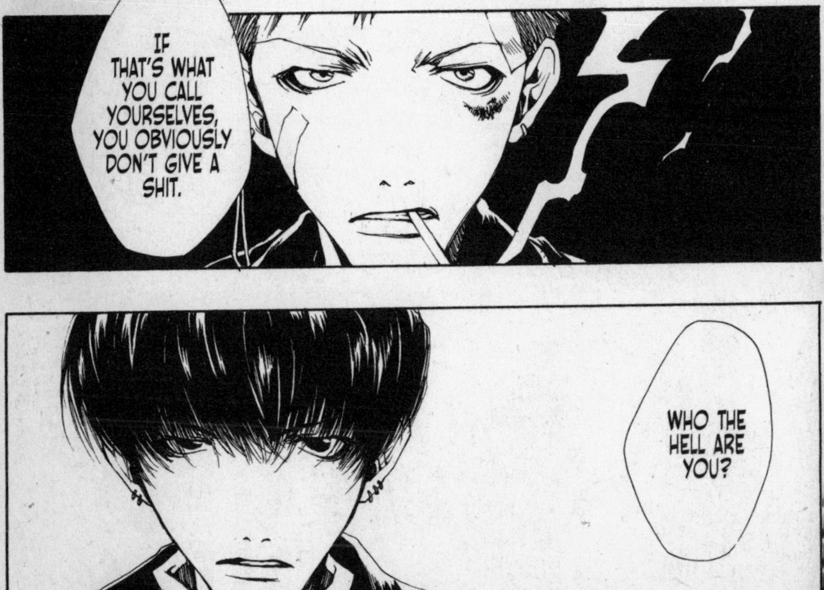
IF THAT'S WHAT YOU CALL YOURSELVES, YOU OBVIOUSLY DON'T GIVE A SHIT.
WHO THE HELL ARE YOU?

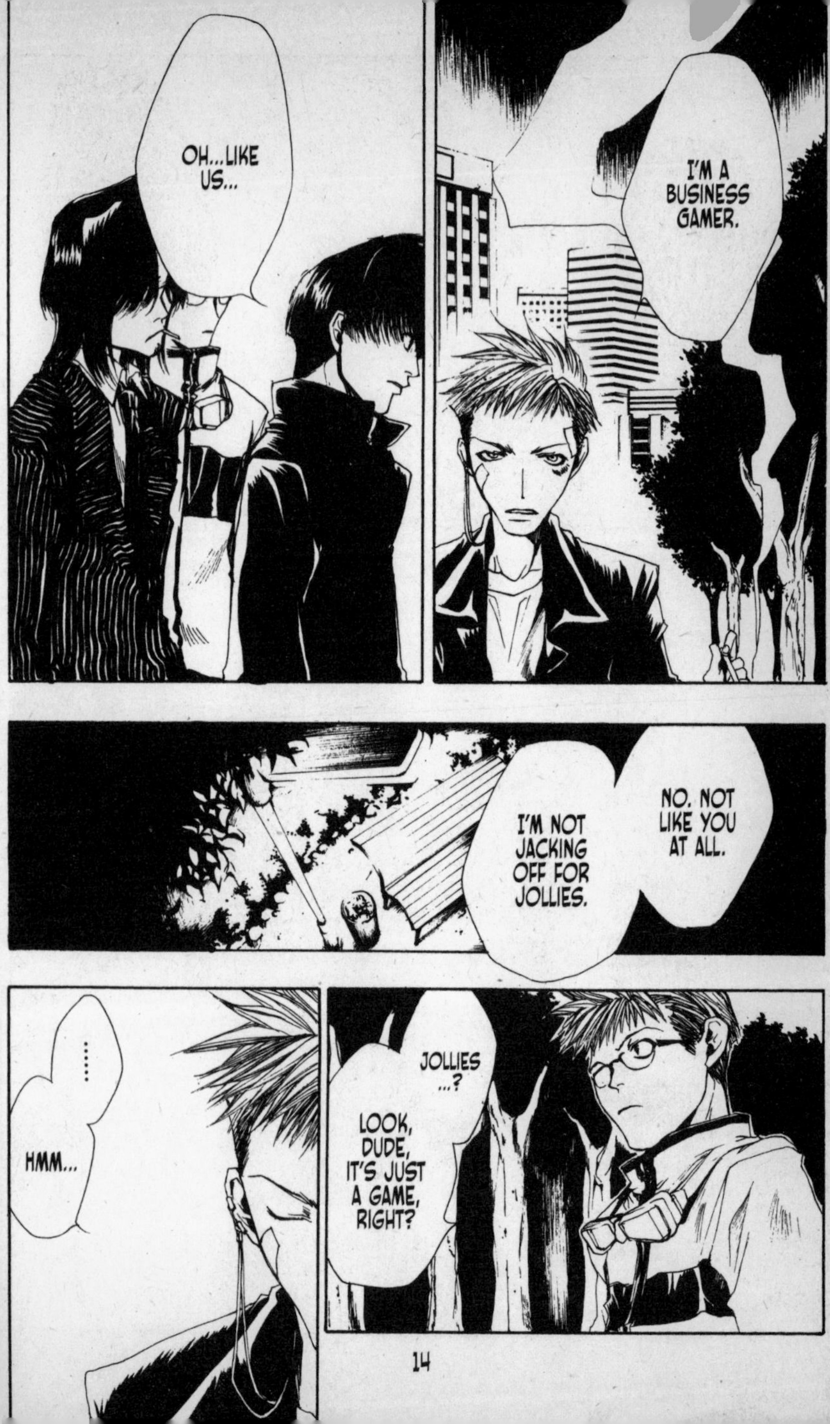
I'M A BUSINESS GAMER.
OH...LIKE US...
NO. NOT LIKE YOU AT ALL.
I'M NOT JACKING OFF FOR JOLLIES.
JOLLIES ...?
LOOK, DUDE, IT'S JUST A GAME, RIGHT?
......
HMM...

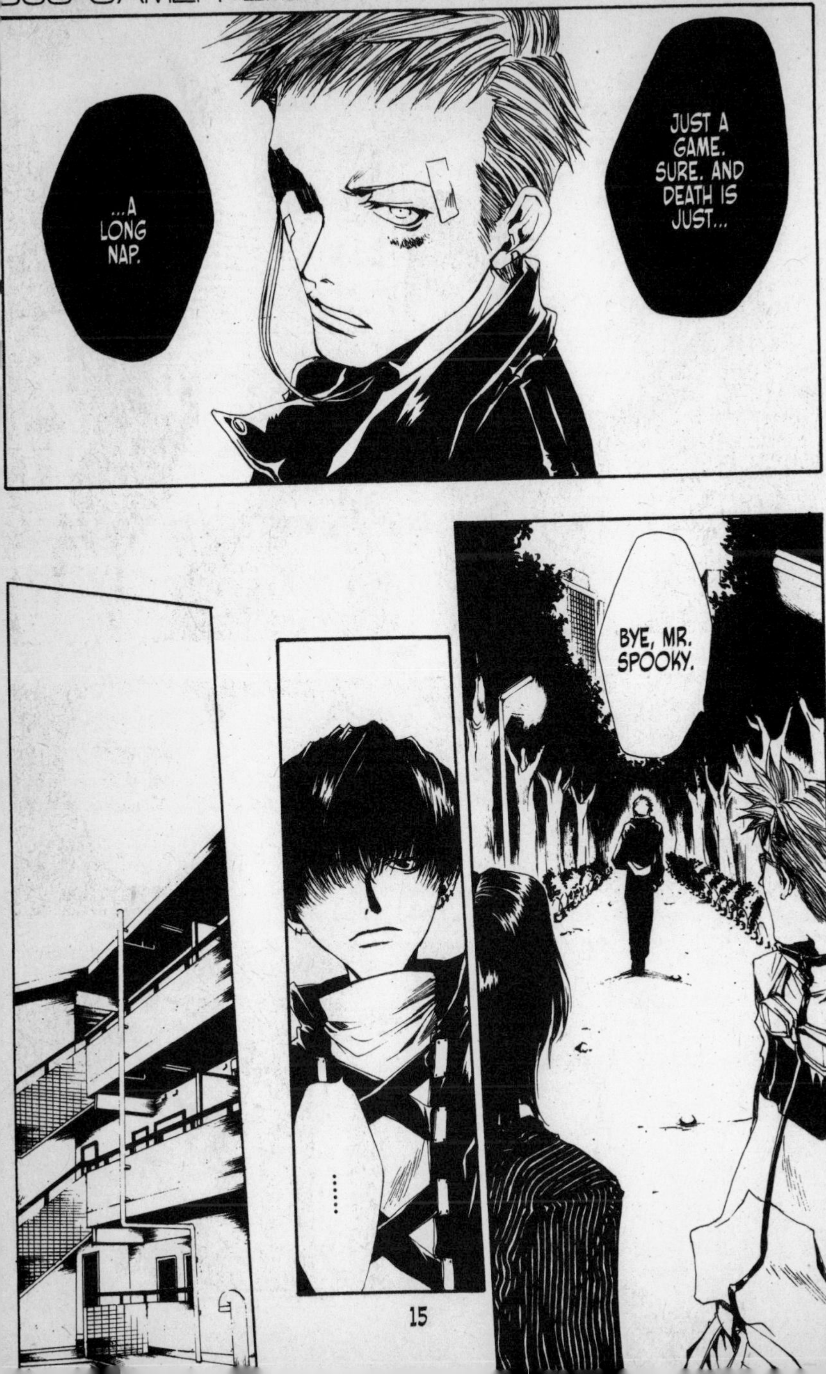
JUST A GAME. SURE. AND DEATH IS JUST...
...A LONG NAP.
BYE, MR. SPOOKY.
......

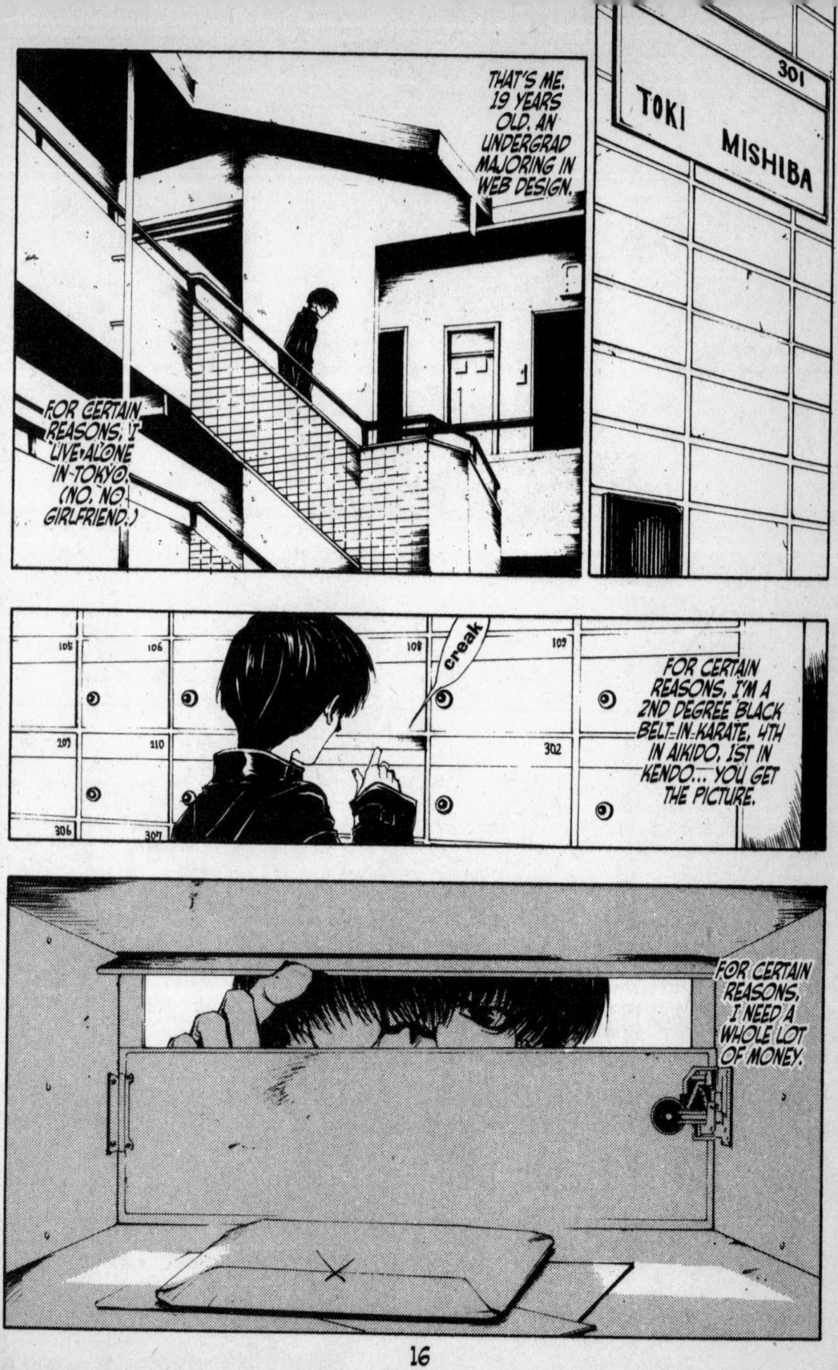
301
TOKI MISHIBA
THAT'S ME. 19 YEARS OLD. AN UNDERGRAD MAJORING IN WEB DESIGN.
FOR CERTAIN REASONS, I LIVE ALONE IN TOKYO. (NO, NO GIRLFRIEND.)
FOR CERTAIN REASONS, I'M A 2ND DEGREE BLACK BELT IN KARATE, 4TH IN AIKIDO, 1ST IN KENDO... YOU GET THE PICTURE.
creak
FOR CERTAIN REASONS, I NEED A WHOLE LOT OF MONEY.

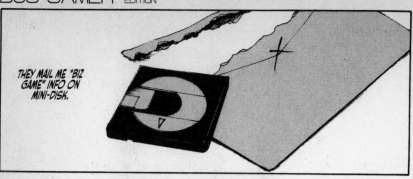

THEY MAIL ME "BIZ GAME" INFO ON MINI-DISK.
THE DATE OF THE GAME, THE NAME OF THE OTHER TEAM, OUR STARTING LOCATION, THE TIME LIMIT...
I'M SUPPOSED TO MEMORIZE ALL OF IT AND DELETE THE DISK.
WE CALL OURSELVES "TEAM AAA." TRIPLE ANONYMOUS. I KEEP WONDERING HOW EXACTLY THEY CHOSE THE THREE OF US TO SLAP TOGETHER.
押ボタン式
"YOU YOUNG MEN HAVE THE SKILL AND TALENT NECESSARY TO WIN OUR GAME, AND I KNOW EACH OF YOU COULD GREATLY USE THE MONEY..."
THAT'S ALL HE SAID. THAT'S WHAT ME, KAZUO SAITOH AND NOBUTO NAKAJYO HAVE IN COMMON.
ONE PAIR CARLTON
100s

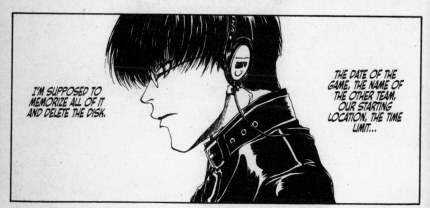

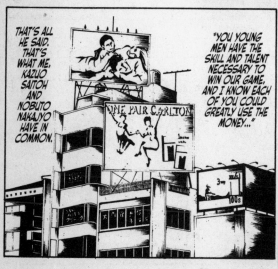

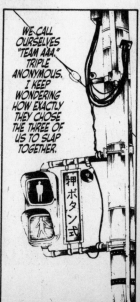

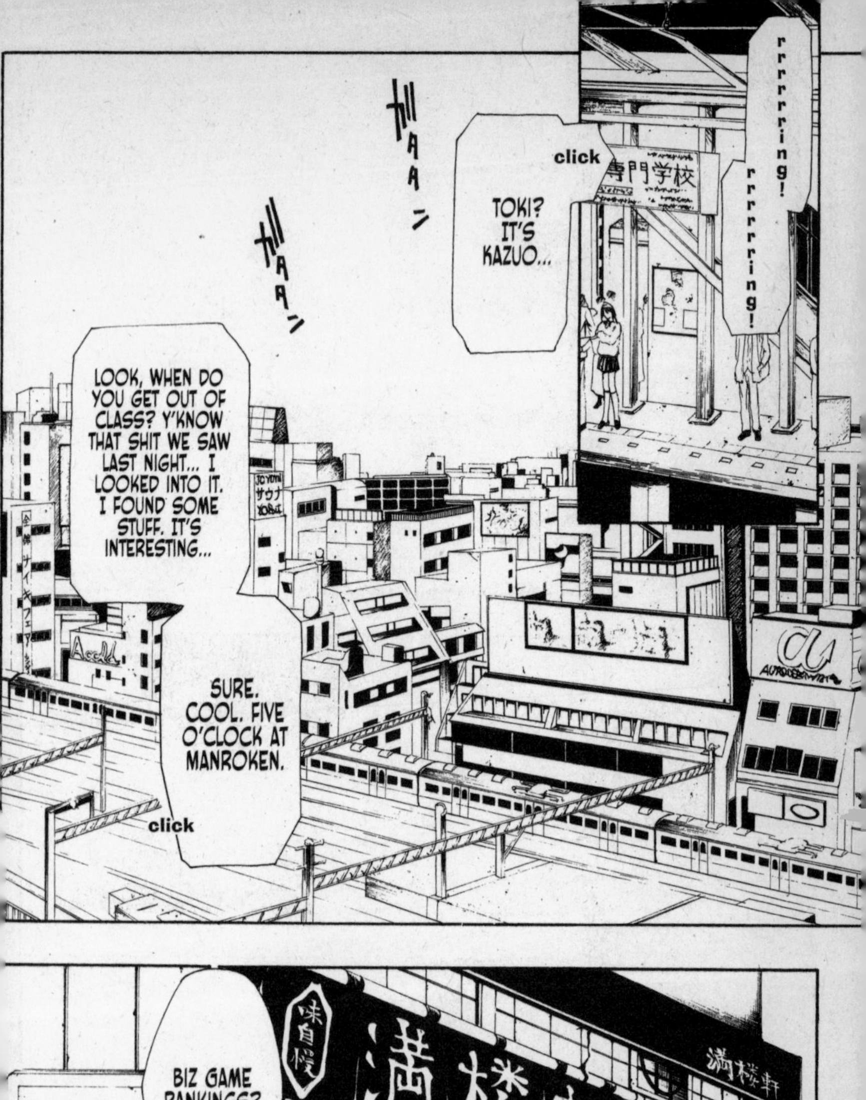
rrrrrring!
rrrrrring!
click
TOKI? IT'S KAZUO...
LOOK, WHEN DO YOU GET OUT OF CLASS? Y'KNOW THAT SHIT WE SAW LAST NIGHT... I LOOKED INTO IT. I FOUND SOME STUFF. IT'S INTERESTING...
SURE. COOL. FIVE O'CLOCK AT MANROKEN.
click

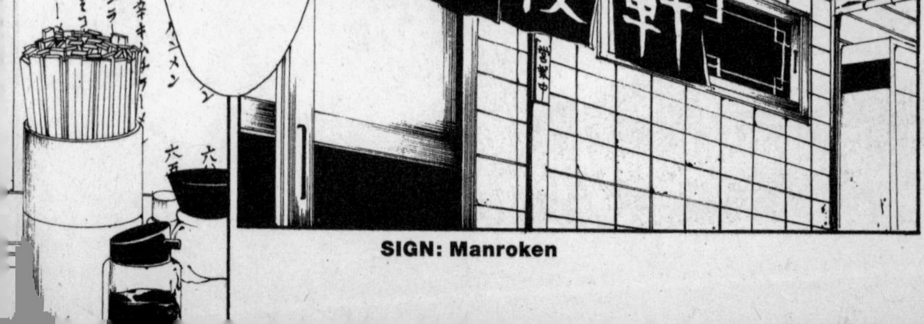
満楼軒
BIZ GAME RANKINGS?

SIGN: Manroken

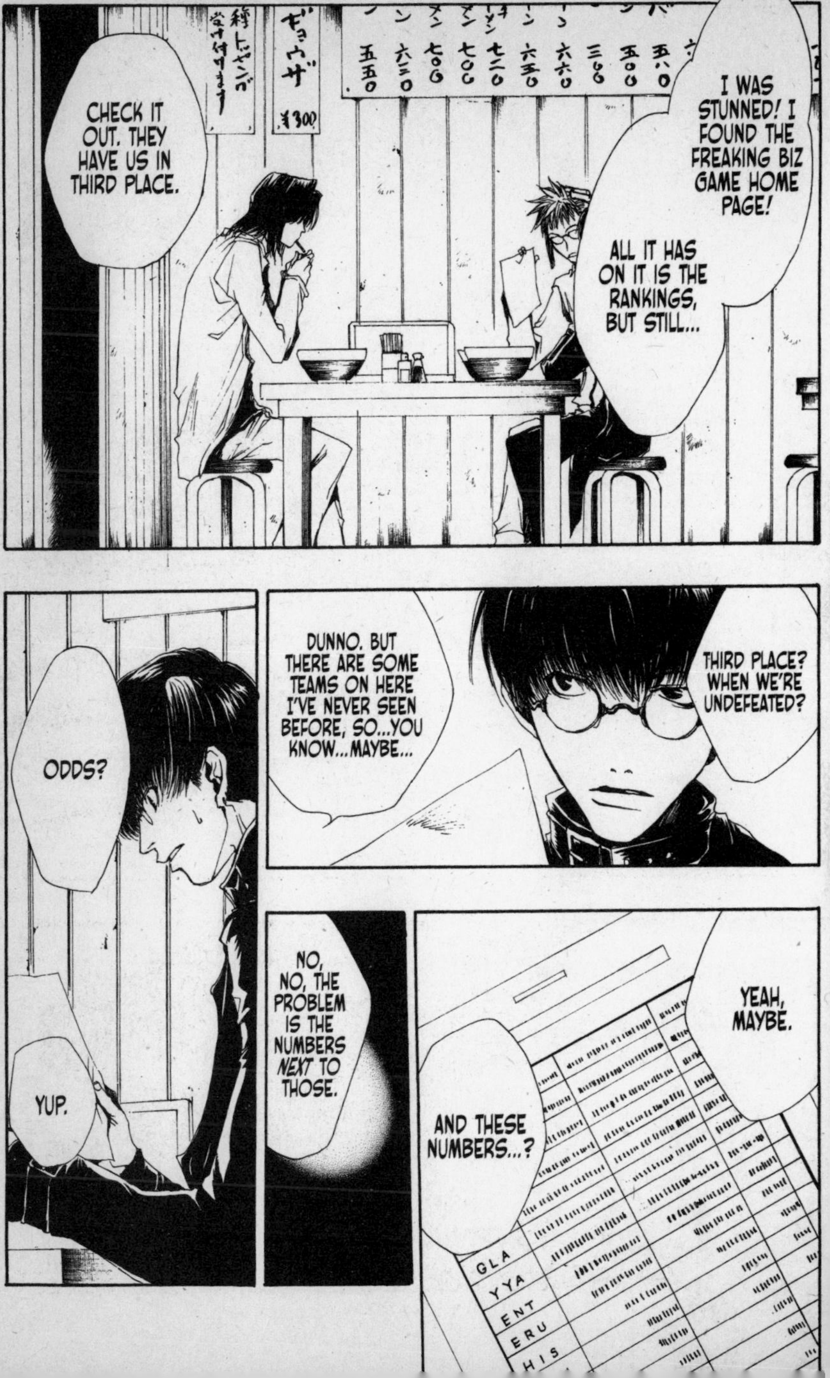
I WAS STUNNED! I FOUND THE FREAKING BIZ GAME HOME PAGE!
ALL IT HAS ON IT IS THE RANKINGS, BUT STILL...
CHECK IT OUT. THEY HAVE US IN THIRD PLACE.
ギョウザ ¥300
THIRD PLACE? WHEN WE'RE UNDEFEATED?
DUNNO. BUT THERE ARE SOME TEAMS ON HERE I'VE NEVER SEEN BEFORE, SO...YOU KNOW...MAYBE...
YEAH, MAYBE.
AND THESE NUMBERS...?
GLA
YYA
ENT
ERU
HIS
NO, NO, THE PROBLEM IS THE NUMBERS *NEXT* TO THOSE.
ODDS?
YUP.

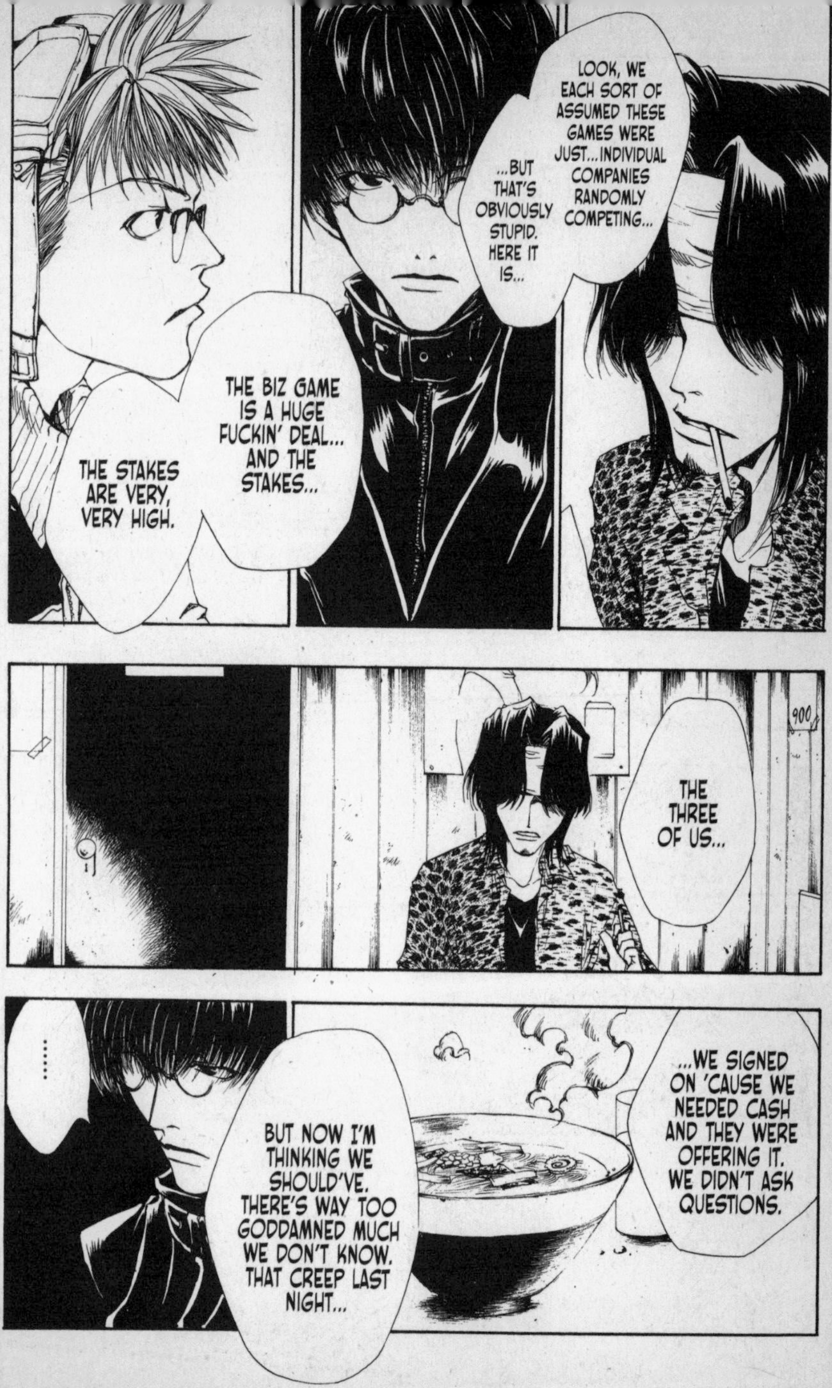
LOOK, WE EACH SORT OF ASSUMED THESE GAMES WERE JUST...INDIVIDUAL COMPANIES RANDOMLY COMPETING...
...BUT THAT'S OBVIOUSLY STUPID. HERE IT IS...
THE BIZ GAME IS A HUGE FUCKIN' DEAL... AND THE STAKES...
THE STAKES ARE VERY, VERY HIGH.
900
THE THREE OF US...
...WE SIGNED ON 'CAUSE WE NEEDED CASH AND THEY WERE OFFERING IT. WE DIDN'T ASK QUESTIONS.
BUT NOW I'M THINKING WE SHOULD'VE. THERE'S WAY TOO GODDAMNED MUCH WE DON'T KNOW. THAT CREEP LAST NIGHT...
......

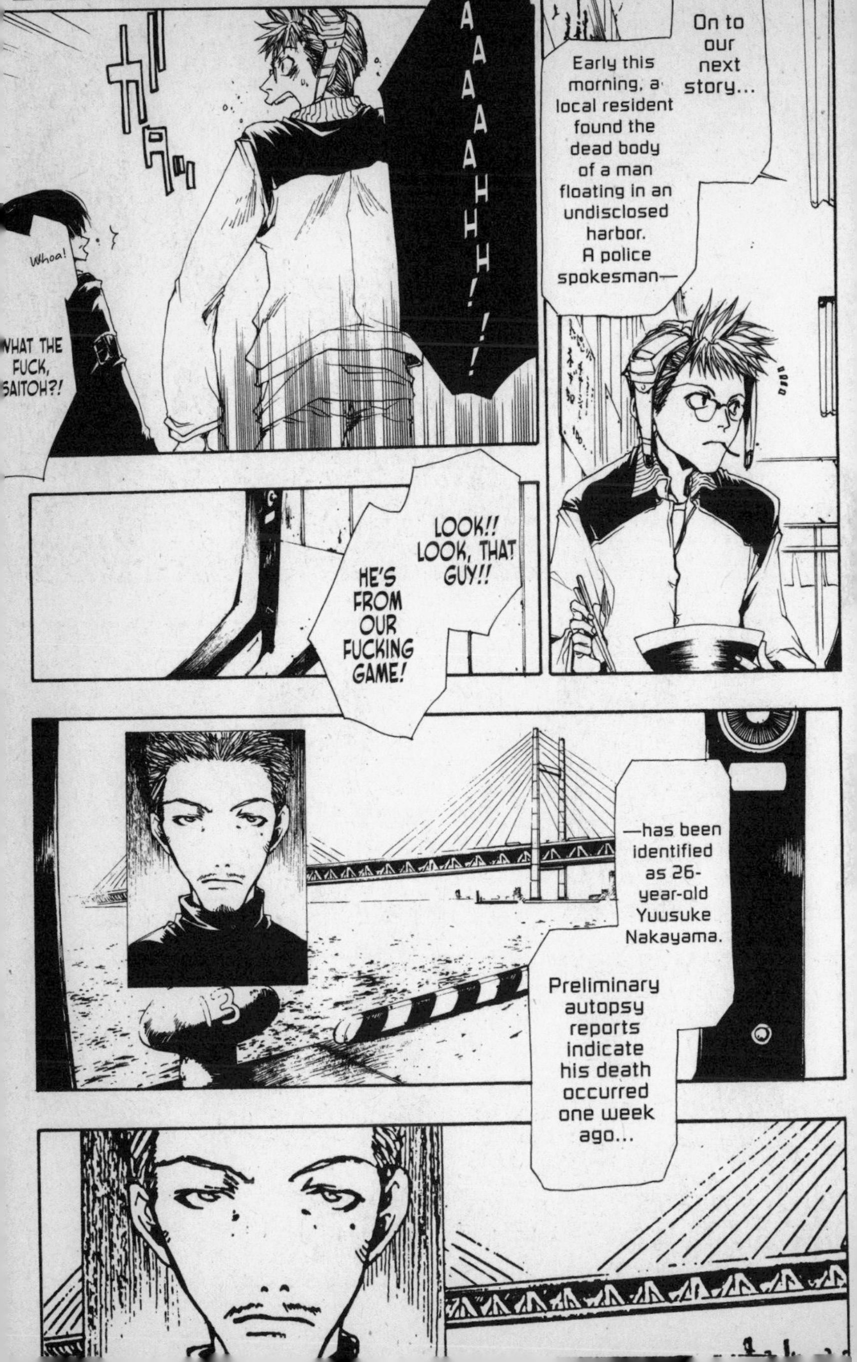
On to our next story...
Early this morning, a local resident found the dead body of a man floating in an undisclosed harbor. A police spokesman—
AAAAAHH!!!
ガタッ
Whoa!
WHAT THE FUCK, SAITOH?!
LOOK!! LOOK, THAT GUY!!
HE'S FROM OUR FUCKING GAME!
—has been identified as 26-year-old Yuusuke Nakayama.
Preliminary autopsy reports indicate his death occurred one week ago...

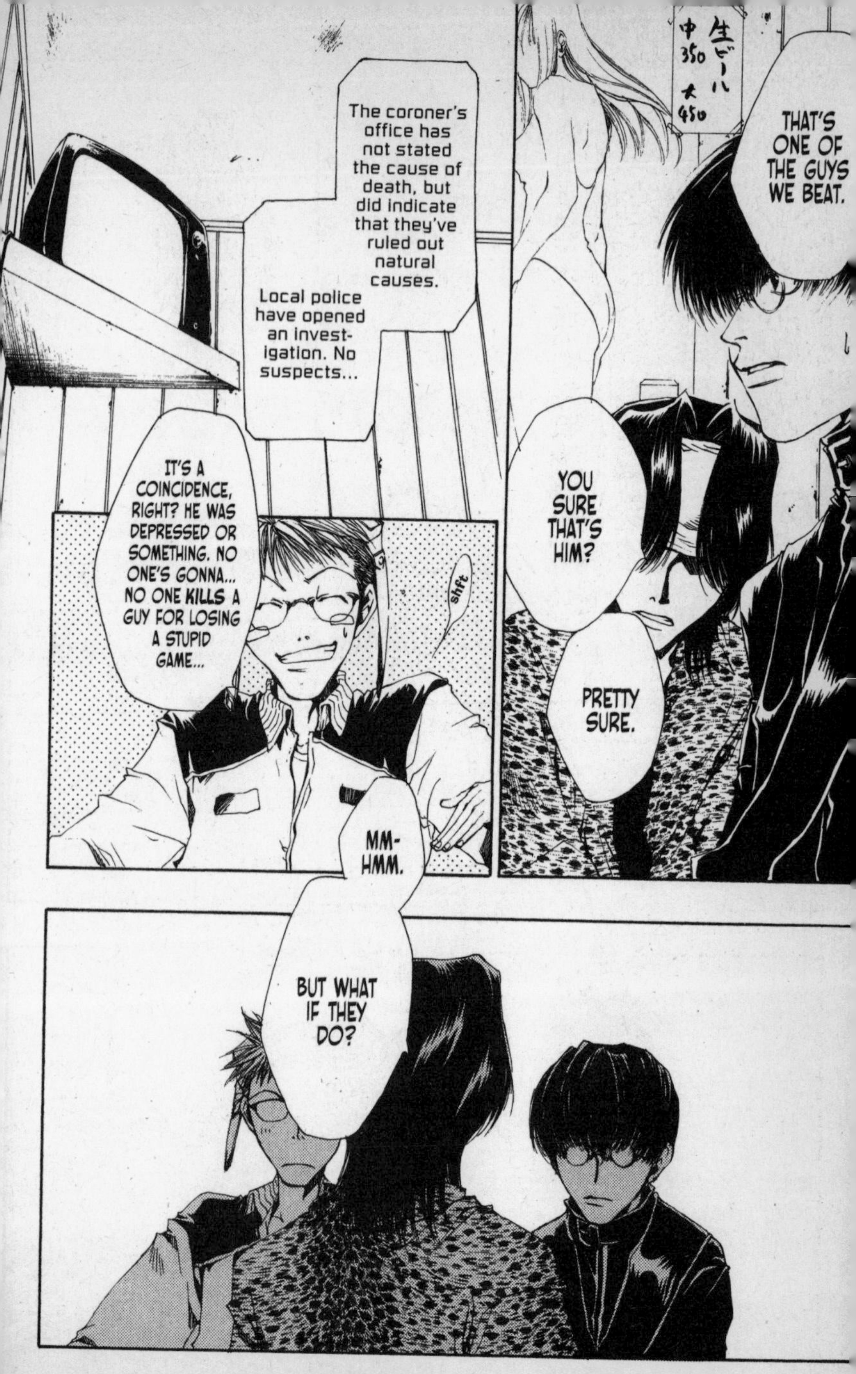
生ビール
中350
大450
THAT'S ONE OF THE GUYS WE BEAT.
YOU SURE THAT'S HIM?
PRETTY SURE.
The coroner's office has not stated the cause of death, but did indicate that they've ruled out natural causes.
Local police have opened an investigation. No suspects...
IT'S A COINCIDENCE, RIGHT? HE WAS DEPRESSED OR SOMETHING. NO ONE'S GONNA... NO ONE **KILLS** A GUY FOR LOSING A STUPID GAME...
shft
MM-HMM.
BUT WHAT IF THEY DO?

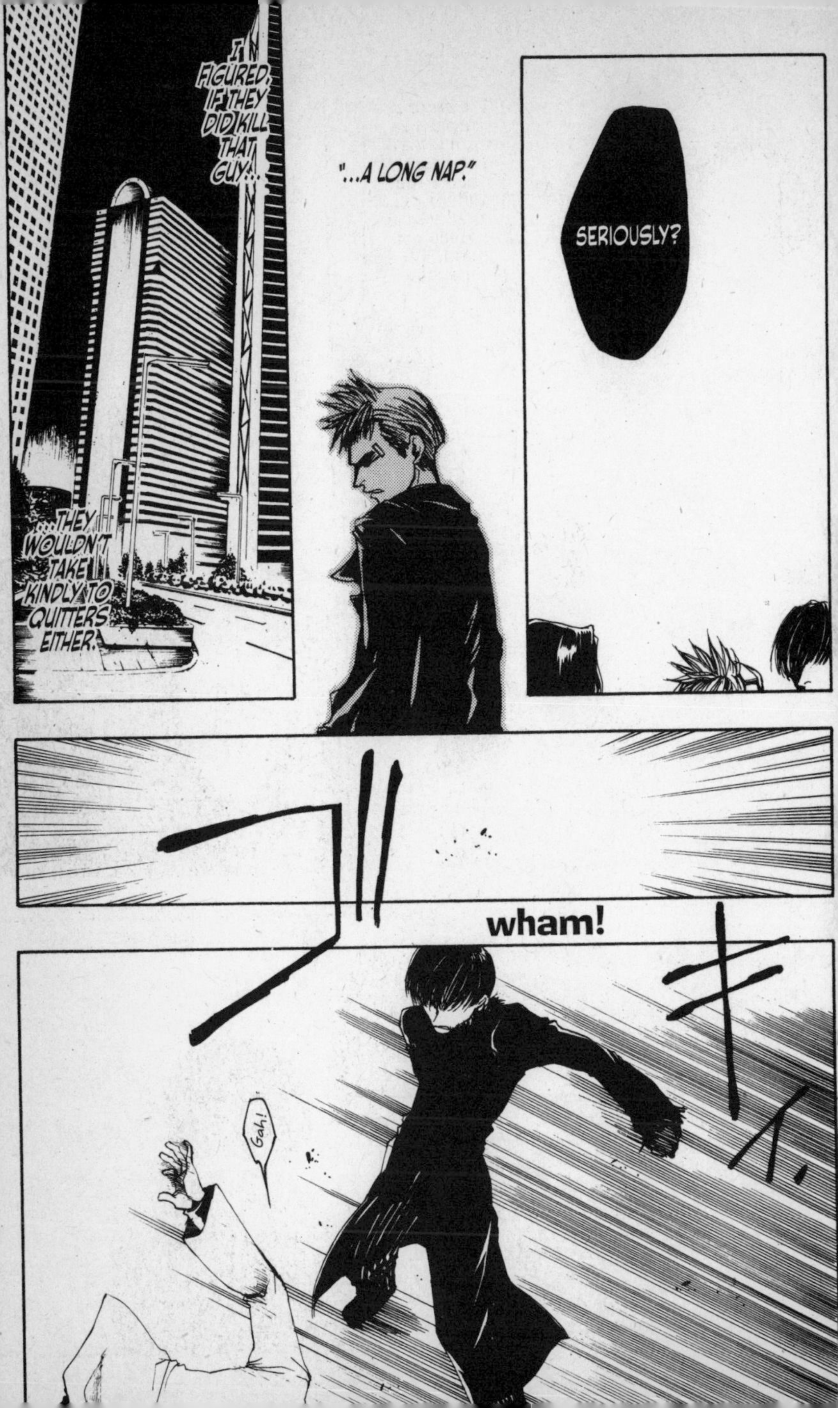
SERIOUSLY?
"...A LONG NAP."
I FIGURED, IF THEY DID KILL THAT GUY...
...THEY WOULDN'T TAKE KINDLY TO QUITTERS EITHER.
wham!
Gah!

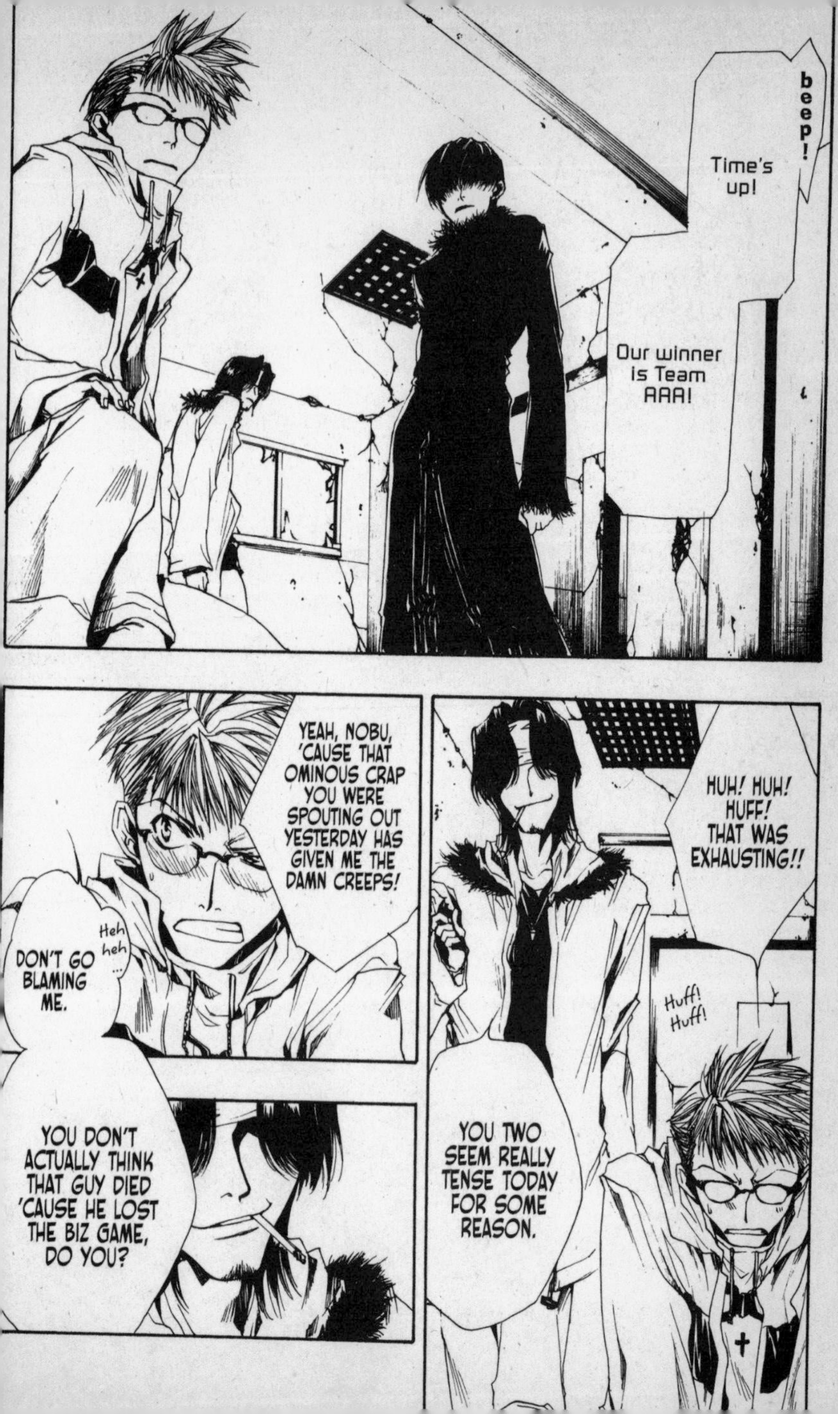
beep!
Time's up!
Our winner is Team AAA!
HUH! HUH! HUFF! THAT WAS EXHAUSTING!!
Huff! Huff!
YOU TWO SEEM REALLY TENSE TODAY FOR SOME REASON.
YEAH, NOBU, 'CAUSE THAT OMINOUS CRAP YOU WERE SPOUTING OUT YESTERDAY HAS GIVEN ME THE DAMN CREEPS!
Heh heh...
DON'T GO BLAMING ME.
YOU DON'T ACTUALLY THINK THAT GUY DIED 'CAUSE HE LOST THE BIZ GAME, DO YOU?

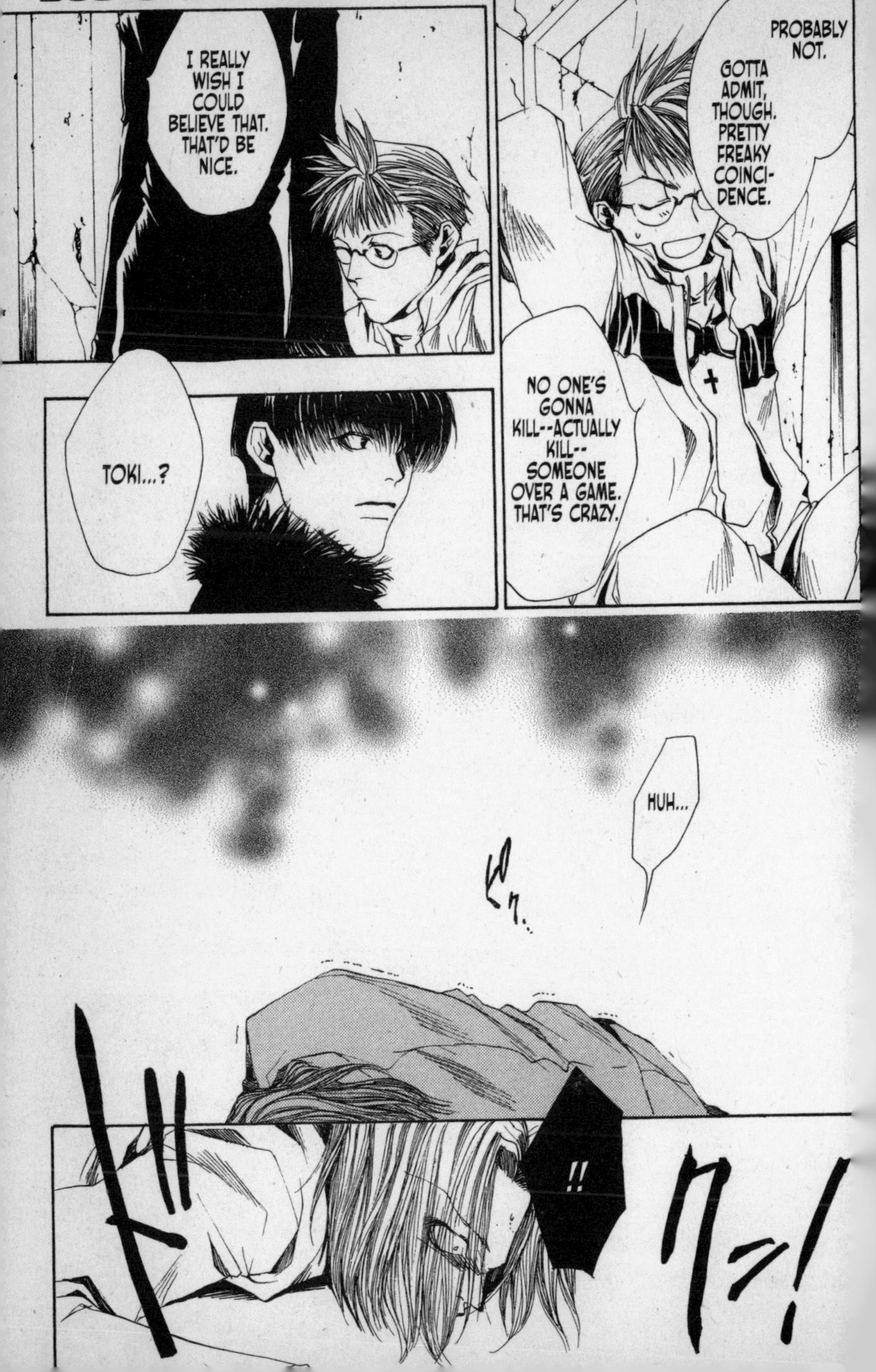
PROBABLY NOT.
GOTTA ADMIT, THOUGH. PRETTY FREAKY COINCI-DENCE.
NO ONE'S GONNA KILL--ACTUALLY KILL--SOMEONE OVER A GAME. THAT'S CRAZY.
I REALLY WISH I COULD BELIEVE THAT. THAT'D BE NICE.
TOKI...?
HUH...
!!

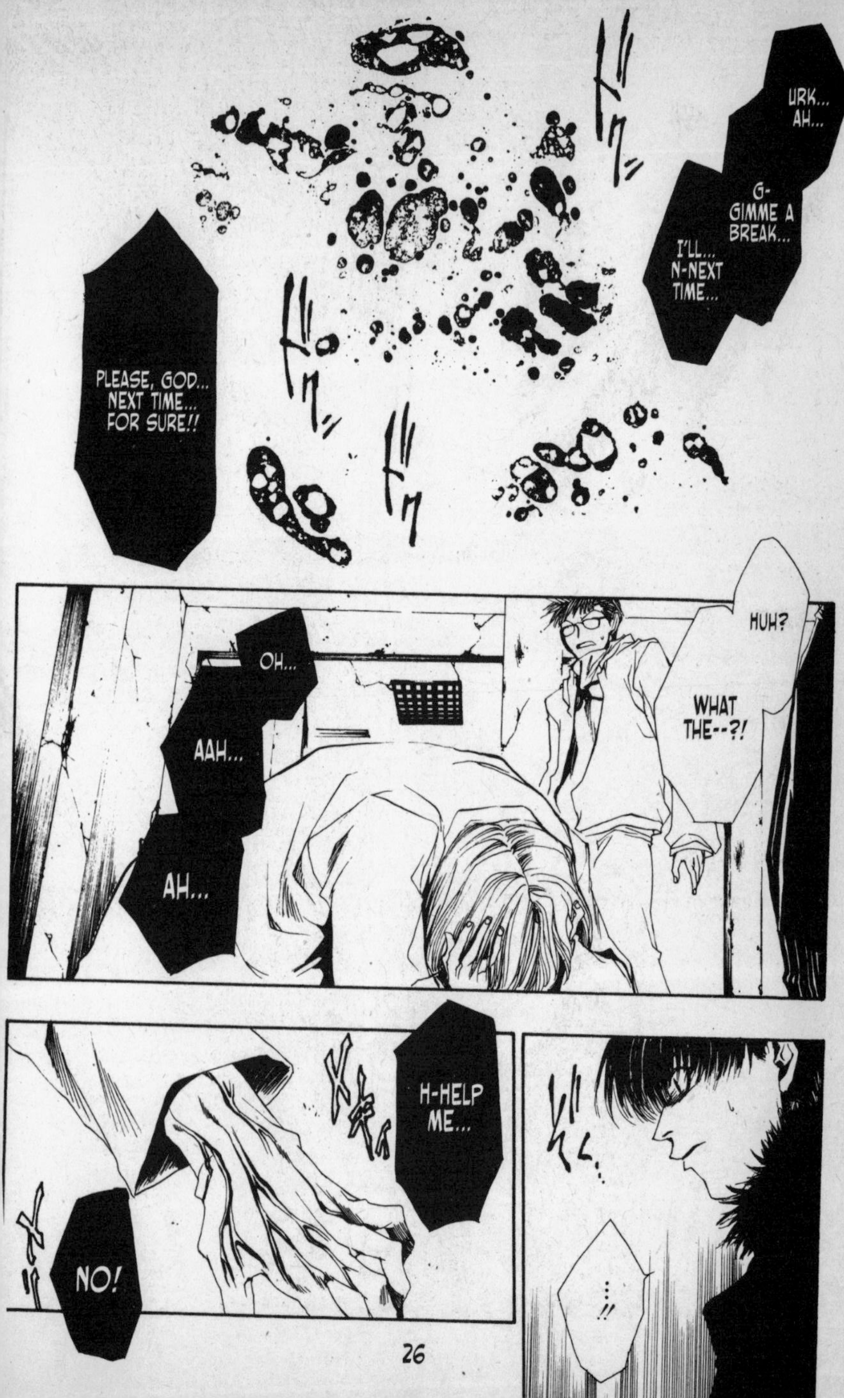
URK... AH...
G- GIMME A BREAK...
I'LL... N-NEXT TIME...
PLEASE, GOD... NEXT TIME... FOR SURE!!
HUH?
WHAT THE--?!
OH...
AAH...
AH...
...!!
H-HELP ME...
NO!

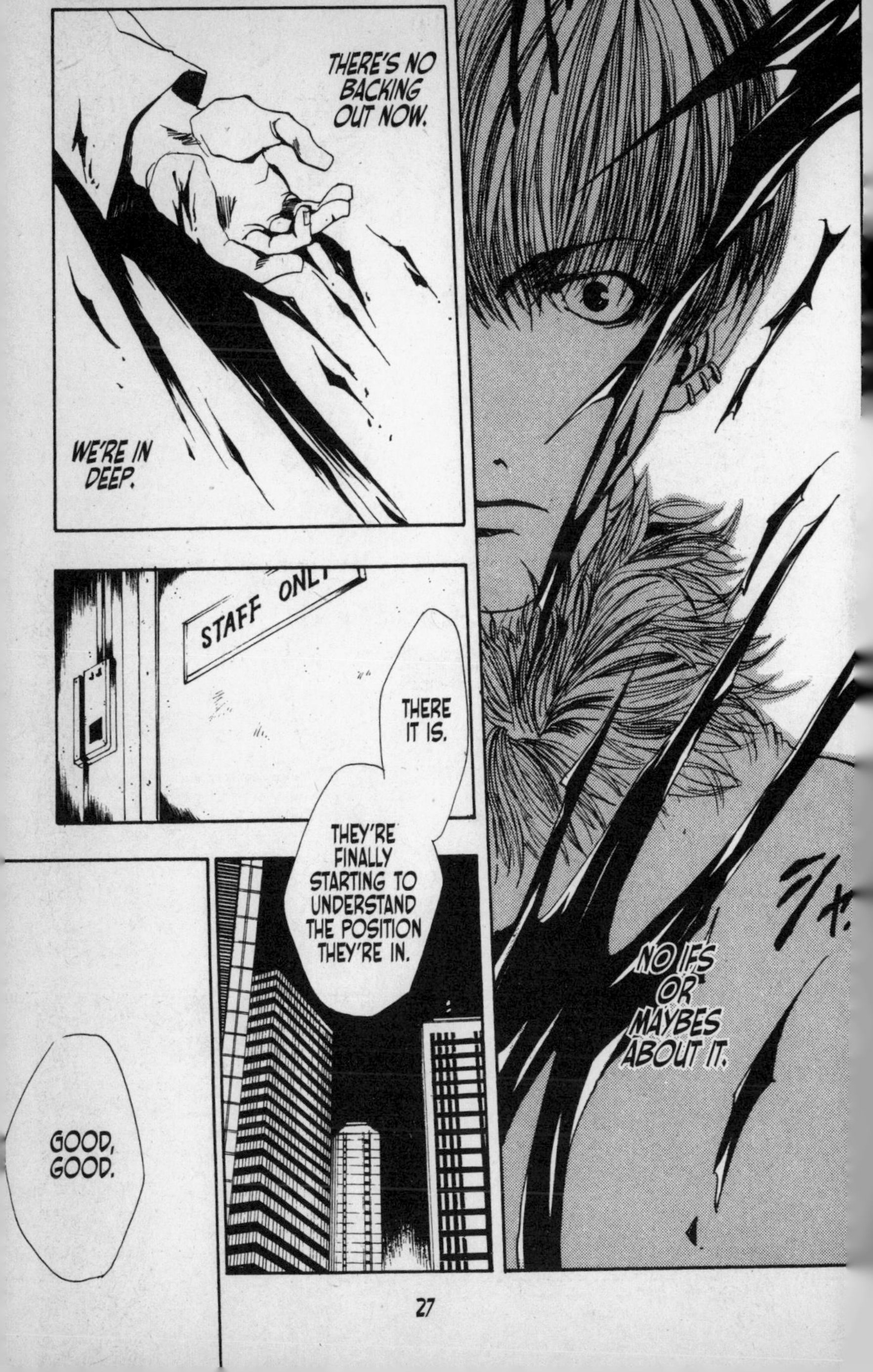
NO IFS OR MAYBES ABOUT IT.
シャ
THERE'S NO BACKING OUT NOW.
WE'RE IN DEEP.
STAFF ONL
THERE IT IS.
THEY'RE FINALLY STARTING TO UNDERSTAND THE POSITION THEY'RE IN.
GOOD, GOOD.

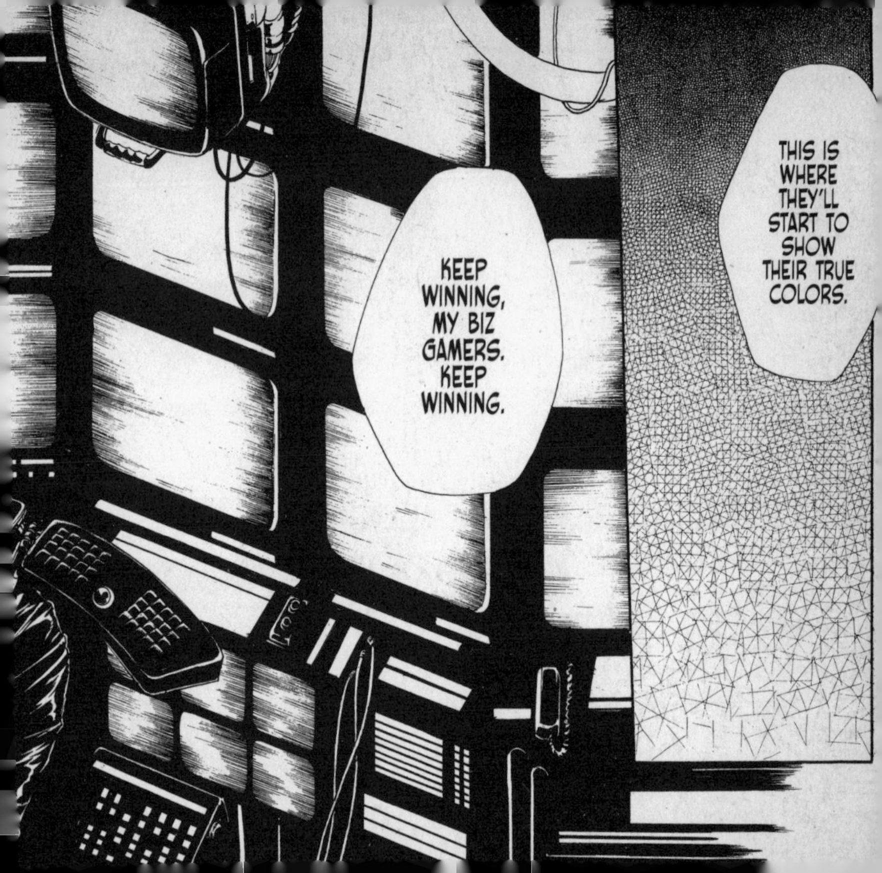
THIS IS WHERE THEY'LL START TO SHOW THEIR TRUE COLORS.
KEEP WINNING, MY BIZ GAMERS. KEEP WINNING.

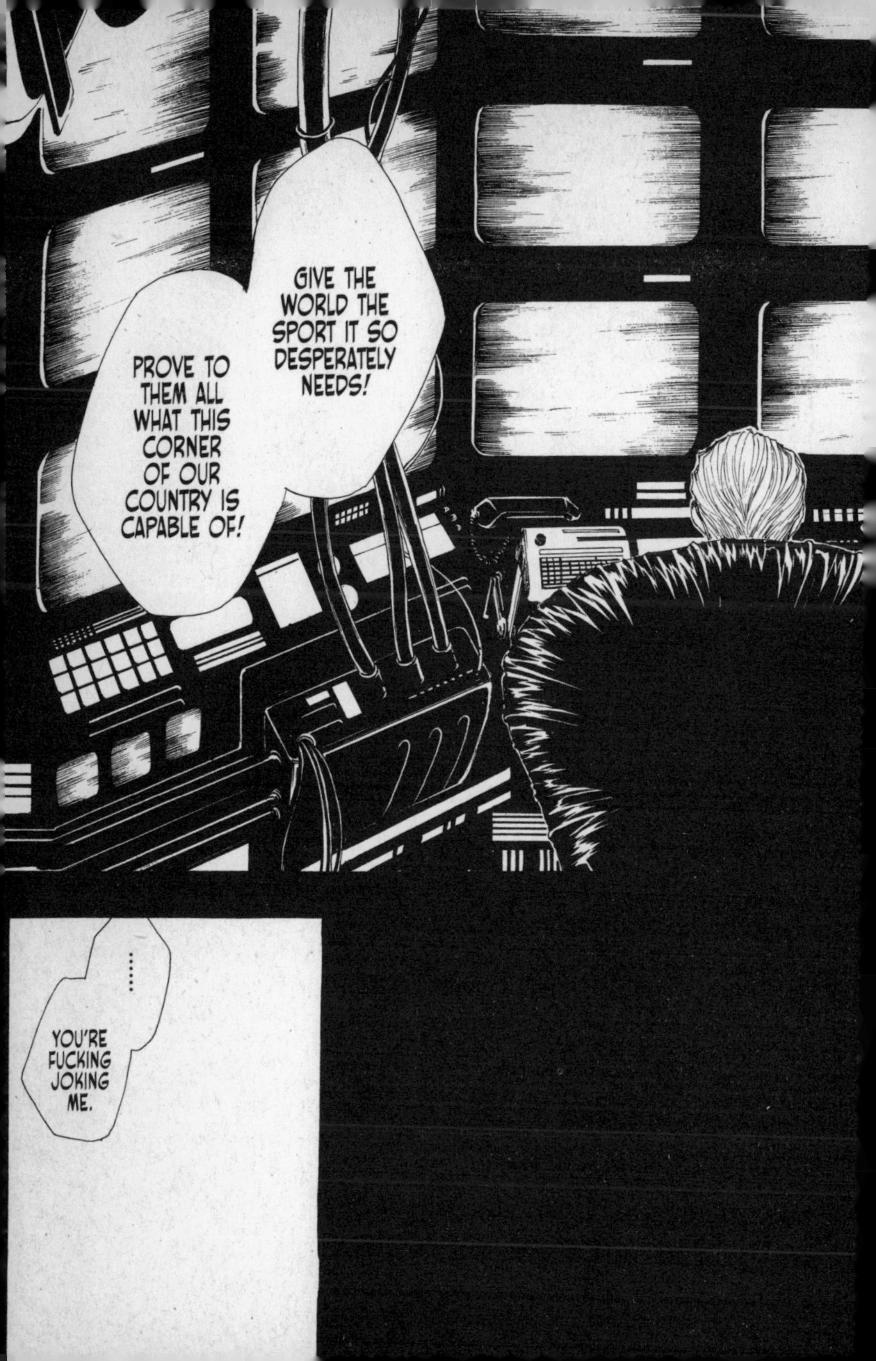
GIVE THE WORLD THE SPORT IT SO DESPERATELY NEEDS!
PROVE TO THEM ALL WHAT THIS CORNER OF OUR COUNTRY IS CAPABLE OF!
......
YOU'RE FUCKING JOKING ME.

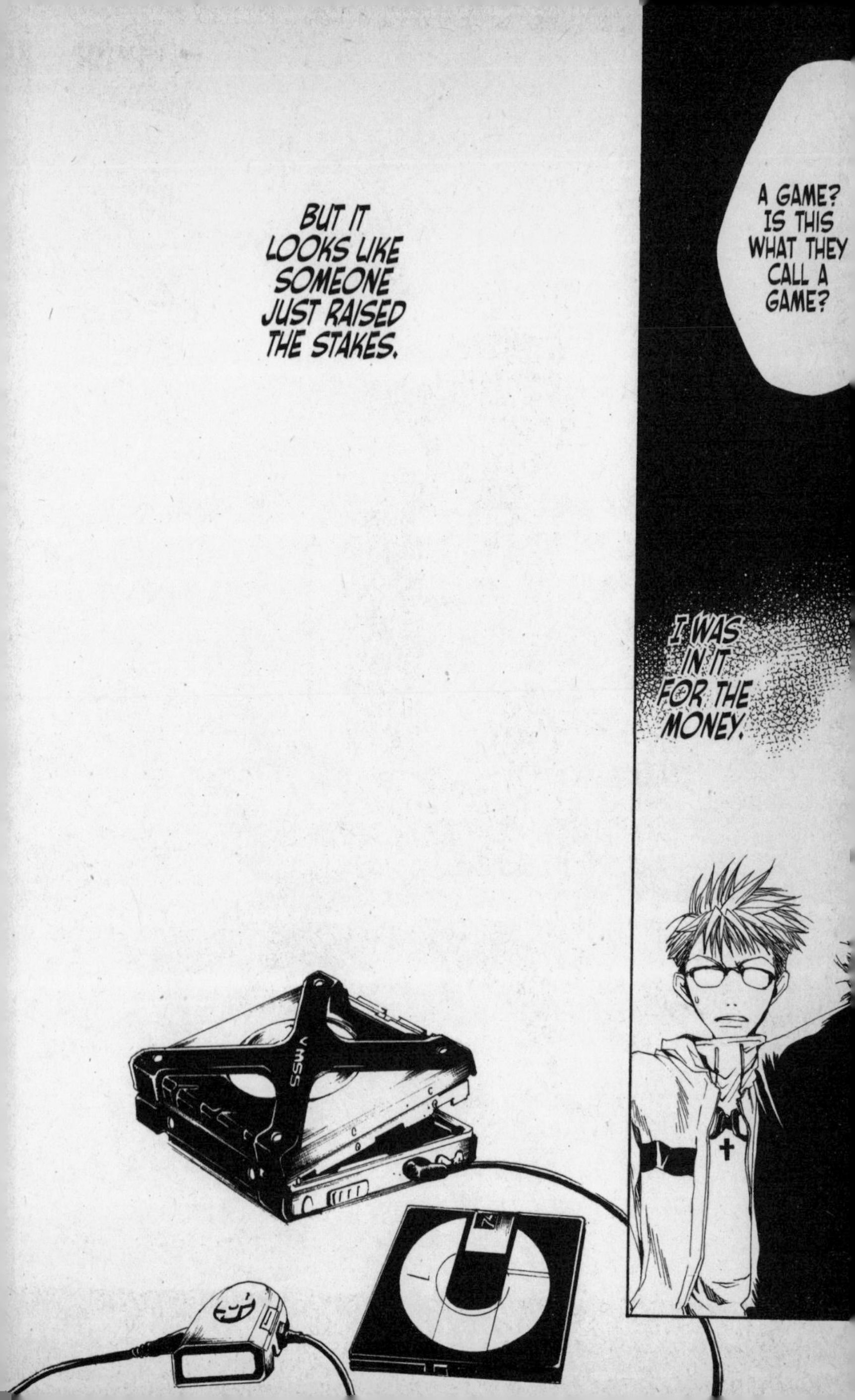
A GAME? IS THIS WHAT THEY CALL A GAME?
I WAS IN IT FOR THE MONEY.
BUT IT LOOKS LIKE SOMEONE JUST RAISED THE STAKES.

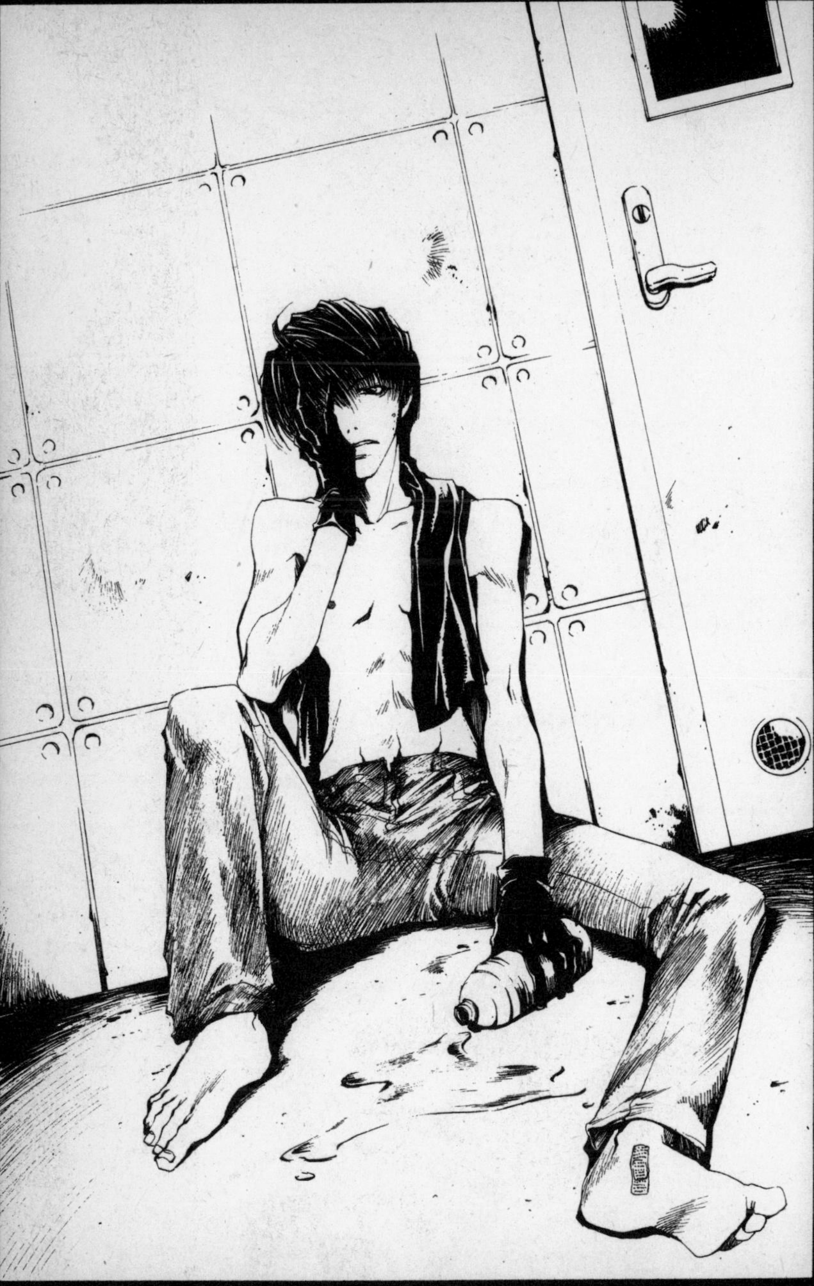

STAGE 2 : Parched Moon

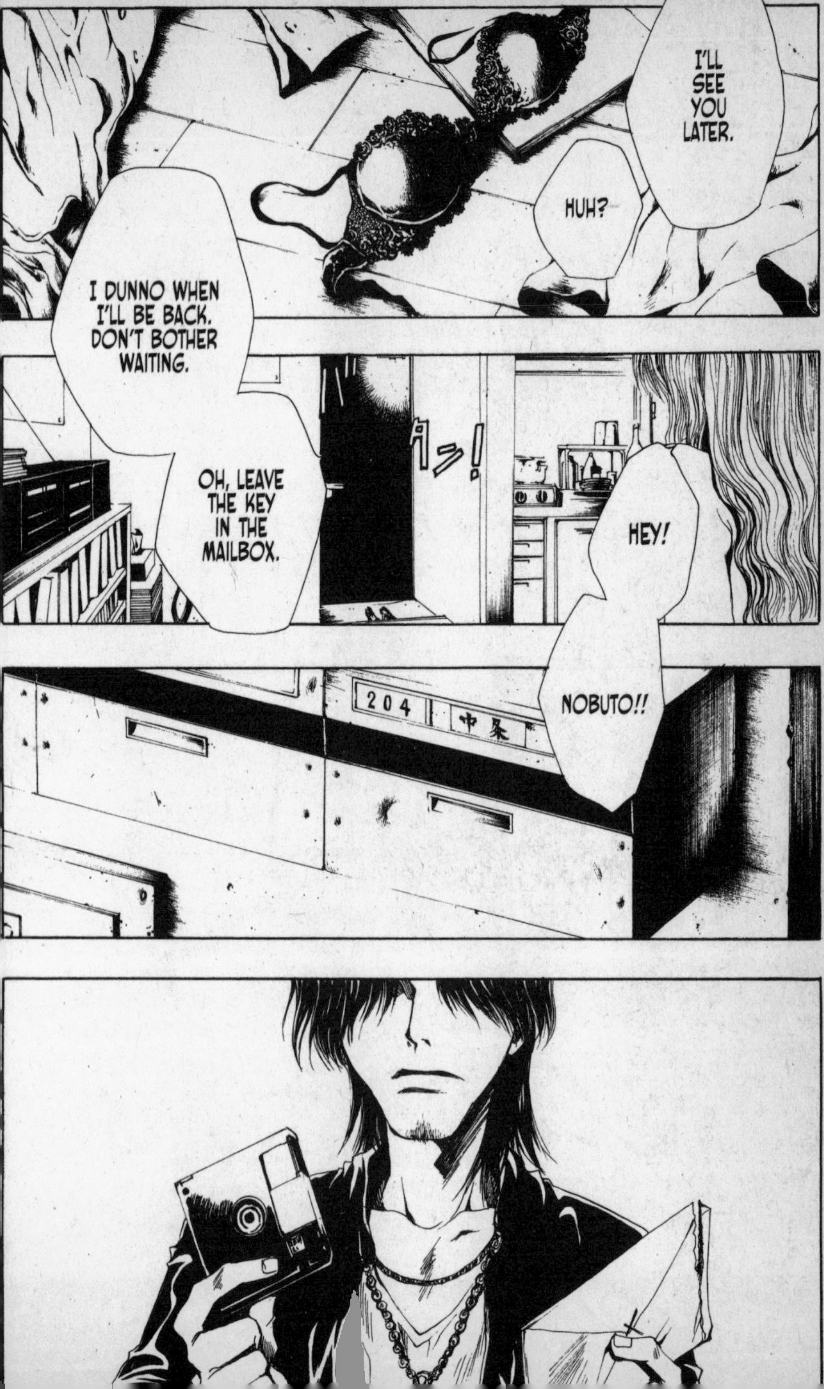
I'LL SEE YOU LATER.
HUH?
I DUNNO WHEN I'LL BE BACK. DON'T BOTHER WAITING.
OH, LEAVE THE KEY IN THE MAILBOX.
HEY!
NOBUTO!!
204
中条

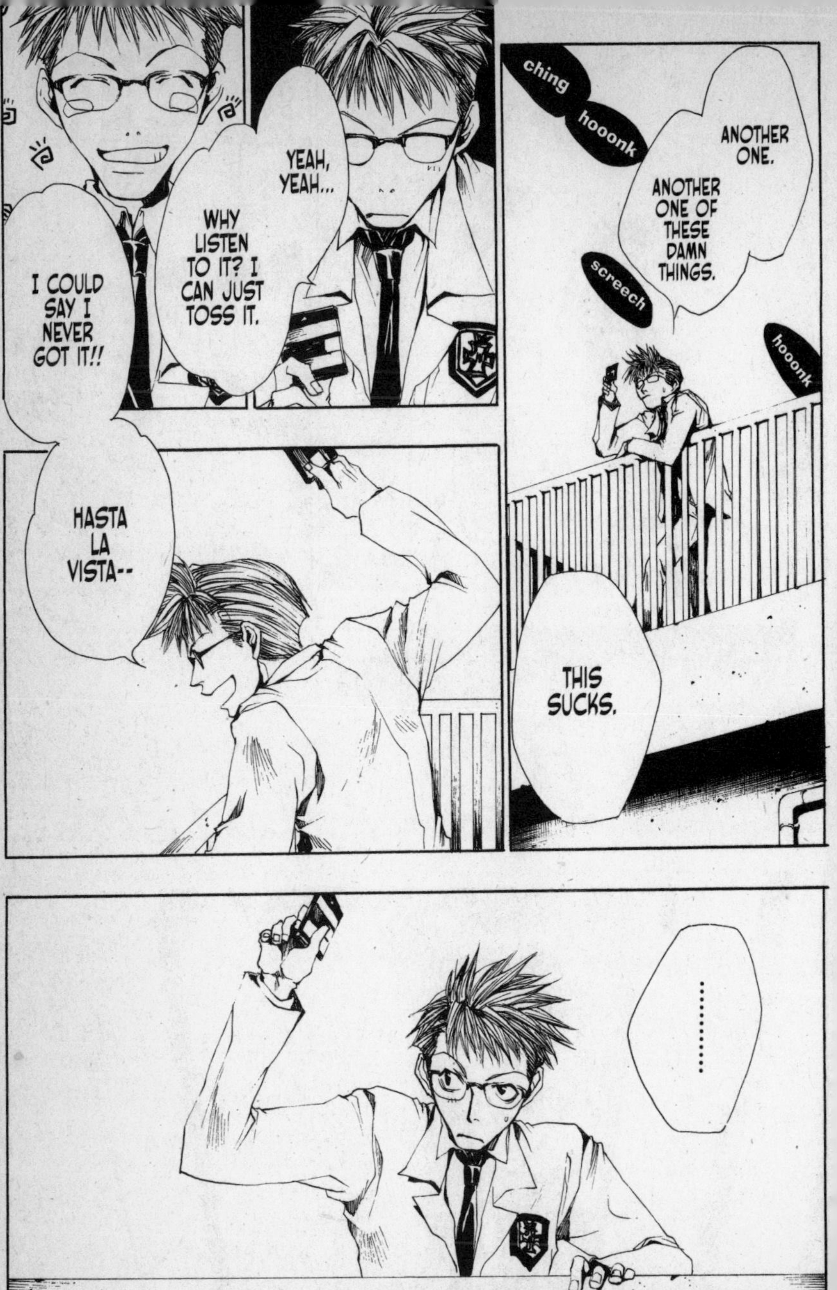
ching
hooonk
ANOTHER ONE.
ANOTHER ONE OF THESE DAMN THINGS.
screech
hooonk
THIS SUCKS.
YEAH, YEAH...
WHY LISTEN TO IT? I CAN JUST TOSS IT.
I COULD SAY I NEVER GOT IT!!
HASTA LA VISTA--
....

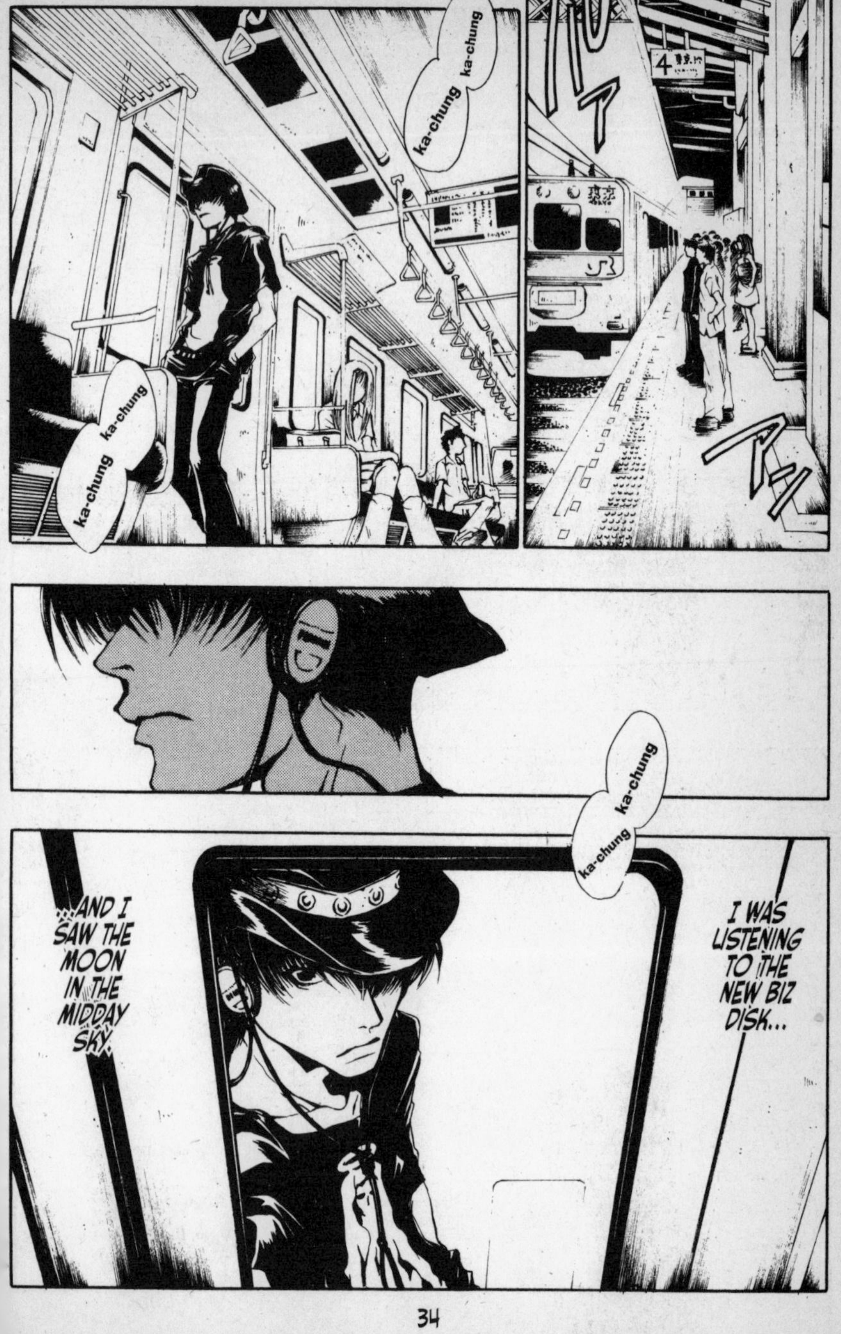
ka-chung ka-chung
ka-chung ka-chung
ka-chung ka-chung
I WAS LISTENING TO THE NEW BIZ DISK...
...AND I SAW THE MOON IN THE MIDDAY SKY.

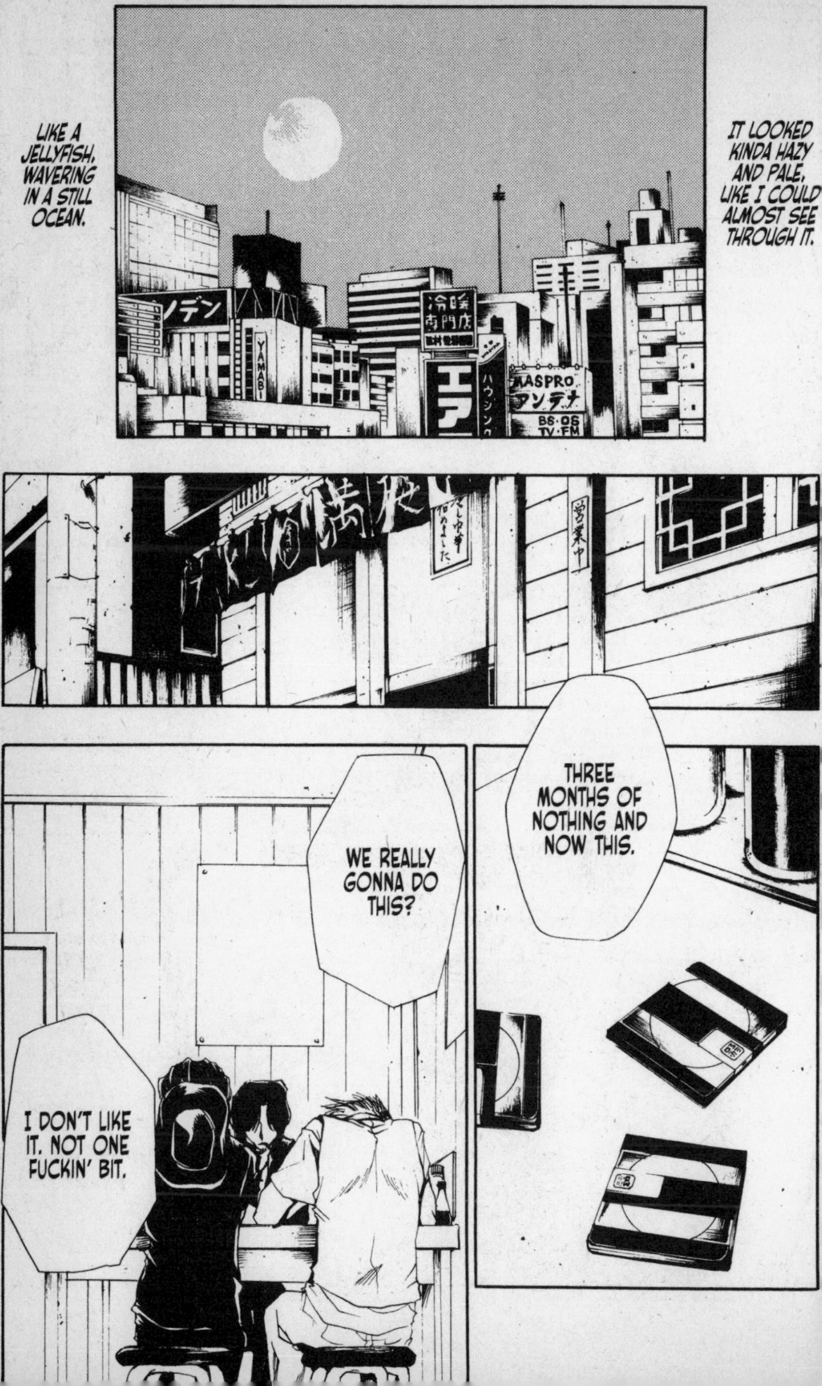
IT LOOKED KINDA HAZY AND PALE. LIKE I COULD ALMOST SEE THROUGH IT.
LIKE A JELLYFISH, WAVERING IN A STILL OCEAN.
YAMABI
MASPRO
アンテナ
BS・CS
TV・FM
営業中
THREE MONTHS OF NOTHING AND NOW THIS.
WE REALLY GONNA DO THIS?
I DON'T LIKE IT. NOT ONE FUCKIN' BIT.

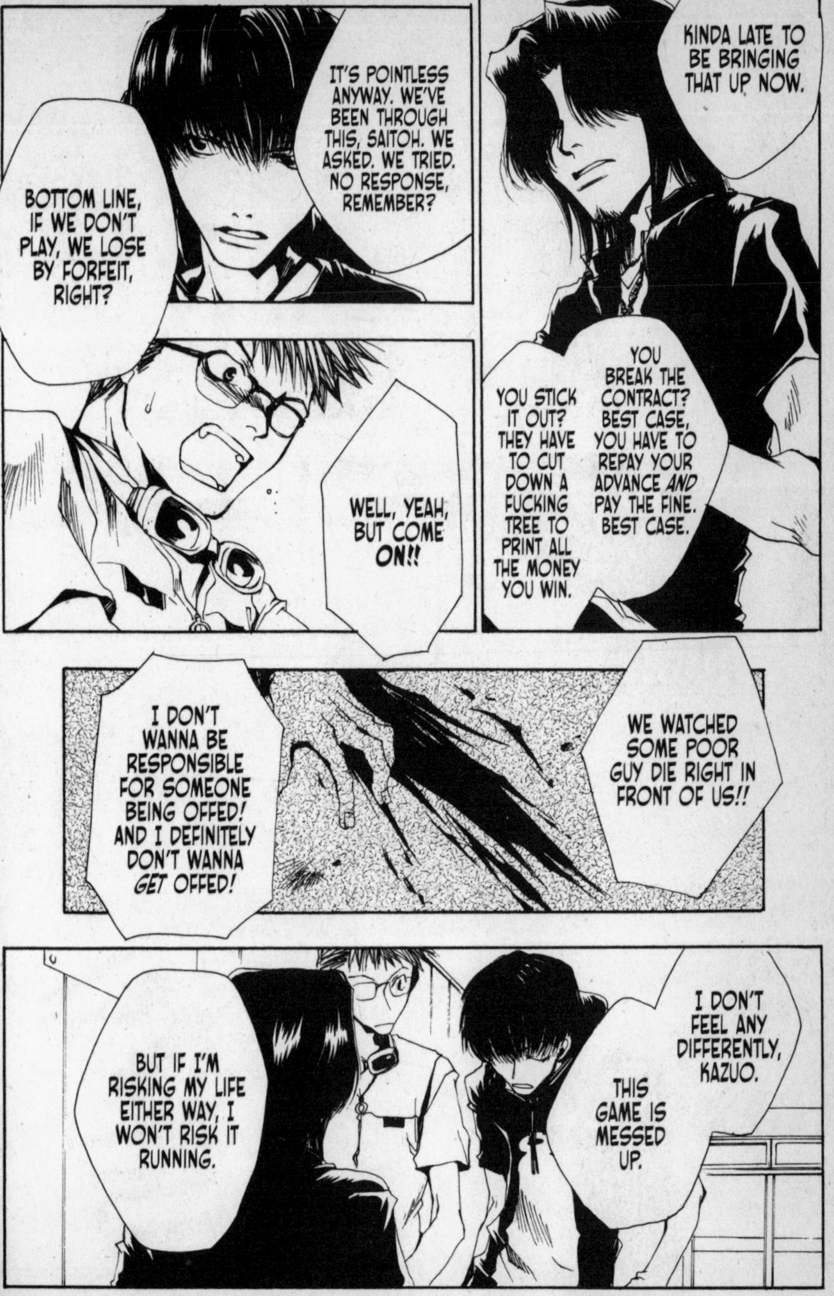
KINDA LATE TO BE BRINGING THAT UP NOW.
YOU BREAK THE CONTRACT? BEST CASE, YOU HAVE TO REPAY YOUR ADVANCE *AND* PAY THE FINE. BEST CASE.
YOU STICK IT OUT? THEY HAVE TO CUT DOWN A FUCKING TREE TO PRINT ALL THE MONEY YOU WIN.
IT'S POINTLESS ANYWAY. WE'VE BEEN THROUGH THIS, SAITOH. WE ASKED. WE TRIED. NO RESPONSE, REMEMBER?
BOTTOM LINE, IF WE DON'T PLAY, WE LOSE BY FORFEIT, RIGHT?
WELL, YEAH, BUT COME **ON!!**
WE WATCHED SOME POOR GUY DIE RIGHT IN FRONT OF US*!!*
I DON'T WANNA BE RESPONSIBLE FOR SOMEONE BEING OFFED*!* AND I DEFINITELY DON'T WANNA *GET* OFFED*!*
I DON'T FEEL ANY DIFFERENTLY, KAZUO.
THIS GAME IS MESSED UP.
BUT IF I'M RISKING MY LIFE EITHER WAY, I WON'T RISK IT RUNNING.

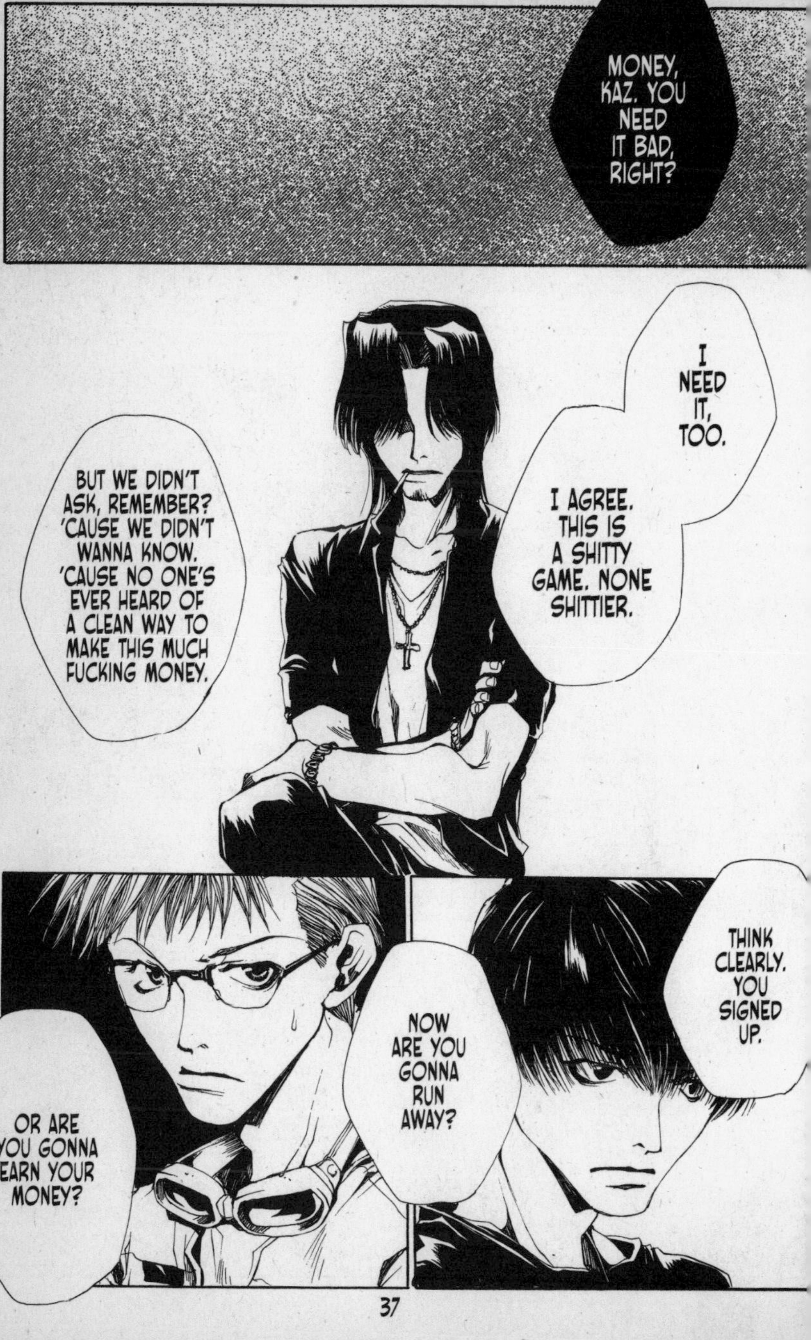
MONEY, KAZ. YOU NEED IT BAD, RIGHT?
I NEED IT, TOO.
I AGREE. THIS IS A SHITTY GAME. NONE SHITTIER.
BUT WE DIDN'T ASK, REMEMBER? 'CAUSE WE DIDN'T WANNA KNOW. 'CAUSE NO ONE'S EVER HEARD OF A CLEAN WAY TO MAKE THIS MUCH FUCKING MONEY.
THINK CLEARLY. YOU SIGNED UP.
NOW ARE YOU GONNA RUN AWAY?
OR ARE YOU GONNA EARN YOUR MONEY?

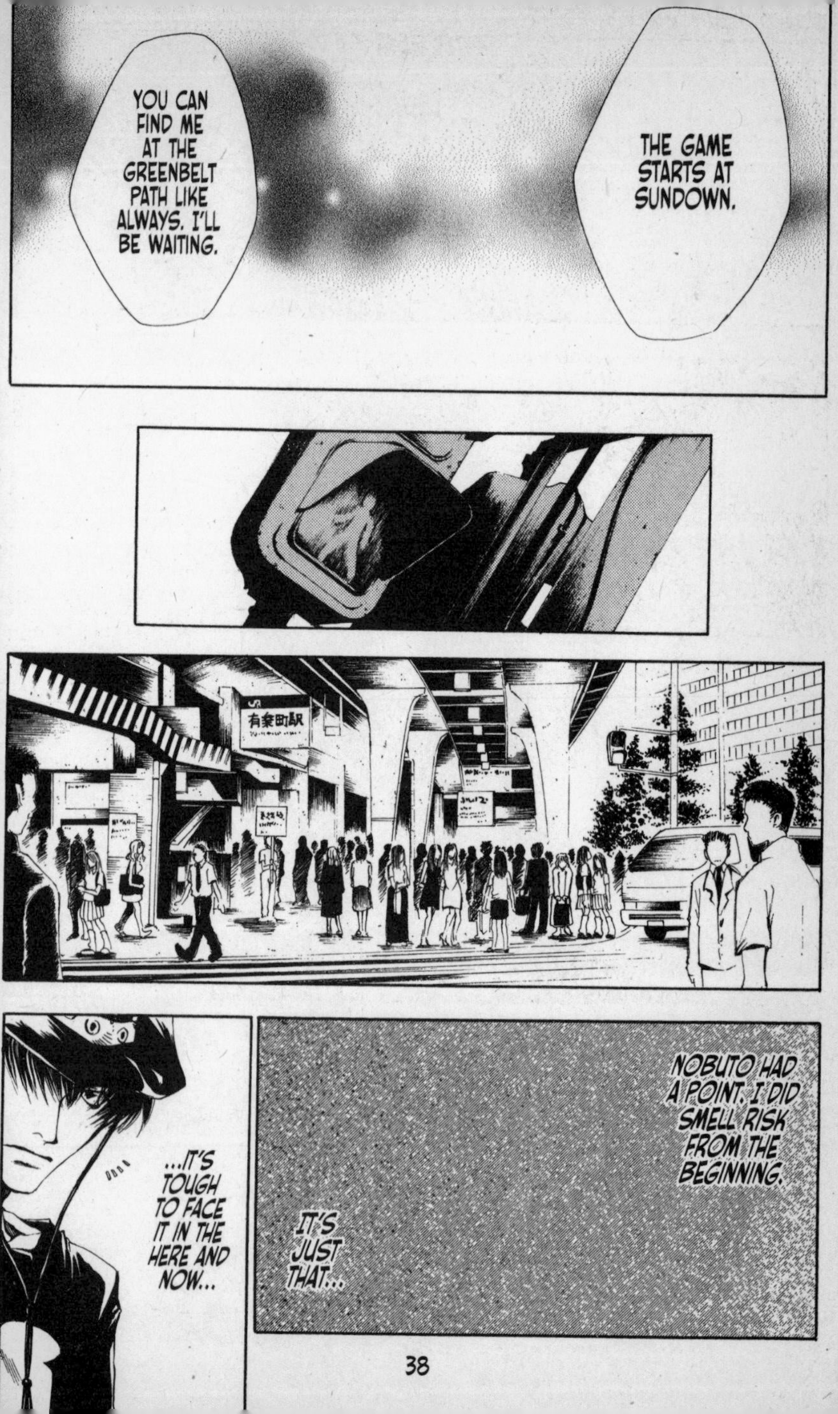
THE GAME STARTS AT SUNDOWN.
YOU CAN FIND ME AT THE GREENBELT PATH LIKE ALWAYS. I'LL BE WAITING.
有楽町駅
NOBUTO HAD A POINT. I DID SMELL RISK FROM THE BEGINNING.
IT'S JUST THAT...
...IT'S TOUGH TO FACE IT IN THE HERE AND NOW...

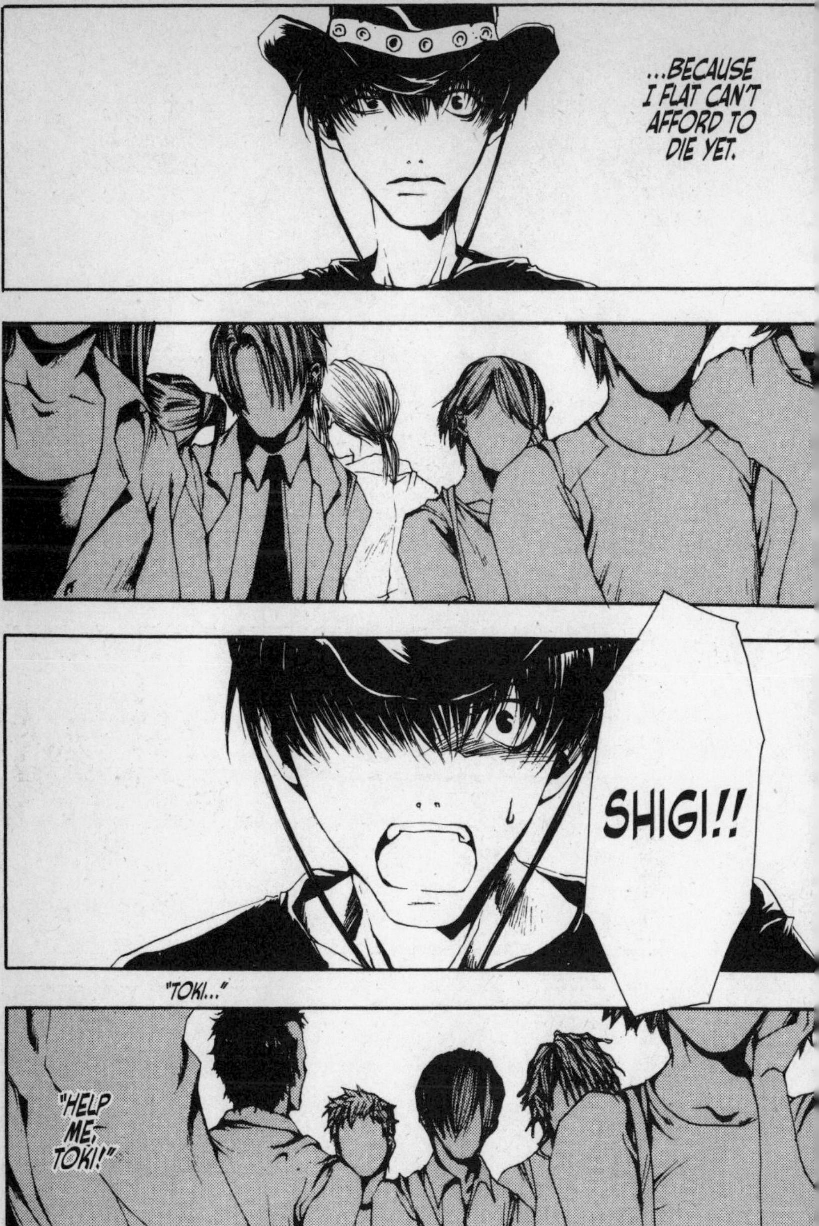
...BECAUSE I FLAT CAN'T AFFORD TO DIE YET.
SHIGI!!
"TOKI..."
"HELP ME, TOKI!"

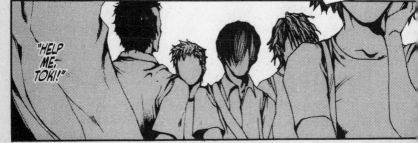

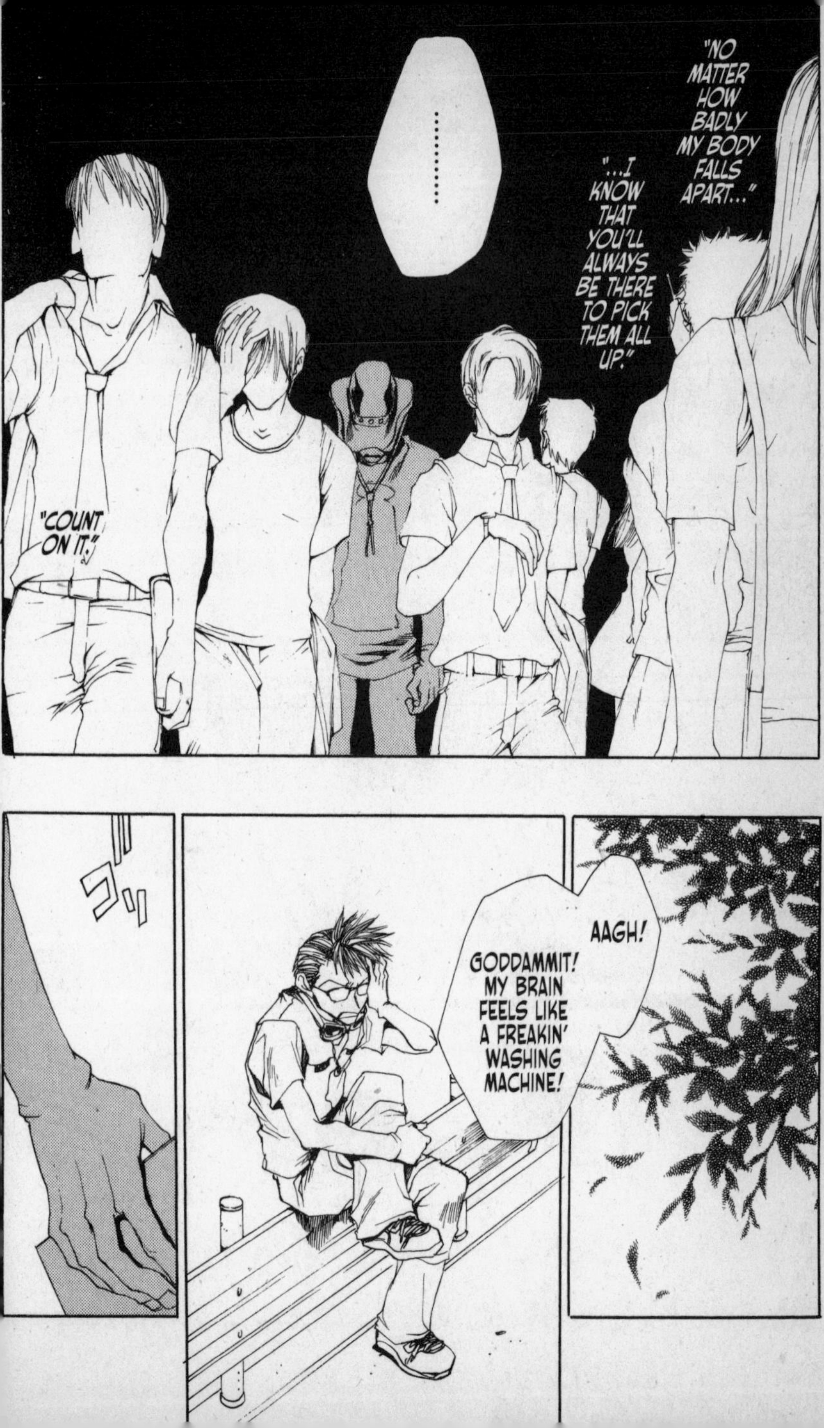
"NO MATTER HOW BADLY MY BODY FALLS APART..."
"...I KNOW THAT YOU'LL ALWAYS BE THERE TO PICK THEM ALL UP."
......
"COUNT ON IT."
AAGH!
GODDAMMIT! MY BRAIN FEELS LIKE A FREAKIN' WASHING MACHINE!
ゴッ

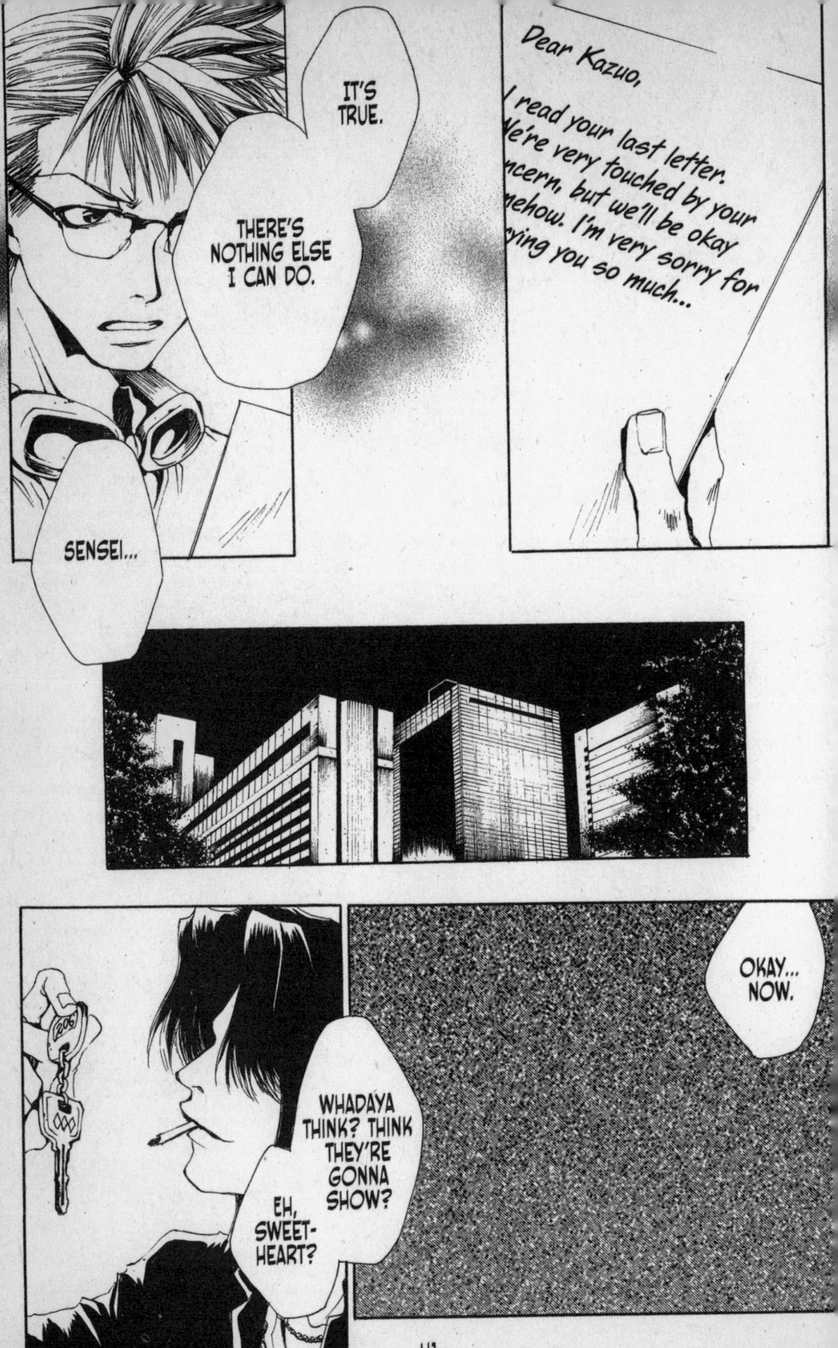
Dear Kazuo,
I read your last letter.
le're very touched by your
ncern, but we'll be okay
mehow. I'm very sorry for
ying you so much...
IT'S TRUE.
THERE'S NOTHING ELSE I CAN DO.
SENSEI...
OKAY... NOW.
WHADAYA THINK? THINK THEY'RE GONNA SHOW?
EH, SWEET-HEART?

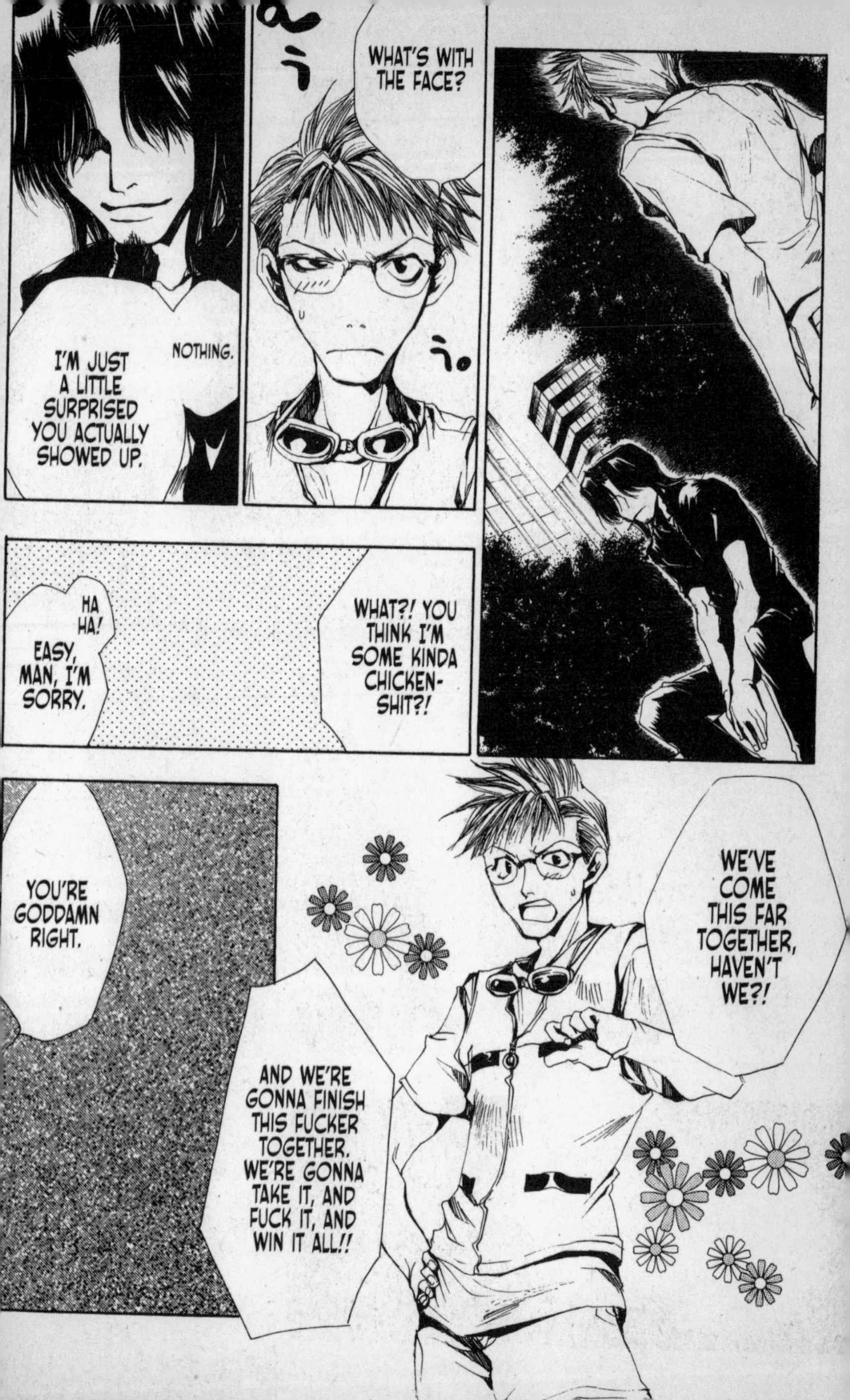
WHAT'S WITH THE FACE?
NOTHING.
I'M JUST A LITTLE SURPRISED YOU ACTUALLY SHOWED UP.
WHAT?! YOU THINK I'M SOME KINDA CHICKEN-SHIT?!
HA HA!
EASY, MAN, I'M SORRY.
WE'VE COME THIS FAR TOGETHER, HAVEN'T WE?!
AND WE'RE GONNA FINISH THIS FUCKER TOGETHER. WE'RE GONNA TAKE IT, AND FUCK IT, AND WIN IT ALL!!
YOU'RE GODDAMN RIGHT.

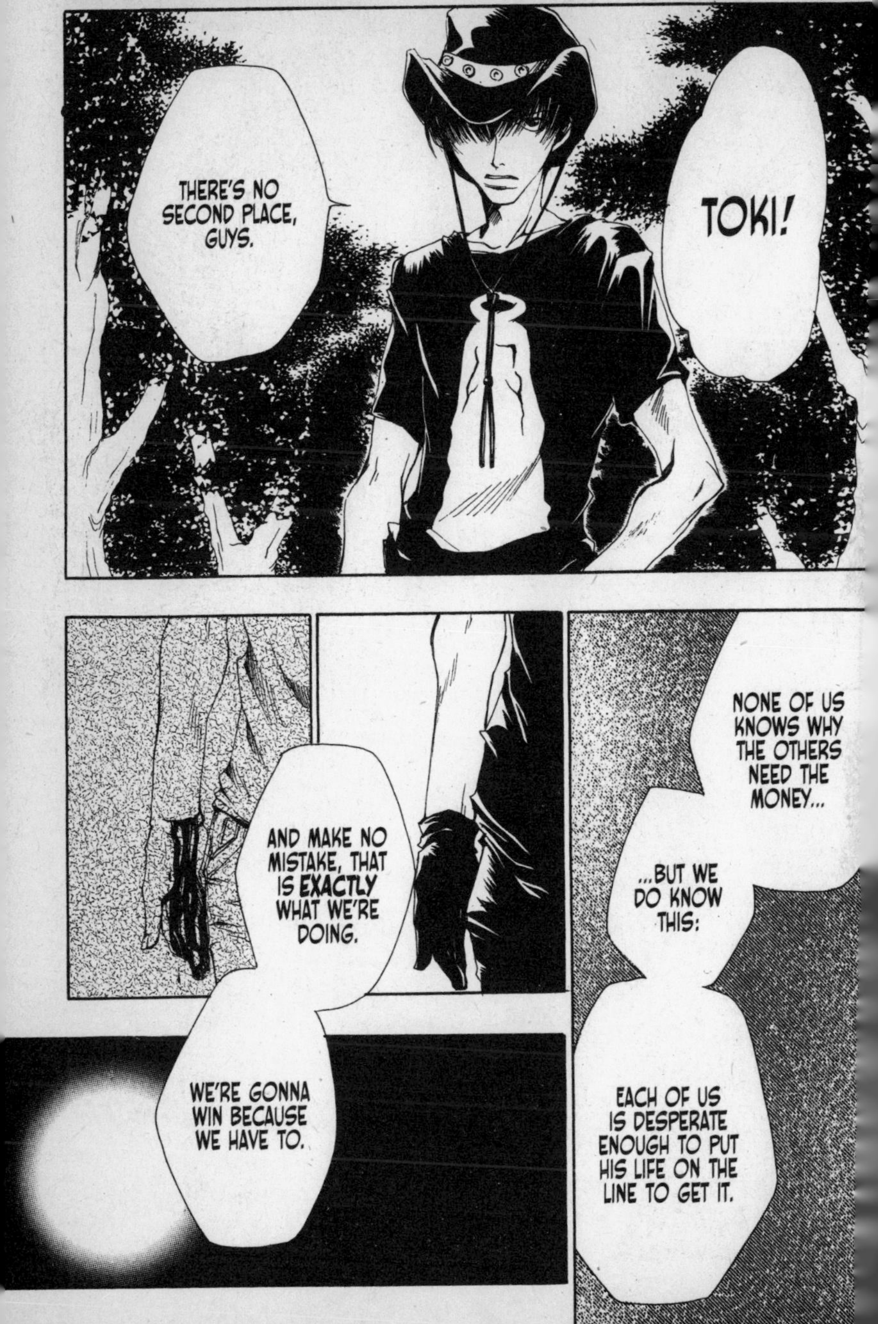
TOKI!
THERE'S NO SECOND PLACE, GUYS.
NONE OF US KNOWS WHY THE OTHERS NEED THE MONEY...
...BUT WE DO KNOW THIS:
EACH OF US IS DESPERATE ENOUGH TO PUT HIS LIFE ON THE LINE TO GET IT.
AND MAKE NO MISTAKE, THAT IS EXACTLY WHAT WE'RE DOING.
WE'RE GONNA WIN BECAUSE WE HAVE TO.

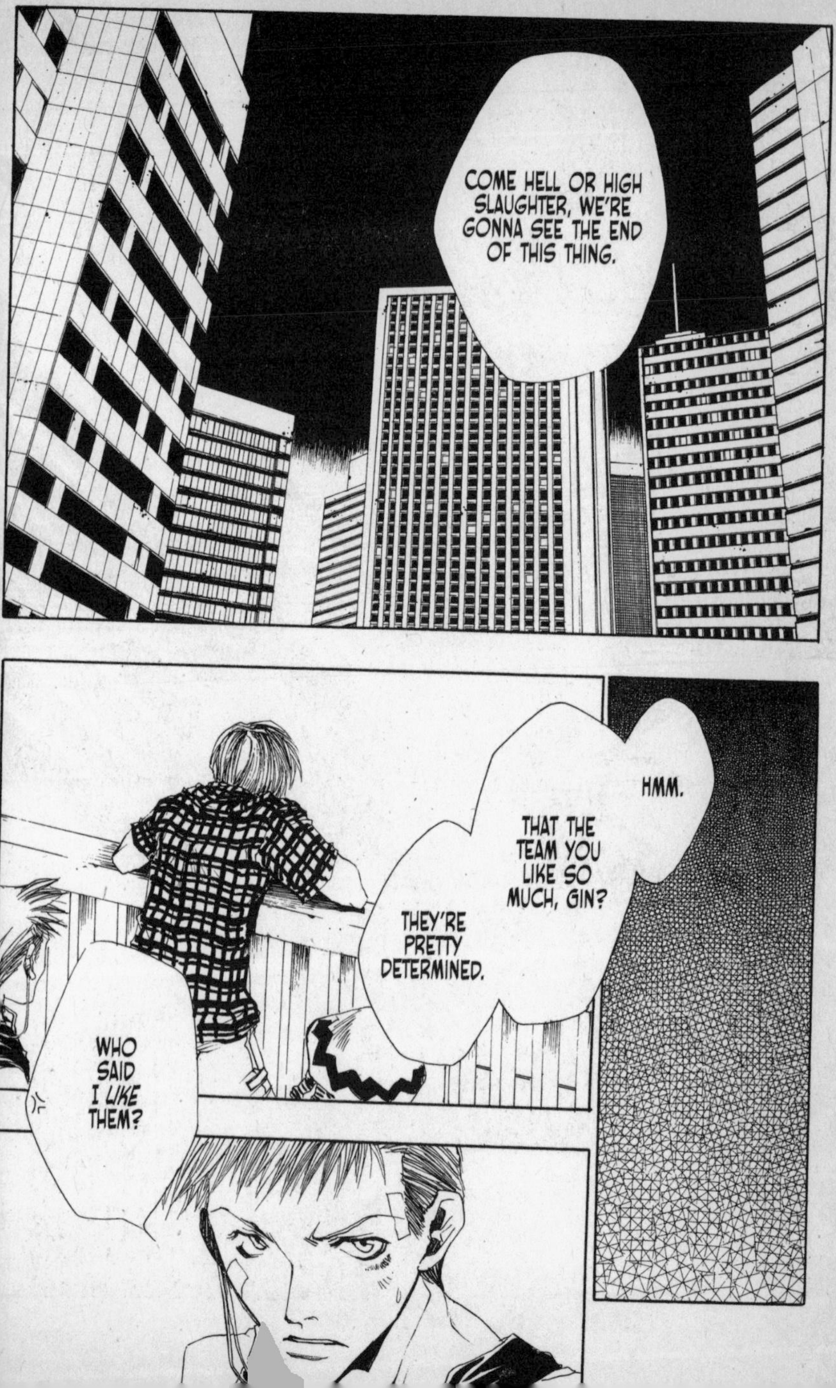
COME HELL OR HIGH SLAUGHTER, WE'RE GONNA SEE THE END OF THIS THING.
HMM.
THAT THE TEAM YOU LIKE SO MUCH, GIN?
THEY'RE PRETTY DETERMINED.
WHO SAID I *LIKE* THEM?

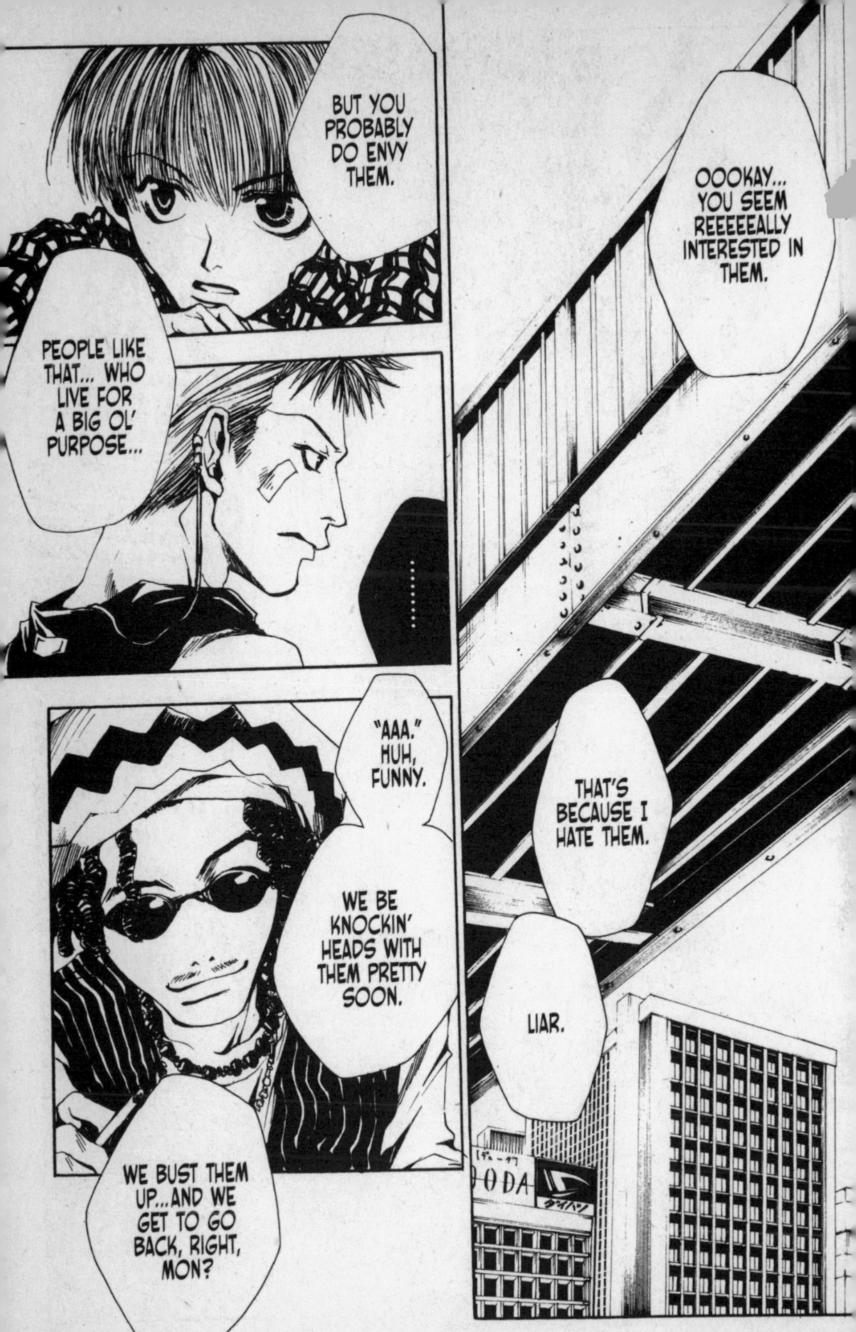
OOOKAY... YOU SEEM REEEEEALLY INTERESTED IN THEM.
THAT'S BECAUSE I HATE THEM.
LIAR.
BUT YOU PROBABLY DO ENVY THEM.
PEOPLE LIKE THAT... WHO LIVE FOR A BIG OL' PURPOSE...
"AAA." HUH, FUNNY.
WE BE KNOCKIN' HEADS WITH THEM PRETTY SOON.
WE BUST THEM UP...AND WE GET TO GO BACK, RIGHT, MON?

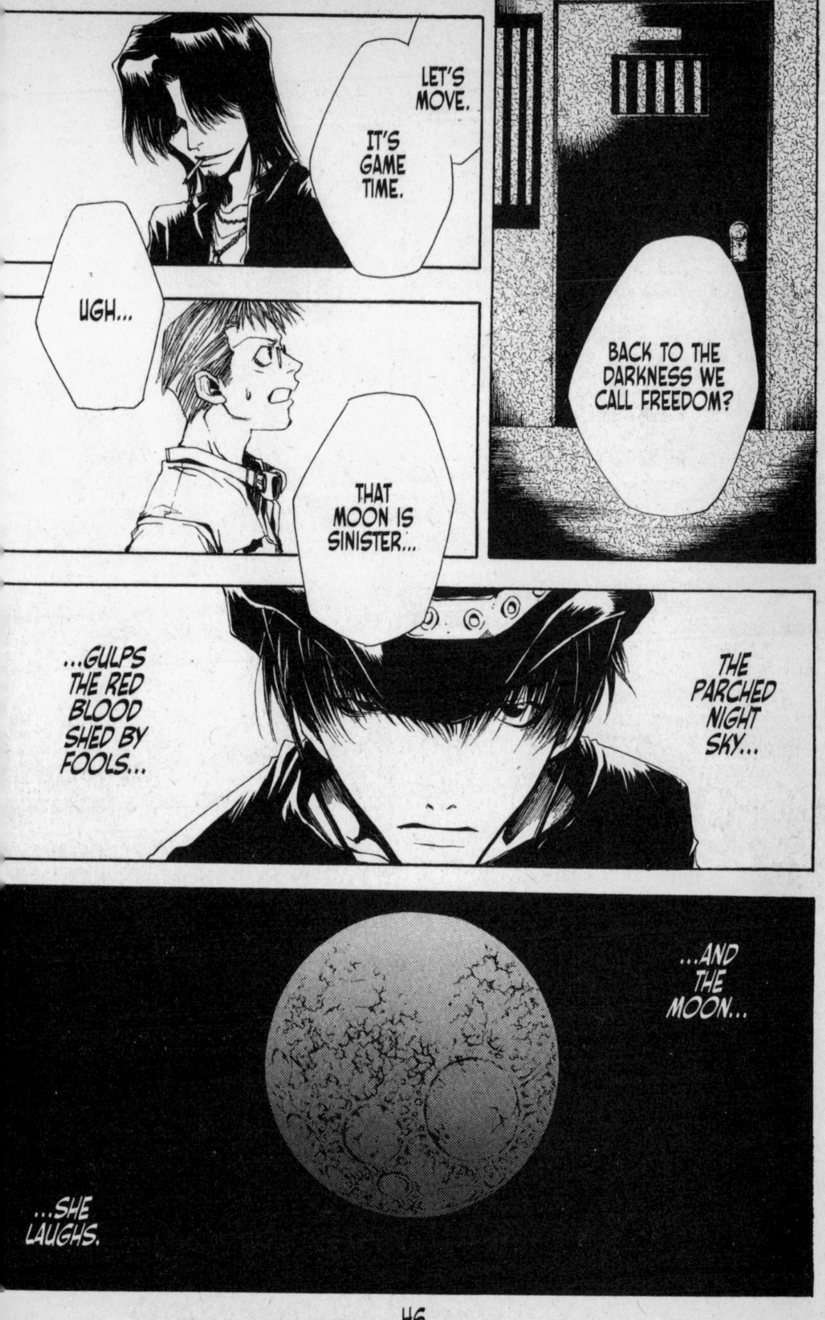
BACK TO THE DARKNESS WE CALL FREEDOM?
LET'S MOVE.
IT'S GAME TIME.
UGH...
THAT MOON IS SINISTER...
THE PARCHED NIGHT SKY...
...GULPS THE RED BLOOD SHED BY FOOLS...
...AND THE MOON...
...SHE LAUGHS.

BIZ GAME

A BATTLE SIMULATION IN WHICH GAMERS, SELECTED BY VARIOUS CORPORATIONS, PLAY THREE-ON-THREE. THE BATTLEGROUND IS USUALLY INSIDE TOKYO.

THE RULES ARE SIMPLE:

ONE TEAM IS SELECTED TO BE HOME AND THE OTHER AWAY.
THE HOME TEAM IS GIVEN A DISK CONTAINING THEIR CORPORATION'S SECRET FILES TO PROTECT. THE AWAY TEAM ATTEMPTS TO STEAL THAT DISK.
AWAY WINS IF THEY CAN STEAL THE DISK WITHIN THE GIVEN TIME LIMIT.
HOME WINS IF THEY CAN KEEP THE DISK SAFE.

THE GAME INFORMATION AND DETAILS ARE DISTRIBUTED TO THE GAMERS VIA MINI-DISK.
THE BUSINESSES PARTICIPATING IN THE BIZ GAME WAGER HUGE SUMS OF MONEY ON EACH GAME, WATCHING THE ACTION FROM A DISTANCE.

IT'S A STUPID GAME. A WAY FOR RICH PEOPLE TO AMUSE THEMSELVES.
AND WE'RE THEIR PAWNS.

IN EXCHANGE FOR PUTTING THEIR LIVES IN GREAT DANGER, GAMERS STAND TO GAIN HUGE SUMS OF MONEY, BOTH THROUGH THEIR CONTRACTS AND BY WINNING PRIZE PURSES.

AT FIRST, I JUST WANTED THE MONEY.

YEAH. AT FIRST.

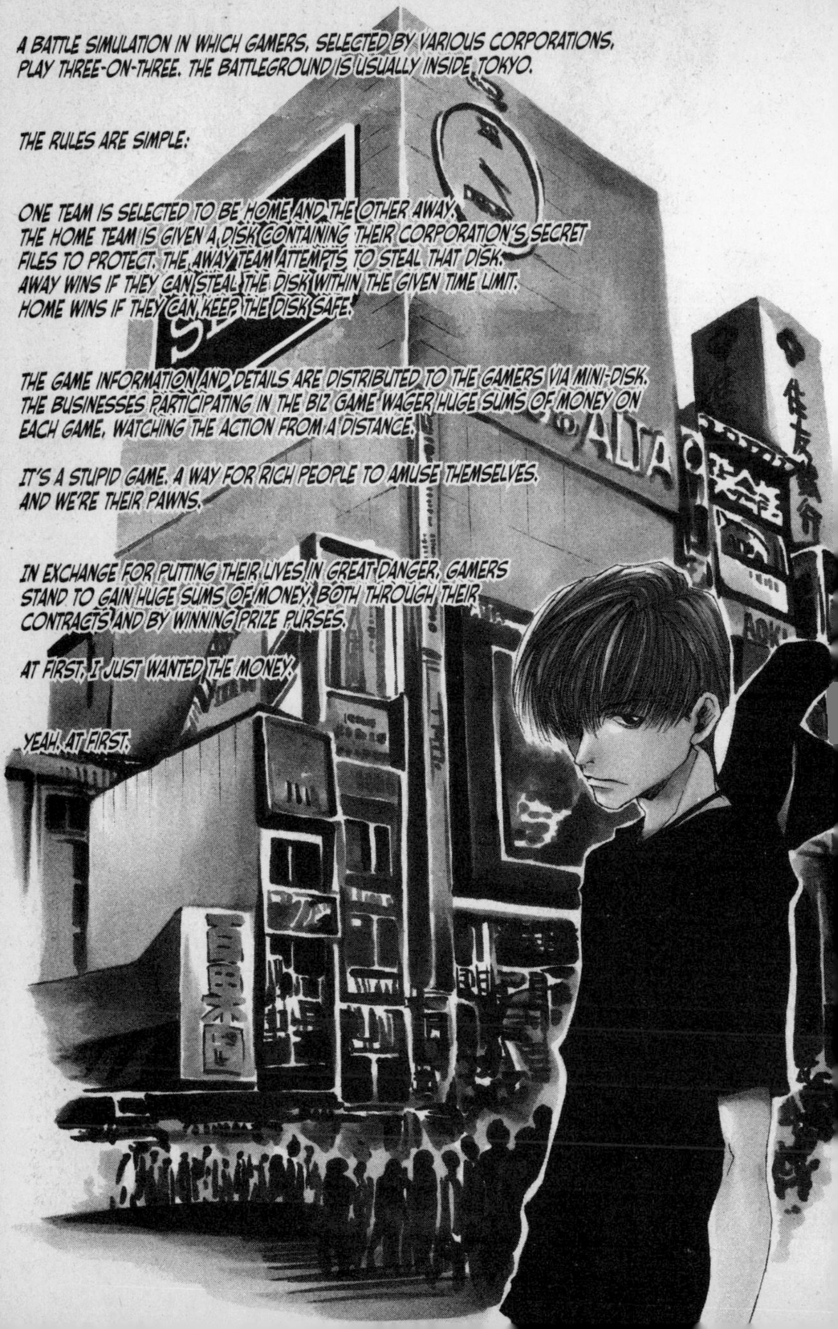
ALTA

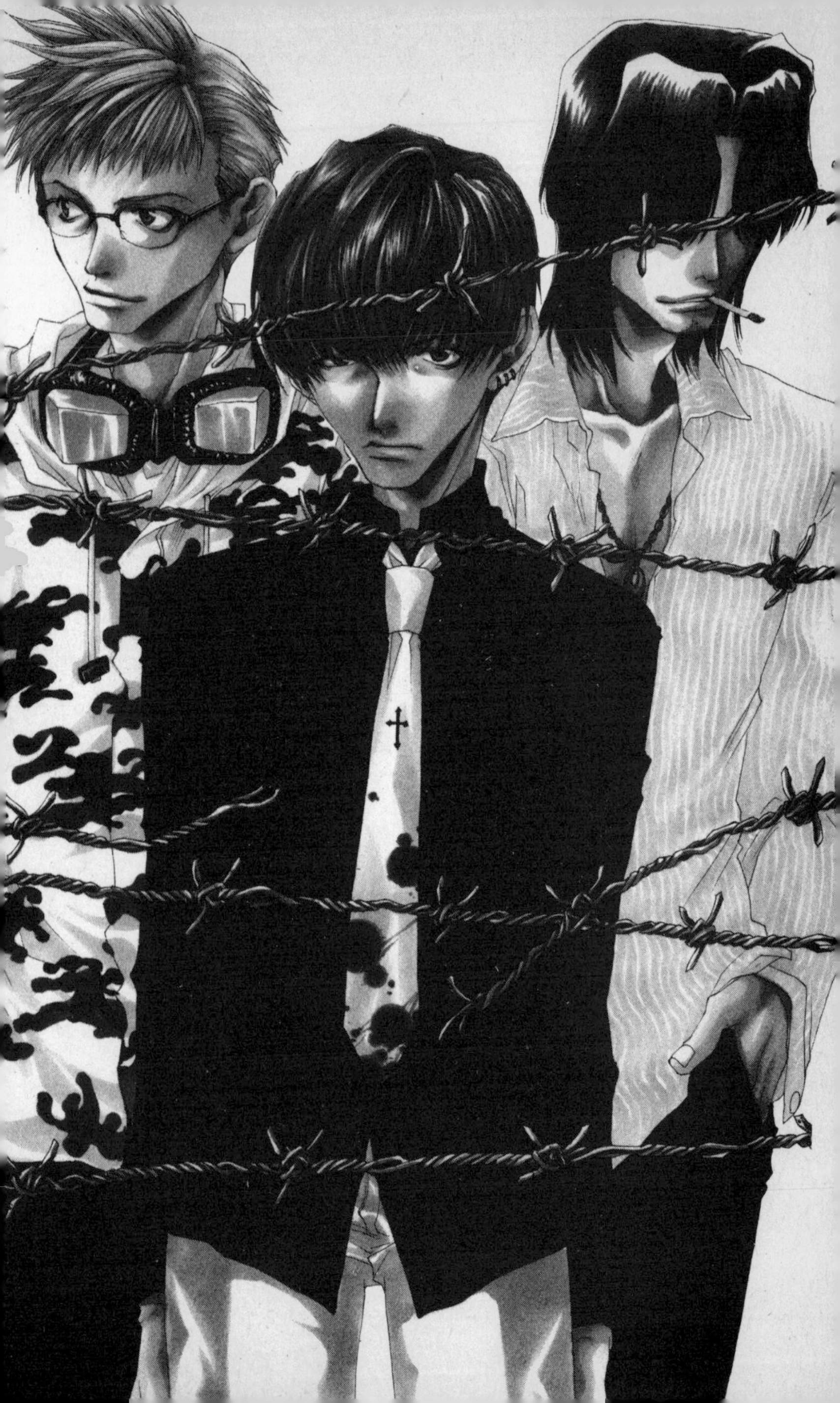

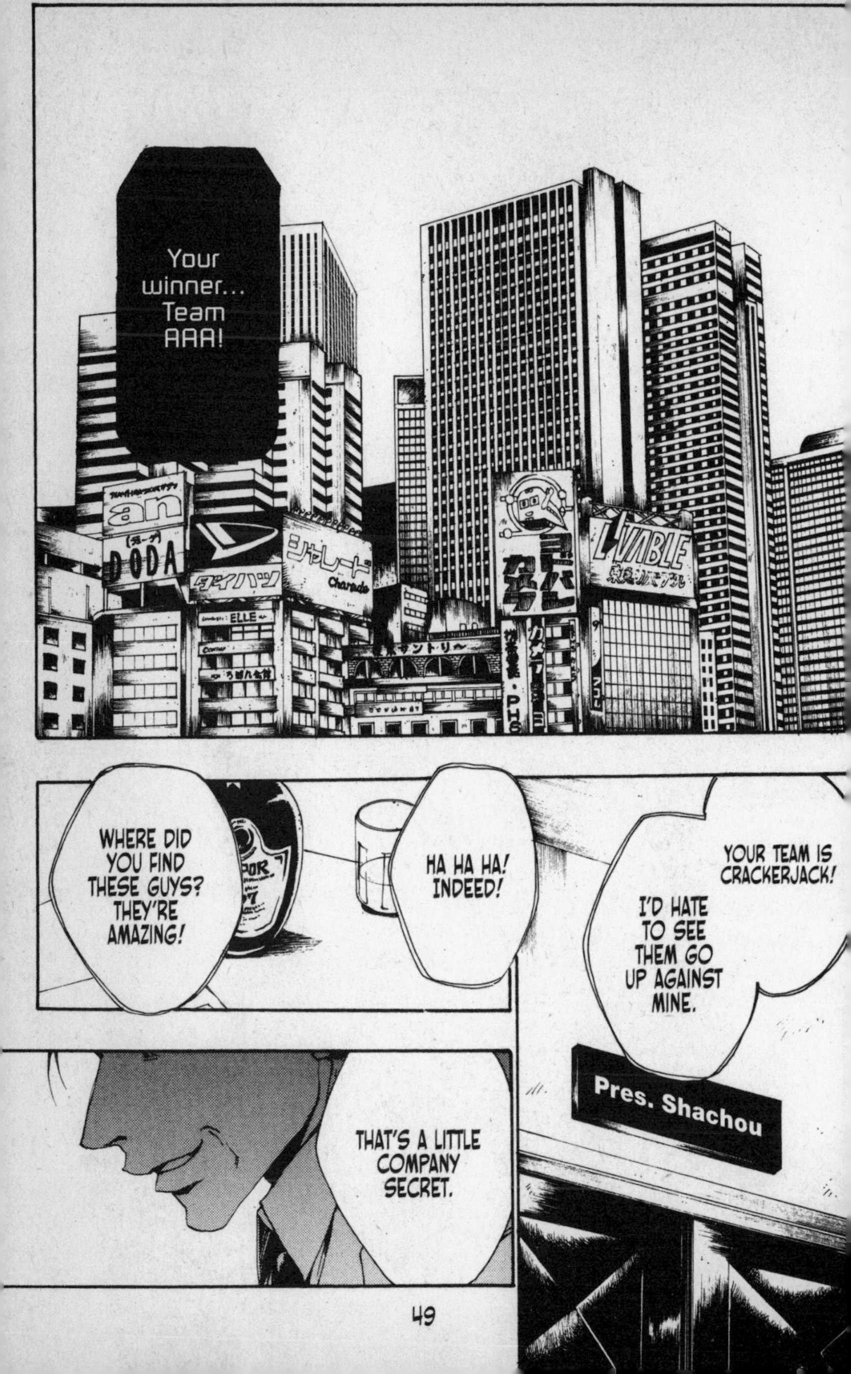
Your winner... Team AAA!
an
DODA
Charade
YOUR TEAM IS CRACKERJACK!
I'D HATE TO SEE THEM GO UP AGAINST MINE.
Pres. Shachou
WHERE DID YOU FIND THESE GUYS? THEY'RE AMAZING!
HA HA HA! INDEED!
THAT'S A LITTLE COMPANY SECRET.

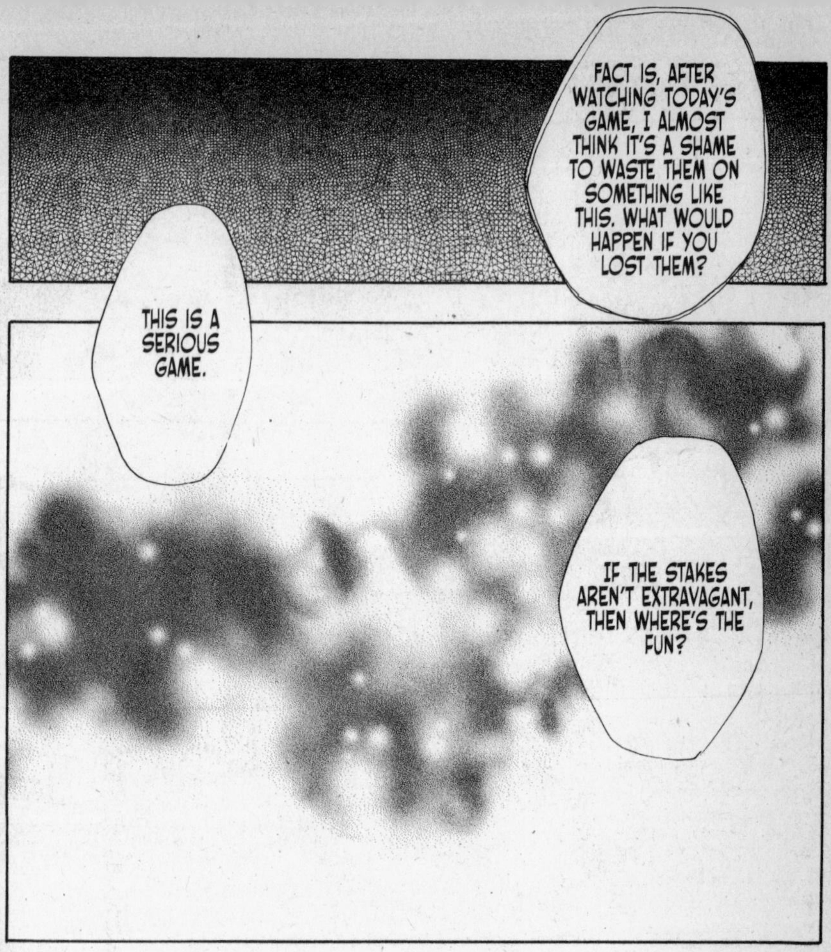
FACT IS, AFTER WATCHING TODAY'S GAME, I ALMOST THINK IT'S A SHAME TO WASTE THEM ON SOMETHING LIKE THIS. WHAT WOULD HAPPEN IF YOU LOST THEM?
THIS IS A SERIOUS GAME.
IF THE STAKES AREN'T EXTRAVAGANT, THEN WHERE'S THE FUN?

STAGE3: Trash Day

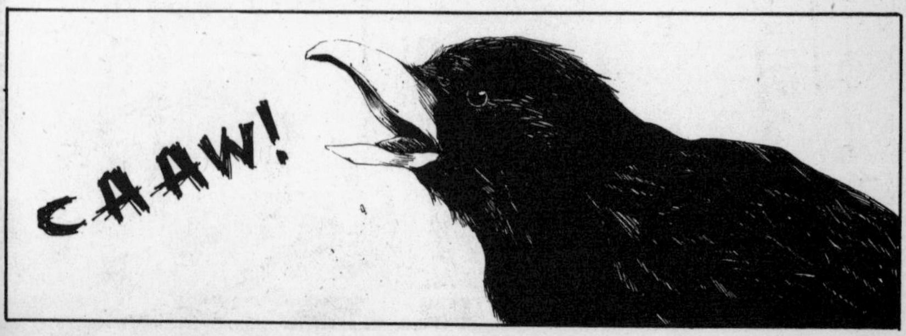
CAAW!

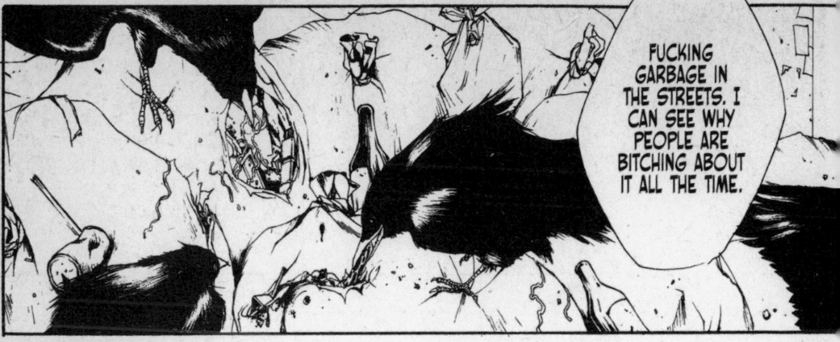
FUCKING GARBAGE IN THE STREETS. I CAN SEE WHY PEOPLE ARE BITCHING ABOUT IT ALL THE TIME.

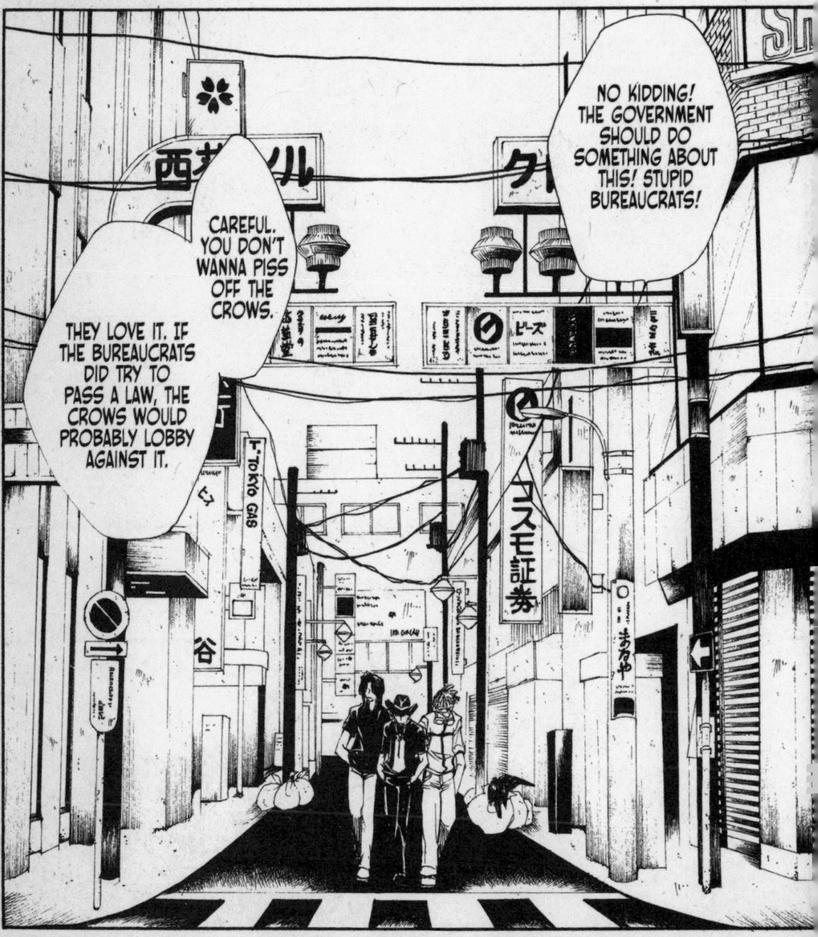
NO KIDDING! THE GOVERNMENT SHOULD DO SOMETHING ABOUT THIS! STUPID BUREAUCRATS!
CAREFUL. YOU DON'T WANNA PISS OFF THE CROWS.
THEY LOVE IT. IF THE BUREAUCRATS DID TRY TO PASS A LAW, THE CROWS WOULD PROBABLY LOBBY AGAINST IT.
コスモ証券
TOKYO GAS

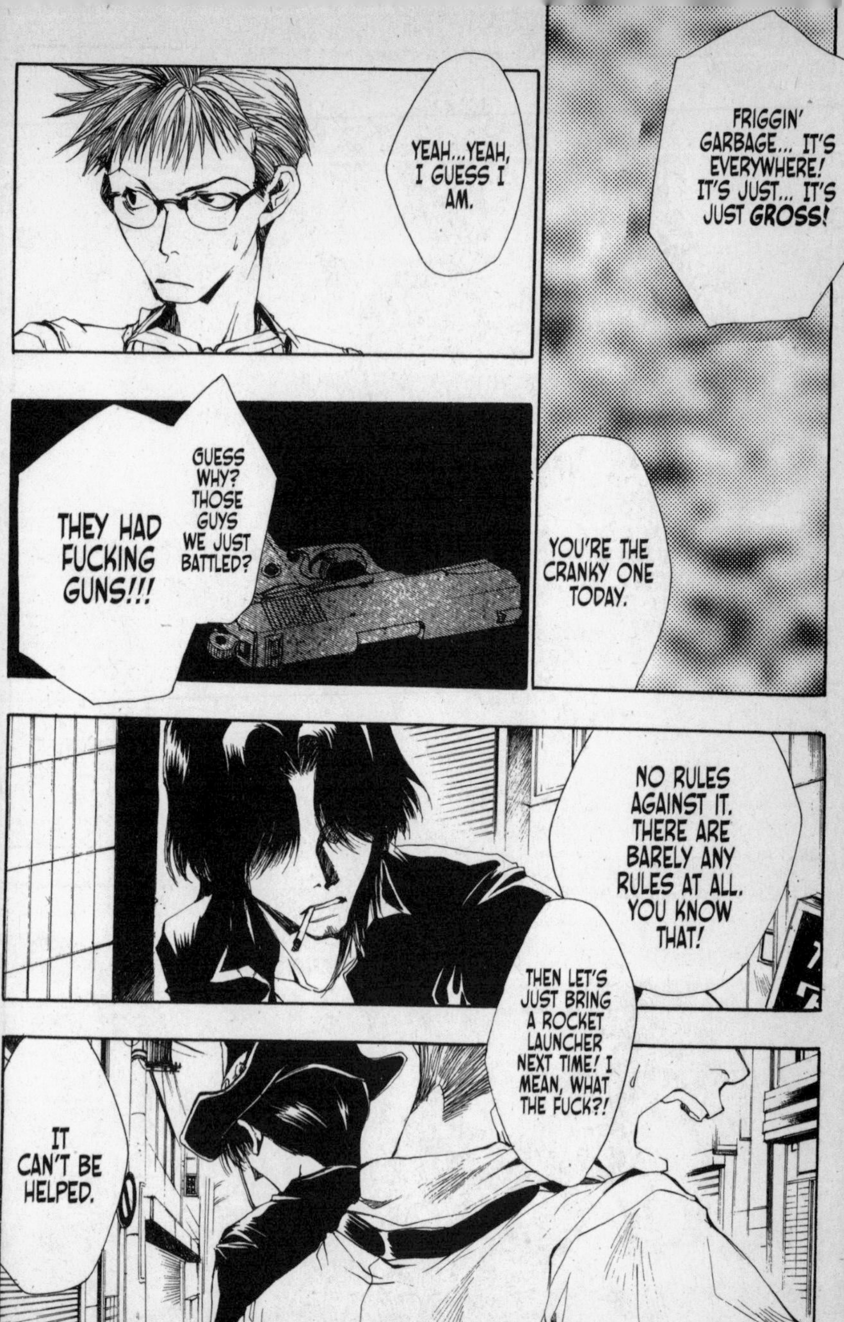
FRIGGIN' GARBAGE... IT'S EVERYWHERE! IT'S JUST... IT'S JUST **GROSS!**
YOU'RE THE CRANKY ONE TODAY.
YEAH...YEAH, I GUESS I AM.
GUESS WHY? THOSE GUYS WE JUST BATTLED?
THEY HAD FUCKING GUNS!!!
NO RULES AGAINST IT. THERE ARE BARELY ANY RULES AT ALL. YOU KNOW THAT!
THEN LET'S JUST BRING A ROCKET LAUNCHER NEXT TIME! I MEAN, WHAT THE FUCK?!
IT CAN'T BE HELPED.

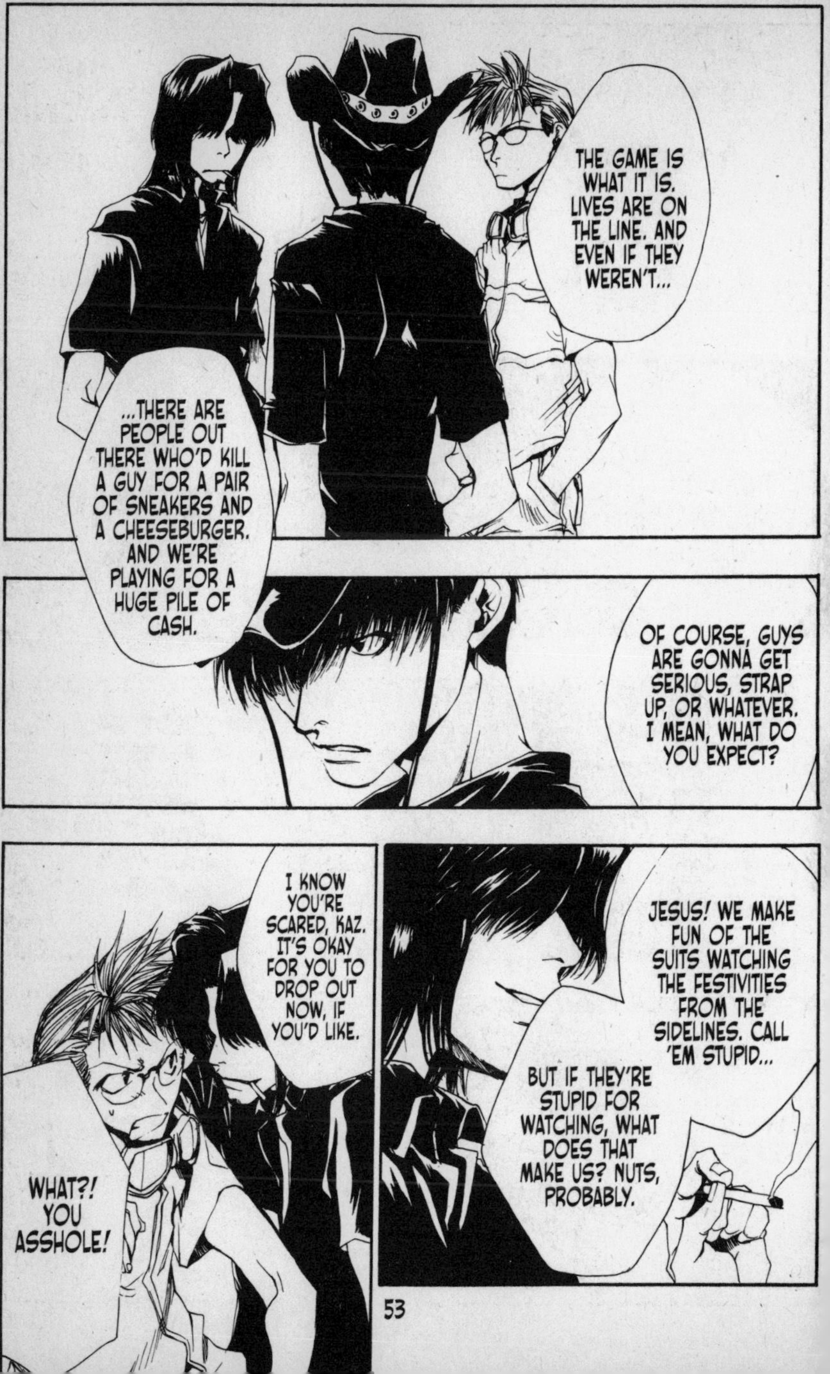
THE GAME IS WHAT IT IS. LIVES ARE ON THE LINE. AND EVEN IF THEY WEREN'T...
...THERE ARE PEOPLE OUT THERE WHO'D KILL A GUY FOR A PAIR OF SNEAKERS AND A CHEESEBURGER. AND WE'RE PLAYING FOR A HUGE PILE OF CASH.
OF COURSE, GUYS ARE GONNA GET SERIOUS, STRAP UP, OR WHATEVER. I MEAN, WHAT DO YOU EXPECT?
JESUS! WE MAKE FUN OF THE SUITS WATCHING THE FESTIVITIES FROM THE SIDELINES. CALL 'EM STUPID...
BUT IF THEY'RE STUPID FOR WATCHING, WHAT DOES THAT MAKE US? NUTS, PROBABLY.
I KNOW YOU'RE SCARED, KAZ. IT'S OKAY FOR YOU TO DROP OUT NOW, IF YOU'D LIKE.
WHAT?! YOU ASSHOLE!

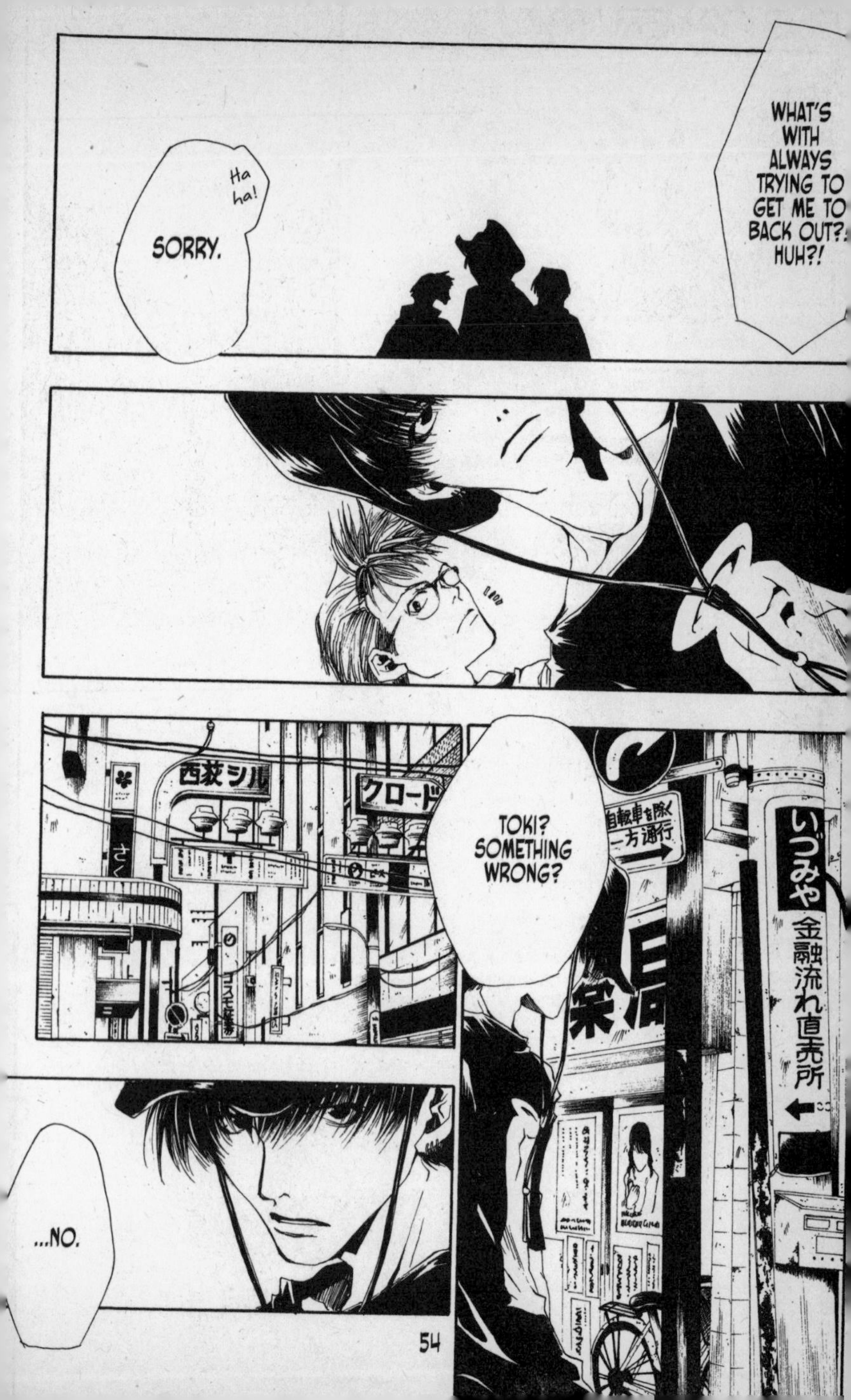
WHAT'S WITH ALWAYS TRYING TO GET ME TO BACK OUT?! HUH?!
Ha ha!
SORRY.
TOKI? SOMETHING WRONG?
いづみや
金融流れ直売所
自転車を除く
一方通行
西荻シル
クロード
...NO.

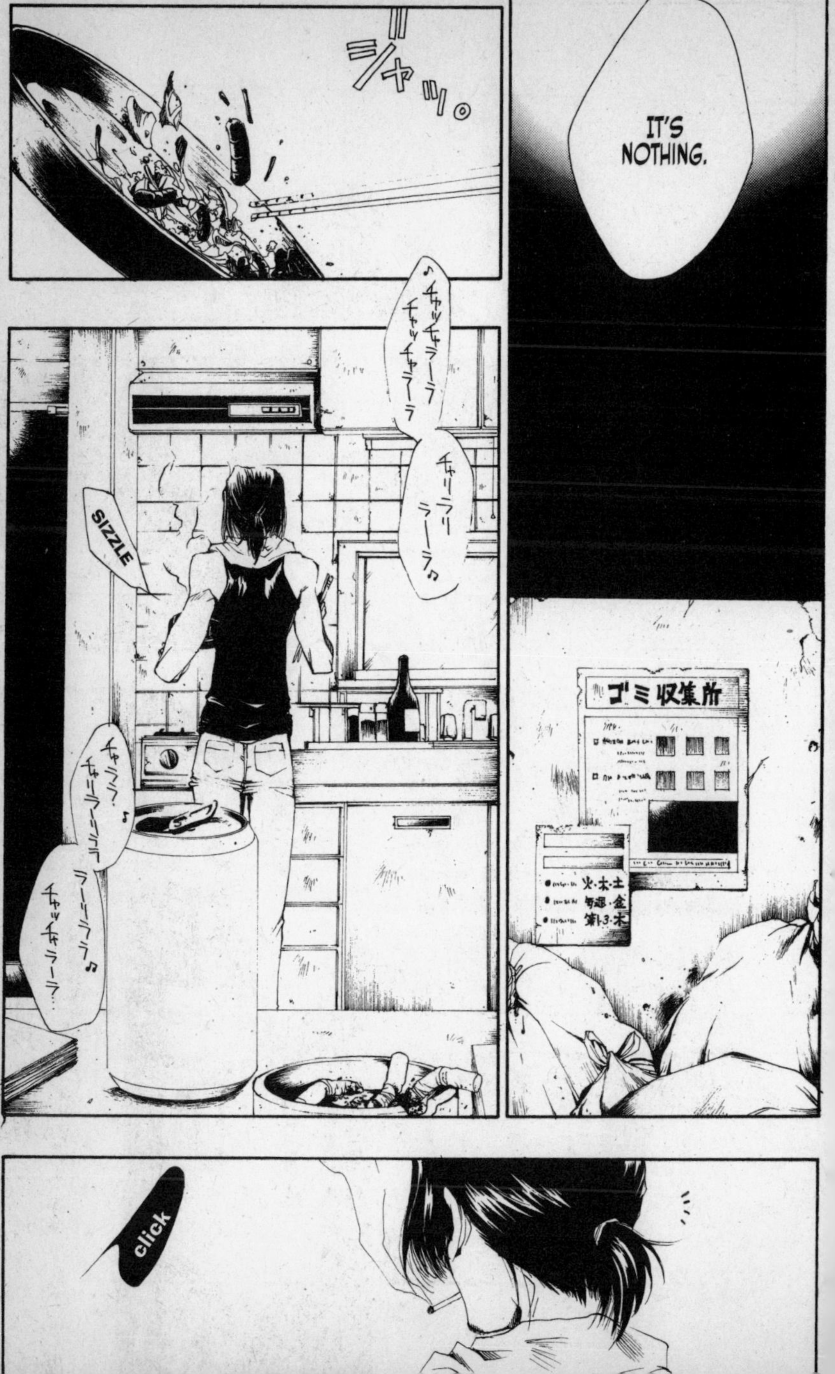
IT'S NOTHING.
ジャッ
♪チャッチャラーラ チャッチャラーラ
チャリラリ ラーラ♪
ゴミ収集所
火・木・土
毎週・金
第1・3・木
SIZZLE
チャララ. チャリラーリララ♪
ラーリララ♪ チャッチャラーラ…
click

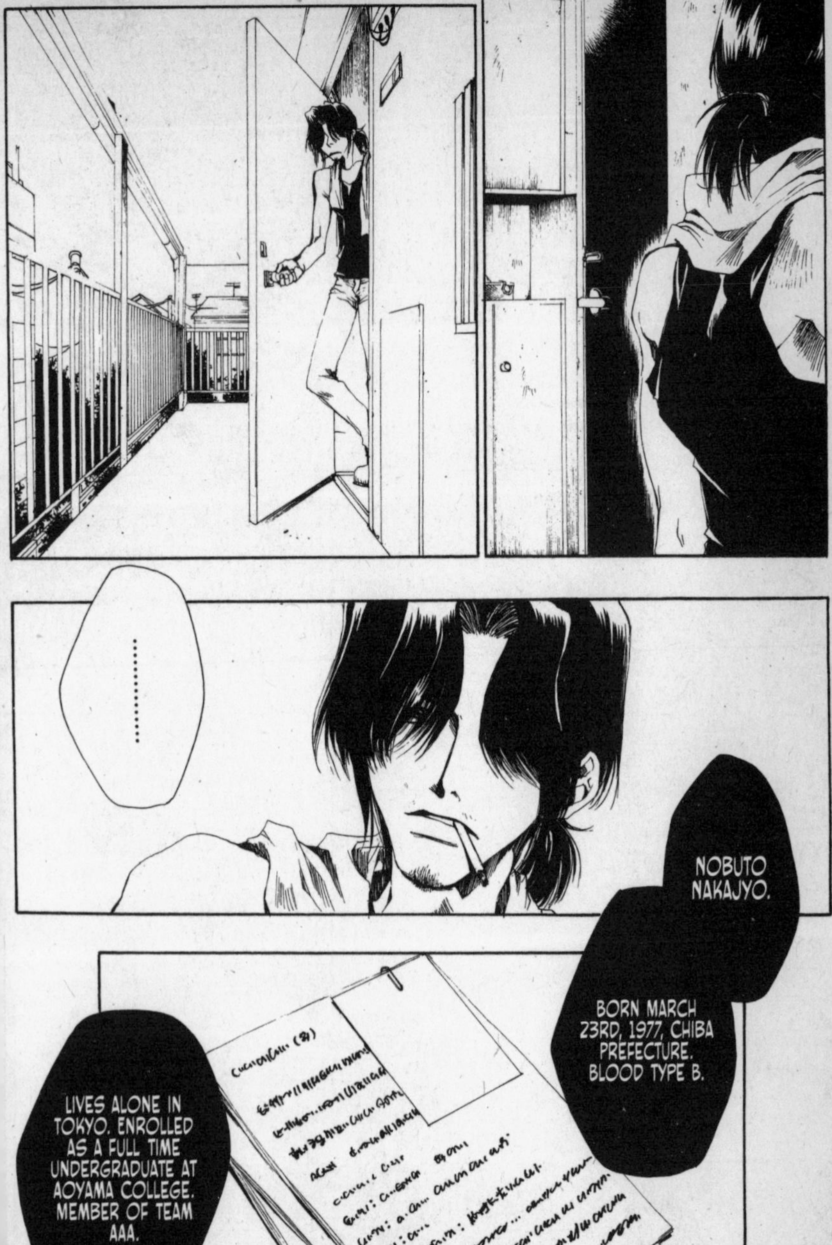
……
NOBUTO NAKAJYO.
BORN MARCH 23RD, 1977, CHIBA PREFECTURE. BLOOD TYPE B.
LIVES ALONE IN TOKYO. ENROLLED AS A FULL TIME UNDERGRADUATE AT AOYAMA COLLEGE. MEMBER OF TEAM AAA.

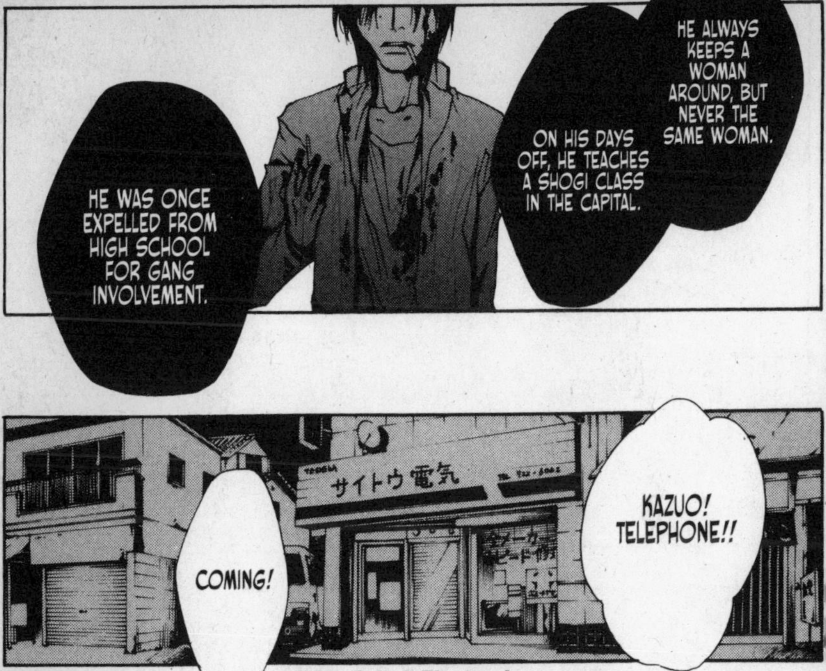
HE ALWAYS KEEPS A WOMAN AROUND, BUT NEVER THE SAME WOMAN.
ON HIS DAYS OFF, HE TEACHES A SHOGI CLASS IN THE CAPITAL.
HE WAS ONCE EXPELLED FROM HIGH SCHOOL FOR GANG INVOLVEMENT.
KAZUO! TELEPHONE!!
COMING!

SIGN: Saitoh Electronics

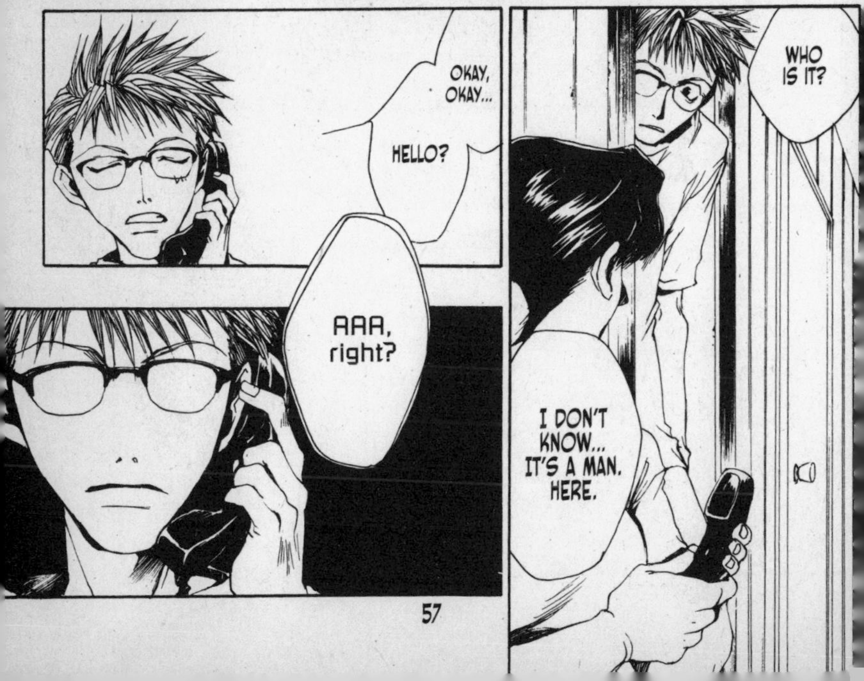
WHO IS IT?
I DON'T KNOW... IT'S A MAN. HERE.
OKAY, OKAY...
HELLO?
AAA, right?

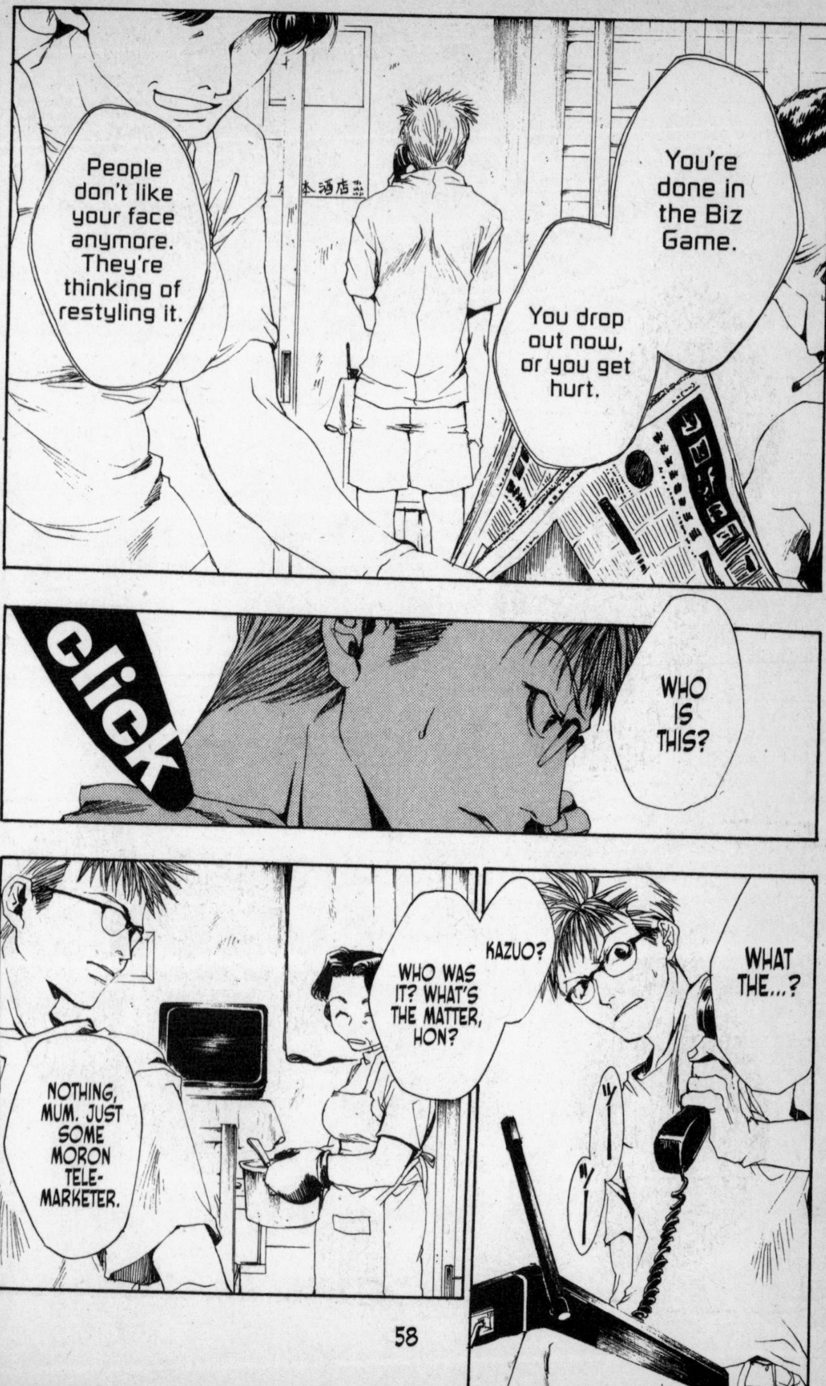
You're done in the Biz Game.
You drop out now, or you get hurt.
People don't like your face anymore. They're thinking of restyling it.
WHO IS THIS?
click
WHAT THE...?
KAZUO?
WHO WAS IT? WHAT'S THE MATTER, HON?
NOTHING, MUM. JUST SOME MORON TELE-MARKETER.

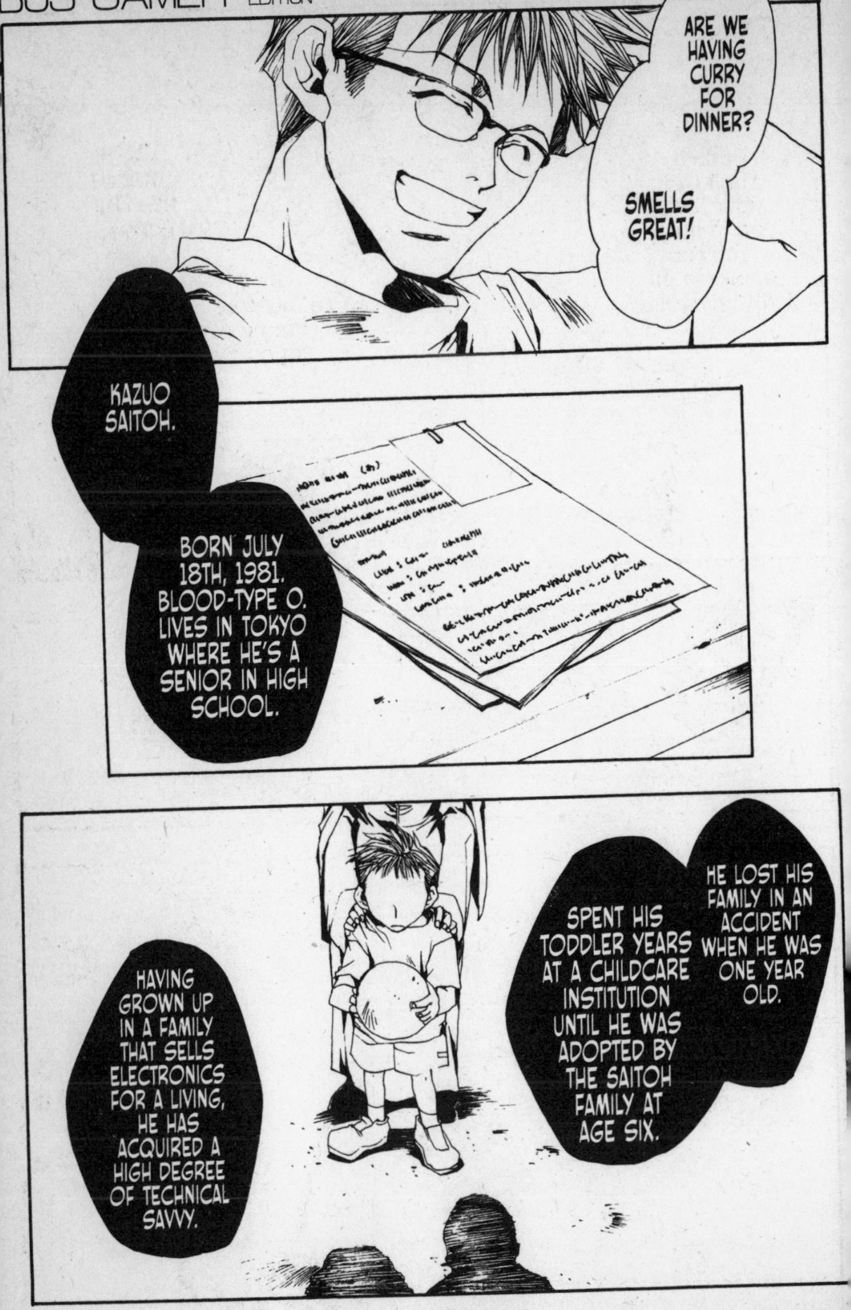
ARE WE HAVING CURRY FOR DINNER?
SMELLS GREAT!
KAZUO SAITOH.
BORN JULY 18TH, 1981. BLOOD-TYPE O. LIVES IN TOKYO WHERE HE'S A SENIOR IN HIGH SCHOOL.
HE LOST HIS FAMILY IN AN ACCIDENT WHEN HE WAS ONE YEAR OLD.
SPENT HIS TODDLER YEARS AT A CHILDCARE INSTITUTION UNTIL HE WAS ADOPTED BY THE SAITOH FAMILY AT AGE SIX.
HAVING GROWN UP IN A FAMILY THAT SELLS ELECTRONICS FOR A LIVING, HE HAS ACQUIRED A HIGH DEGREE OF TECHNICAL SAVVY.

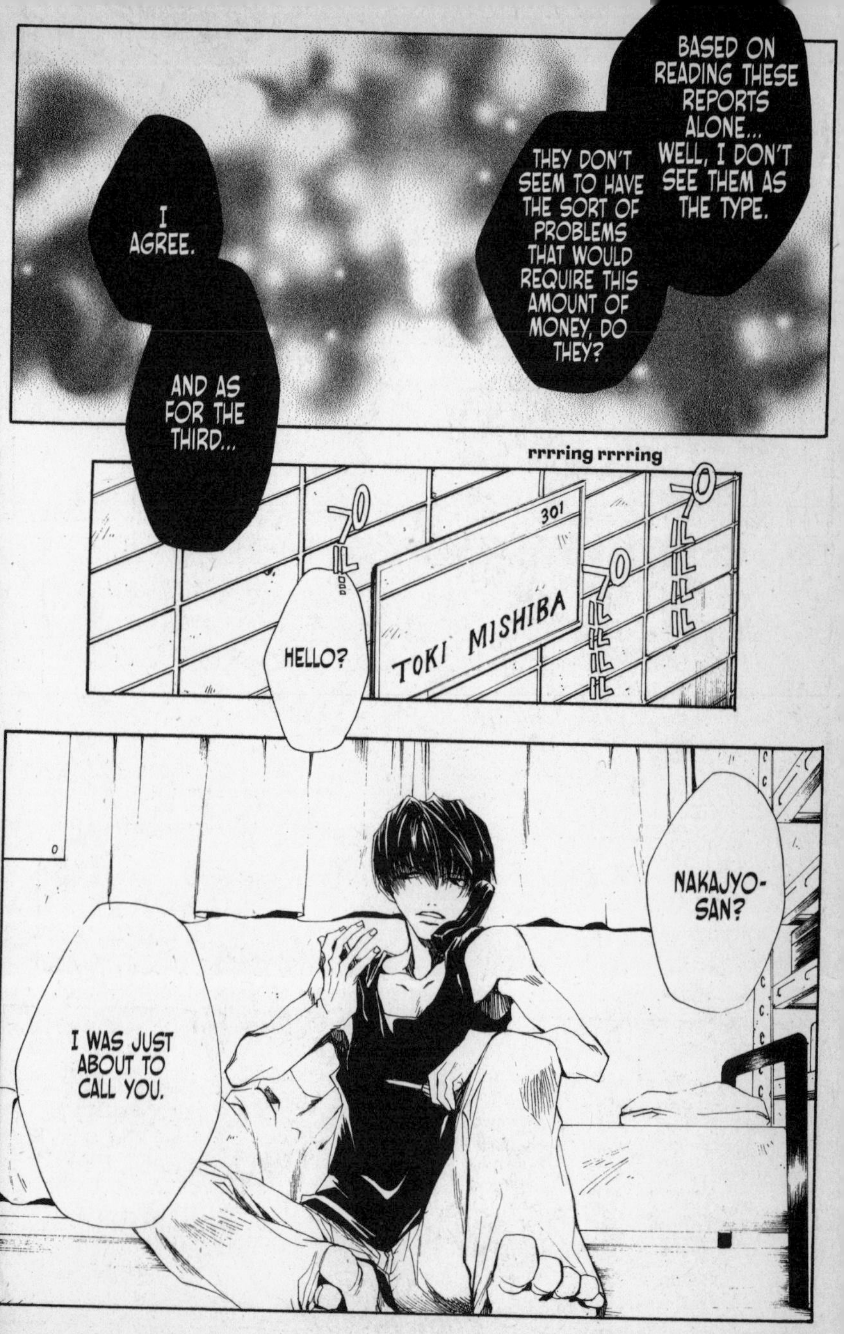
BASED ON READING THESE REPORTS ALONE... WELL, I DON'T SEE THEM AS THE TYPE.
THEY DON'T SEEM TO HAVE THE SORT OF PROBLEMS THAT WOULD REQUIRE THIS AMOUNT OF MONEY, DO THEY?
I AGREE.
AND AS FOR THE THIRD...
rrrring rrrring
301
TOKI MISHIBA
HELLO?
NAKAJYO-SAN?
I WAS JUST ABOUT TO CALL YOU.

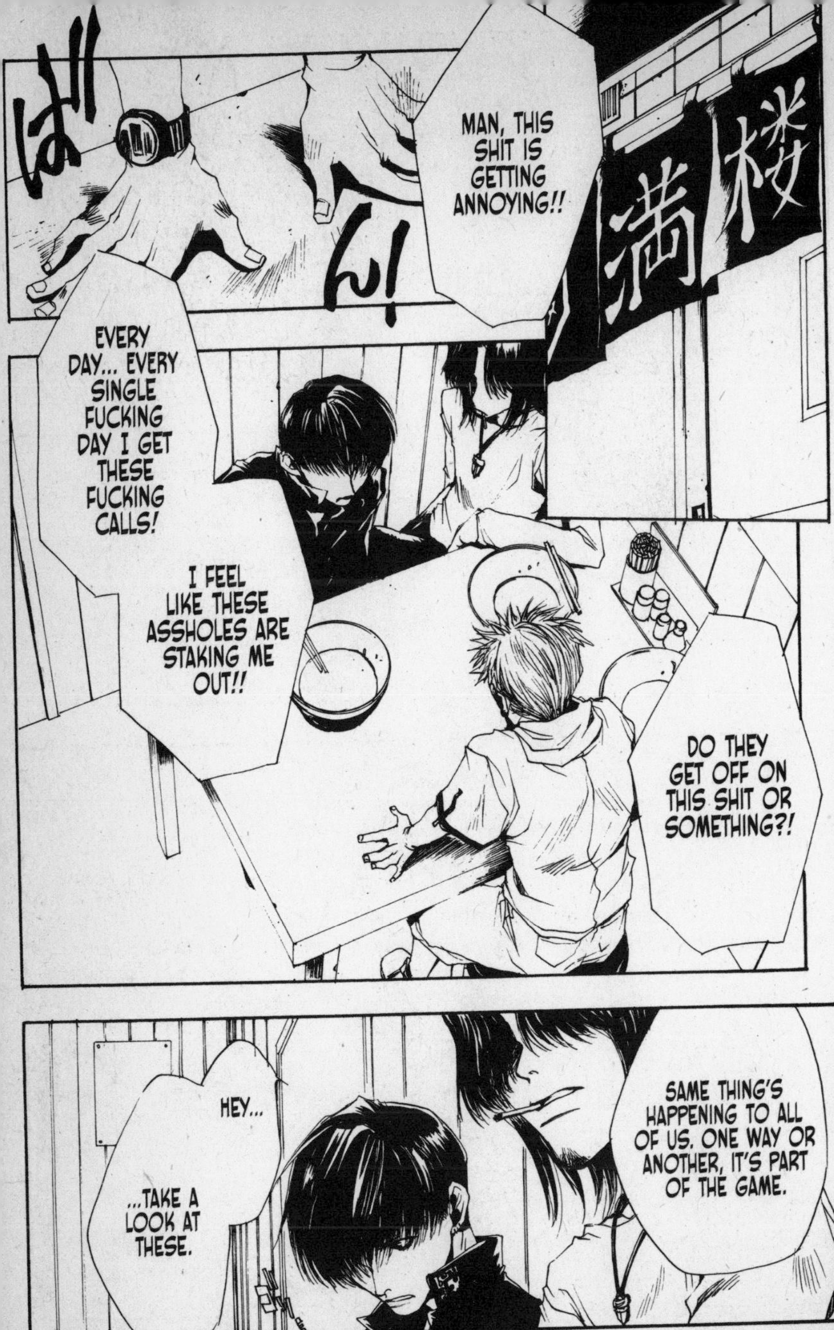

満楼
ばん!
MAN, THIS SHIT IS GETTING ANNOYING!!
EVERY DAY... EVERY SINGLE FUCKING DAY I GET THESE FUCKING CALLS!
I FEEL LIKE THESE ASSHOLES ARE STAKING ME OUT!!
DO THEY GET OFF ON THIS SHIT OR SOMETHING?!
SAME THING'S HAPPENING TO ALL OF US. ONE WAY OR ANOTHER, IT'S PART OF THE GAME.
HEY...
...TAKE A LOOK AT THESE.

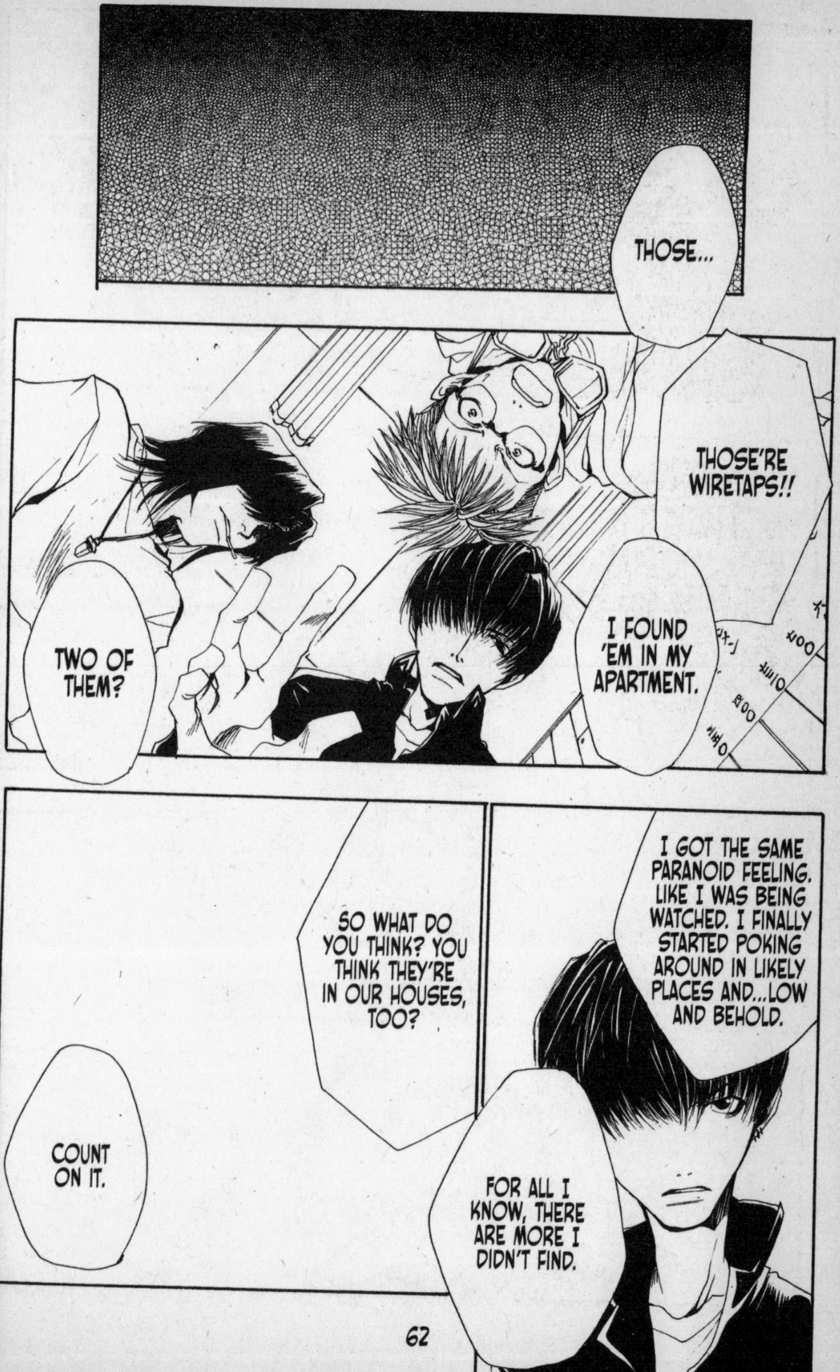
THOSE...
THOSE'RE WIRETAPS!!
I FOUND 'EM IN MY APARTMENT.
TWO OF THEM?
I GOT THE SAME PARANOID FEELING. LIKE I WAS BEING WATCHED. I FINALLY STARTED POKING AROUND IN LIKELY PLACES AND...LOW AND BEHOLD.
FOR ALL I KNOW, THERE ARE MORE I DIDN'T FIND.
SO WHAT DO YOU THINK? YOU THINK THEY'RE IN OUR HOUSES, TOO?
COUNT ON IT.

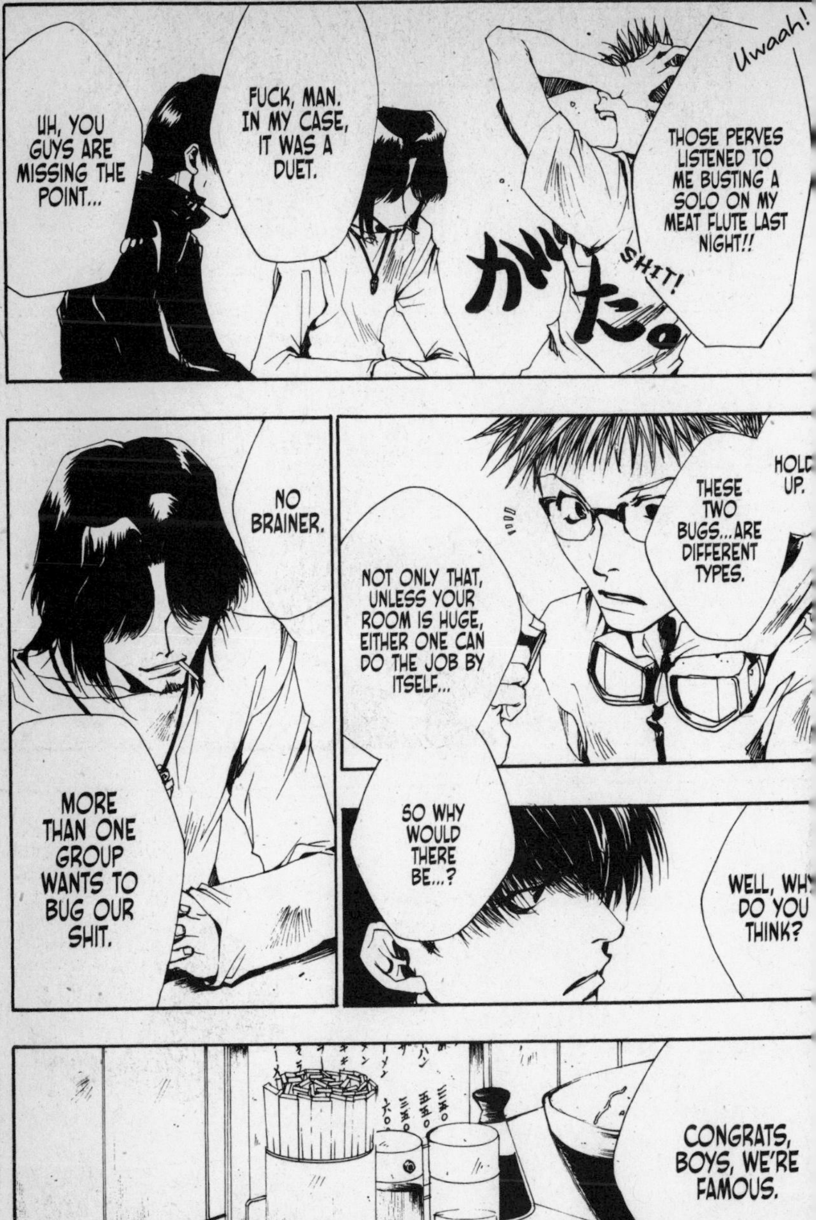
Uwaah!
THOSE PERVES LISTENED TO ME BUSTING A SOLO ON MY MEAT FLUTE LAST NIGHT!!
SHIT!
FUCK, MAN. IN MY CASE, IT WAS A DUET.
UH, YOU GUYS ARE MISSING THE POINT...
HOLD UP.
THESE TWO BUGS...ARE DIFFERENT TYPES.
NOT ONLY THAT, UNLESS YOUR ROOM IS HUGE, EITHER ONE CAN DO THE JOB BY ITSELF...
WELL, WHY DO YOU THINK?
SO WHY WOULD THERE BE...?
NO BRAINER.
MORE THAN ONE GROUP WANTS TO BUG OUR SHIT.
CONGRATS, BOYS, WE'RE FAMOUS.

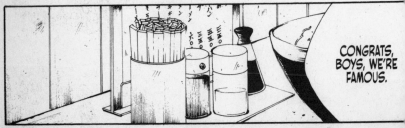

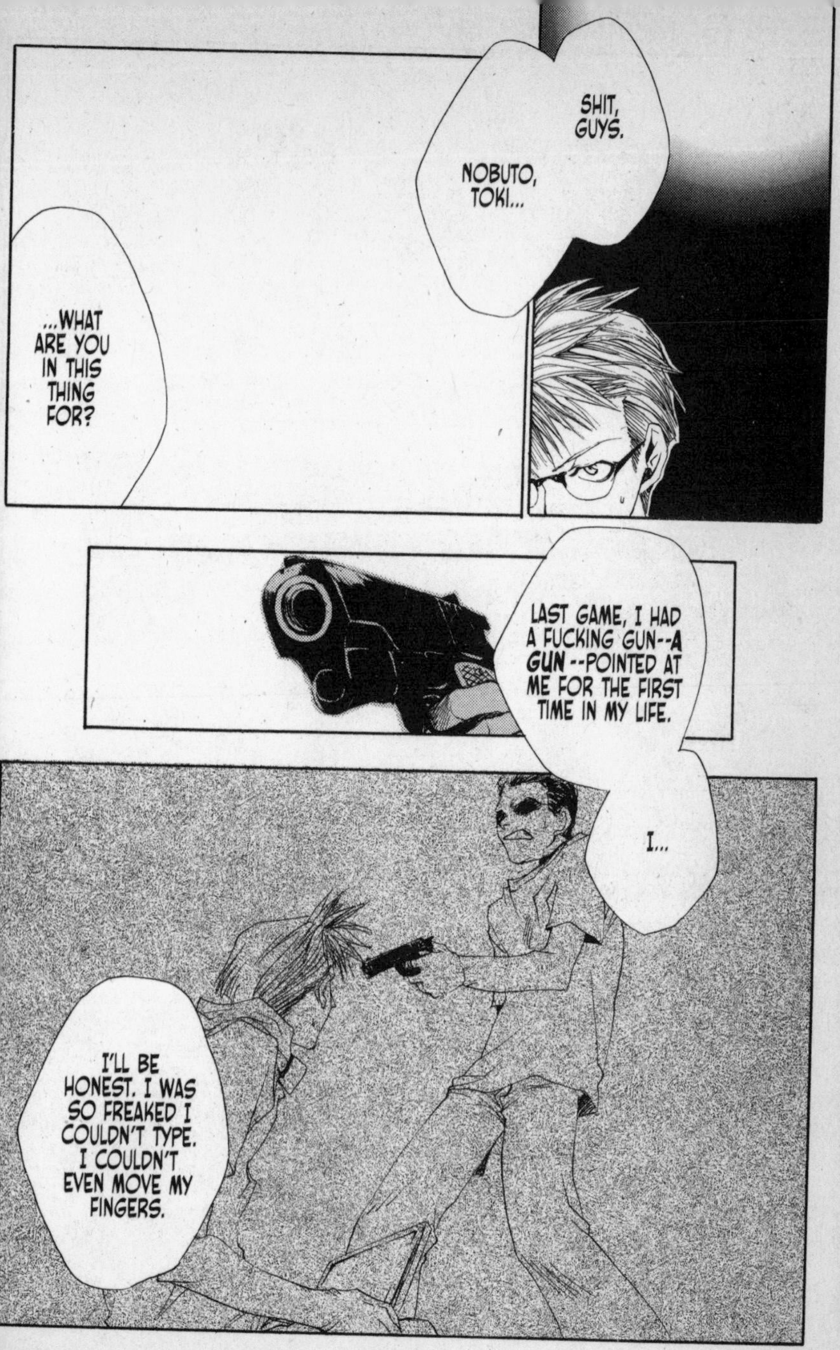
SHIT, GUYS.
NOBUTO, TOKI...
...WHAT ARE YOU IN THIS THING FOR?
LAST GAME, I HAD A FUCKING GUN--A **GUN**--POINTED AT ME FOR THE FIRST TIME IN MY LIFE.
I...
I'LL BE HONEST. I WAS SO FREAKED I COULDN'T TYPE. I COULDN'T EVEN MOVE MY FINGERS.

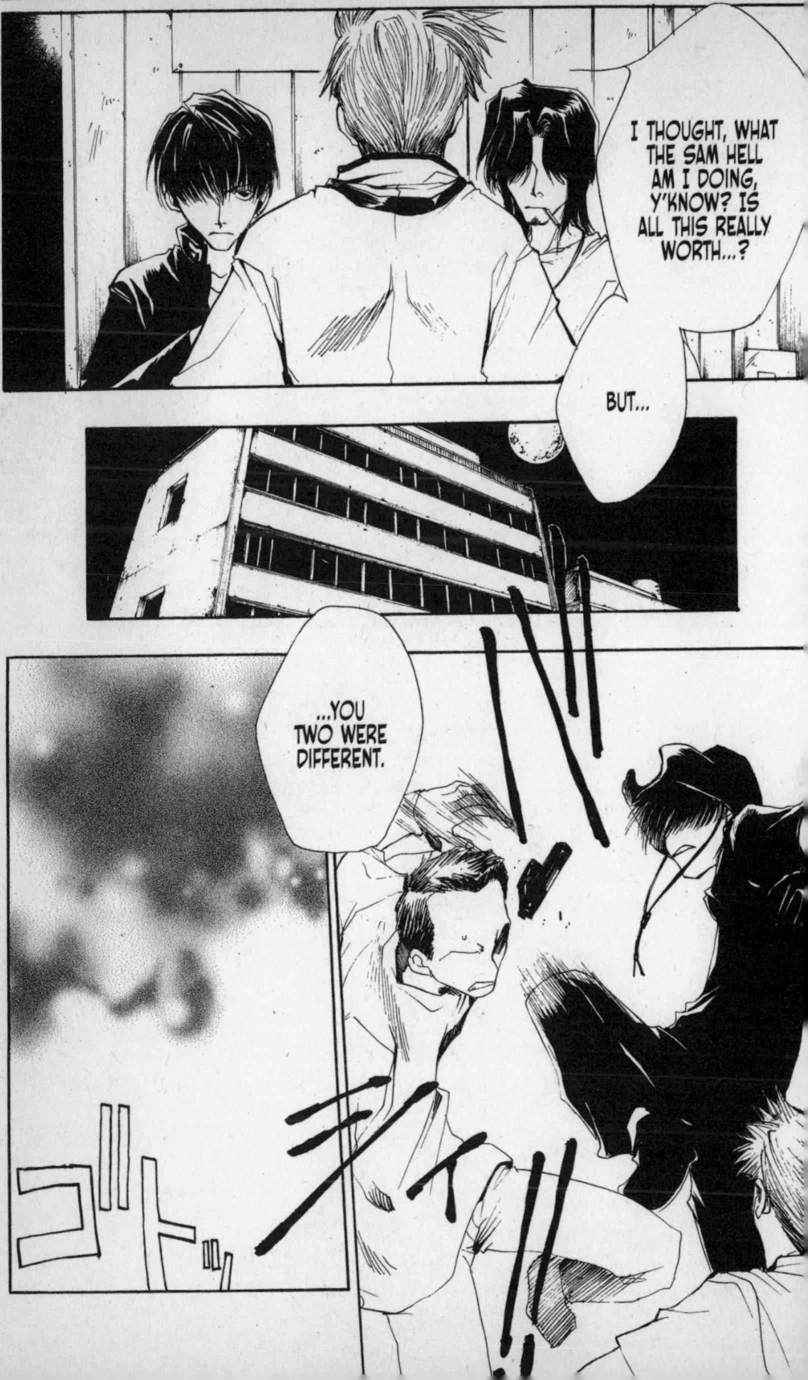
I THOUGHT, WHAT THE SAM HELL AM I DOING, Y'KNOW? IS ALL THIS REALLY WORTH...?
BUT...
...YOU TWO WERE DIFFERENT.
ゴトッ

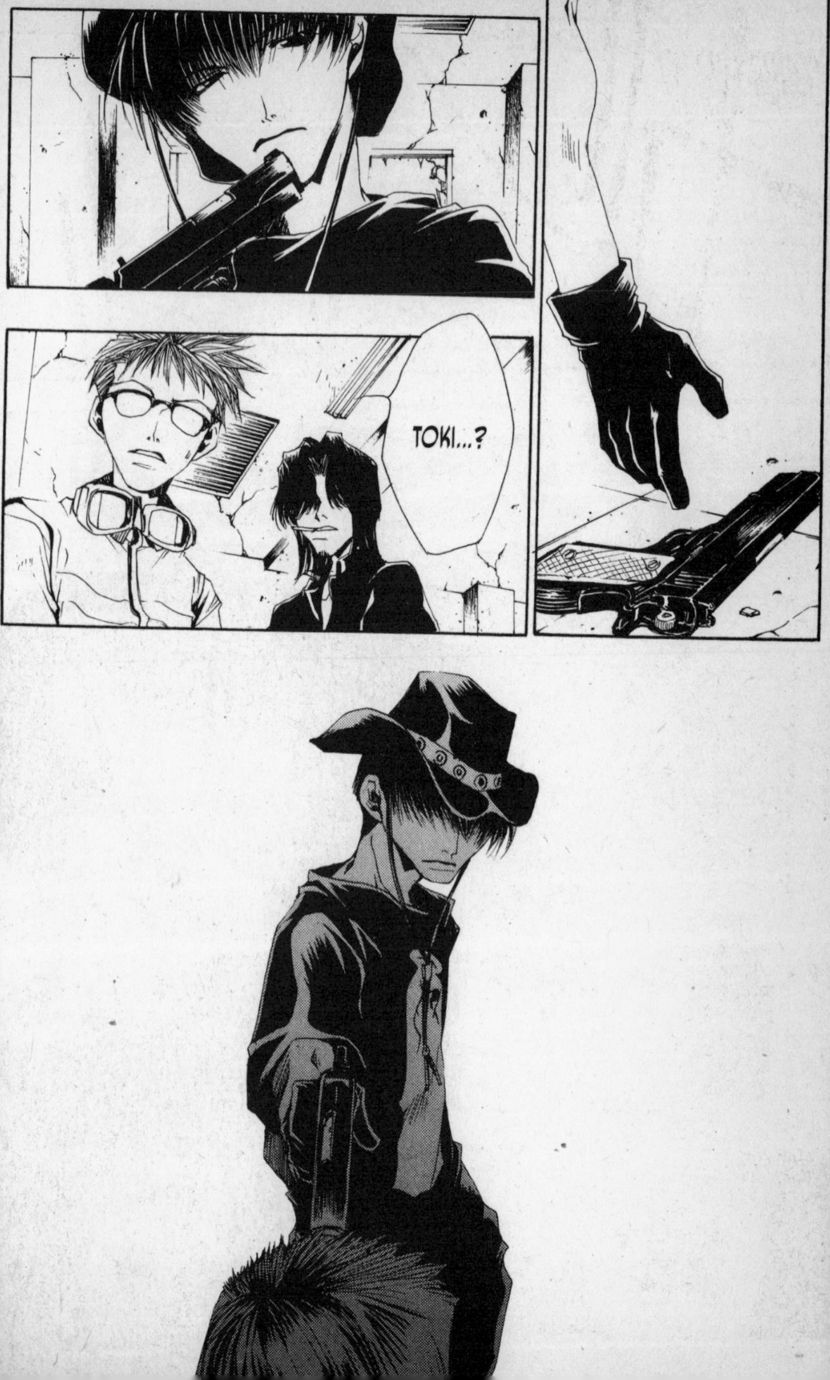
TOKI...?

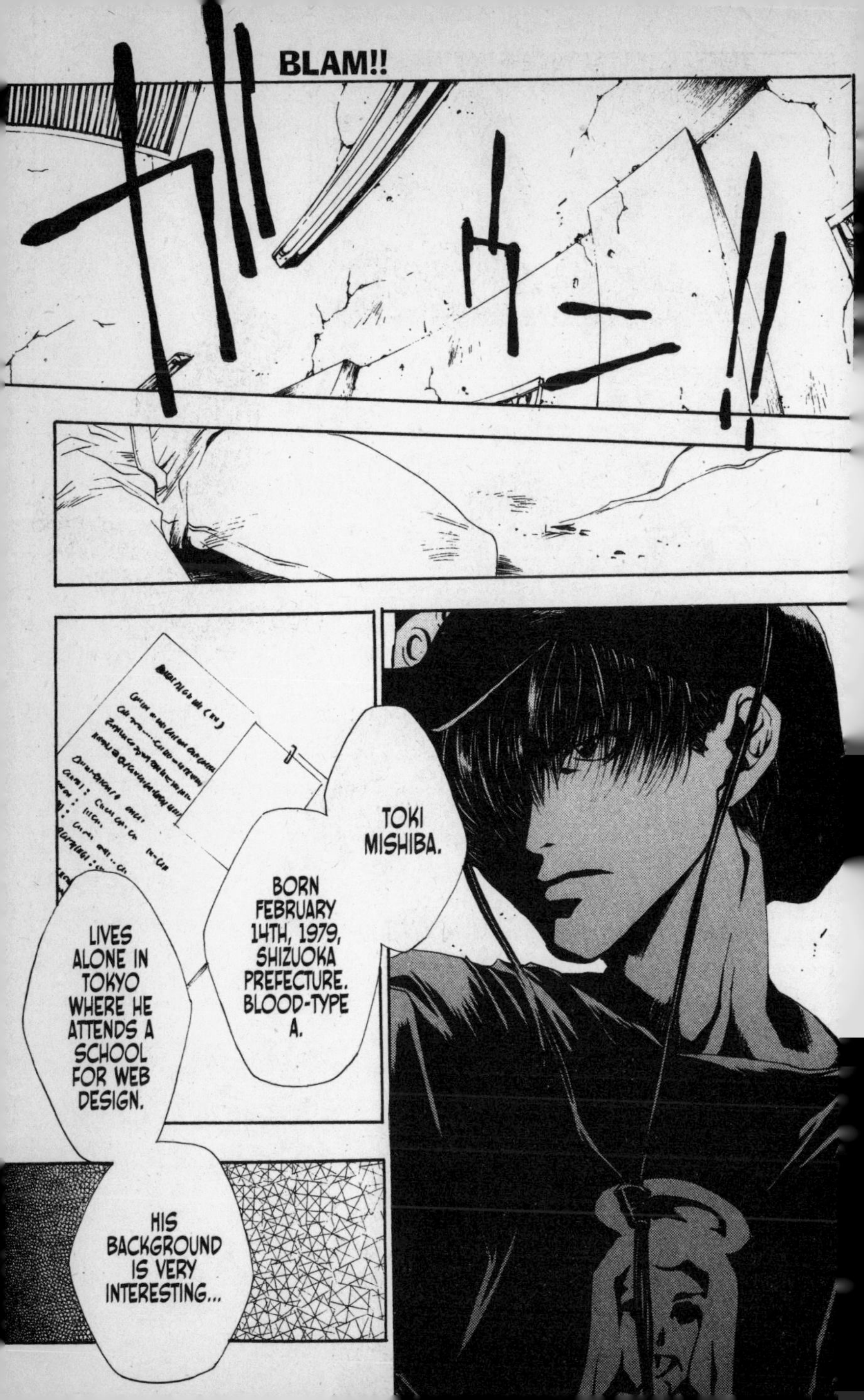
BLAM!!
TOKI MISHIBA.
BORN FEBRUARY 14TH, 1979, SHIZUOKA PREFECTURE. BLOOD-TYPE A.
LIVES ALONE IN TOKYO WHERE HE ATTENDS A SCHOOL FOR WEB DESIGN.
HIS BACKGROUND IS VERY INTERESTING...

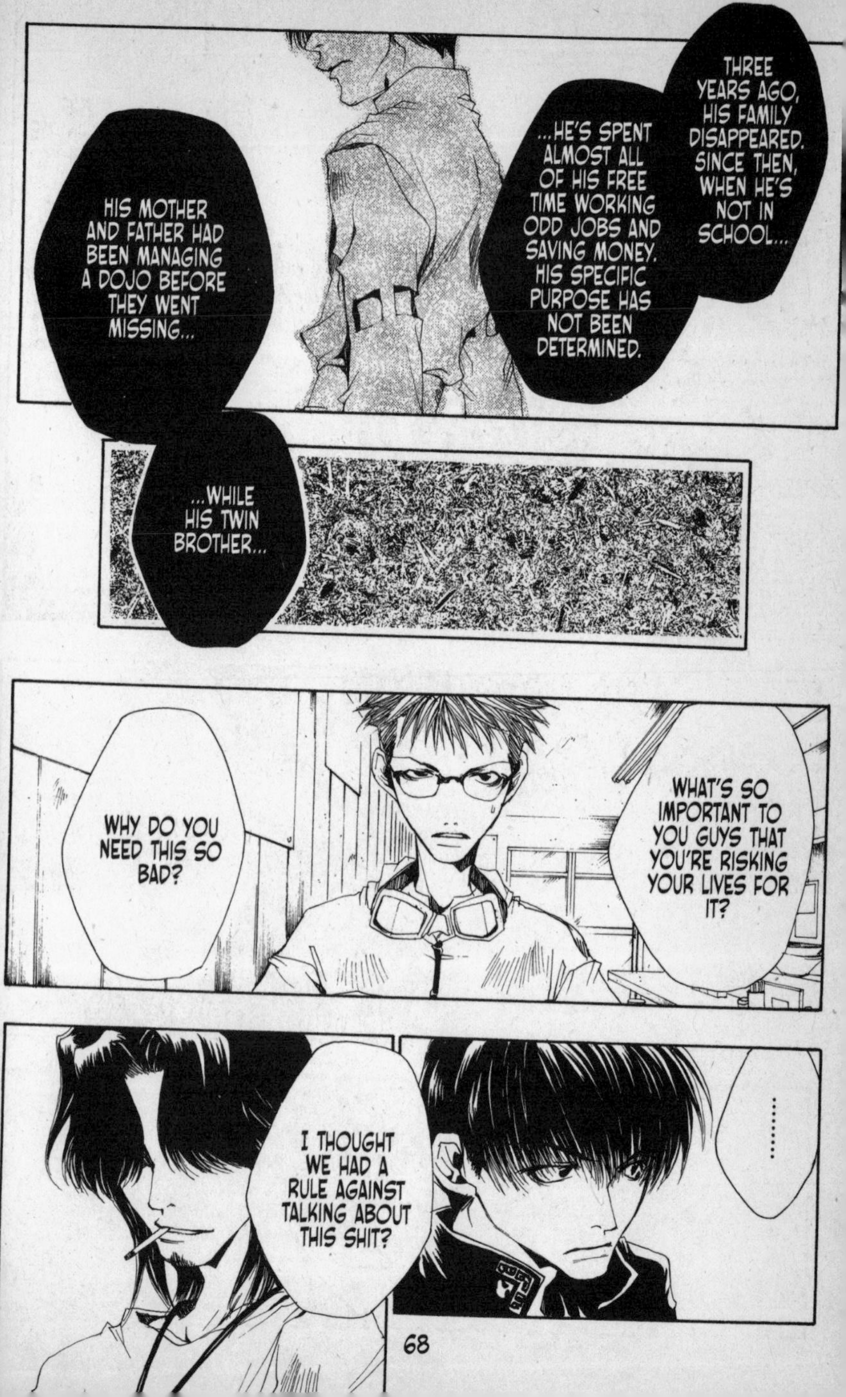
THREE YEARS AGO, HIS FAMILY DISAPPEARED. SINCE THEN, WHEN HE'S NOT IN SCHOOL...
...HE'S SPENT ALMOST ALL OF HIS FREE TIME WORKING ODD JOBS AND SAVING MONEY. HIS SPECIFIC PURPOSE HAS NOT BEEN DETERMINED.
HIS MOTHER AND FATHER HAD BEEN MANAGING A DOJO BEFORE THEY WENT MISSING...
...WHILE HIS TWIN BROTHER...
WHAT'S SO IMPORTANT TO YOU GUYS THAT YOU'RE RISKING YOUR LIVES FOR IT?
WHY DO YOU NEED THIS SO BAD?
......
I THOUGHT WE HAD A RULE AGAINST TALKING ABOUT THIS SHIT?

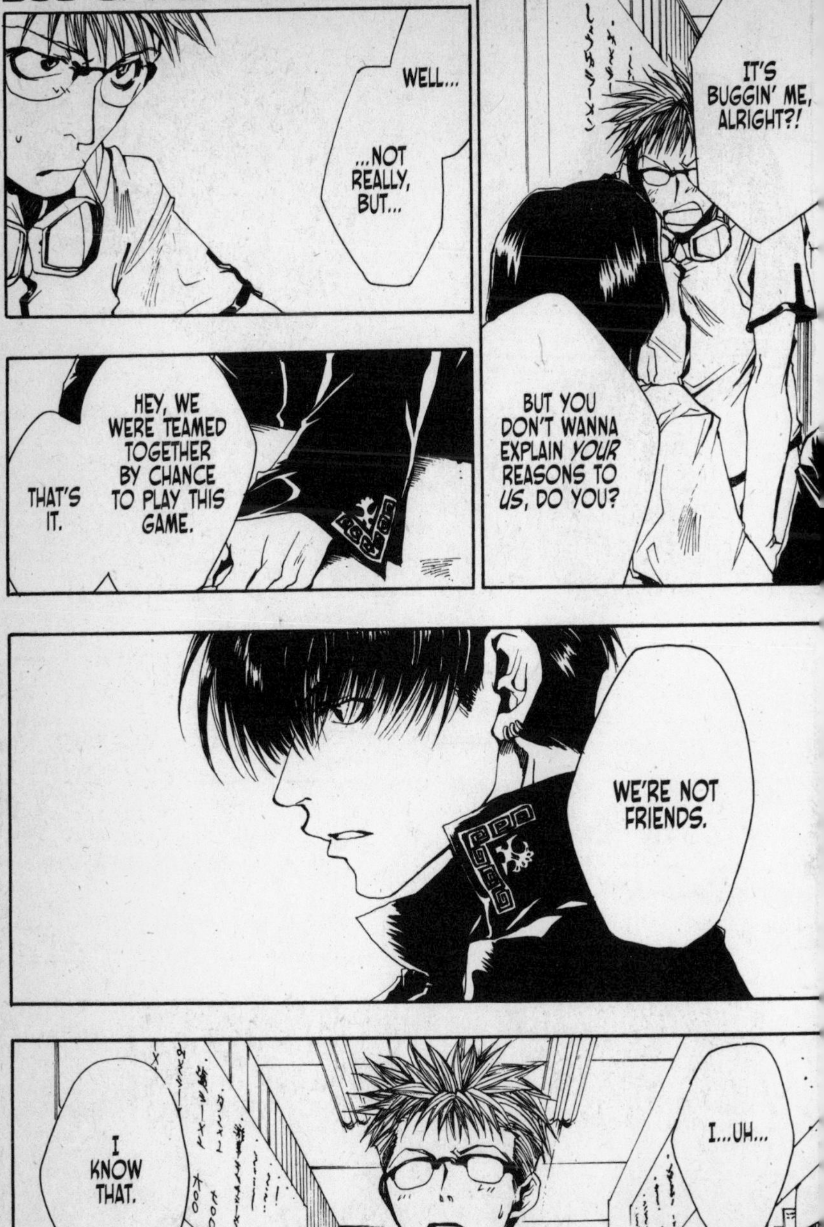
IT'S BUGGIN' ME, ALRIGHT?!
BUT YOU DON'T WANNA EXPLAIN *YOUR* REASONS TO *US*, DO YOU?
WELL...
...NOT REALLY, BUT...
HEY, WE WERE TEAMED TOGETHER BY CHANCE TO PLAY THIS GAME.
THAT'S IT.
WE'RE NOT FRIENDS.
I...UH...
I KNOW THAT.

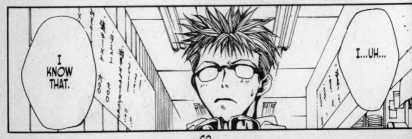

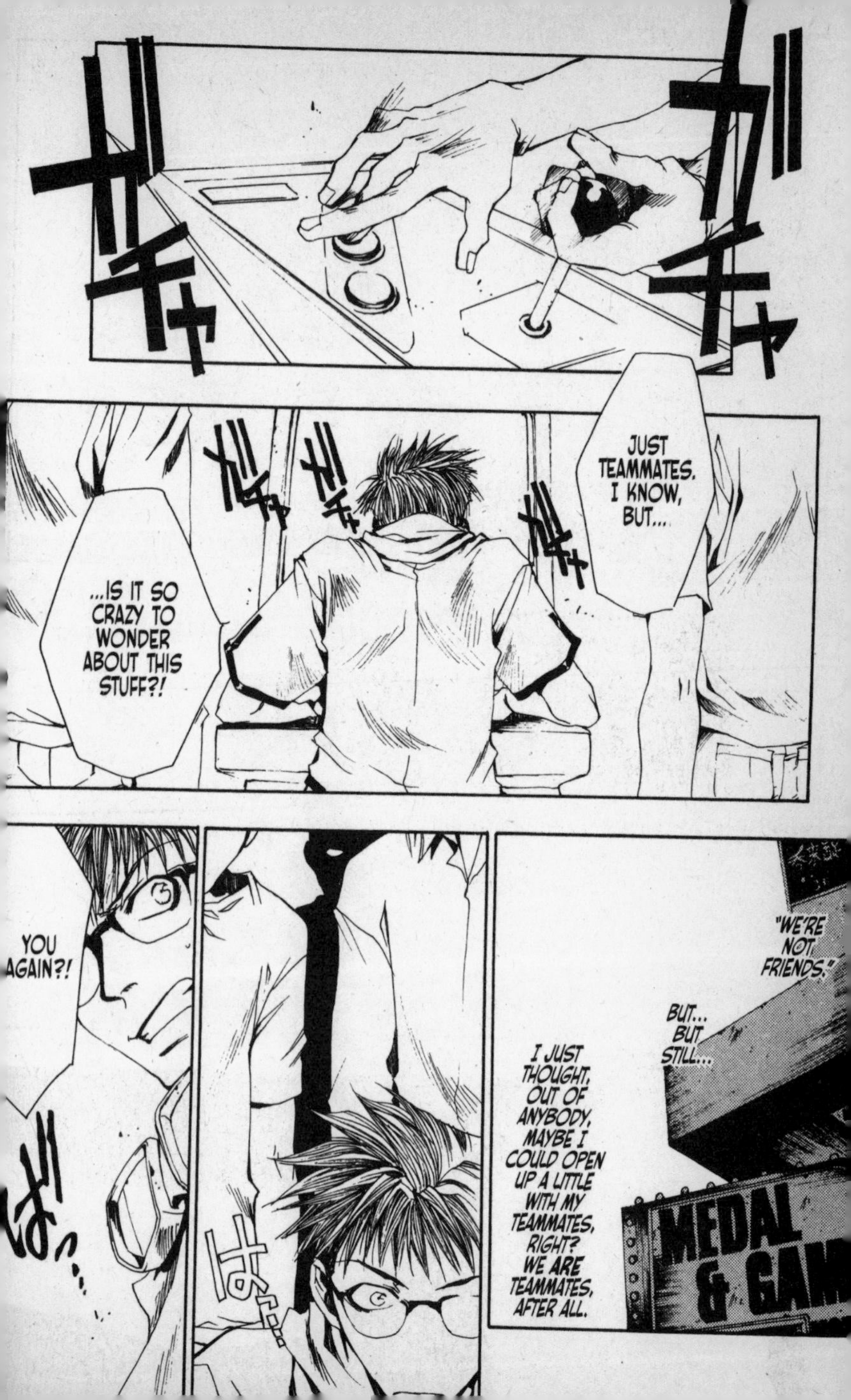
ガチャ
ガチャ
JUST TEAMMATES. I KNOW, BUT...
...IS IT SO CRAZY TO WONDER ABOUT THIS STUFF?!
"WE'RE NOT FRIENDS."
BUT... BUT STILL...
I JUST THOUGHT, OUT OF ANYBODY, MAYBE I COULD OPEN UP A LITTLE WITH MY TEAMMATES, RIGHT? WE ARE TEAMMATES, AFTER ALL.
MEDAL & GAM
YOU AGAIN?!

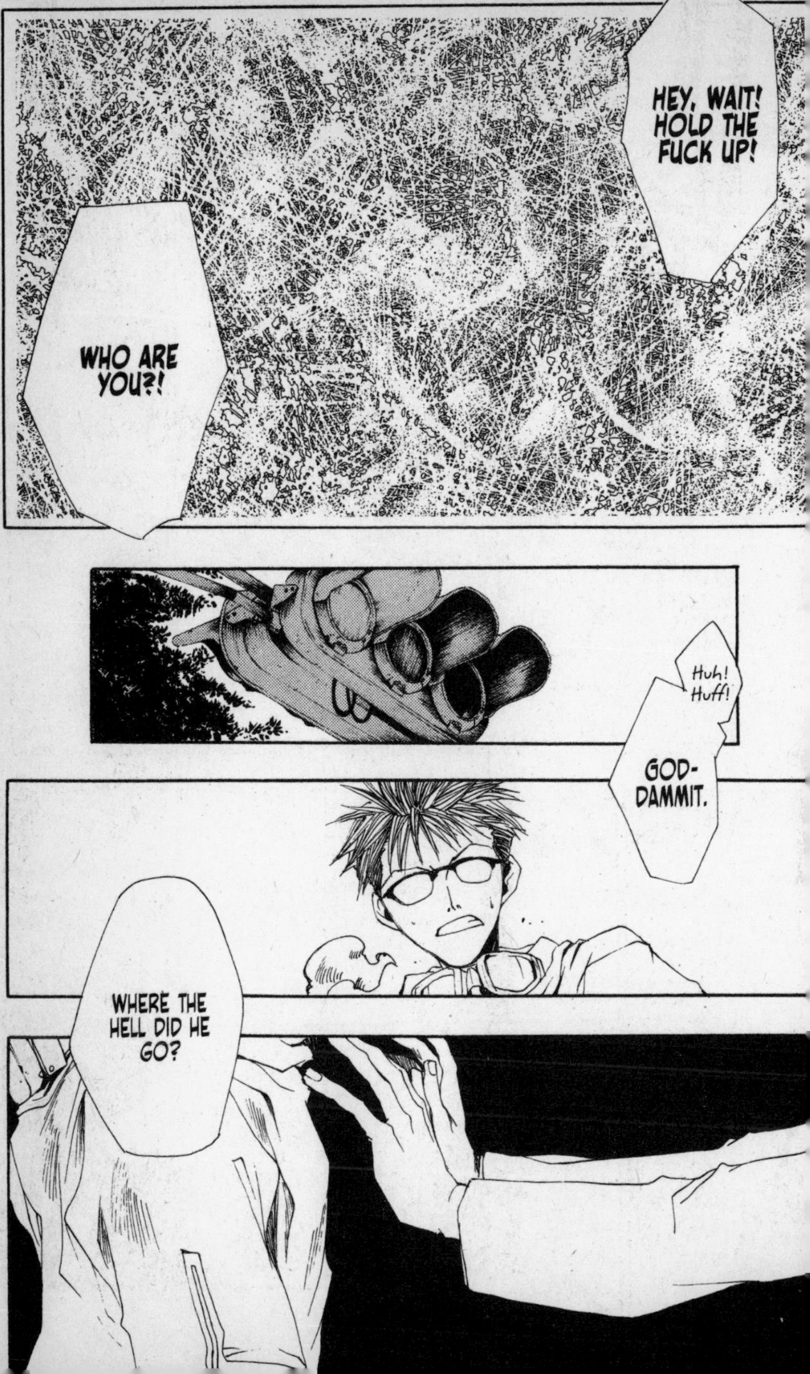
HEY, WAIT! HOLD THE FUCK UP!
WHO ARE YOU?!
Huh! Huff!
GOD-DAMMIT.
WHERE THE HELL DID HE GO?

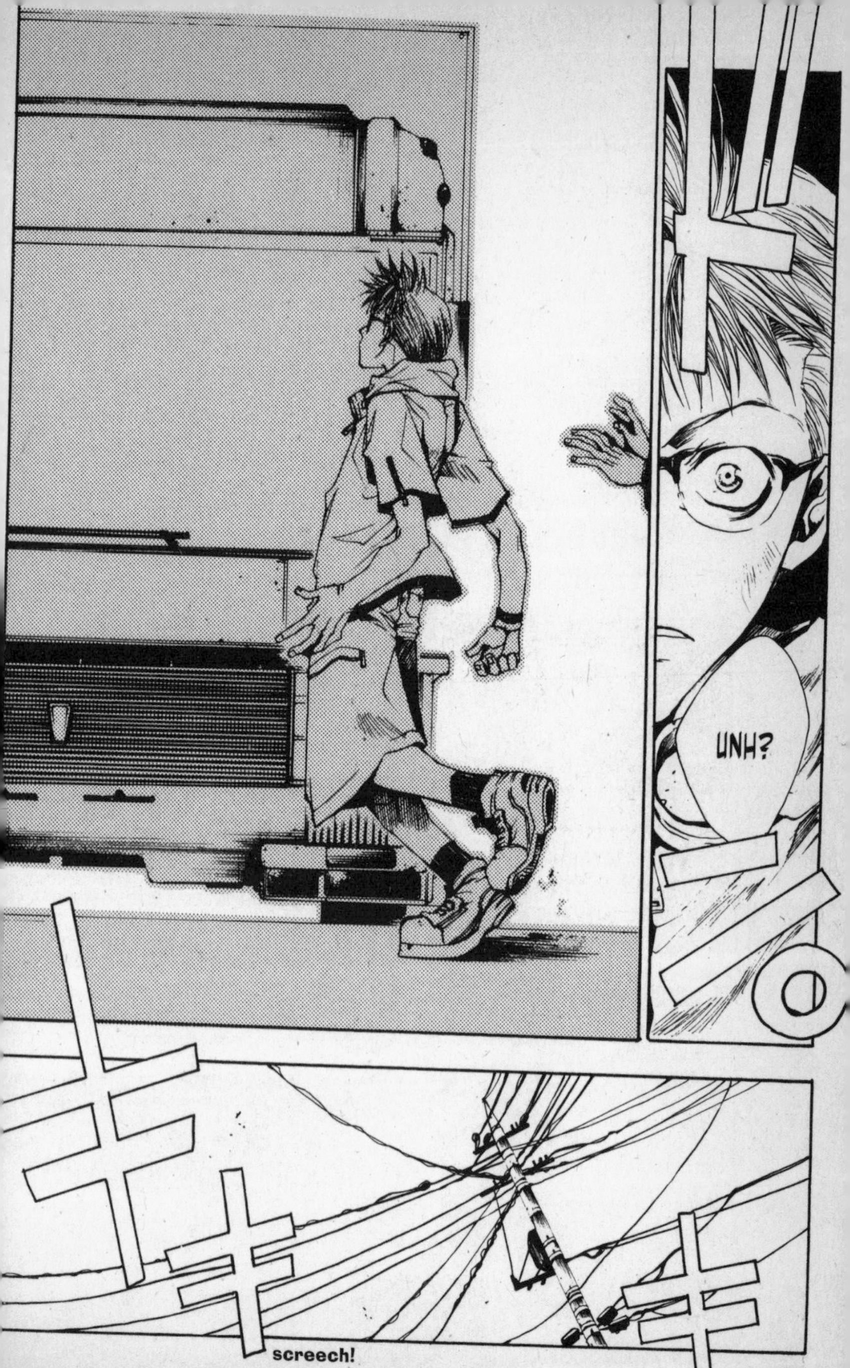
UNH?
screech!

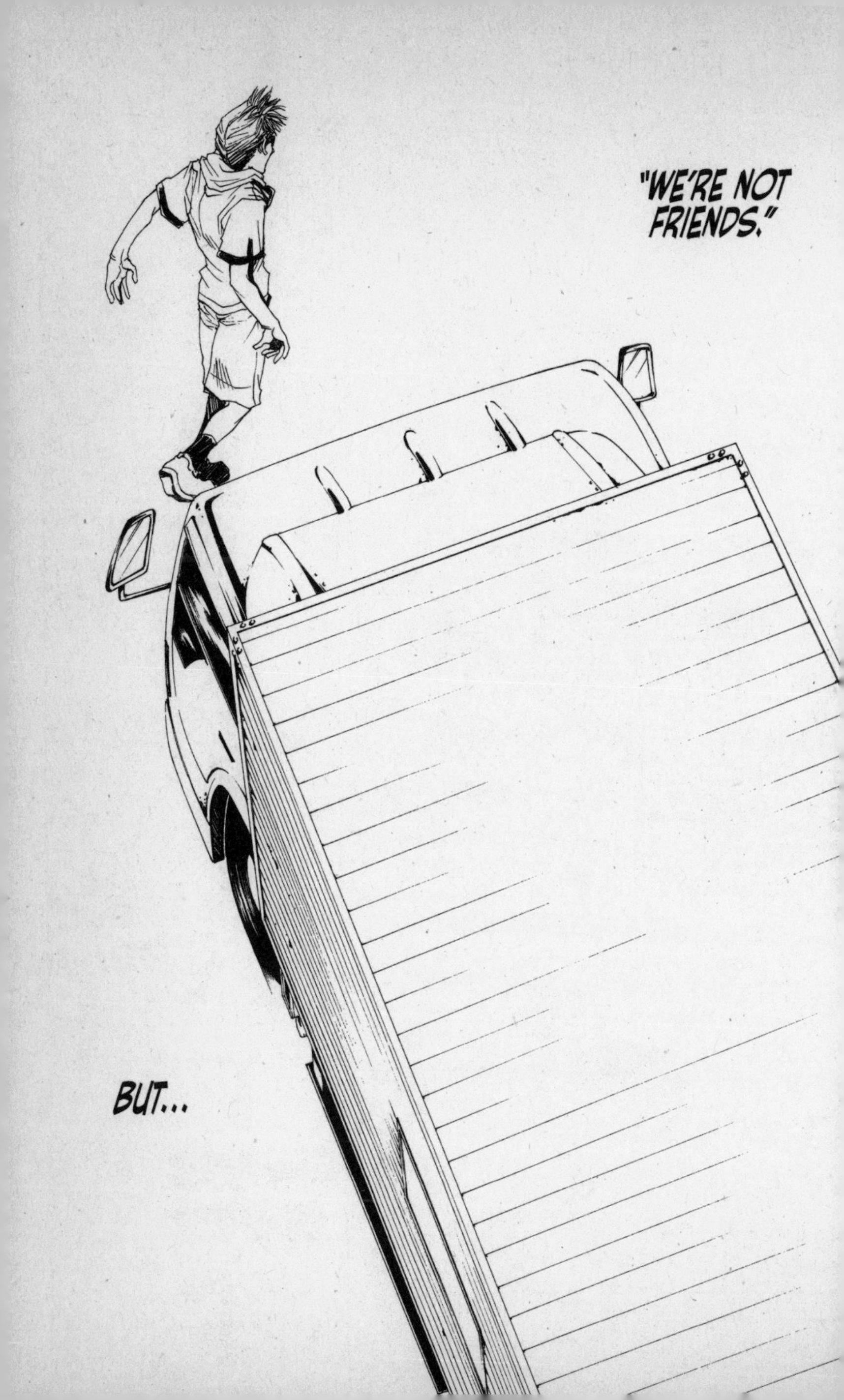
"WE'RE NOT FRIENDS."
BUT...

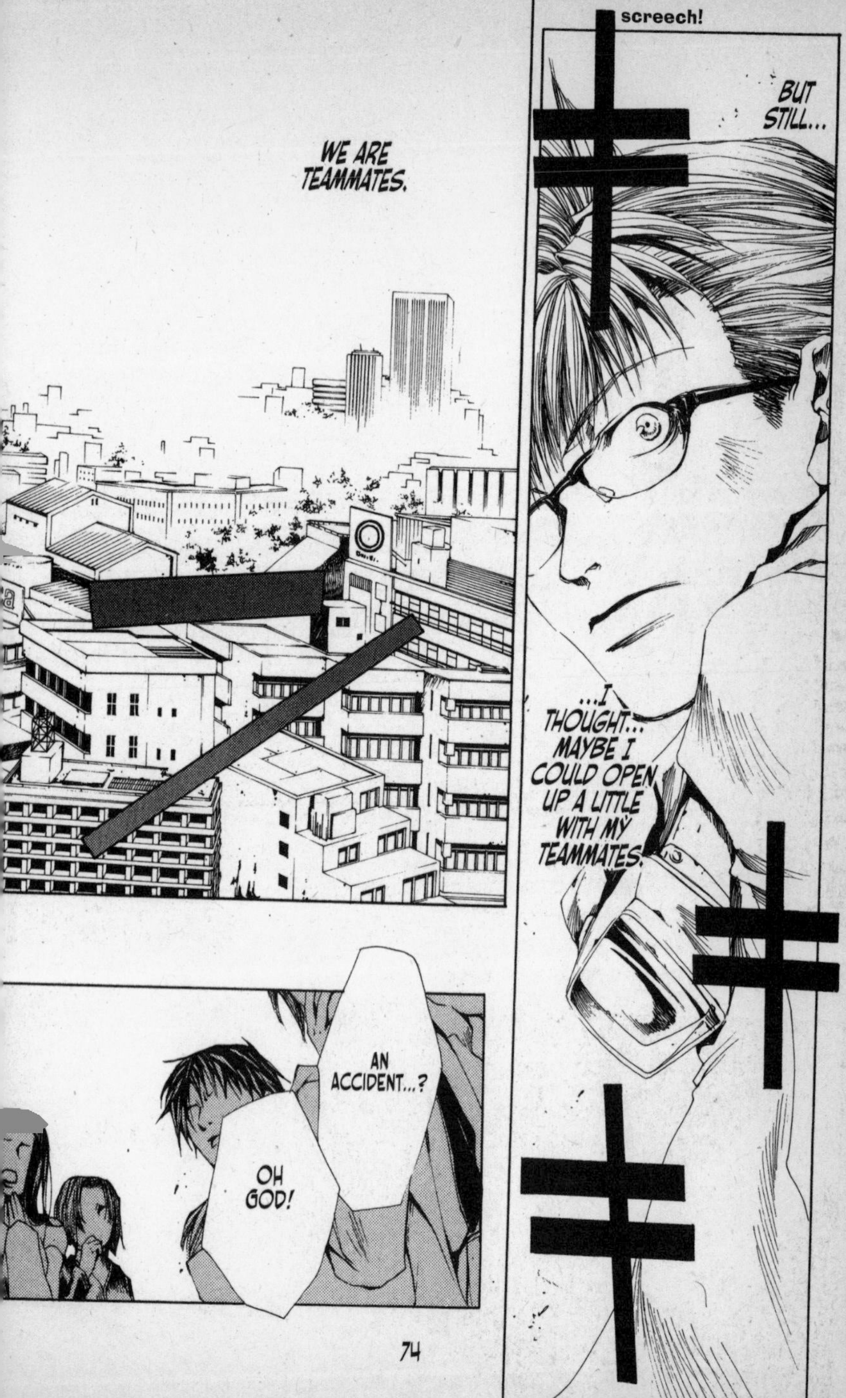
screech!
BUT STILL...
...I THOUGHT... MAYBE I COULD OPEN UP A LITTLE WITH MY TEAMMATES.
WE ARE TEAMMATES.
AN ACCIDENT...?
OH GOD!

STAGE 4: Out of Bounds

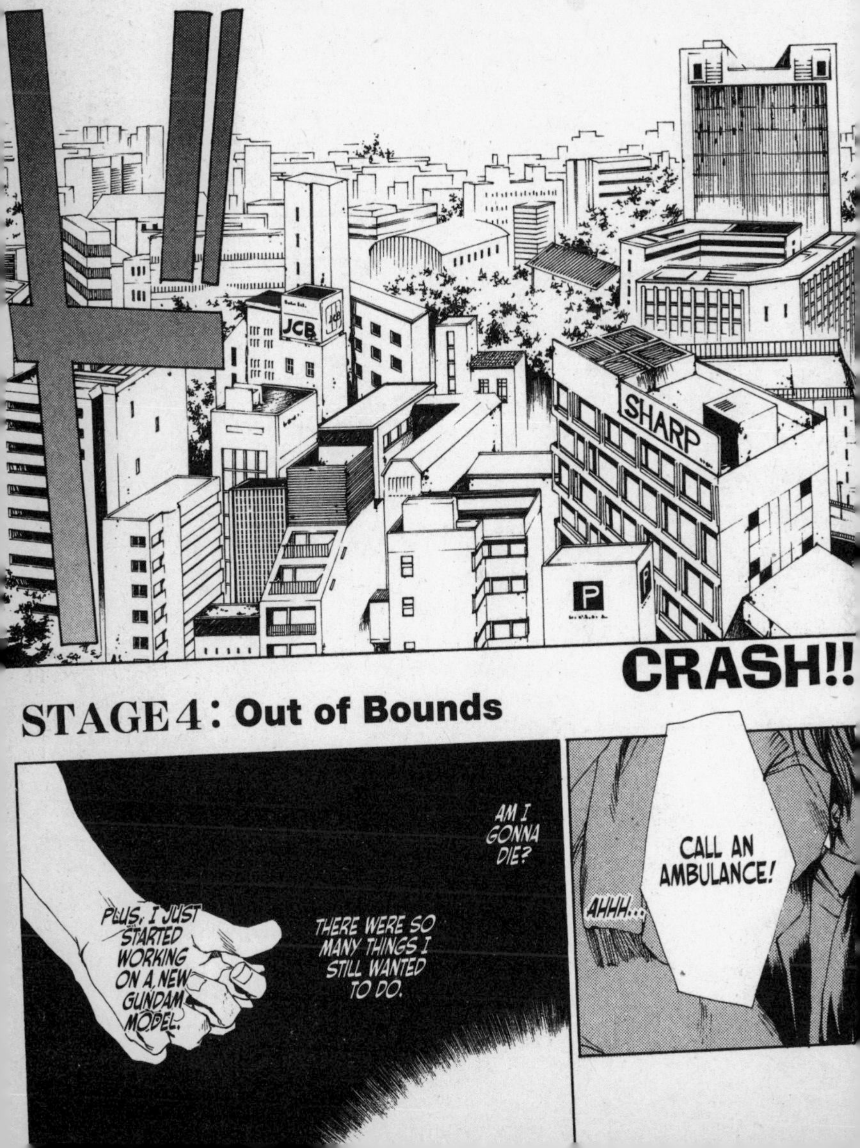
JCB
SHARP
P
CRASH!!
CALL AN AMBULANCE!
AHHH...
AM I GONNA DIE?
THERE WERE SO MANY THINGS I STILL WANTED TO DO.
PLUS, I JUST STARTED WORKING ON A NEW GUNDAM MODEL.

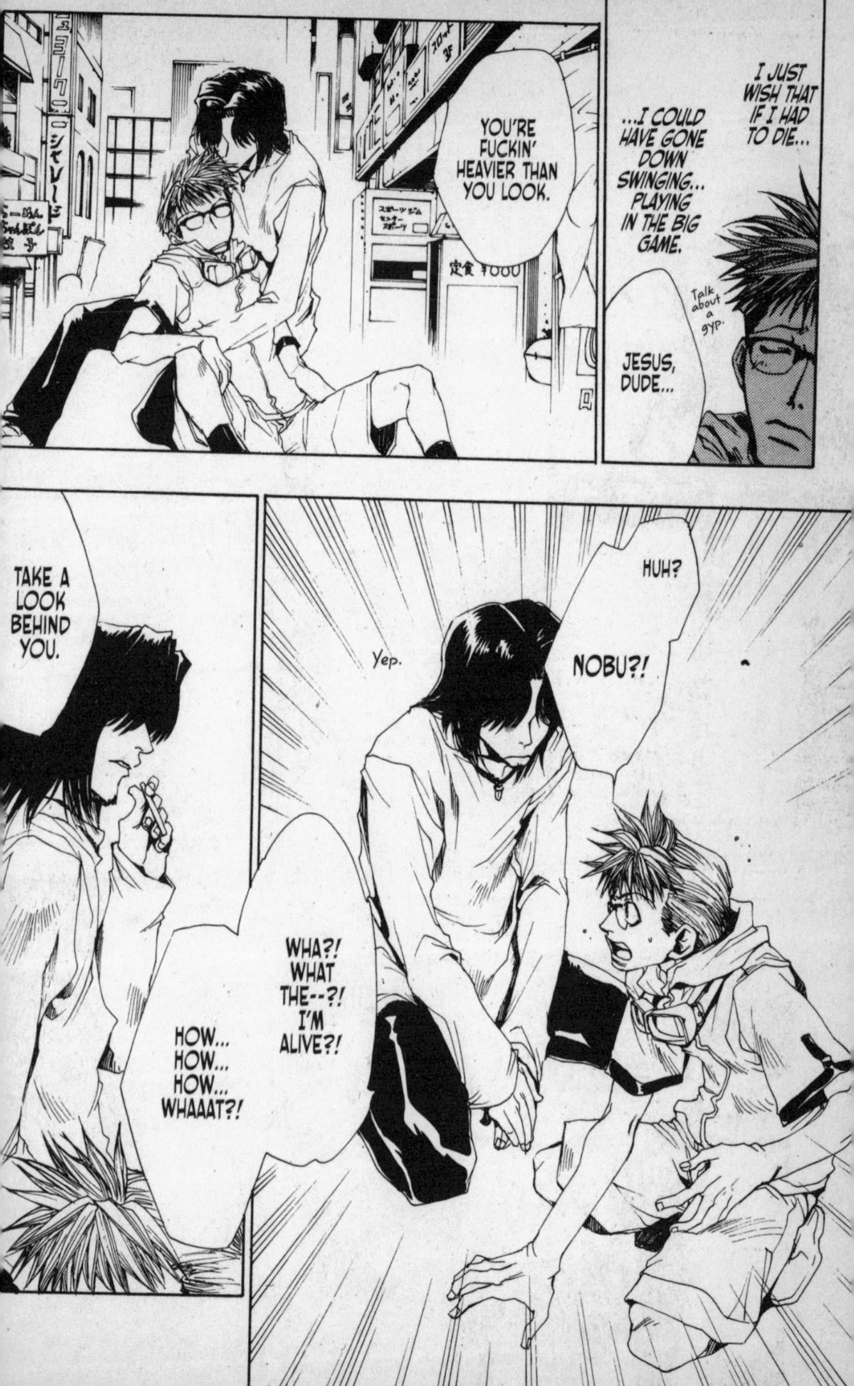
I JUST WISH THAT IF I HAD TO DIE...
...I COULD HAVE GONE DOWN SWINGING... PLAYING IN THE BIG GAME.
Talk about a gyp.
JESUS, DUDE...
YOU'RE FUCKIN' HEAVIER THAN YOU LOOK.
HUH?
NOBU?!
Yep.
WHA?! WHAT THE--?! I'M ALIVE?!
HOW... HOW... HOW... WHAAAT?!
TAKE A LOOK BEHIND YOU.

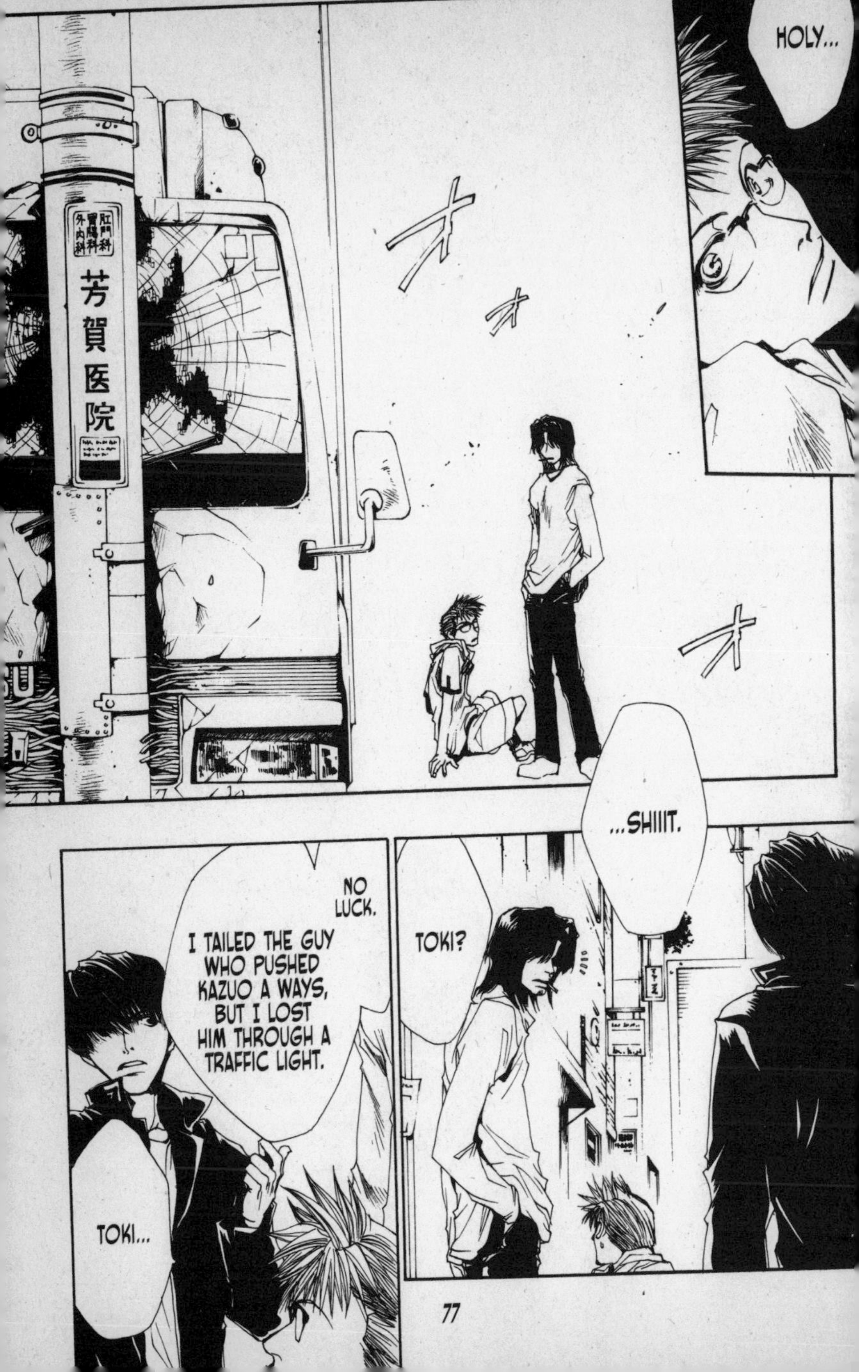
HOLY...
肛門科 胃腸科 外内科
芳賀医院
...SHIIIT.
TOKI?
NO LUCK.
I TAILED THE GUY WHO PUSHED KAZUO A WAYS, BUT I LOST HIM THROUGH A TRAFFIC LIGHT.
TOKI...

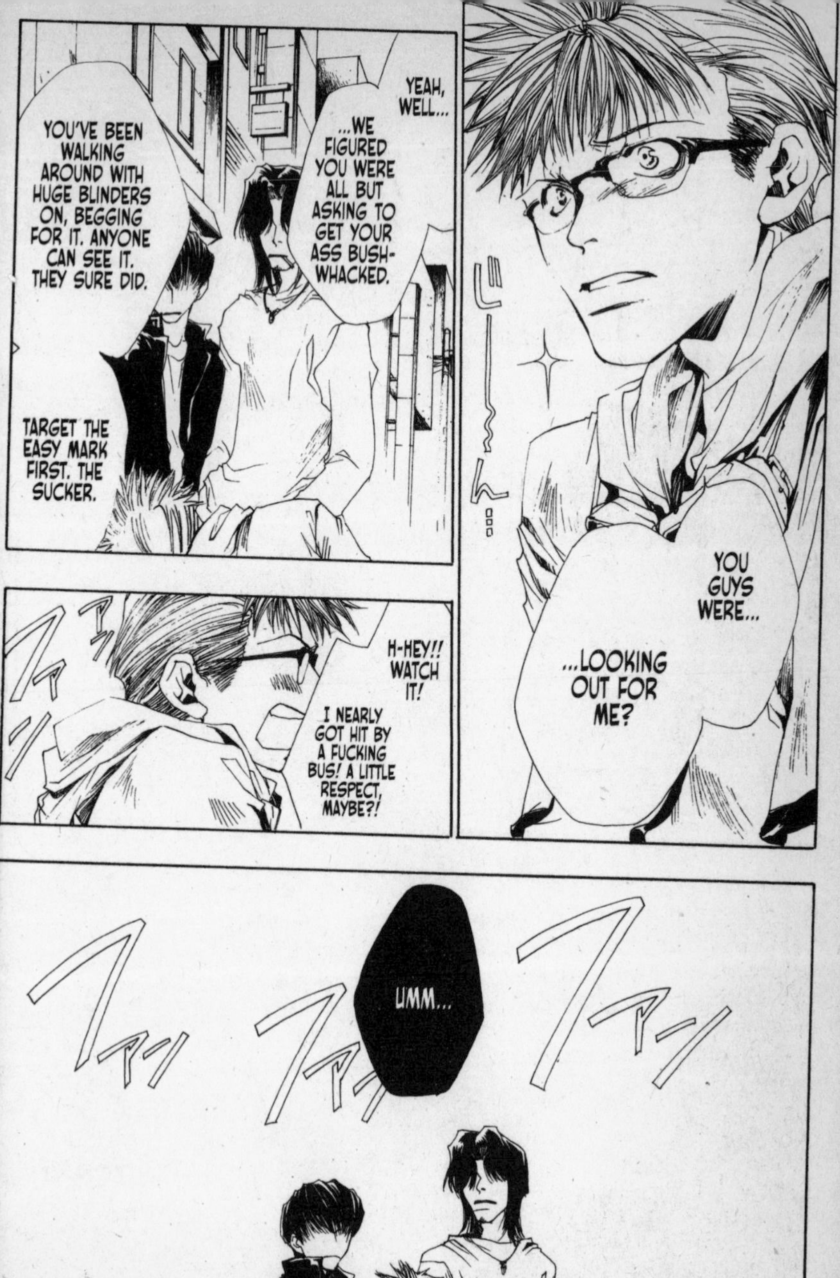
じーーん…
YOU GUYS WERE...
...LOOKING OUT FOR ME?
YEAH, WELL...
...WE FIGURED YOU WERE ALL BUT ASKING TO GET YOUR ASS BUSH-WHACKED.
YOU'VE BEEN WALKING AROUND WITH HUGE BLINDERS ON, BEGGING FOR IT. ANYONE CAN SEE IT. THEY SURE DID.
TARGET THE EASY MARK FIRST. THE SUCKER.
H-HEY!! WATCH IT!
I NEARLY GOT HIT BY A FUCKING BUS! A LITTLE RESPECT, MAYBE?!
UMM...

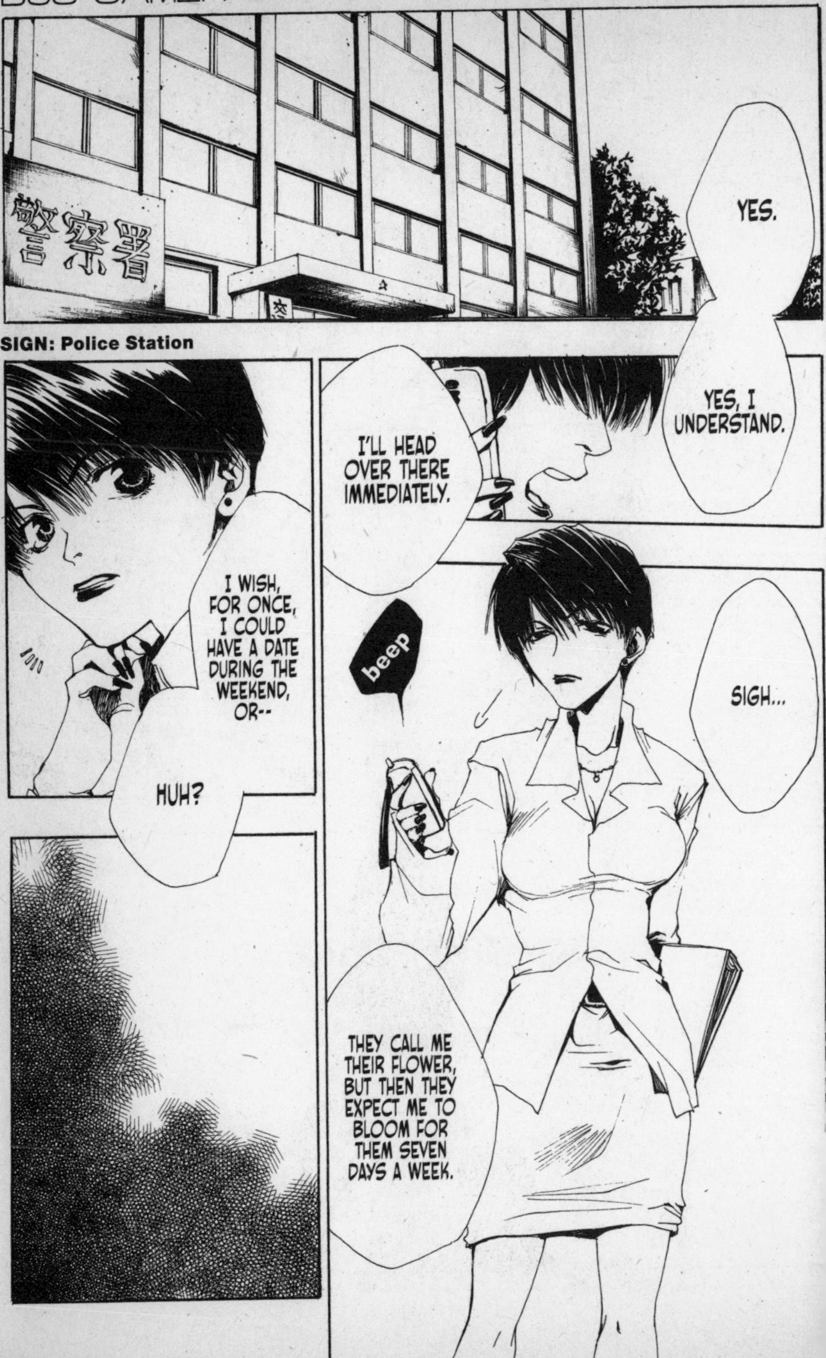
警察署
YES.
YES, I UNDERSTAND.
I'LL HEAD OVER THERE IMMEDIATELY.
beep
SIGH...
THEY CALL ME THEIR FLOWER, BUT THEN THEY EXPECT ME TO BLOOM FOR THEM SEVEN DAYS A WEEK.
I WISH, FOR ONCE, I COULD HAVE A DATE DURING THE WEEKEND, OR--
HUH?

SIGN: Police Station

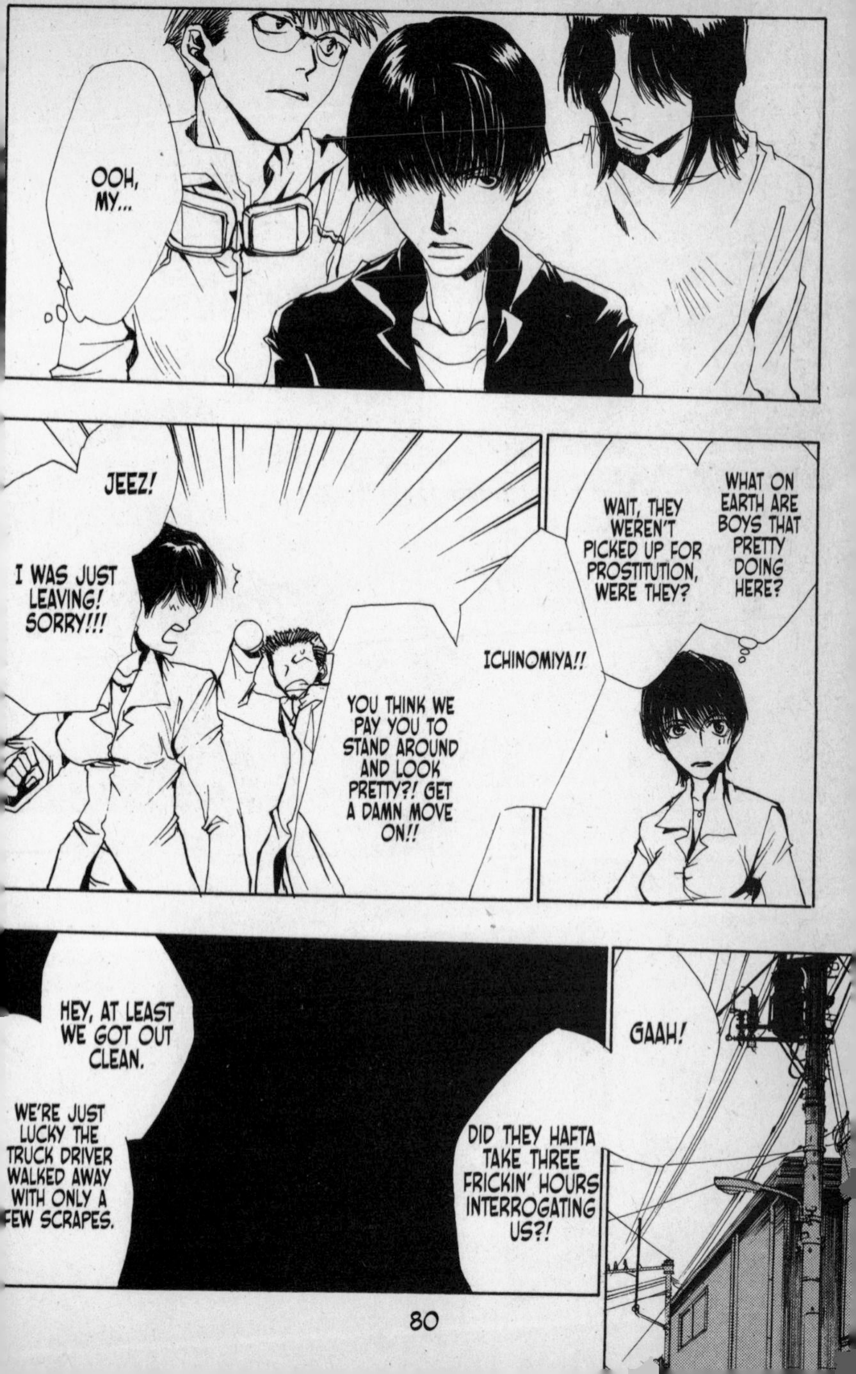
OOH, MY...
WHAT ON EARTH ARE BOYS THAT PRETTY DOING HERE?
WAIT, THEY WEREN'T PICKED UP FOR PROSTITUTION, WERE THEY?
ICHINOMIYA!!
YOU THINK WE PAY YOU TO STAND AROUND AND LOOK PRETTY?! GET A DAMN MOVE ON!!
JEEZ!
I WAS JUST LEAVING! SORRY!!!
GAAH!
DID THEY HAFTA TAKE THREE FRICKIN' HOURS INTERROGATING US?!
HEY, AT LEAST WE GOT OUT CLEAN.
WE'RE JUST LUCKY THE TRUCK DRIVER WALKED AWAY WITH ONLY A FEW SCRAPES.

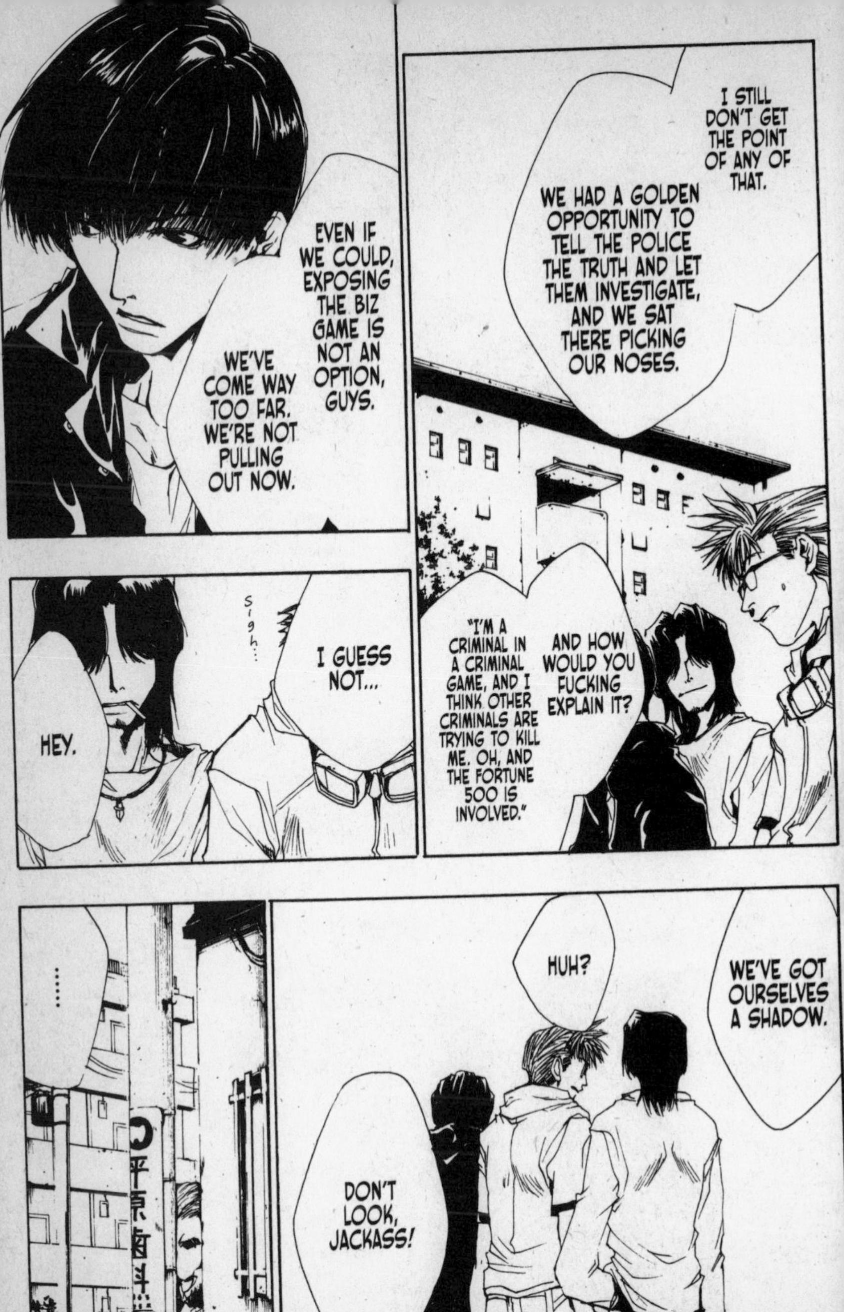

I STILL DON'T GET THE POINT OF ANY OF THAT.
WE HAD A GOLDEN OPPORTUNITY TO TELL THE POLICE THE TRUTH AND LET THEM INVESTIGATE, AND WE SAT THERE PICKING OUR NOSES.
AND HOW WOULD YOU FUCKING EXPLAIN IT?
"I'M A CRIMINAL IN A CRIMINAL GAME, AND I THINK OTHER CRIMINALS ARE TRYING TO KILL ME. OH, AND THE FORTUNE 500 IS INVOLVED."
EVEN IF WE COULD, EXPOSING THE BIZ GAME IS NOT AN OPTION, GUYS.
WE'VE COME WAY TOO FAR. WE'RE NOT PULLING OUT NOW.
I GUESS NOT...
Sigh...
HEY.
WE'VE GOT OURSELVES A SHADOW.
HUH?
DON'T LOOK, JACKASS!
......

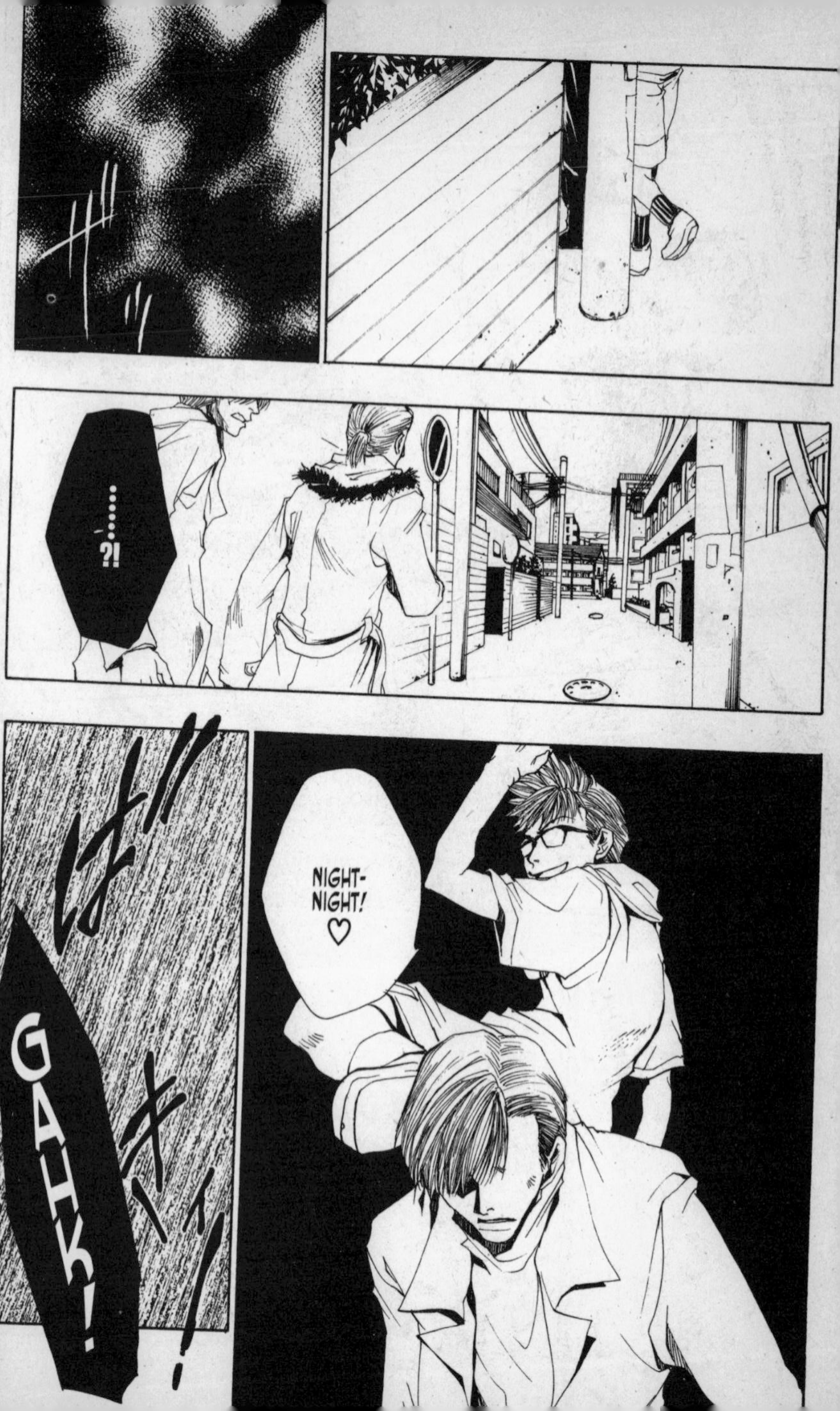
......?!
NIGHT-NIGHT! ♡
GAHK!!

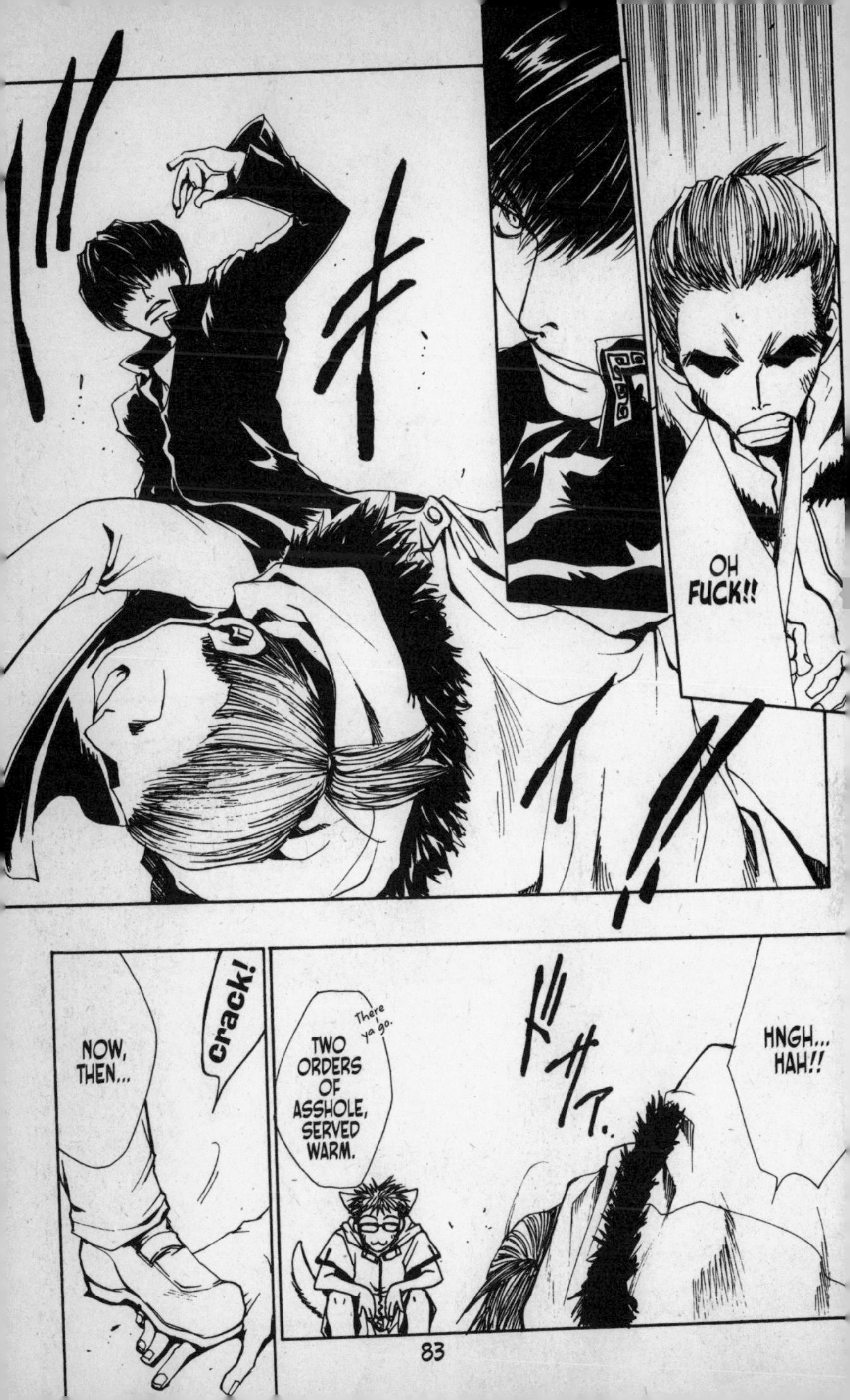
OH FUCK!!
HNGH... HAH!!
ドサァ..
TWO ORDERS OF ASSHOLE, SERVED WARM.
There ya go.
crack!
NOW, THEN...

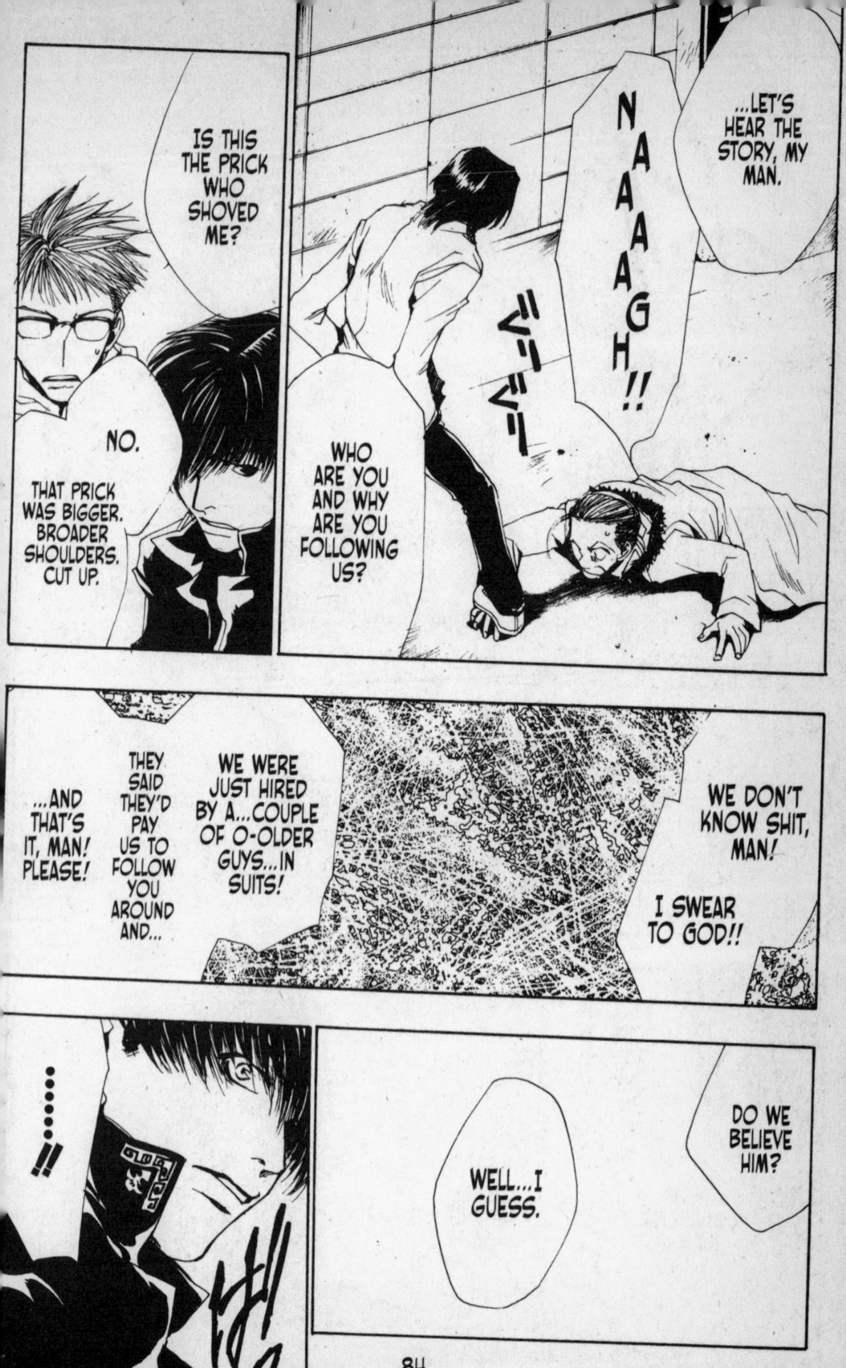
...LET'S HEAR THE STORY, MY MAN.
NAAAAGH!!
WHO ARE YOU AND WHY ARE YOU FOLLOWING US?
IS THIS THE PRICK WHO SHOVED ME?
NO.
THAT PRICK WAS BIGGER. BROADER SHOULDERS. CUT UP.
WE DON'T KNOW SHIT, MAN!
I SWEAR TO GOD!!
WE WERE JUST HIRED BY A...COUPLE OF O-OLDER GUYS...IN SUITS!
THEY SAID THEY'D PAY US TO FOLLOW YOU AROUND AND...
...AND THAT'S IT, MAN! PLEASE!
DO WE BELIEVE HIM?
WELL...I GUESS.
......!!

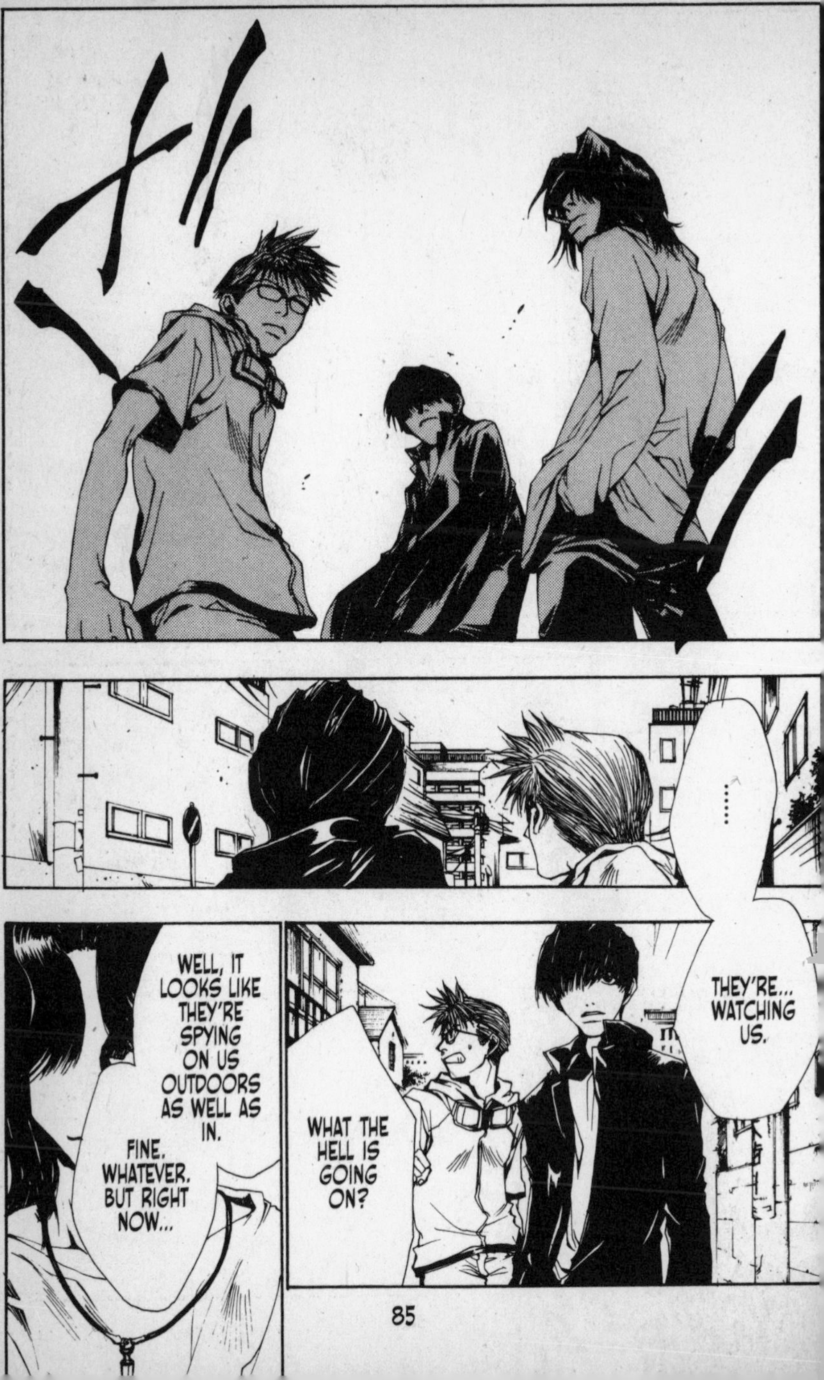
......
THEY'RE... WATCHING US.
WHAT THE HELL IS GOING ON?
WELL, IT LOOKS LIKE THEY'RE SPYING ON US OUTDOORS AS WELL AS IN.
FINE. WHATEVER. BUT RIGHT NOW...

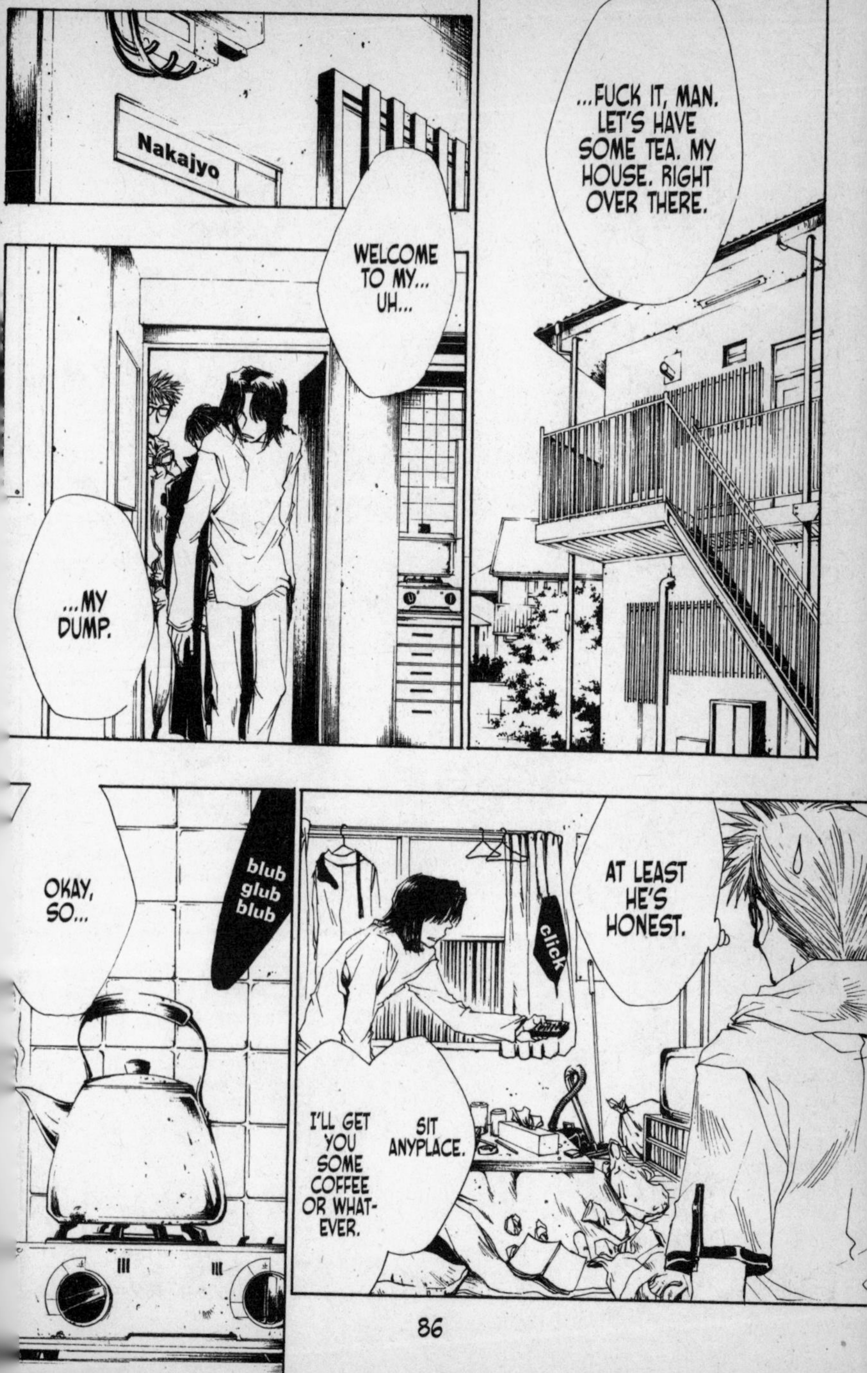
...FUCK IT, MAN. LET'S HAVE SOME TEA. MY HOUSE. RIGHT OVER THERE.
Nakajyo
WELCOME TO MY... UH...
...MY DUMP.
AT LEAST HE'S HONEST.
click
SIT ANYPLACE.
I'LL GET YOU SOME COFFEE OR WHAT-EVER.
blub glub blub
OKAY, SO...

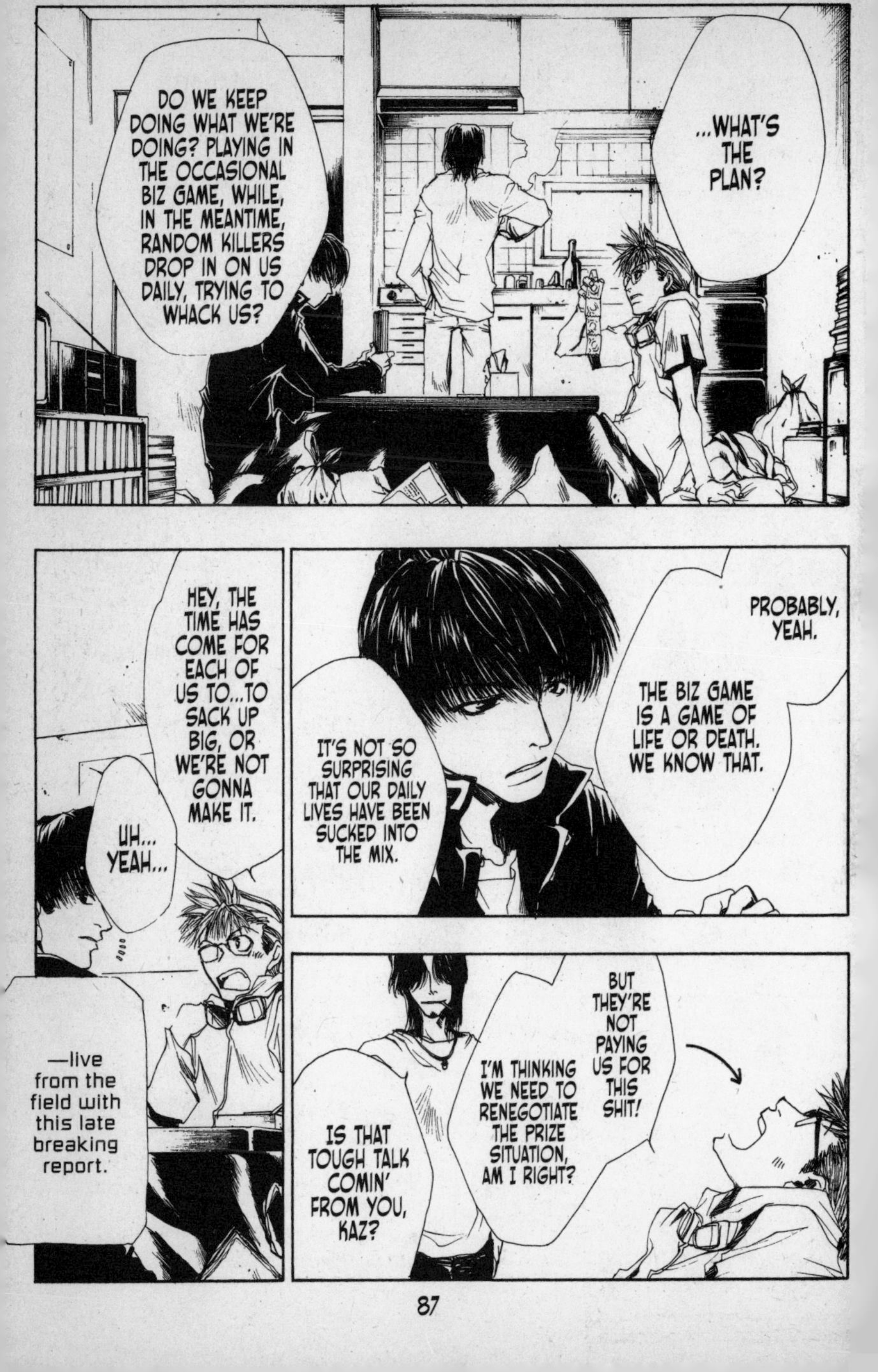
...WHAT'S THE PLAN?
DO WE KEEP DOING WHAT WE'RE DOING? PLAYING IN THE OCCASIONAL BIZ GAME, WHILE, IN THE MEANTIME, RANDOM KILLERS DROP IN ON US DAILY, TRYING TO WHACK US?
PROBABLY, YEAH.
THE BIZ GAME IS A GAME OF LIFE OR DEATH. WE KNOW THAT.
IT'S NOT SO SURPRISING THAT OUR DAILY LIVES HAVE BEEN SUCKED INTO THE MIX.
BUT THEY'RE NOT PAYING US FOR THIS SHIT!
I'M THINKING WE NEED TO RENEGOTIATE THE PRIZE SITUATION, AM I RIGHT?
IS THAT TOUGH TALK COMIN' FROM YOU, KAZ?
HEY, THE TIME HAS COME FOR EACH OF US TO...TO SACK UP BIG, OR WE'RE NOT GONNA MAKE IT.
UH... YEAH...
—live from the field with this late breaking report.

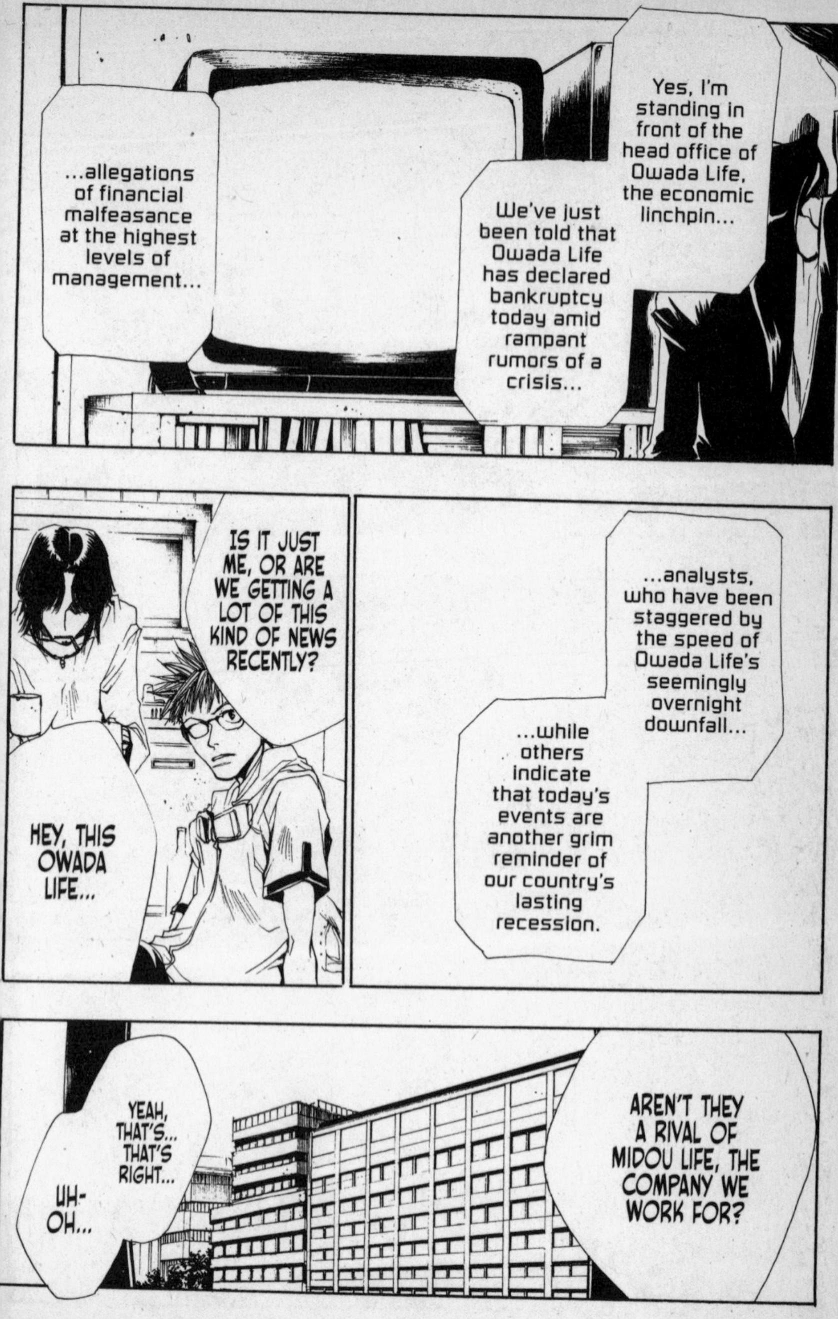
Yes, I'm standing in front of the head office of Owada Life, the economic linchpin...
We've just been told that Owada Life has declared bankruptcy today amid rampant rumors of a crisis...
...allegations of financial malfeasance at the highest levels of management...
...analysts, who have been staggered by the speed of Owada Life's seemingly overnight downfall...
...while others indicate that today's events are another grim reminder of our country's lasting recession.
IS IT JUST ME, OR ARE WE GETTING A LOT OF THIS KIND OF NEWS RECENTLY?
HEY, THIS OWADA LIFE...
AREN'T THEY A RIVAL OF MIDOU LIFE, THE COMPANY WE WORK FOR?
YEAH, THAT'S... THAT'S RIGHT...
UH-OH...

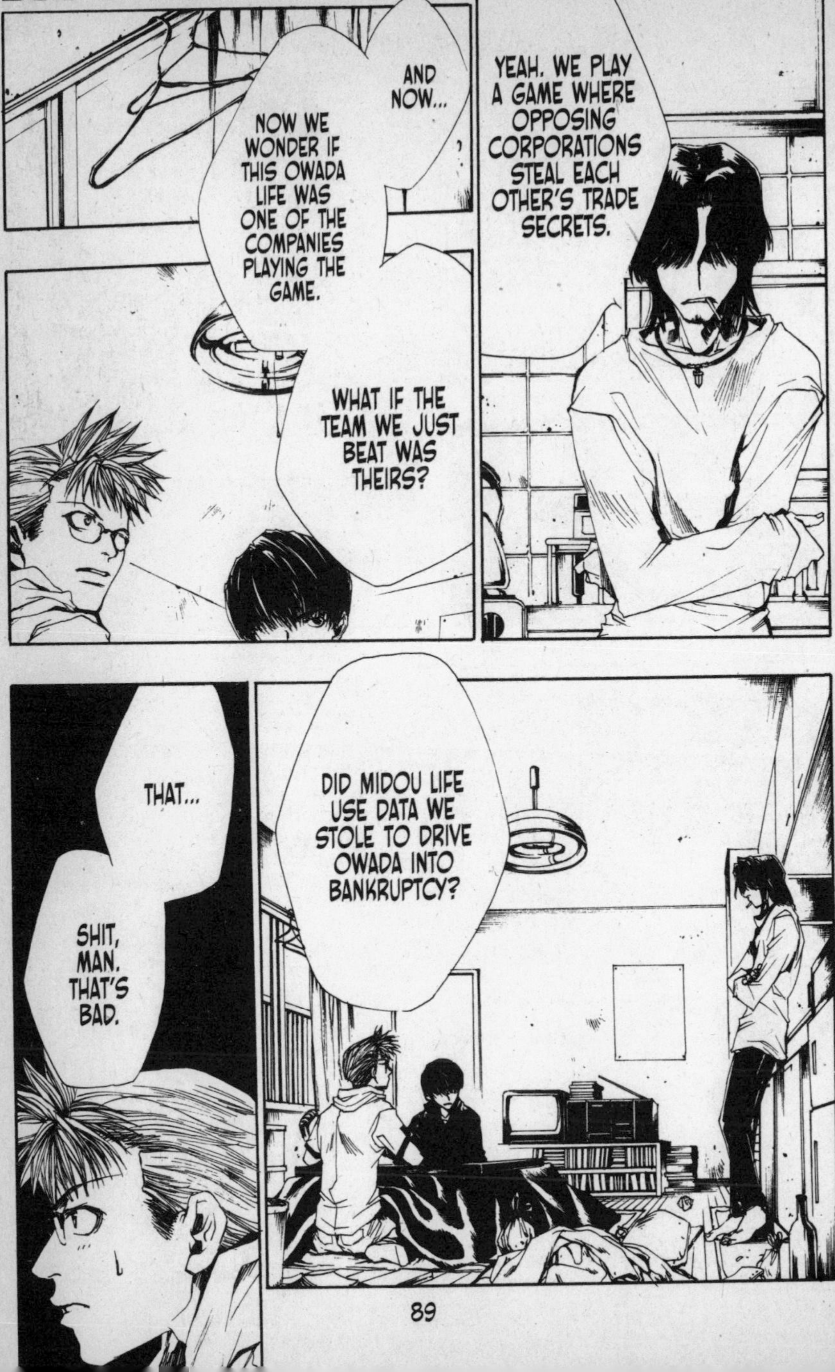
YEAH. WE PLAY A GAME WHERE OPPOSING CORPORATIONS STEAL EACH OTHER'S TRADE SECRETS.
AND NOW...
NOW WE WONDER IF THIS OWADA LIFE WAS ONE OF THE COMPANIES PLAYING THE GAME.
WHAT IF THE TEAM WE JUST BEAT WAS THEIRS?
DID MIDOU LIFE USE DATA WE STOLE TO DRIVE OWADA INTO BANKRUPTCY?
THAT...
SHIT, MAN. THAT'S BAD.

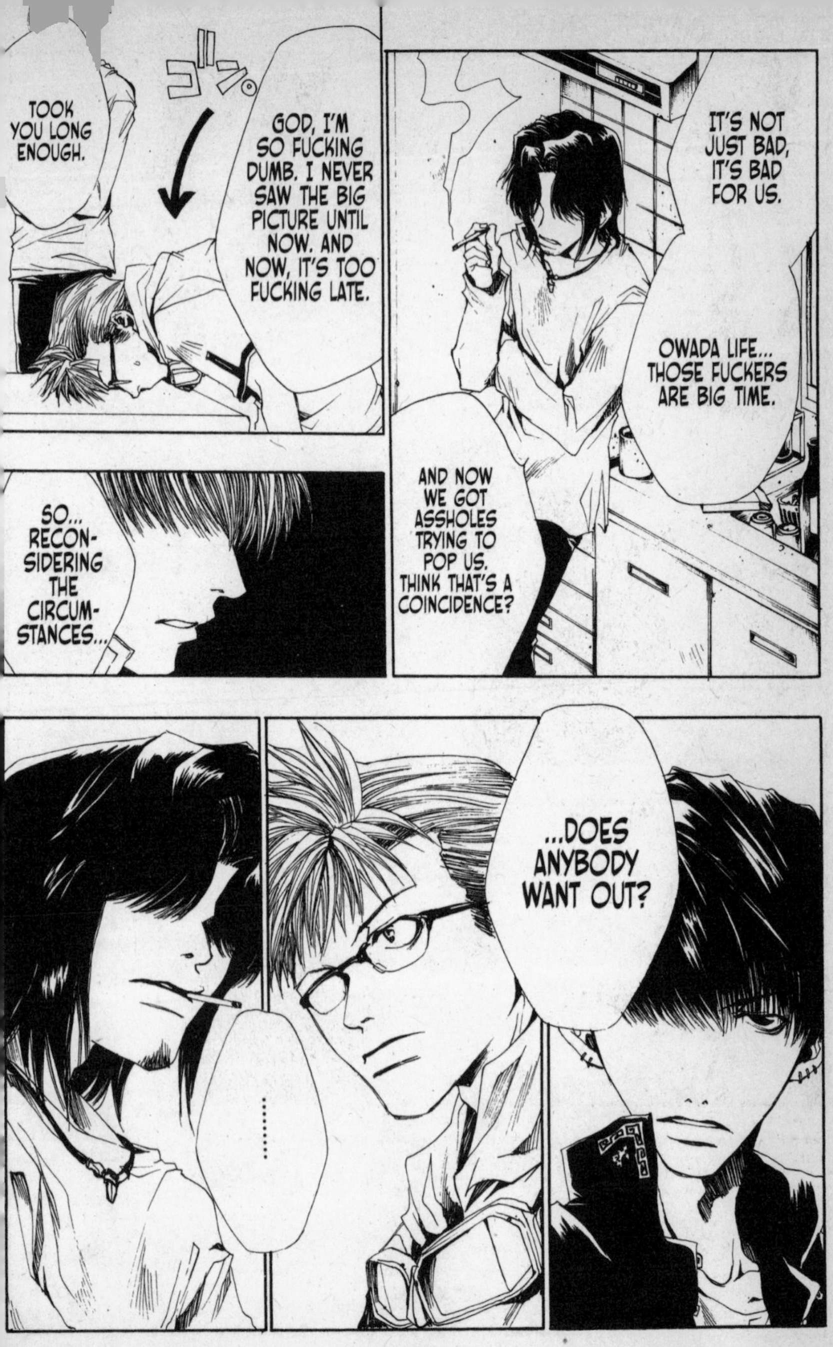
IT'S NOT JUST BAD, IT'S BAD FOR US.
OWADA LIFE... THOSE FUCKERS ARE BIG TIME.
AND NOW WE GOT ASSHOLES TRYING TO POP US. THINK THAT'S A COINCIDENCE?
GOD, I'M SO FUCKING DUMB. I NEVER SAW THE BIG PICTURE UNTIL NOW. AND NOW, IT'S TOO FUCKING LATE.
TOOK YOU LONG ENOUGH.
SO... RECONSIDERING THE CIRCUMSTANCES...
...DOES ANYBODY WANT OUT?
......

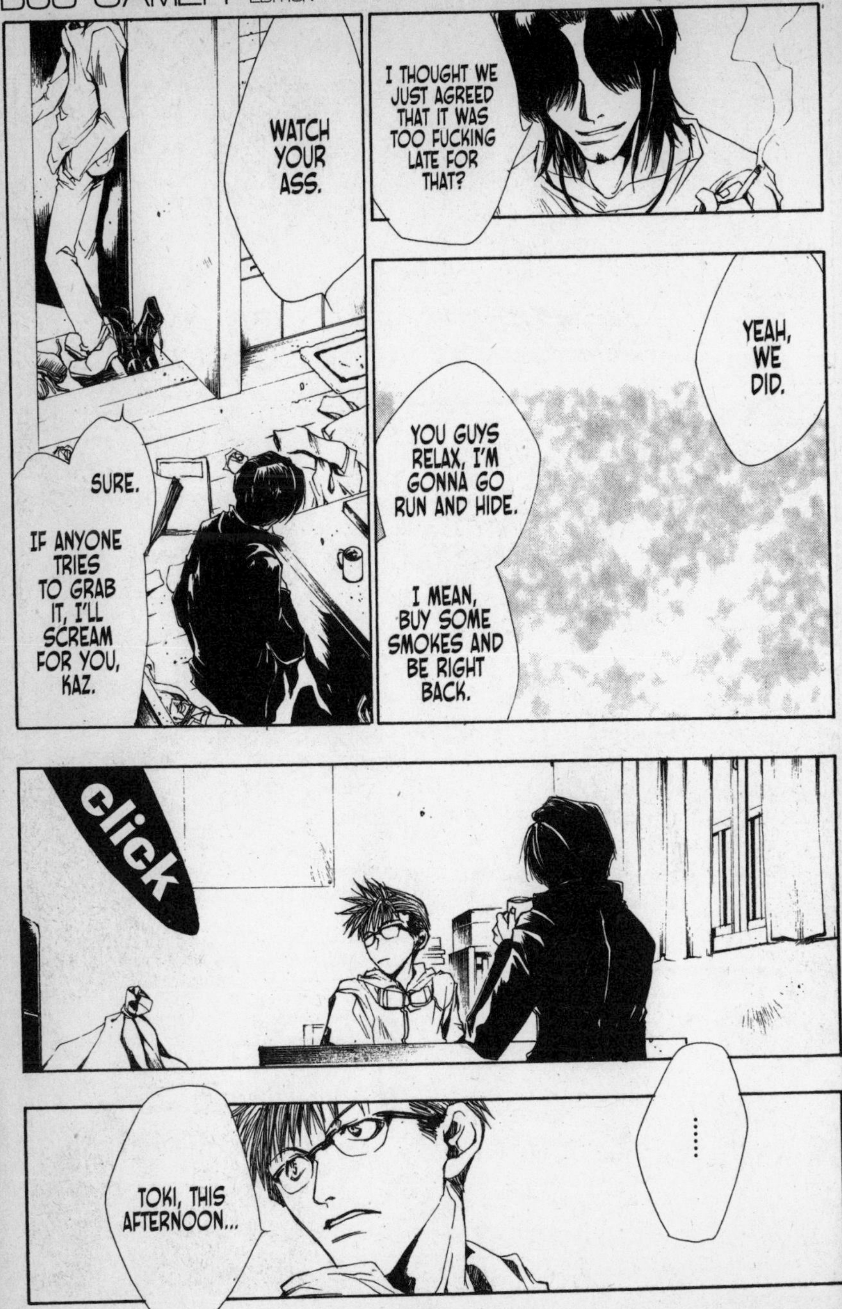
I THOUGHT WE JUST AGREED THAT IT WAS TOO FUCKING LATE FOR THAT?
YEAH, WE DID.
YOU GUYS RELAX, I'M GONNA GO RUN AND HIDE.
I MEAN, BUY SOME SMOKES AND BE RIGHT BACK.
WATCH YOUR ASS.
SURE.
IF ANYONE TRIES TO GRAB IT, I'LL SCREAM FOR YOU, KAZ.
click
......
TOKI, THIS AFTERNOON...

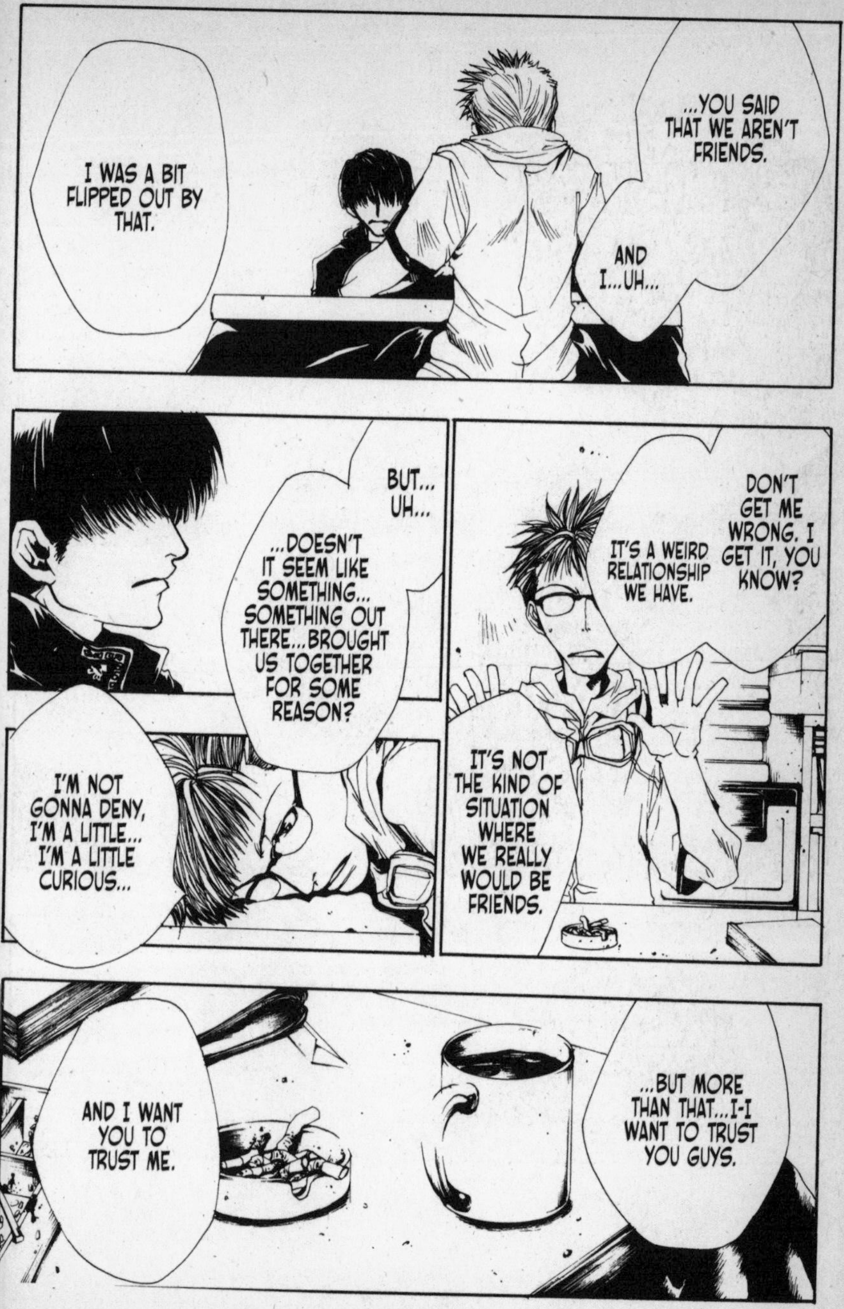
...YOU SAID THAT WE AREN'T FRIENDS.
AND I...UH...
I WAS A BIT FLIPPED OUT BY THAT.
DON'T GET ME WRONG. I GET IT, YOU KNOW?
IT'S A WEIRD RELATIONSHIP WE HAVE.
IT'S NOT THE KIND OF SITUATION WHERE WE REALLY WOULD BE FRIENDS.
BUT... UH...
...DOESN'T IT SEEM LIKE SOMETHING... SOMETHING OUT THERE...BROUGHT US TOGETHER FOR SOME REASON?
I'M NOT GONNA DENY, I'M A LITTLE... I'M A LITTLE CURIOUS...
...BUT MORE THAN THAT...I-I WANT TO TRUST YOU GUYS.
AND I WANT YOU TO TRUST ME.

I WANT TO KNOW MORE.

WHO IS NOBUTO NAKAJYO?

AND TOKI, WHO ARE YOU?

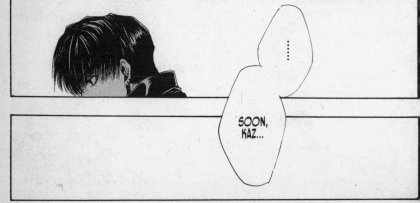

....

SOON, KAZ...

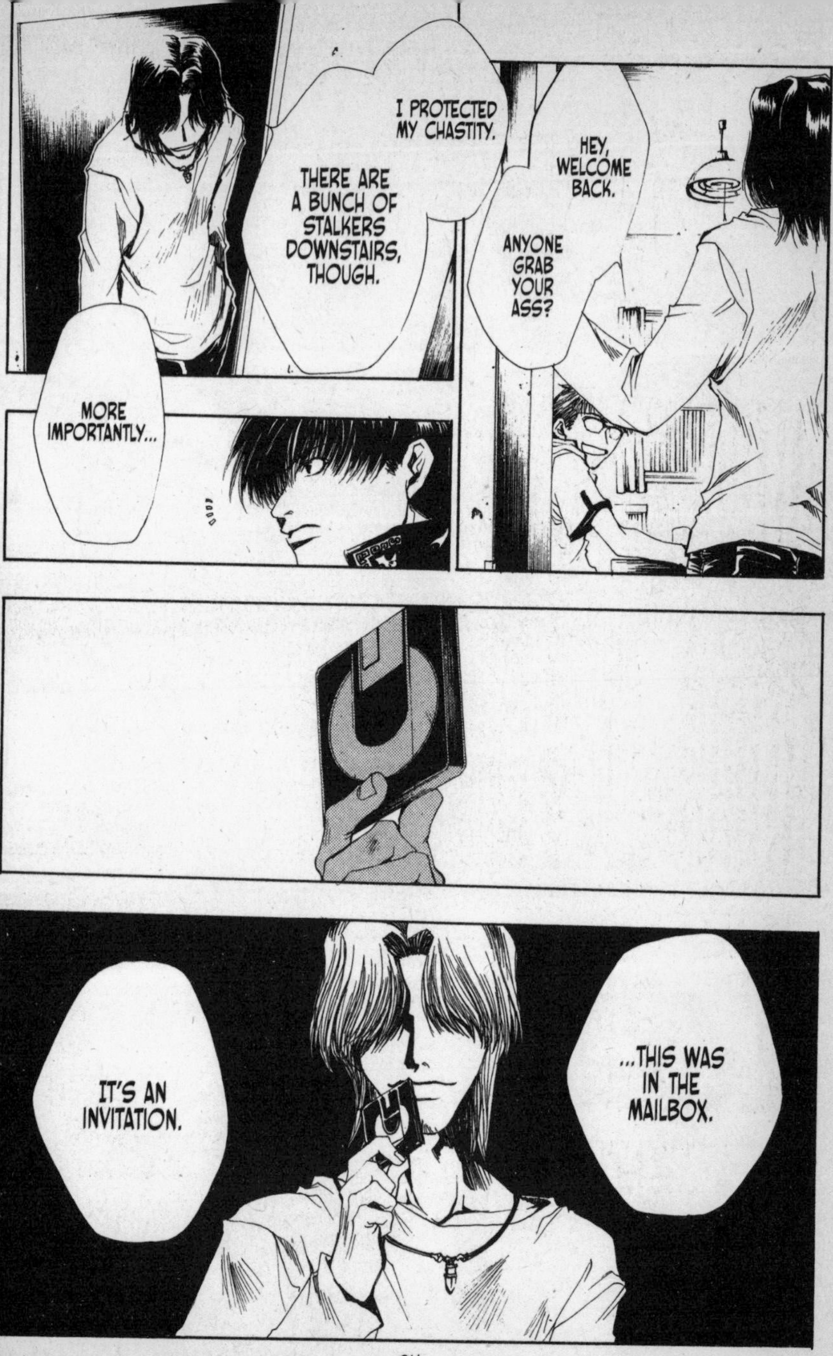
HEY, WELCOME BACK.
ANYONE GRAB YOUR ASS?
I PROTECTED MY CHASTITY.
THERE ARE A BUNCH OF STALKERS DOWNSTAIRS, THOUGH.
MORE IMPORTANTLY...
...THIS WAS IN THE MAILBOX.
IT'S AN INVITATION.

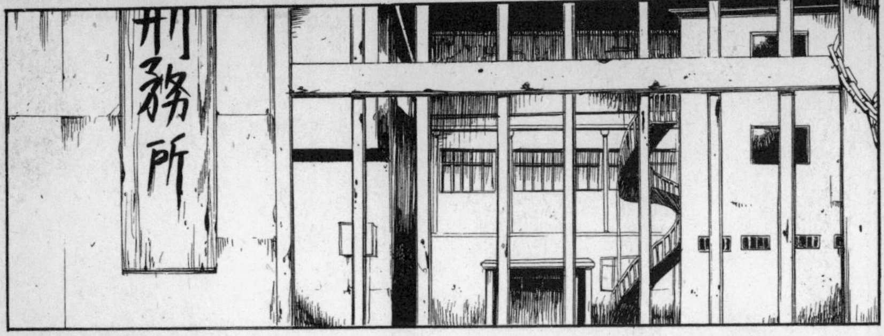
刑務所

SIGN: Prison

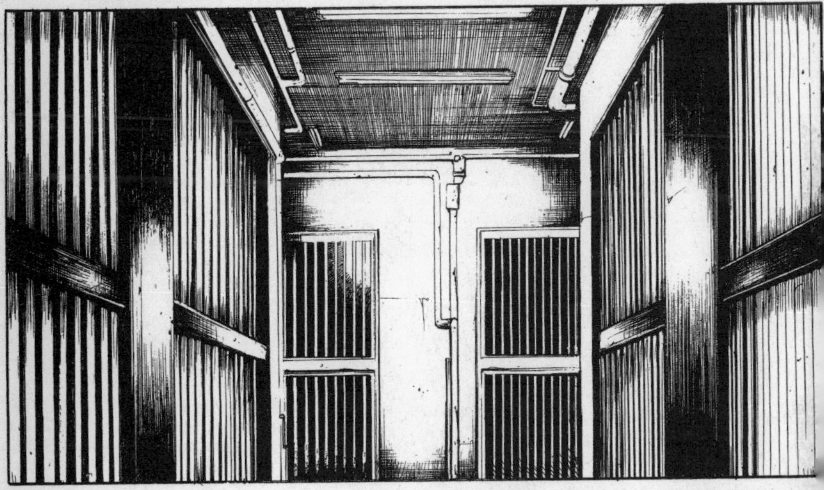

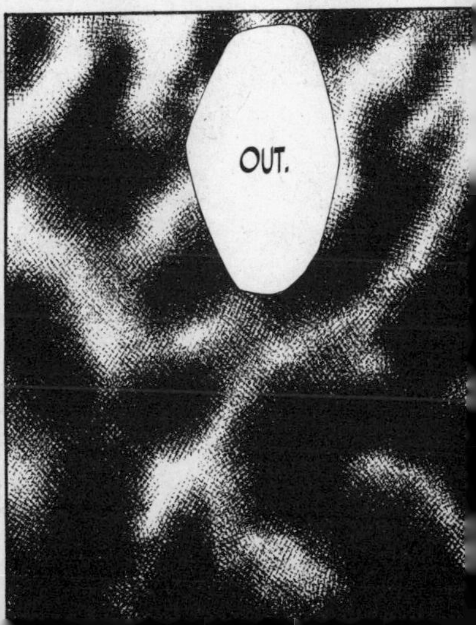
OUT.

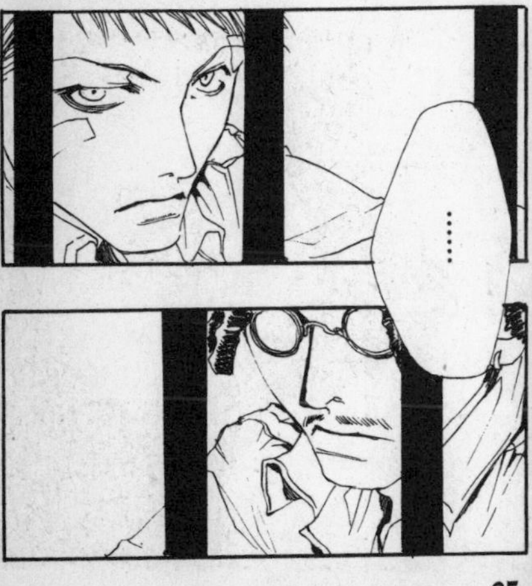
......

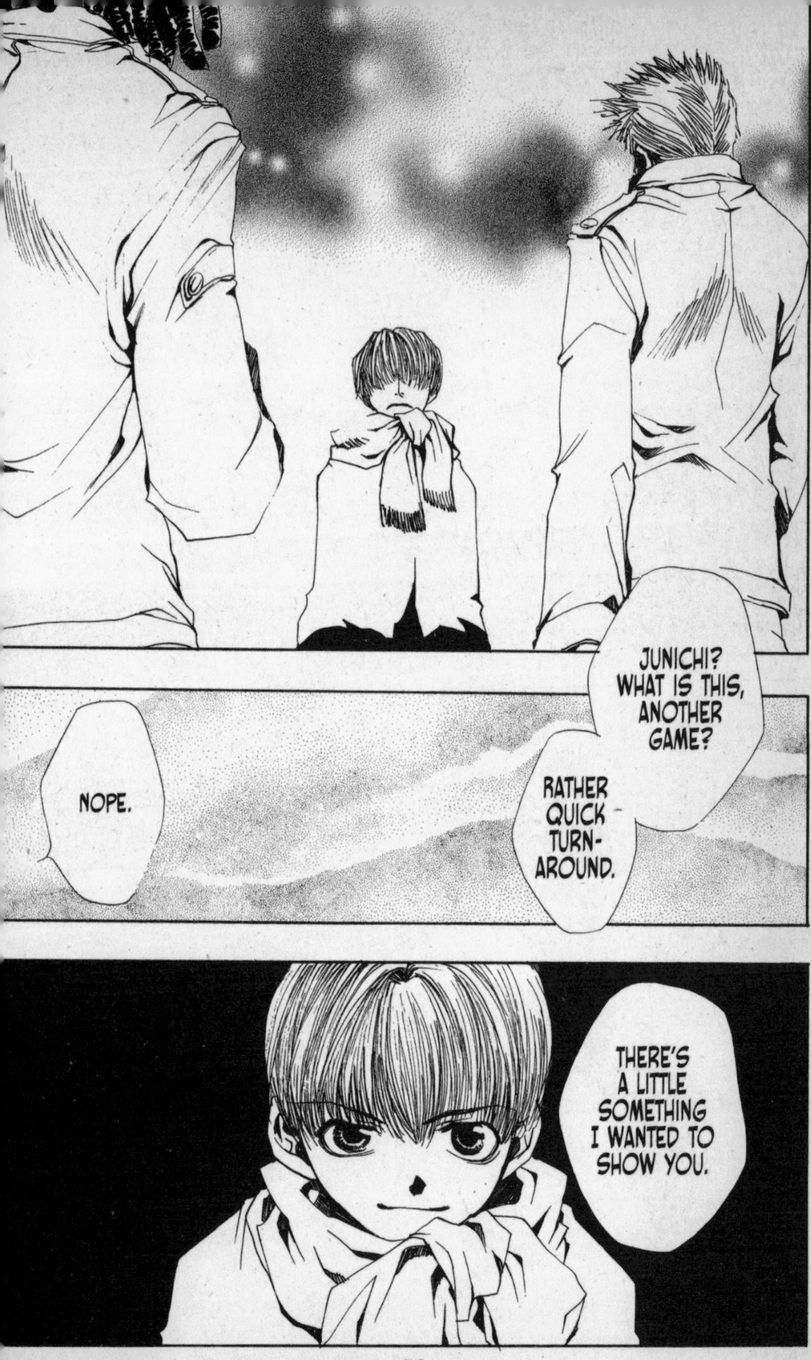
JUNICHI? WHAT IS THIS, ANOTHER GAME?
RATHER QUICK TURN-AROUND.
NOPE.
THERE'S A LITTLE SOMETHING I WANTED TO SHOW YOU.

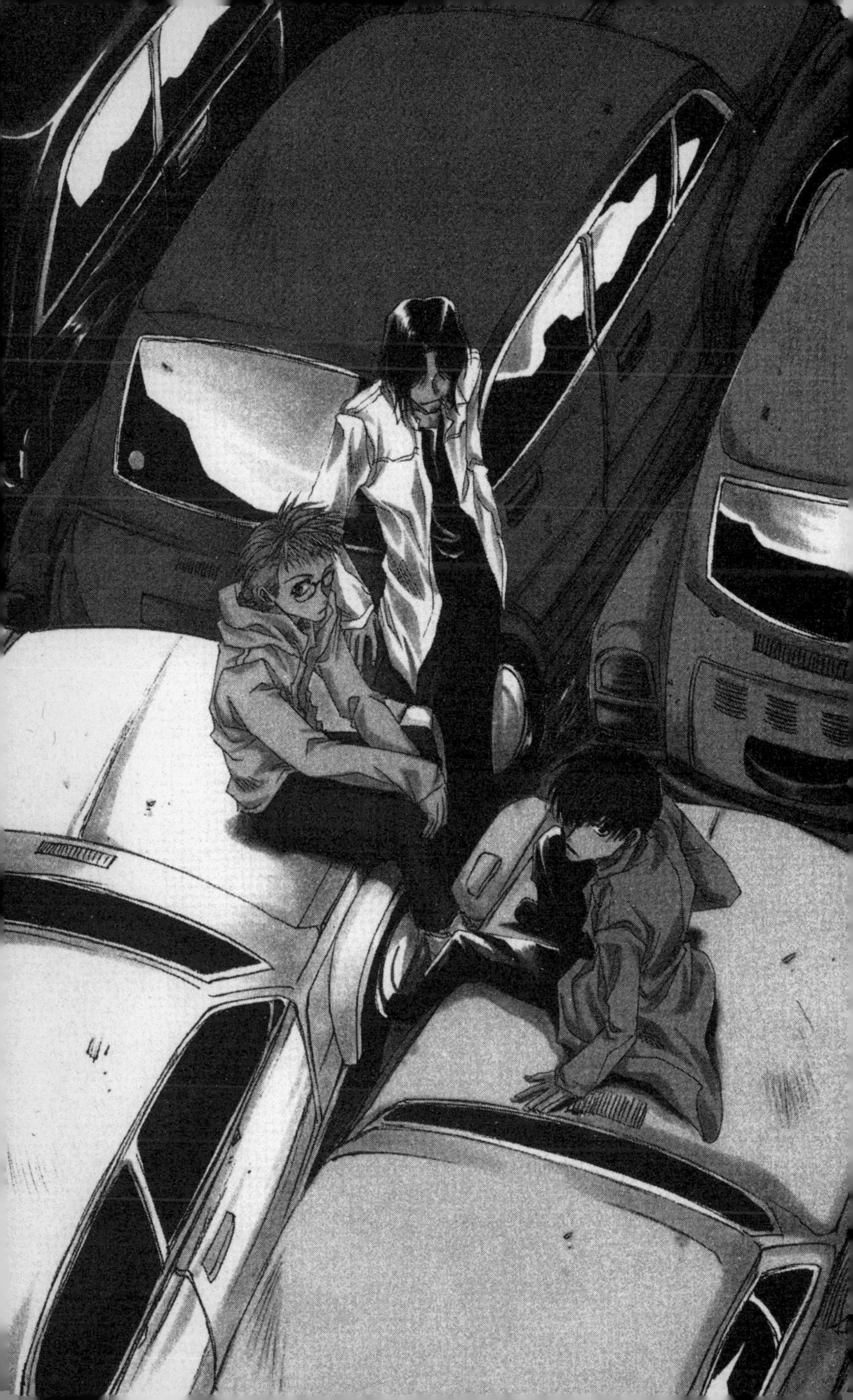

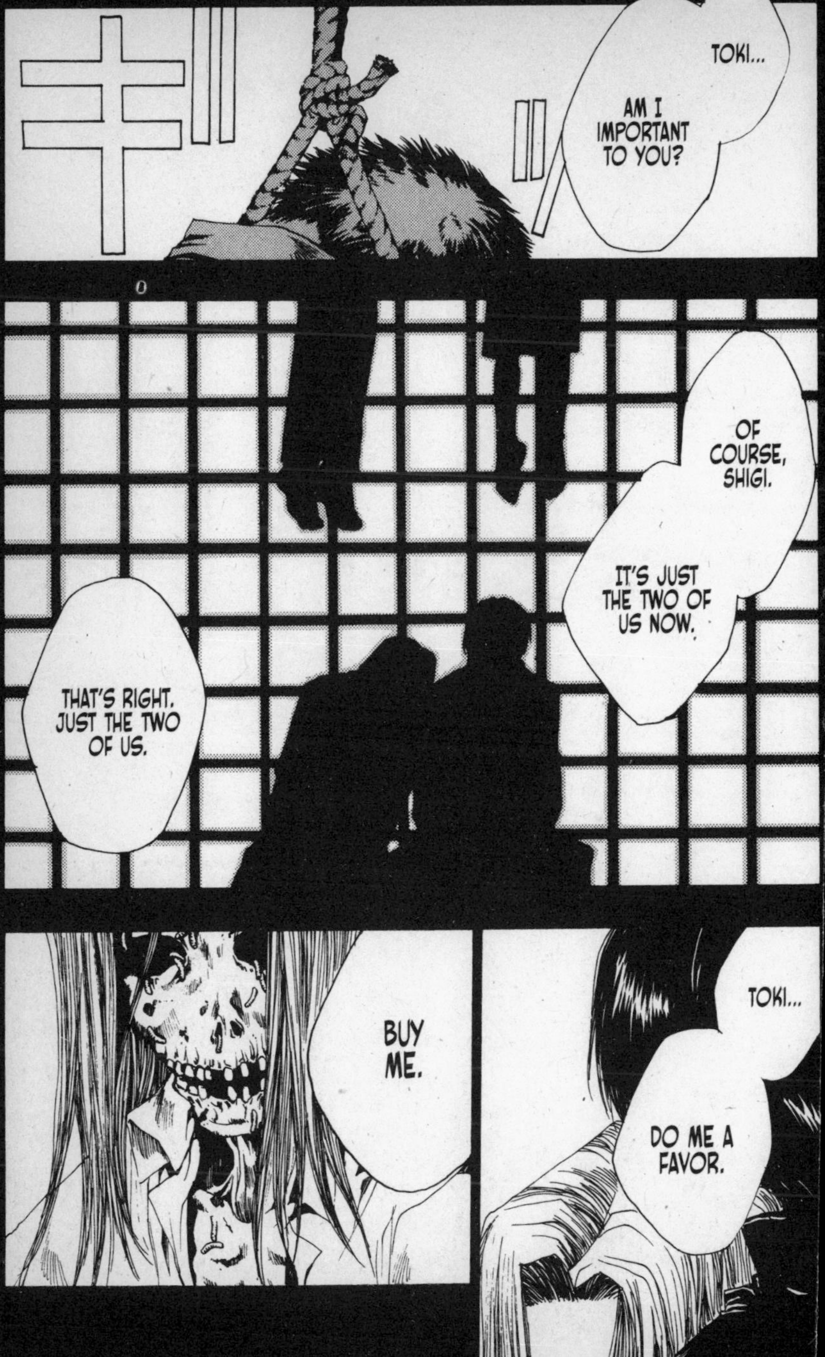
TOKI...
AM I IMPORTANT TO YOU?
OF COURSE, SHIGI.
IT'S JUST THE TWO OF US NOW.
THAT'S RIGHT. JUST THE TWO OF US.
TOKI...
DO ME A FAVOR.
BUY ME.

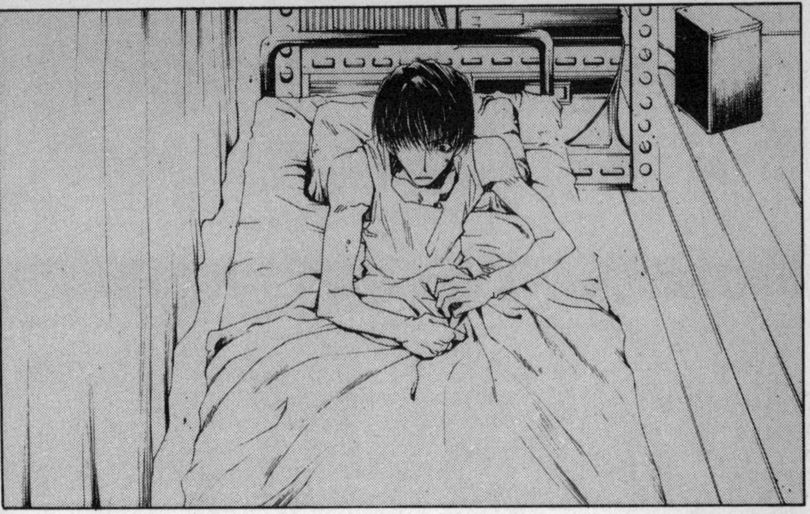

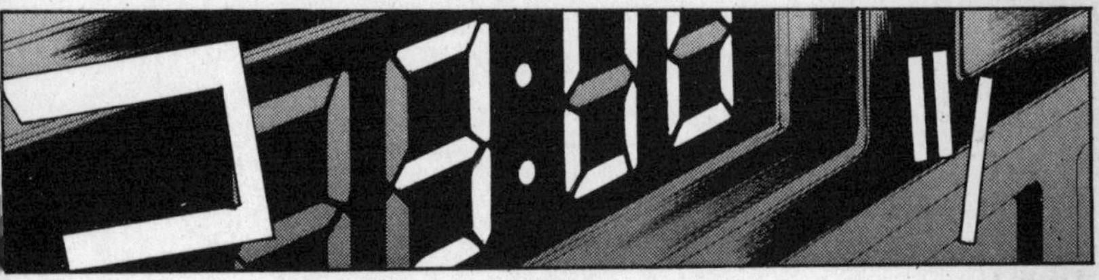

STAGE 5: Starting Now

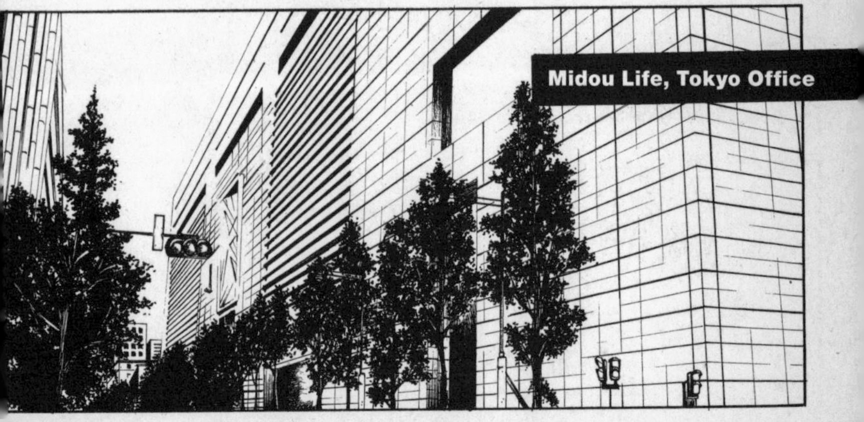
Midou Life, Tokyo Office

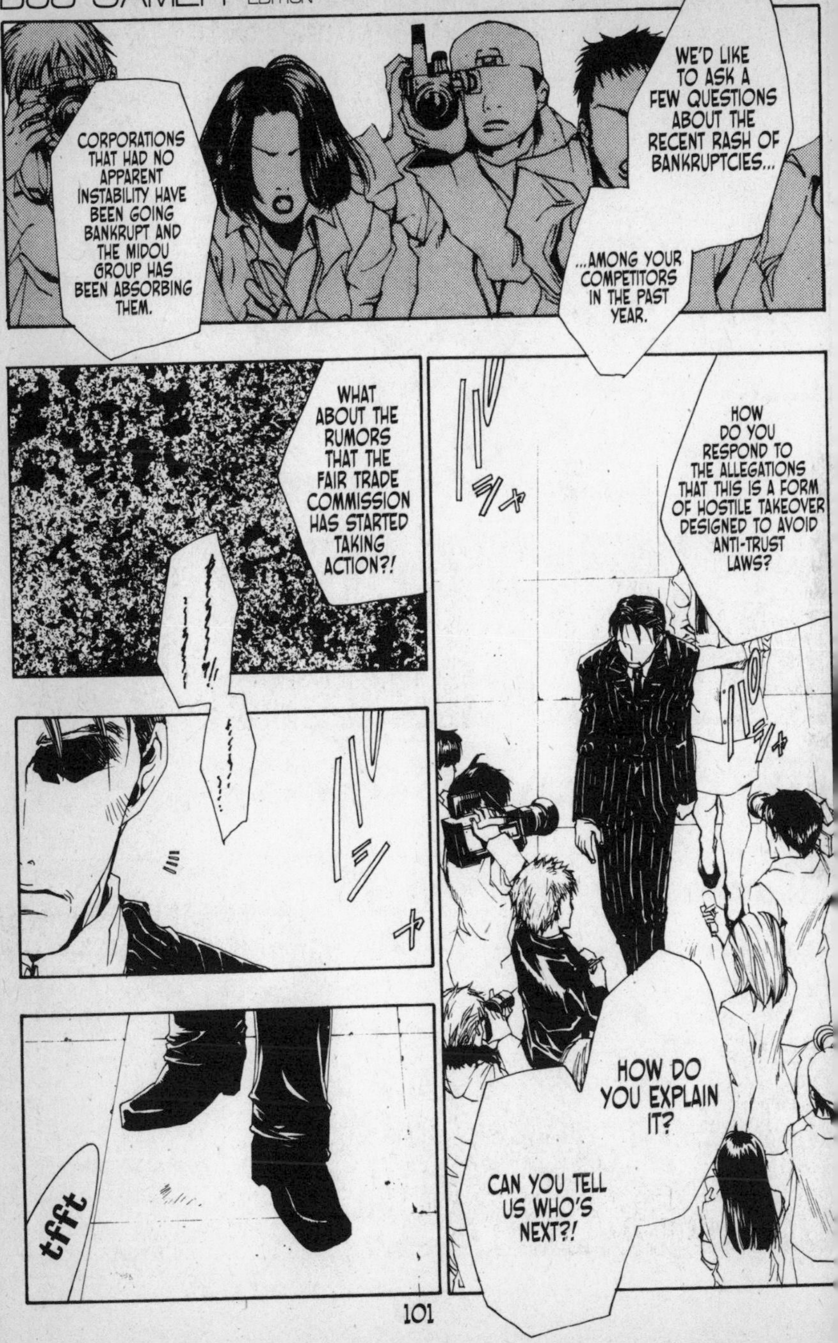
WE'D LIKE TO ASK A FEW QUESTIONS ABOUT THE RECENT RASH OF BANKRUPTCIES...
...AMONG YOUR COMPETITORS IN THE PAST YEAR.
CORPORATIONS THAT HAD NO APPARENT INSTABILITY HAVE BEEN GOING BANKRUPT AND THE MIDOU GROUP HAS BEEN ABSORBING THEM.
HOW DO YOU RESPOND TO THE ALLEGATIONS THAT THIS IS A FORM OF HOSTILE TAKEOVER DESIGNED TO AVOID ANTI-TRUST LAWS?
HOW DO YOU EXPLAIN IT?
CAN YOU TELL US WHO'S NEXT?!
WHAT ABOUT THE RUMORS THAT THE FAIR TRADE COMMISSION HAS STARTED TAKING ACTION?!
tfft

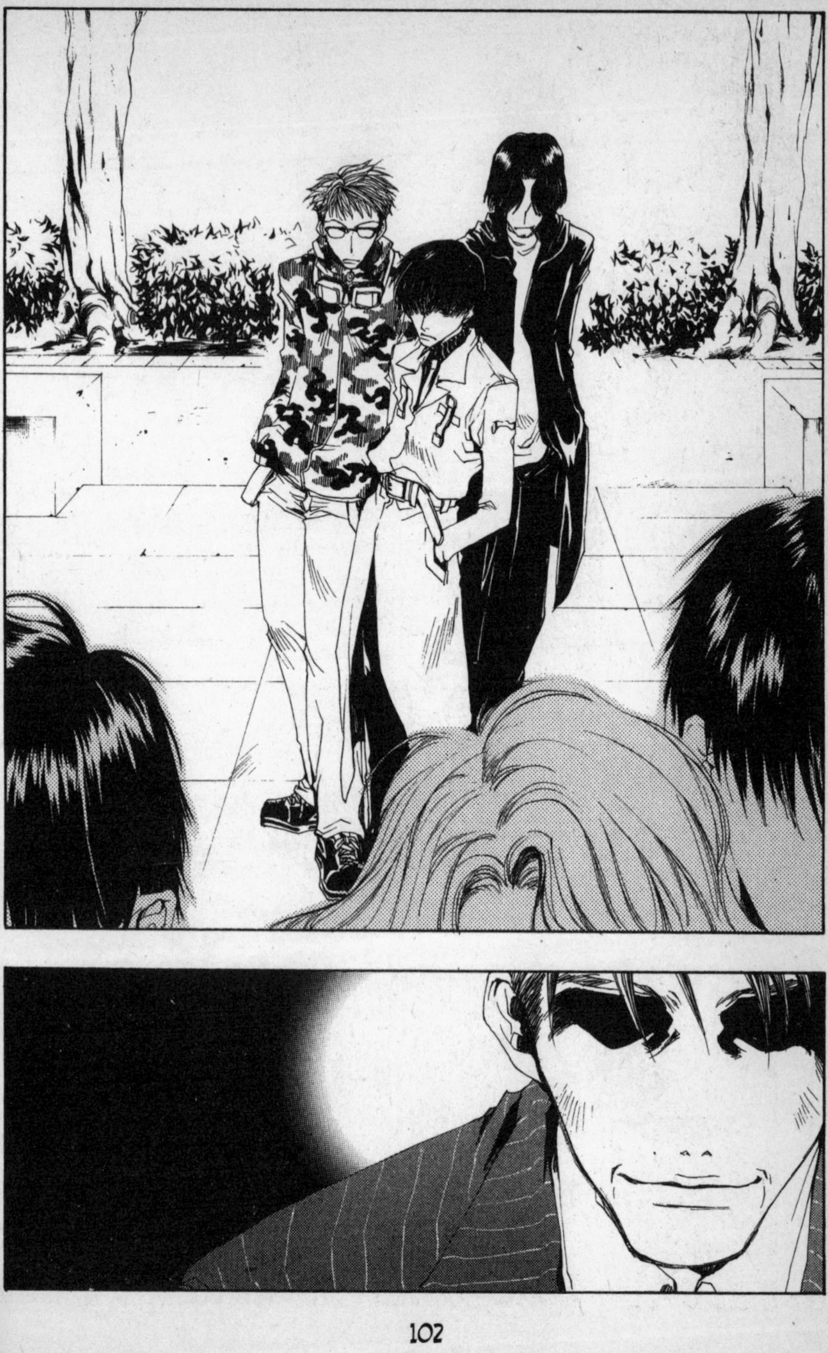

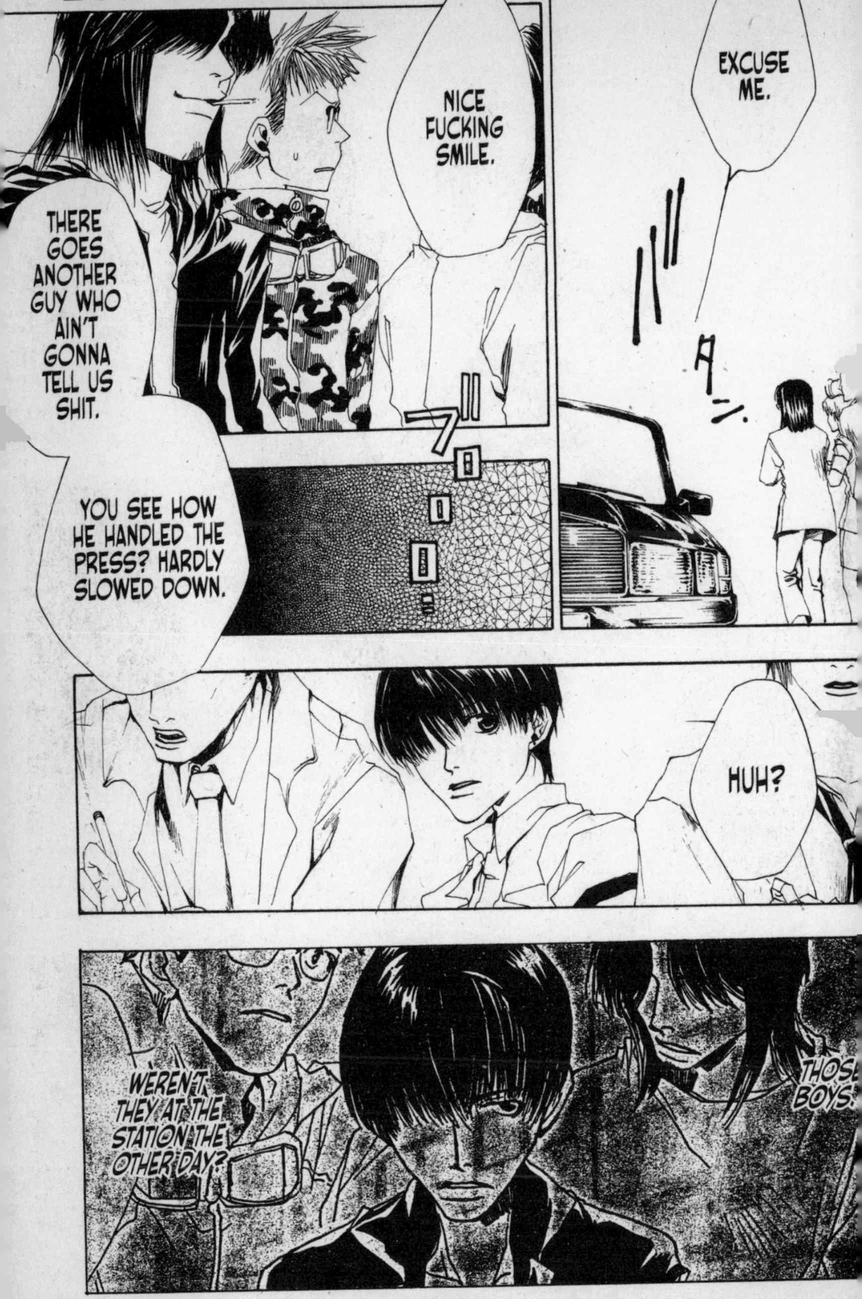
EXCUSE ME.
NICE FUCKING SMILE.
THERE GOES ANOTHER GUY WHO AIN'T GONNA TELL US SHIT.
YOU SEE HOW HE HANDLED THE PRESS? HARDLY SLOWED DOWN.
HUH?
THOSE BOYS.
WEREN'T THEY AT THE STATION THE OTHER DAY?

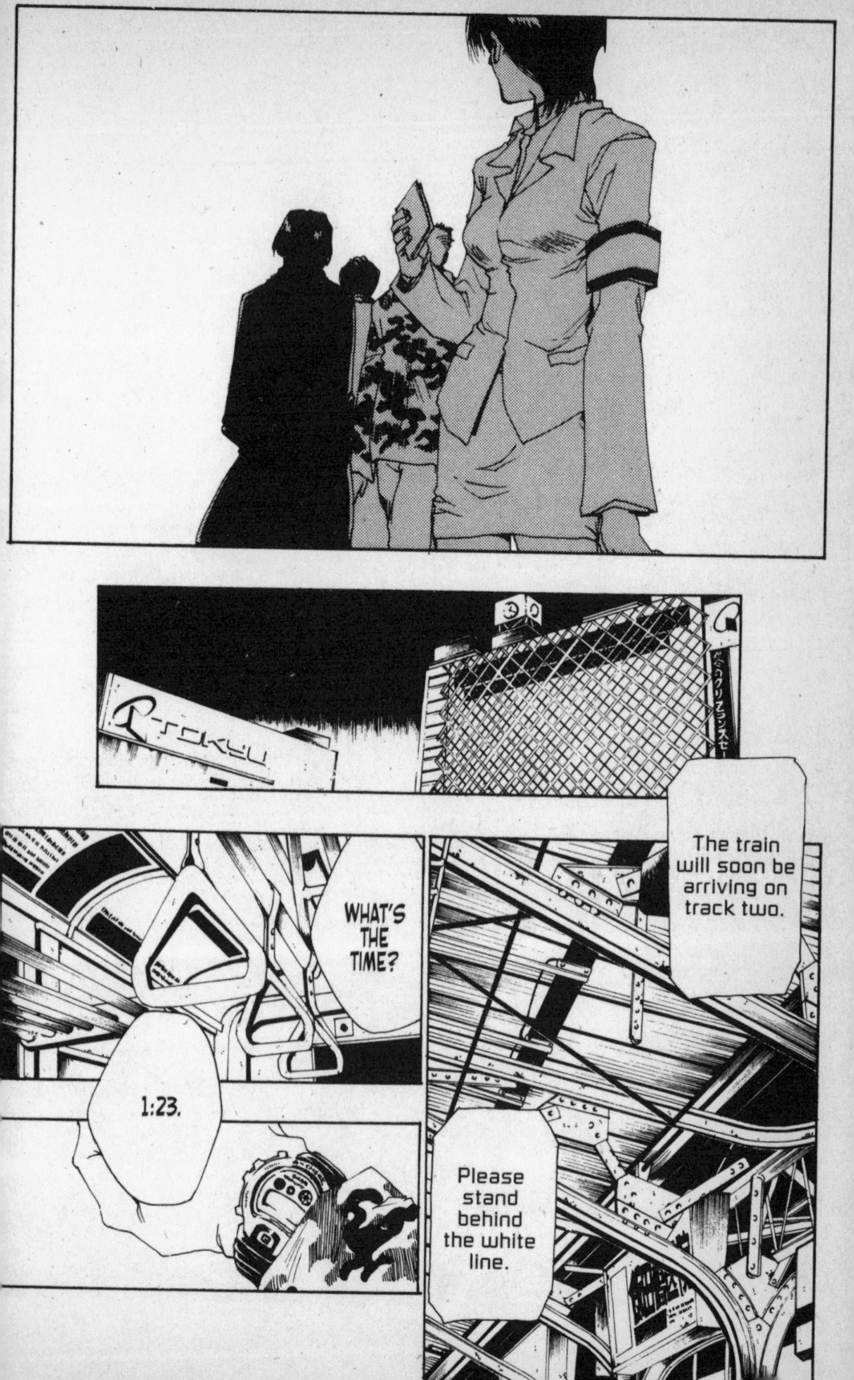
The train will soon be arriving on track two.
Please stand behind the white line.
WHAT'S THE TIME?
1:23.

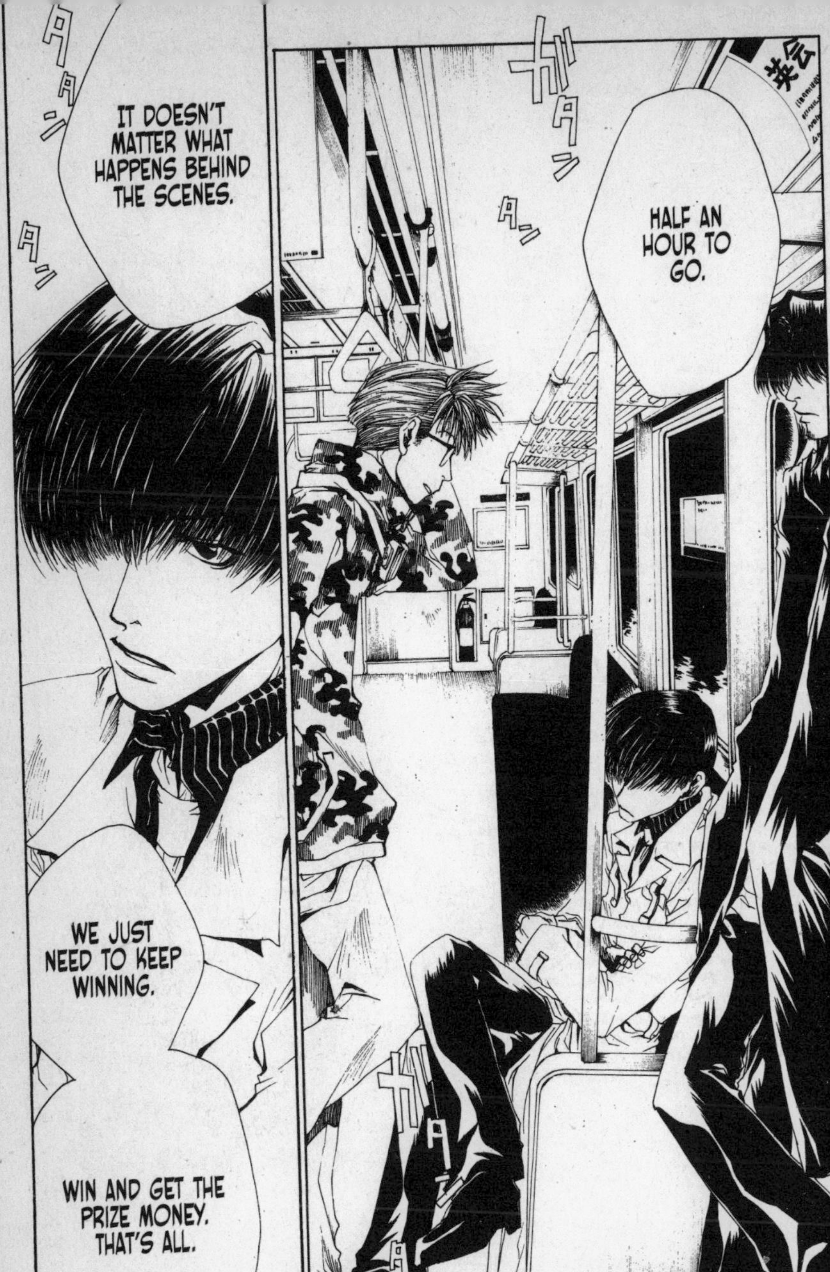
ガタン
タン
HALF AN HOUR TO GO.
タタン
IT DOESN'T MATTER WHAT HAPPENS BEHIND THE SCENES.
タン
WE JUST NEED TO KEEP WINNING.
WIN AND GET THE PRIZE MONEY. THAT'S ALL.

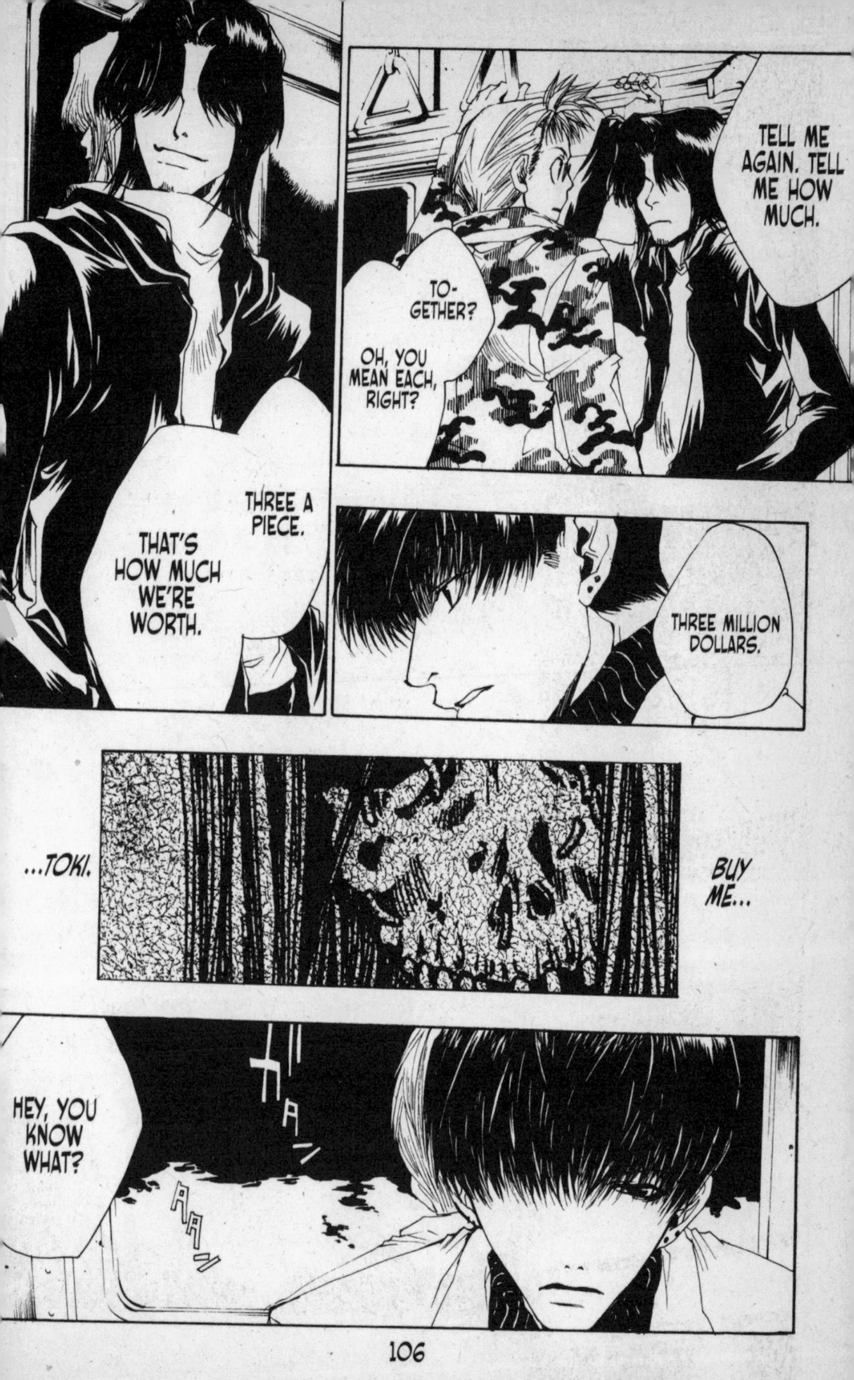

TELL ME AGAIN. TELL ME HOW MUCH.
TO-GETHER?
OH, YOU MEAN EACH, RIGHT?
THREE MILLION DOLLARS.
THREE A PIECE.
THAT'S HOW MUCH WE'RE WORTH.
BUY ME...
...TOKI.
HEY, YOU KNOW WHAT?

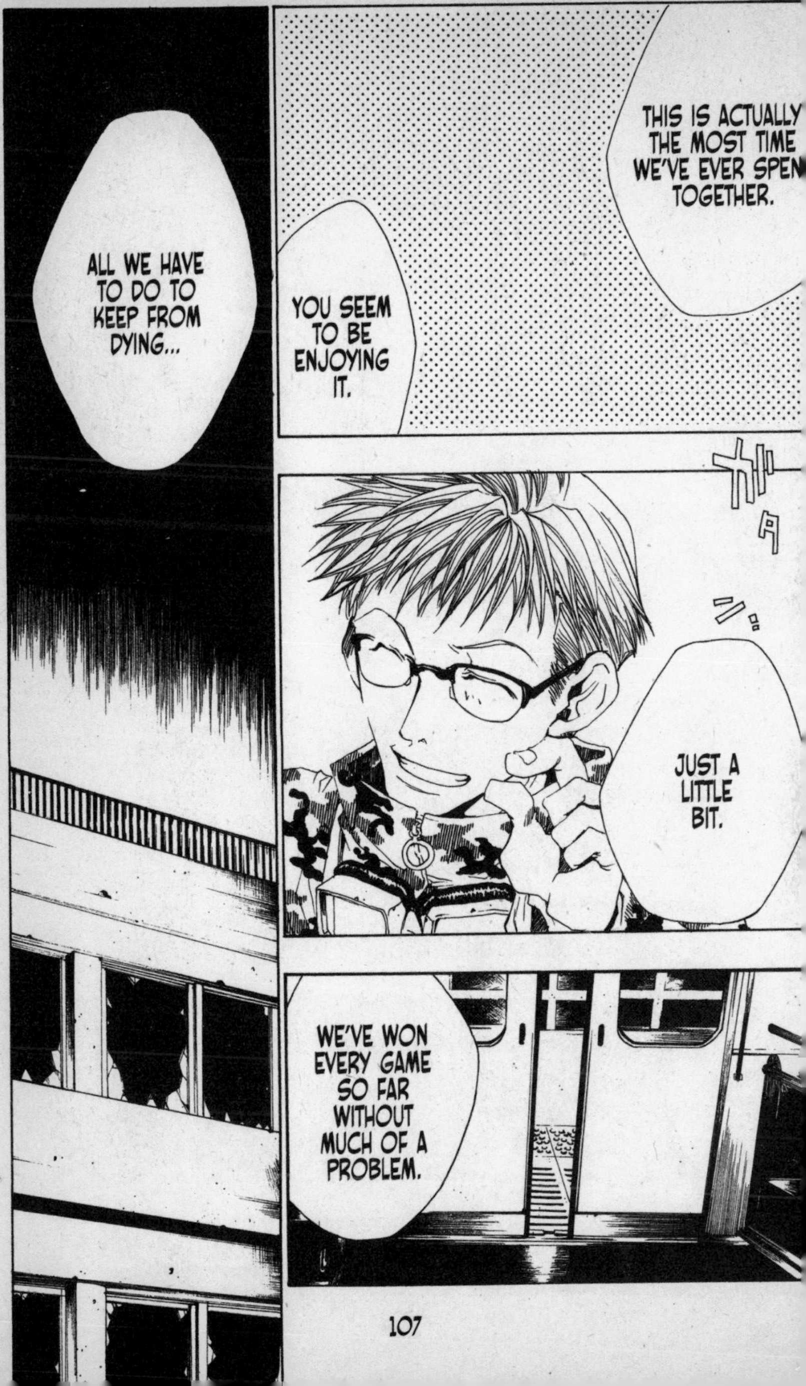
THIS IS ACTUALLY THE MOST TIME WE'VE EVER SPEN TOGETHER.
YOU SEEM TO BE ENJOYING IT.
JUST A LITTLE BIT.
WE'VE WON EVERY GAME SO FAR WITHOUT MUCH OF A PROBLEM.
ALL WE HAVE TO DO TO KEEP FROM DYING...

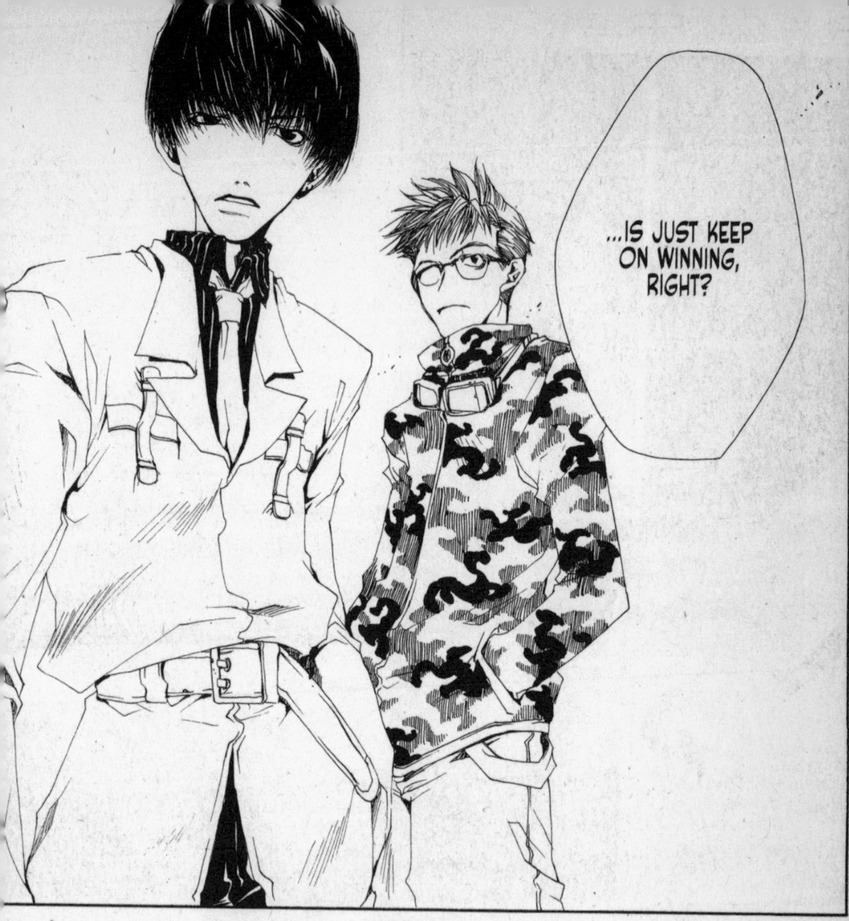
...IS JUST KEEP ON WINNING, RIGHT?
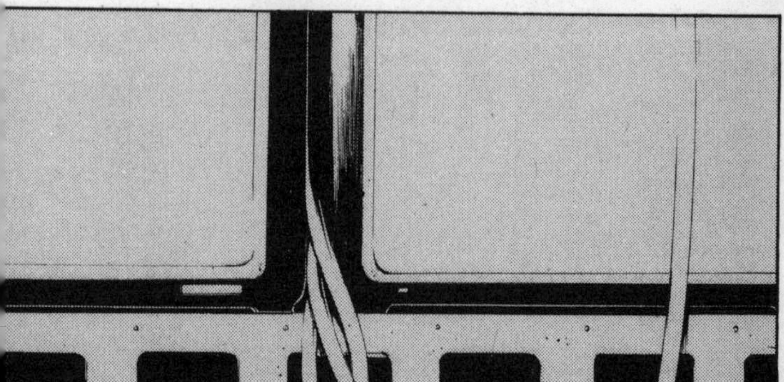

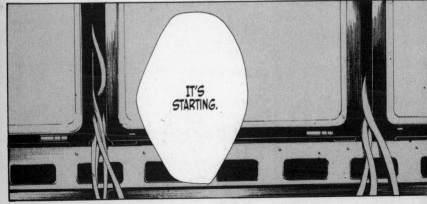

IT'S
STARTING.

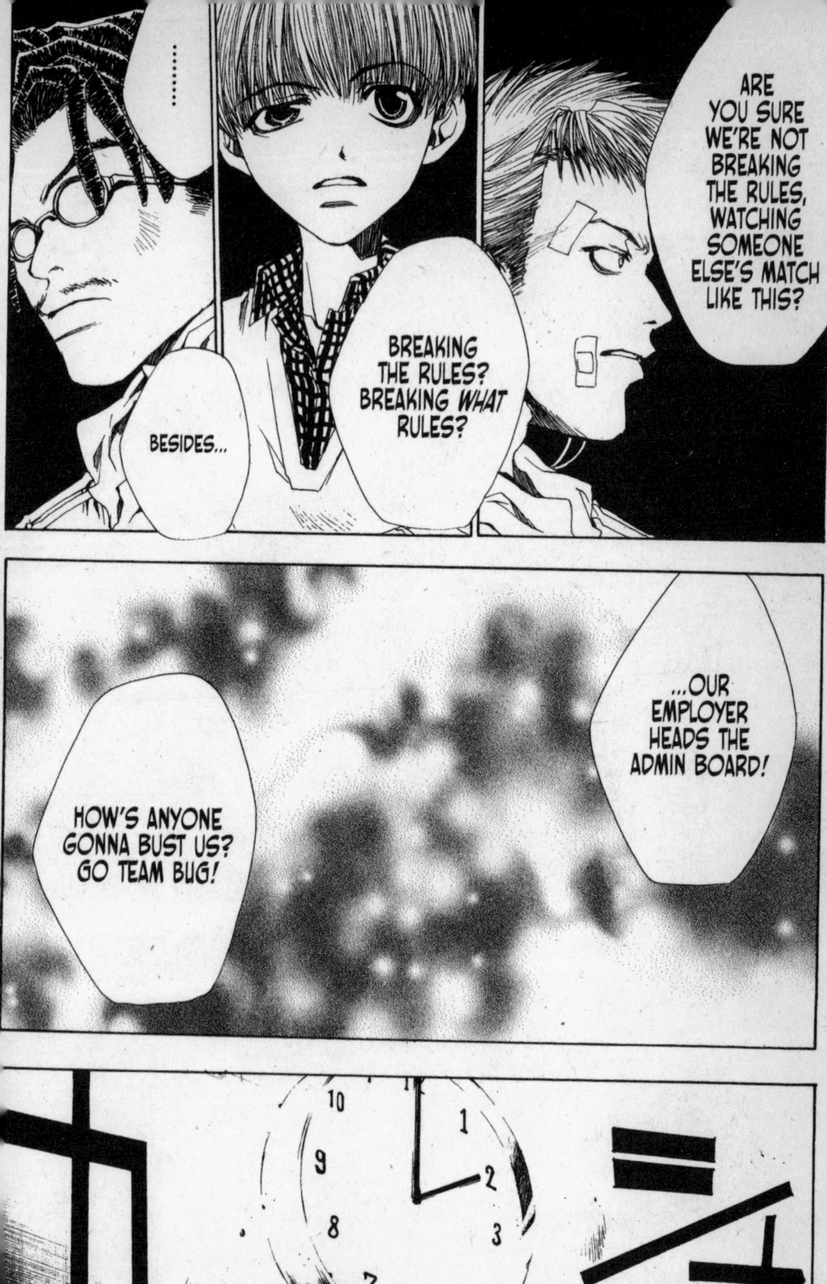
ARE YOU SURE WE'RE NOT BREAKING THE RULES, WATCHING SOMEONE ELSE'S MATCH LIKE THIS?
BREAKING THE RULES? BREAKING *WHAT* RULES?
......
BESIDES...
...OUR EMPLOYER HEADS THE ADMIN BOARD!
HOW'S ANYONE GONNA BUST US? GO TEAM BUG!

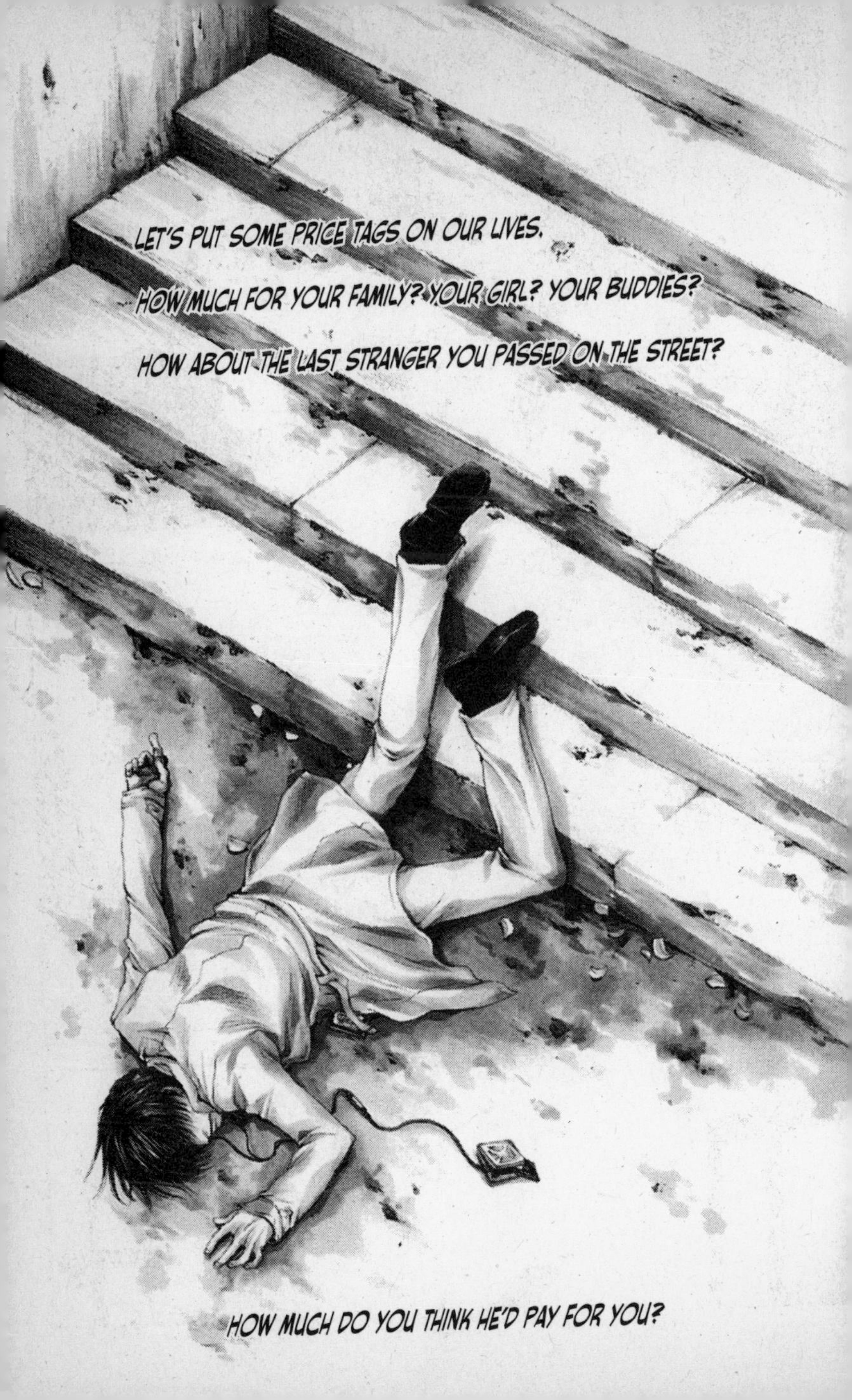
LET'S PUT SOME PRICE TAGS ON OUR LIVES.
HOW MUCH FOR YOUR FAMILY? YOUR GIRL? YOUR BUDDIES?
HOW ABOUT THE LAST STRANGER YOU PASSED ON THE STREET?
HOW MUCH DO YOU THINK HE'D PAY FOR YOU?

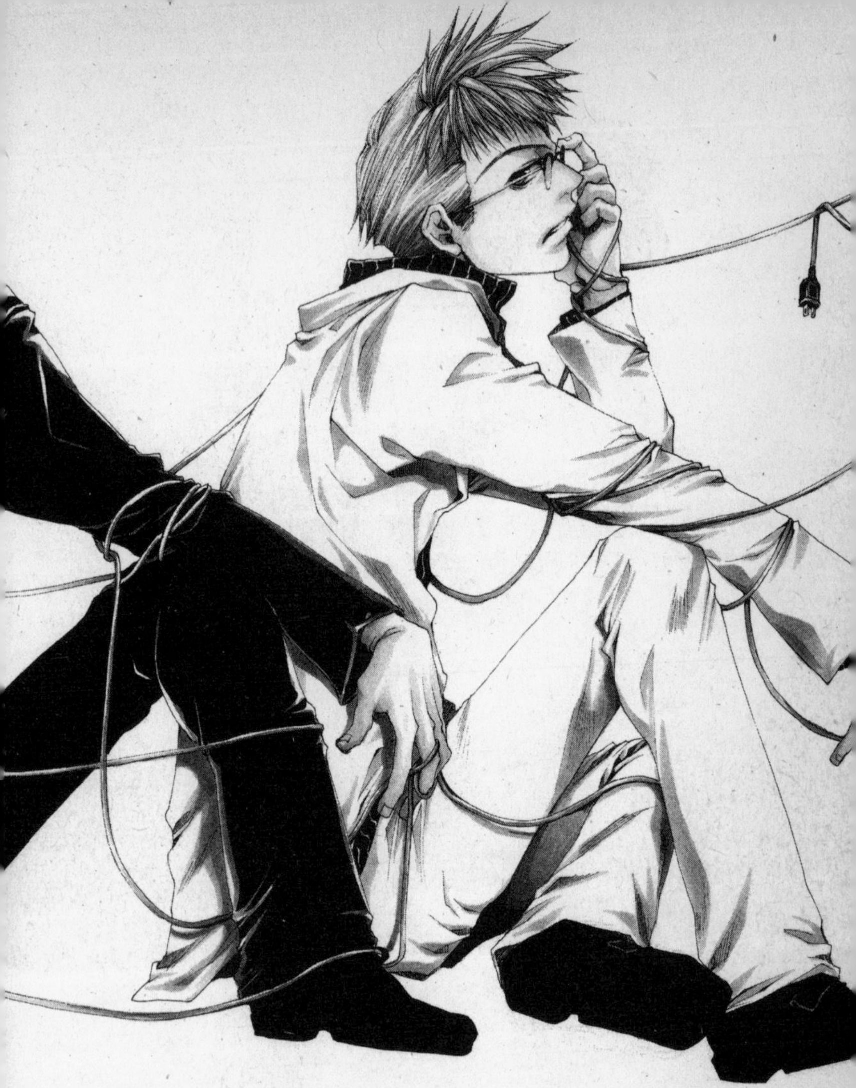

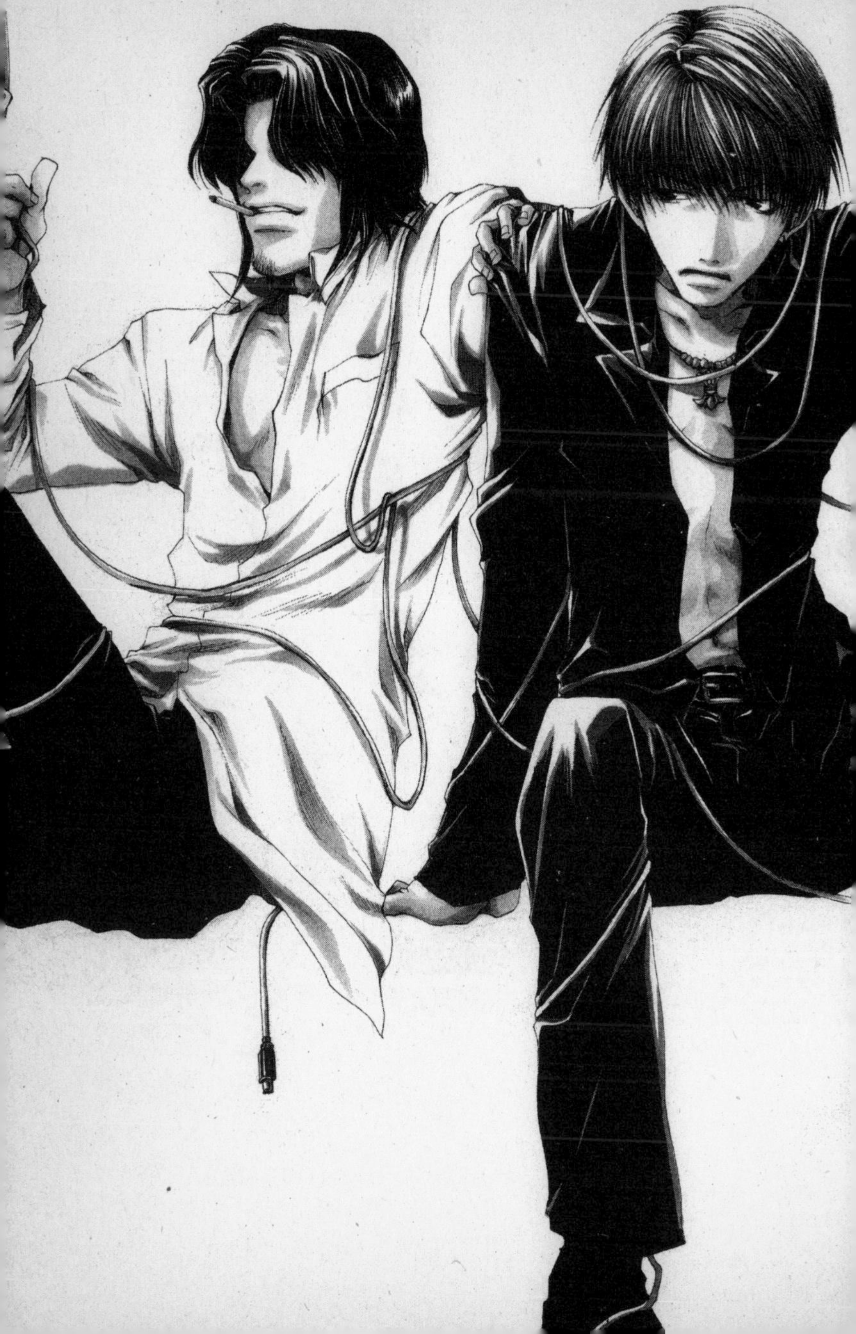

Toki Mishiba

Birthday: February 14th
Age: 20
Occupation: Student
Blood Type: A
Height: 5 ft. 6 in.
Weight: 119 lbs.
Hobby: Meditation (aka zoning out)
Special Skill: High proficiency in several martial arts, needlework
Favorite Foods: Salmon, Manroken's super-spicy kimchi ramen
Note: If you call him and he doesn't answer, it's probably because he's not listening.

Unusually solitary, guarded and alert, Toki maintains a large personal space, avoiding crowds at all costs. This tends to make him appear lonesome and has the paradoxical effect of drawing out concerned do-gooder types who try to engage him in conversation, much to his chagrin. He has cultivated an expressionless demeanor, his face as blank and handsome as a mannequin's. Despite his efforts, there are times when the magma inside him does erupt. He considers his goal of making money "absolute," even to the detriment of his own life.

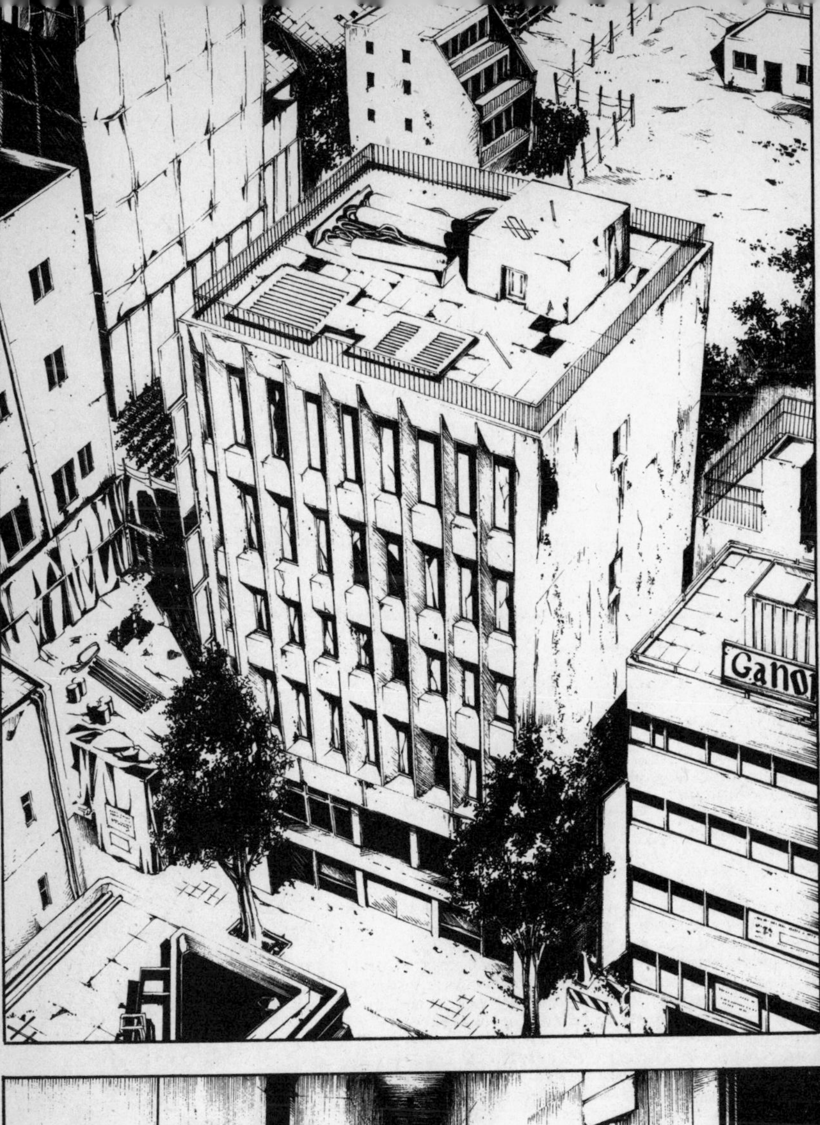
Gano
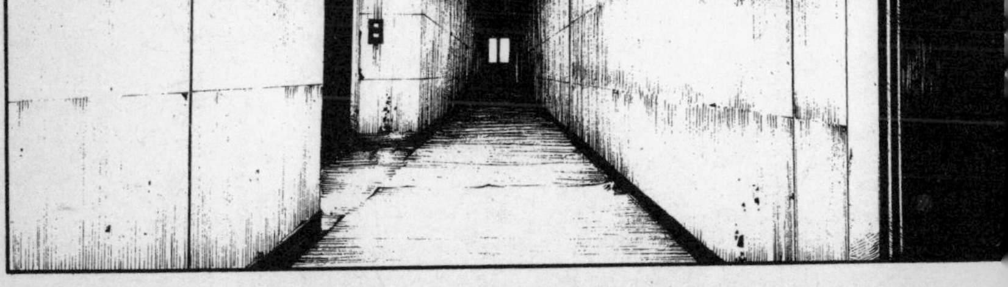

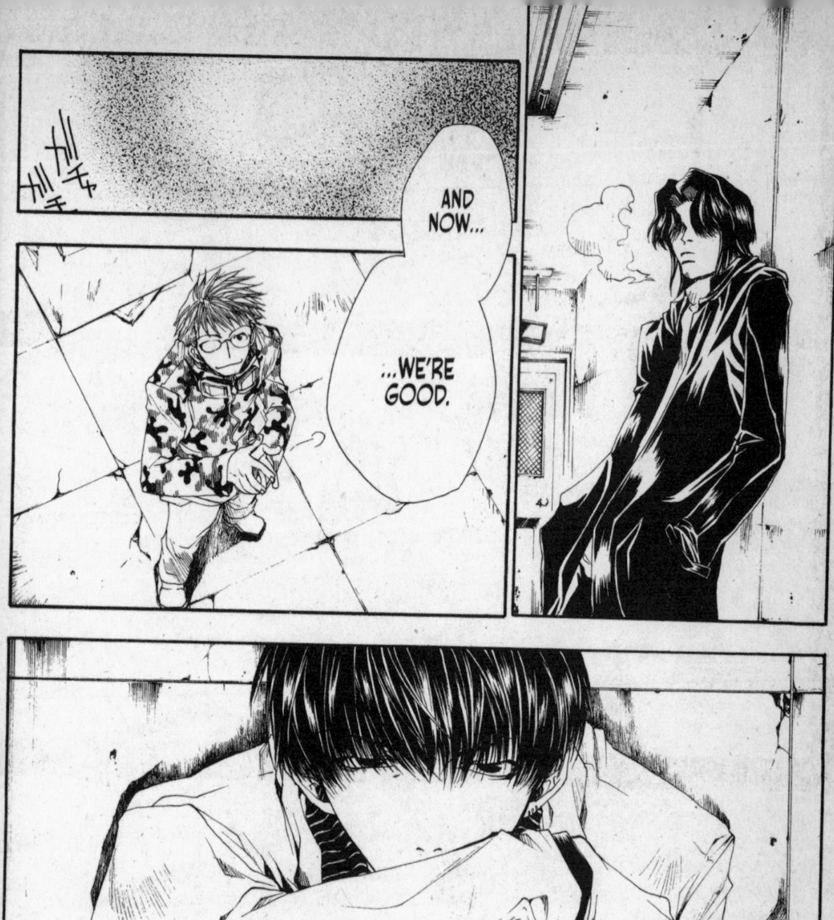
AND NOW...
...WE'RE GOOD.

STAGE 6: The Price of Tomorrow, Part 1

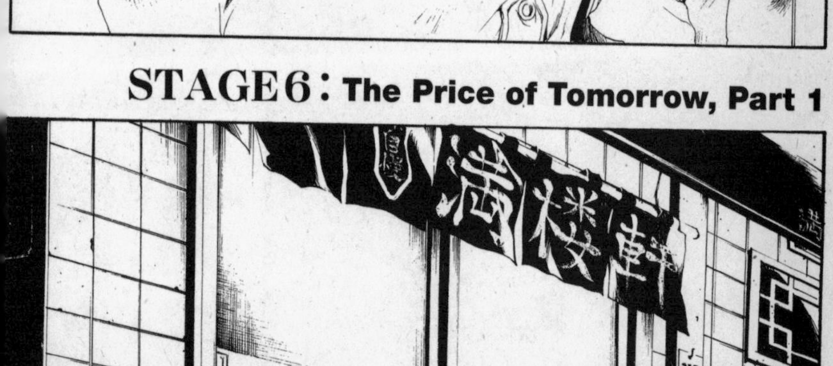

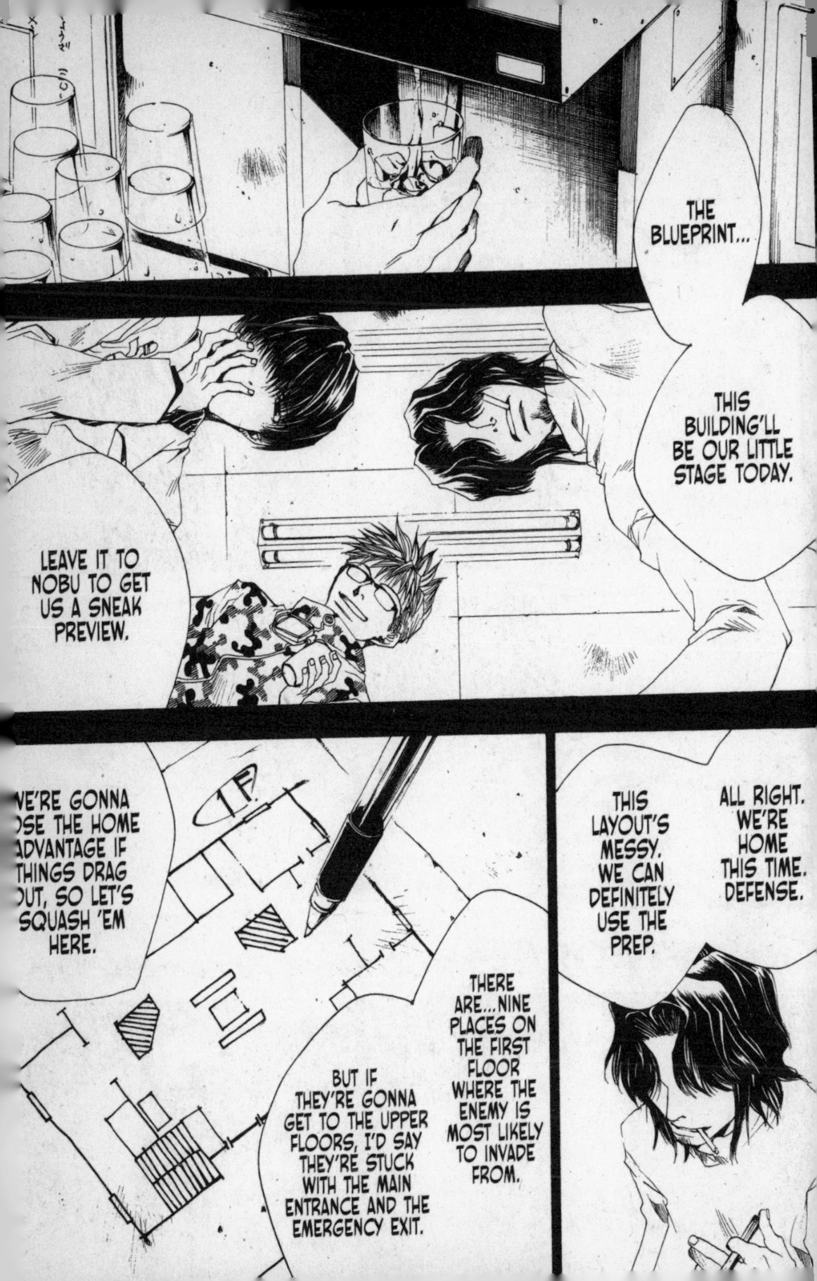
THE BLUEPRINT...
THIS BUILDING'LL BE OUR LITTLE STAGE TODAY.
LEAVE IT TO NOBU TO GET US A SNEAK PREVIEW.
ALL RIGHT. WE'RE HOME THIS TIME. DEFENSE.
THIS LAYOUT'S MESSY. WE CAN DEFINITELY USE THE PREP.
THERE ARE...NINE PLACES ON THE FIRST FLOOR WHERE THE ENEMY IS MOST LIKELY TO INVADE FROM.
BUT IF THEY'RE GONNA GET TO THE UPPER FLOORS, I'D SAY THEY'RE STUCK WITH THE MAIN ENTRANCE AND THE EMERGENCY EXIT.
1F
VE'RE GONNA OSE THE HOME ADVANTAGE IF THINGS DRAG OUT, SO LET'S SQUASH 'EM HERE.

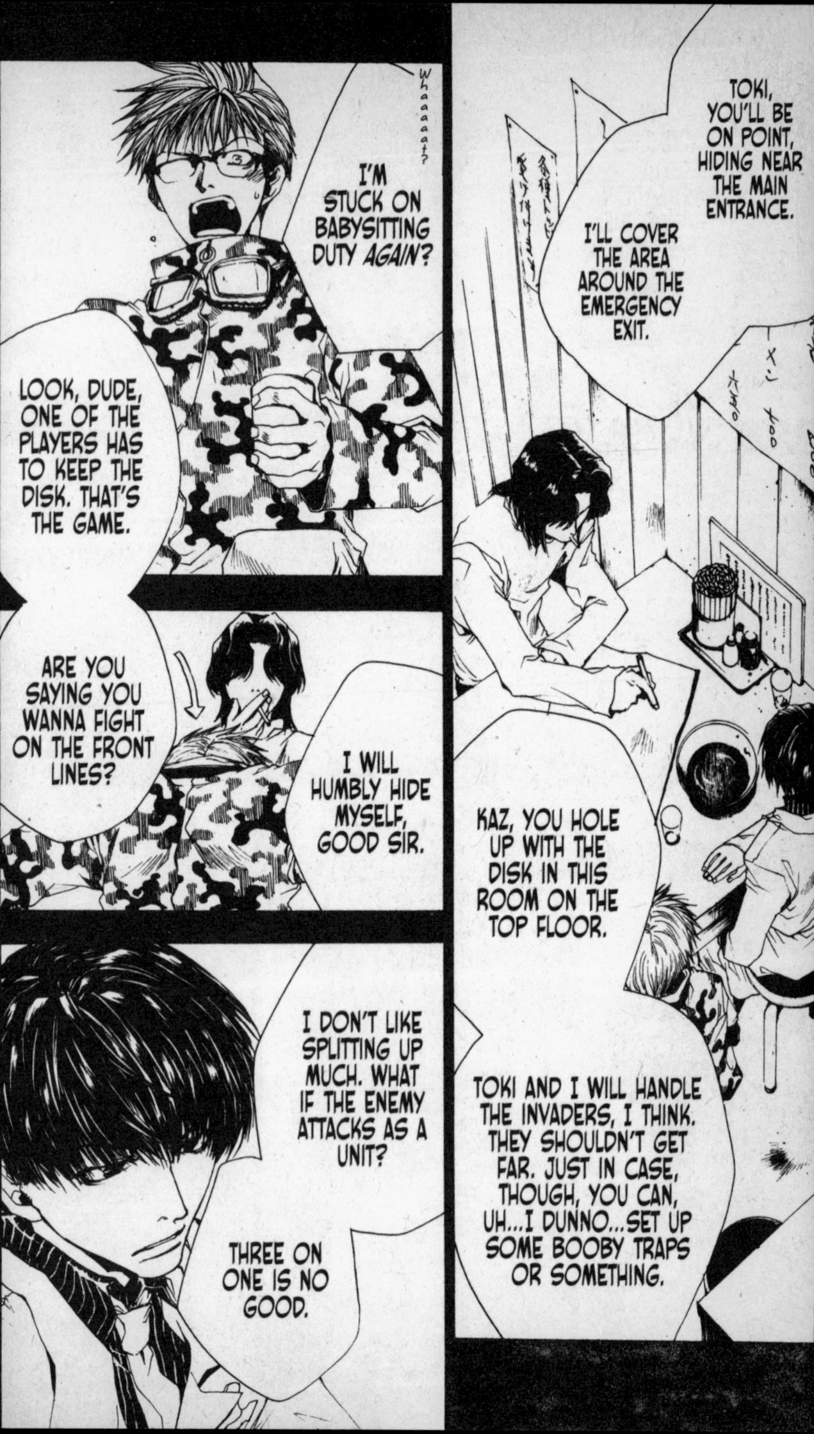
TOKI, YOU'LL BE ON POINT, HIDING NEAR THE MAIN ENTRANCE.
I'LL COVER THE AREA AROUND THE EMERGENCY EXIT.
KAZ, YOU HOLE UP WITH THE DISK IN THIS ROOM ON THE TOP FLOOR.
TOKI AND I WILL HANDLE THE INVADERS, I THINK. THEY SHOULDN'T GET FAR. JUST IN CASE, THOUGH, YOU CAN, UH...I DUNNO...SET UP SOME BOOBY TRAPS OR SOMETHING.
Whaaaaaat?
I'M STUCK ON BABYSITTING DUTY *AGAIN*?
LOOK, DUDE, ONE OF THE PLAYERS HAS TO KEEP THE DISK. THAT'S THE GAME.
ARE YOU SAYING YOU WANNA FIGHT ON THE FRONT LINES?
I WILL HUMBLY HIDE MYSELF, GOOD SIR.
I DON'T LIKE SPLITTING UP MUCH. WHAT IF THE ENEMY ATTACKS AS A UNIT?
THREE ON ONE IS NO GOOD.

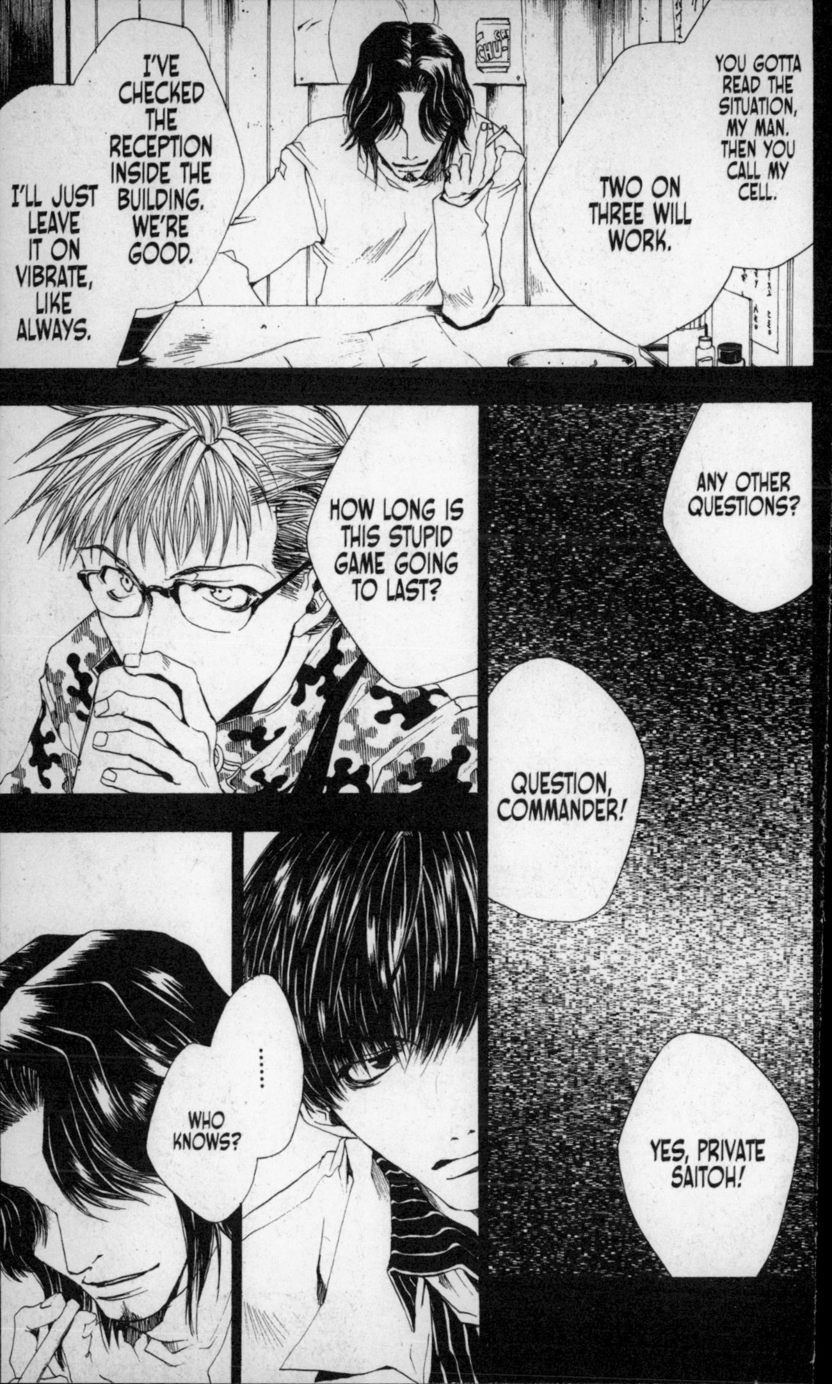
YOU GOTTA READ THE SITUATION, MY MAN. THEN YOU CALL MY CELL.
TWO ON THREE WILL WORK.
I'VE CHECKED THE RECEPTION INSIDE THE BUILDING. WE'RE GOOD.
I'LL JUST LEAVE IT ON VIBRATE, LIKE ALWAYS.
ANY OTHER QUESTIONS?
QUESTION, COMMANDER!
YES, PRIVATE SAITOH!
HOW LONG IS THIS STUPID GAME GOING TO LAST?
......
WHO KNOWS?

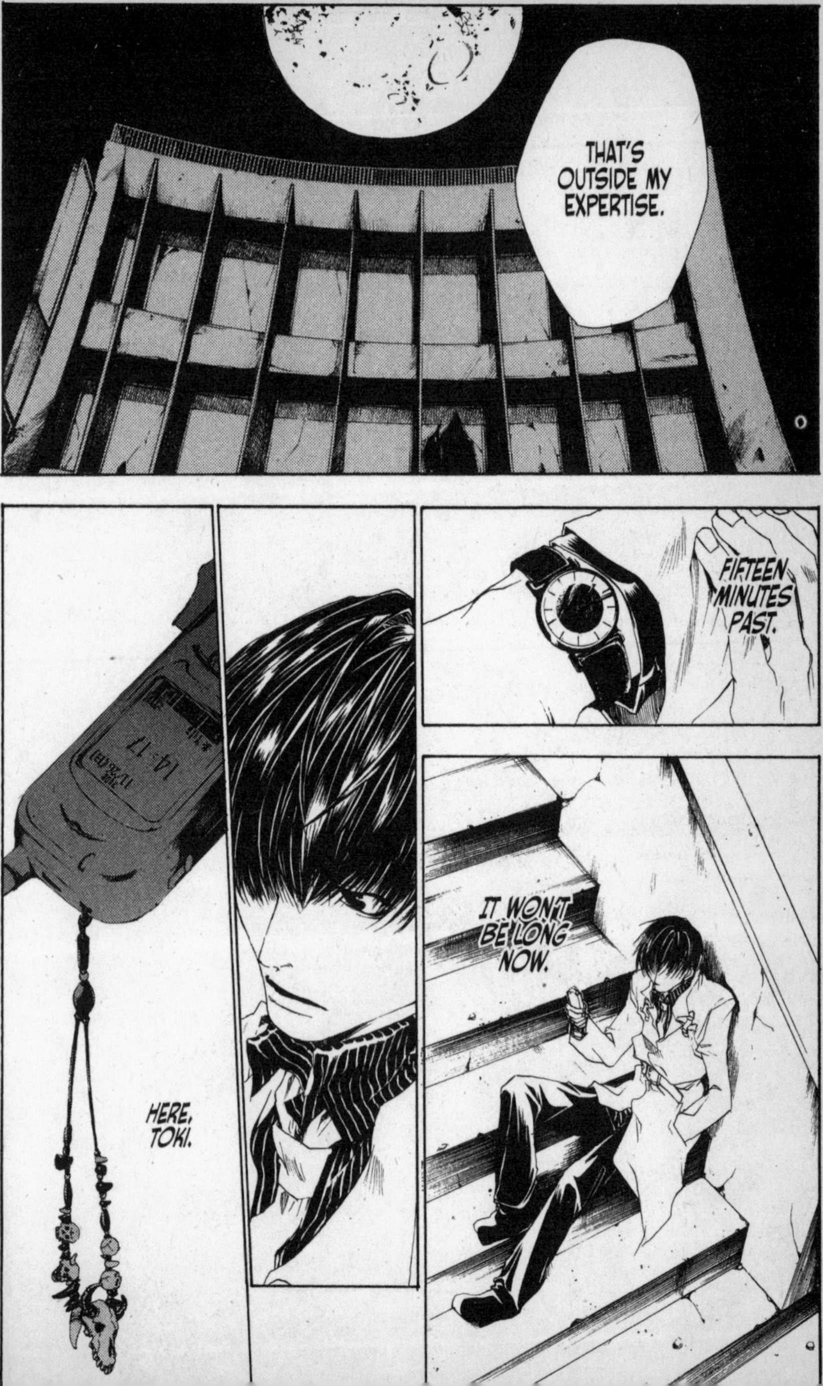
THAT'S OUTSIDE MY EXPERTISE.
FIFTEEN MINUTES PAST.
IT WON'T BE LONG NOW.
HERE, TOKI.

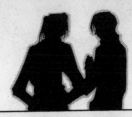

WHAT'S THIS?
A CELL PHONE STRAP. I MADE IT.
YOU DIDN'T MAKE ANY... OTHERS, DID YOU?
WHAT, YOU DON'T LIKE IT?
NO, I DO. THANKS...
...SHIGI.
shfft
THEY'RE HERE.
shffle
shfft
SOUNDS LIKE IT'S JUST ONE.
rattle
I GUESS THE OTHER TWO ARE HEADING TOWARD NOBUTO.
whap!

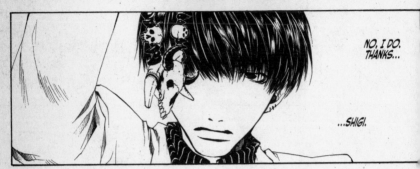

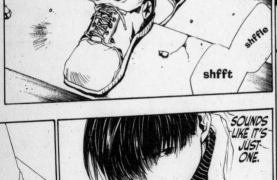

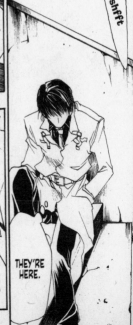

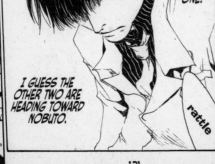

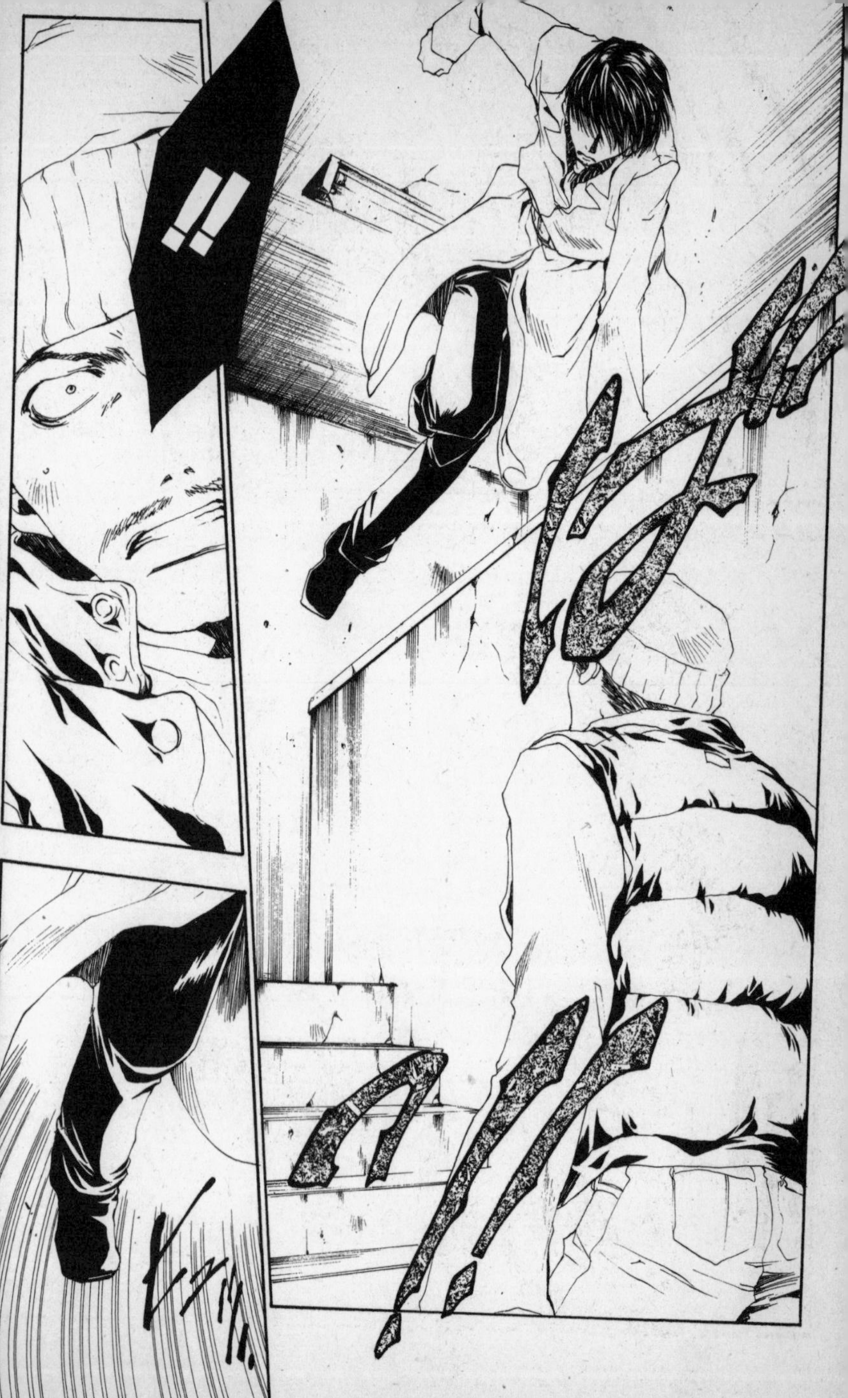
!!

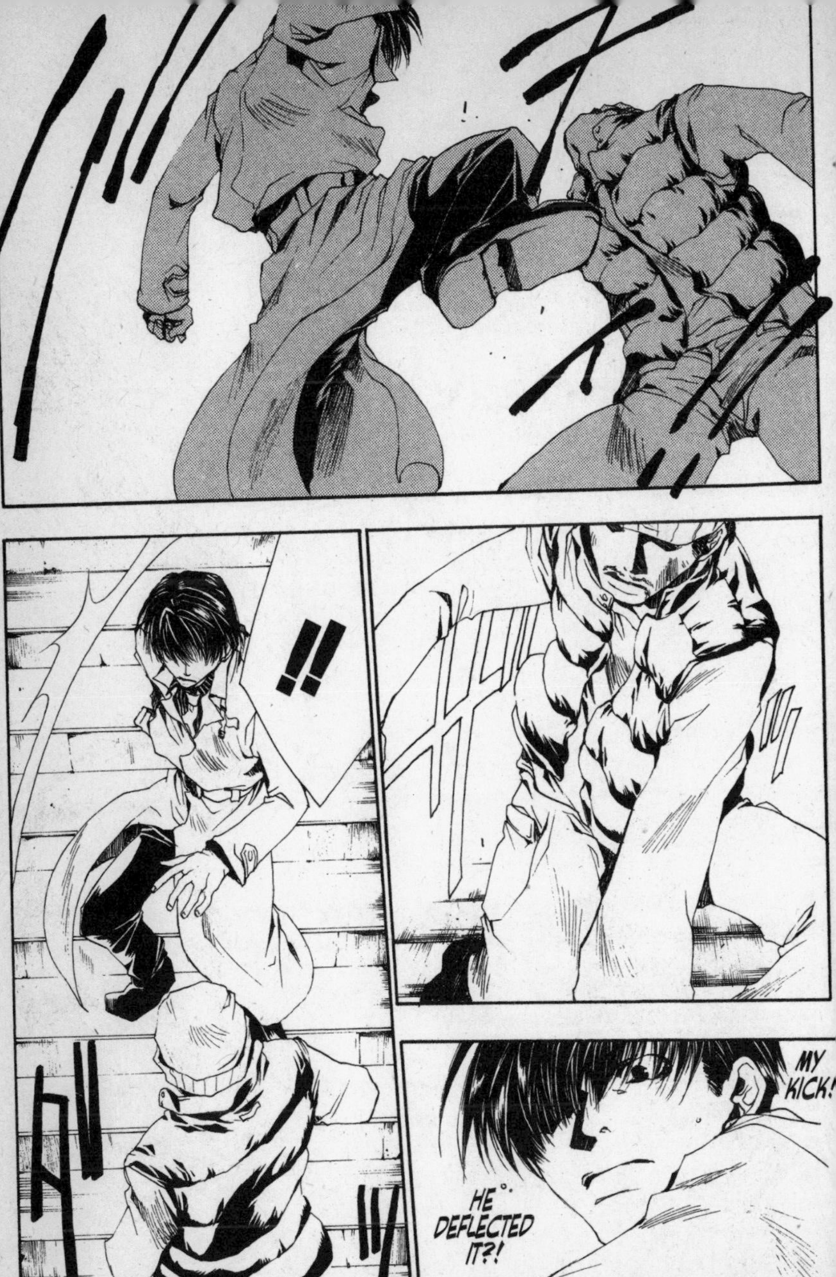
!!
MY KICK!
HE DEFLECTED IT?!

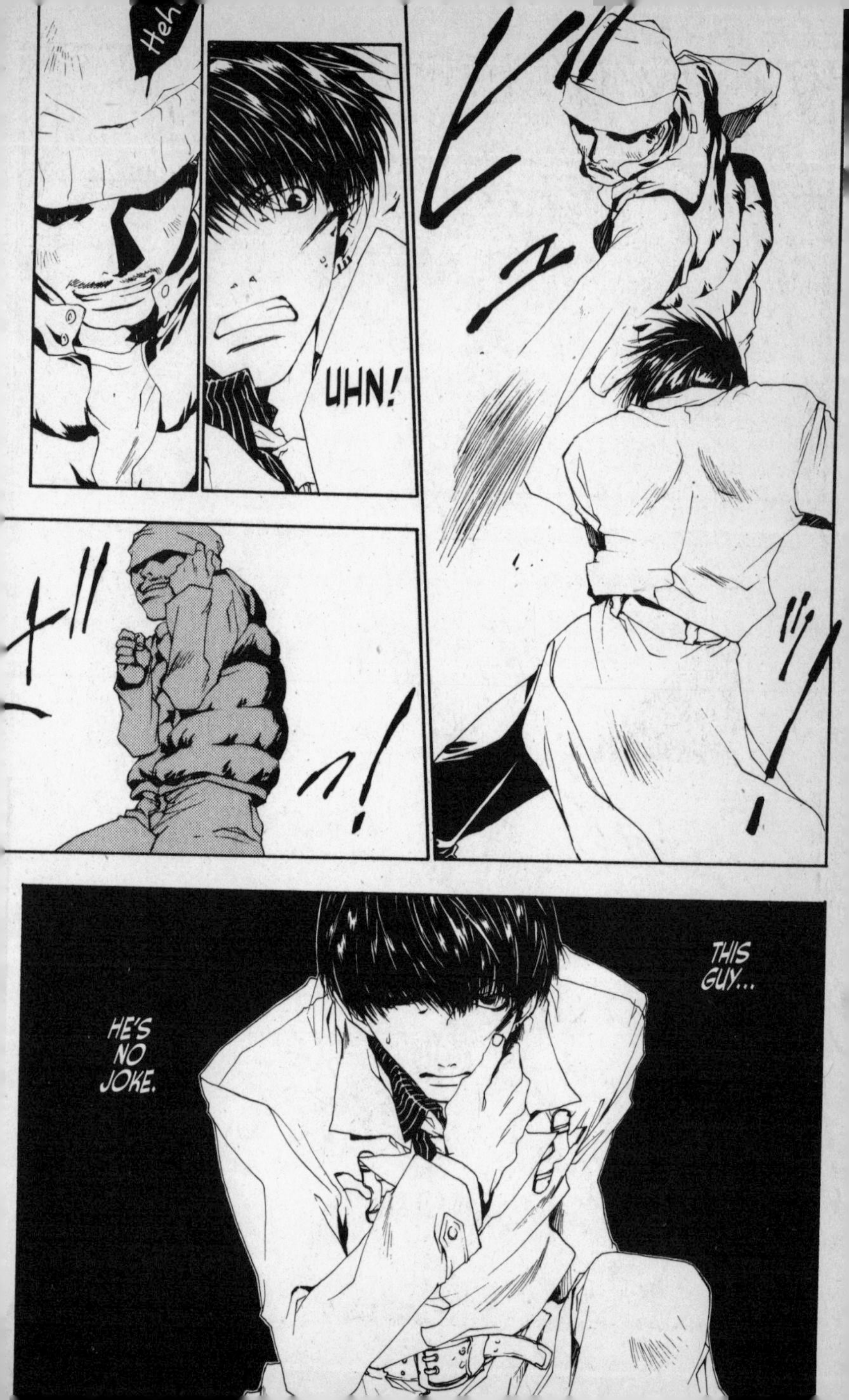
UHN!
Heh
THIS GUY...
HE'S NO JOKE.

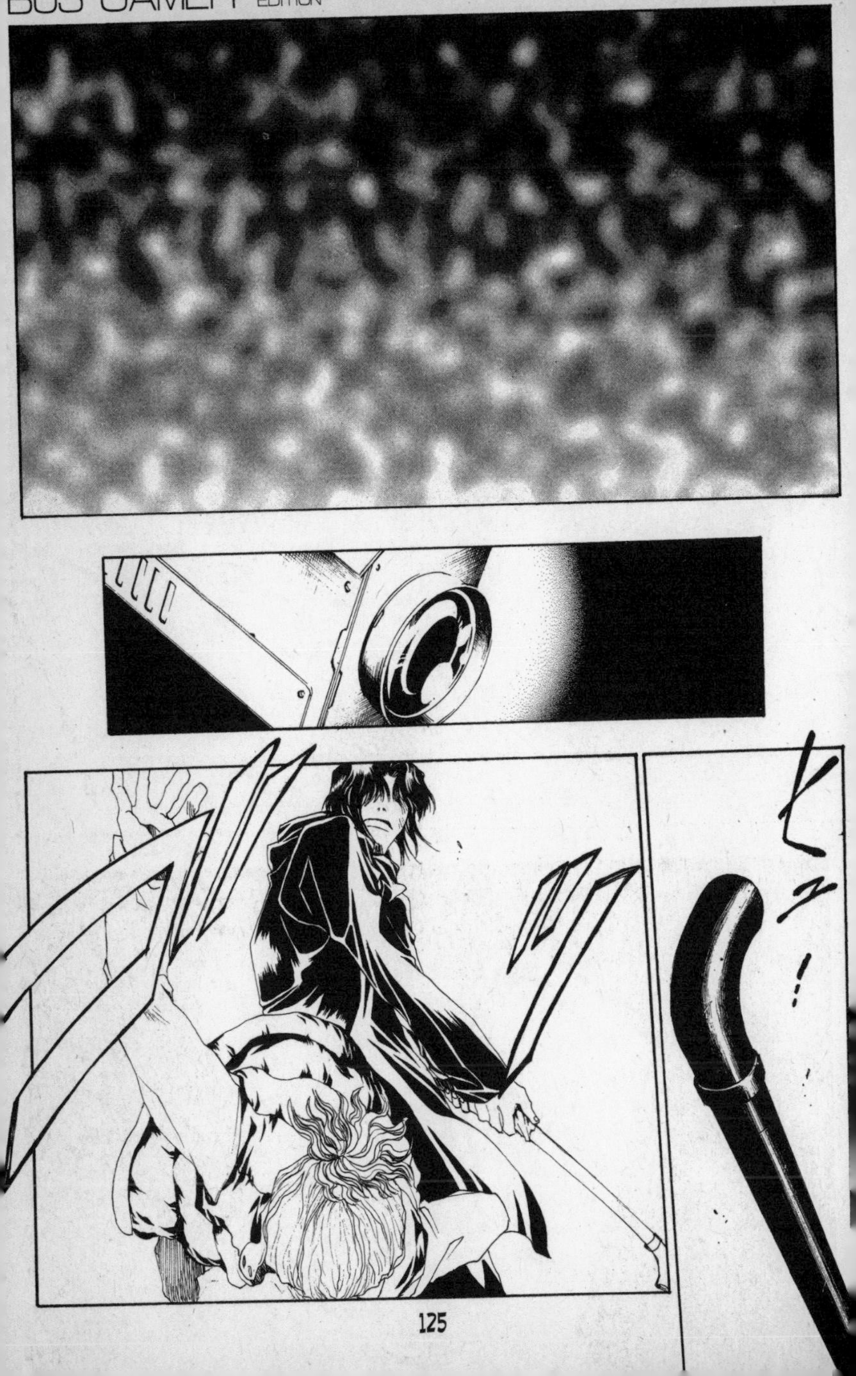
ヒュ!!

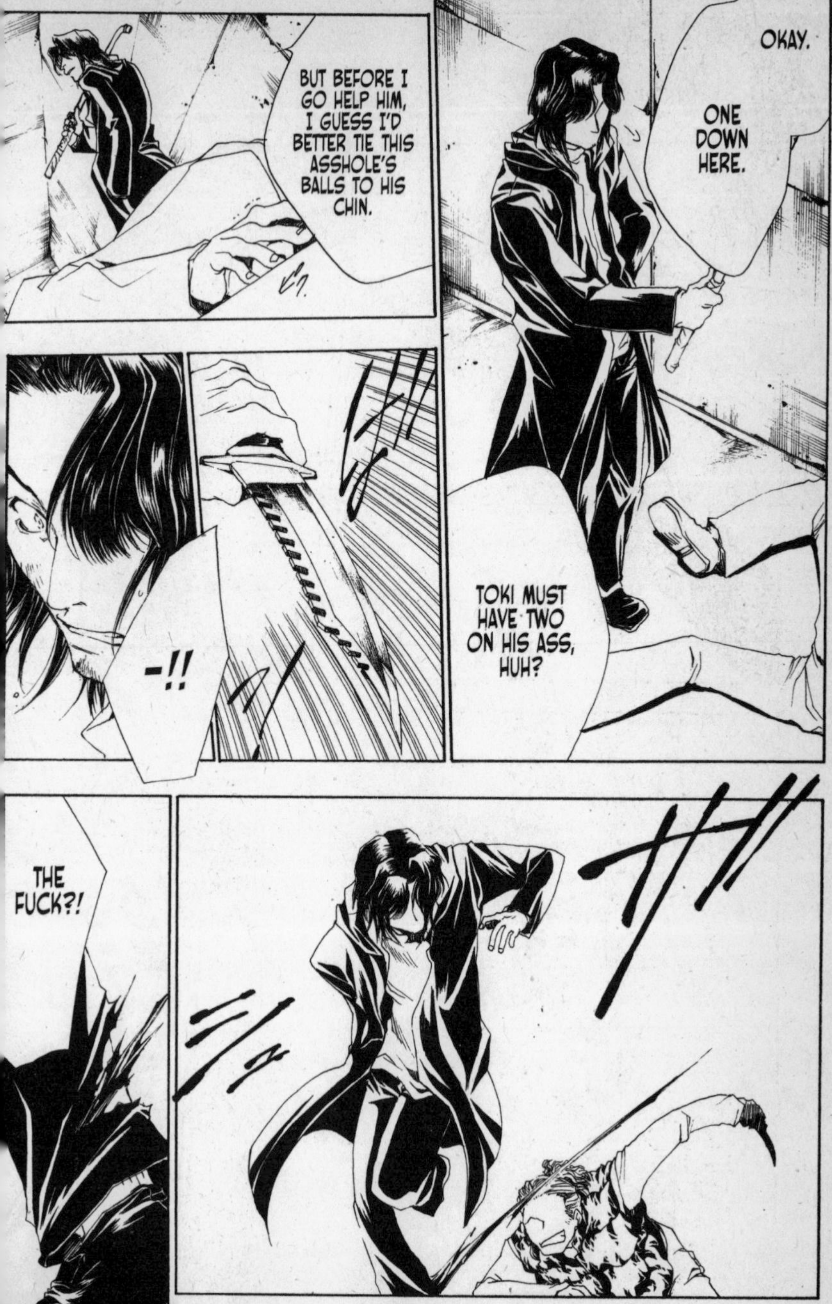

OKAY.
ONE DOWN HERE.
TOKI MUST HAVE TWO ON HIS ASS, HUH?
BUT BEFORE I GO HELP HIM, I GUESS I'D BETTER TIE THIS ASSHOLE'S BALLS TO HIS CHIN.
-!!
THE FUCK?!

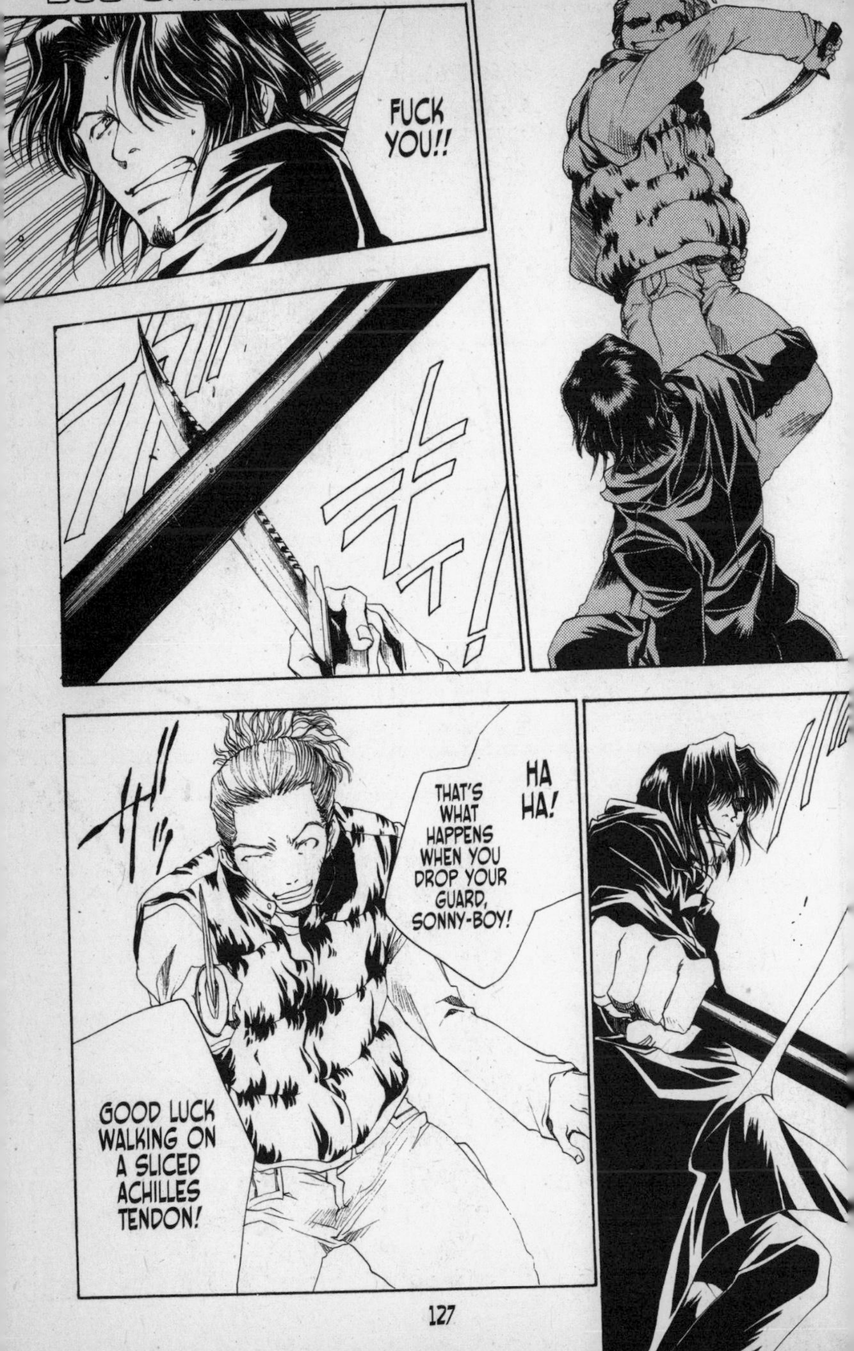
FUCK YOU!!
HA HA!
THAT'S WHAT HAPPENS WHEN YOU DROP YOUR GUARD, SONNY-BOY!
GOOD LUCK WALKING ON A SLICED ACHILLES TENDON!

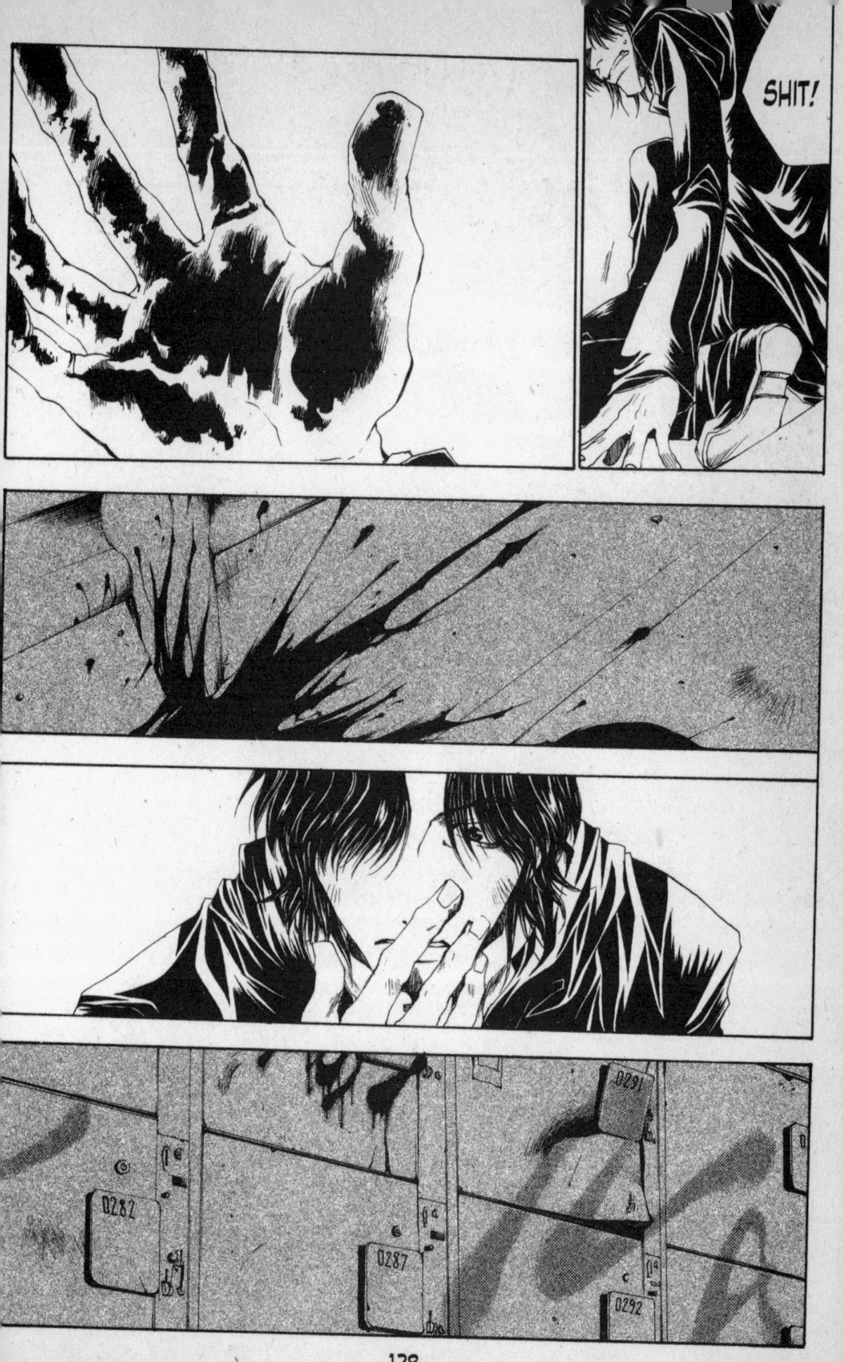
SHIT!
0291
0282
0287
0292

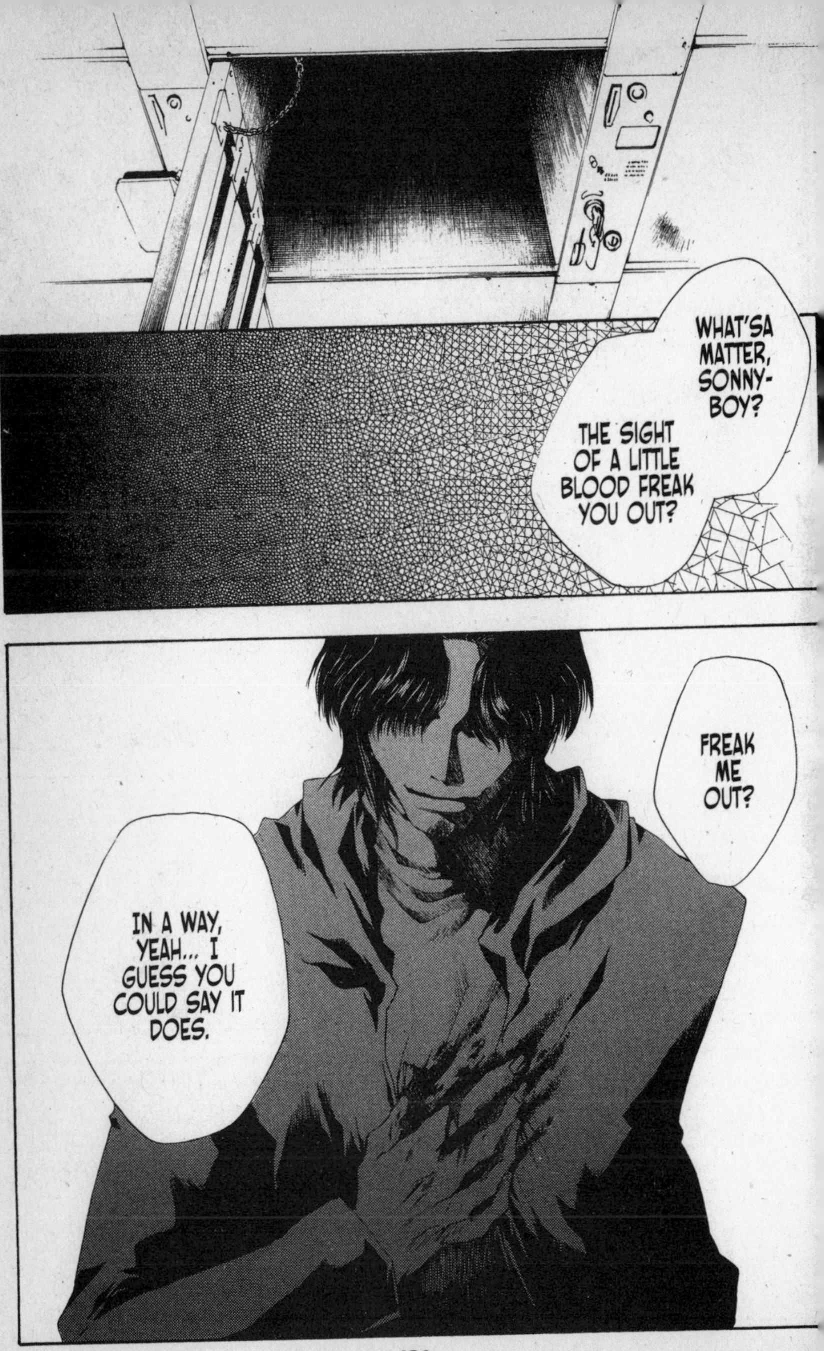
WHAT'SA MATTER, SONNY-BOY?
THE SIGHT OF A LITTLE BLOOD FREAK YOU OUT?
FREAK ME OUT?
IN A WAY, YEAH... I GUESS YOU COULD SAY IT DOES.

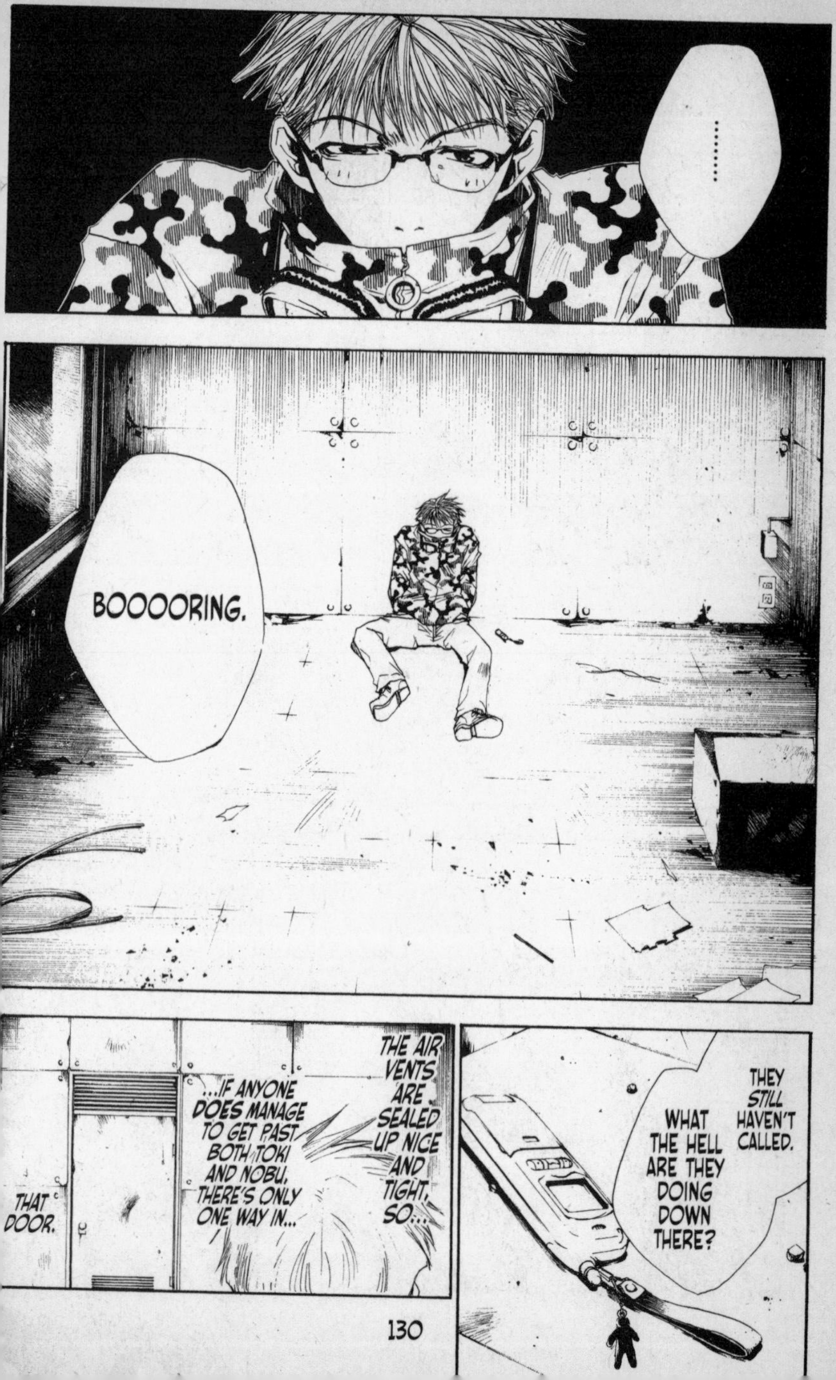
......
BOOOORING.
THEY STILL HAVEN'T CALLED.
WHAT THE HELL ARE THEY DOING DOWN THERE?
THE AIR VENTS ARE SEALED UP NICE AND TIGHT, SO...
...IF ANYONE DOES MANAGE TO GET PAST BOTH TOKI AND NOBU, THERE'S ONLY ONE WAY IN...
THAT DOOR.

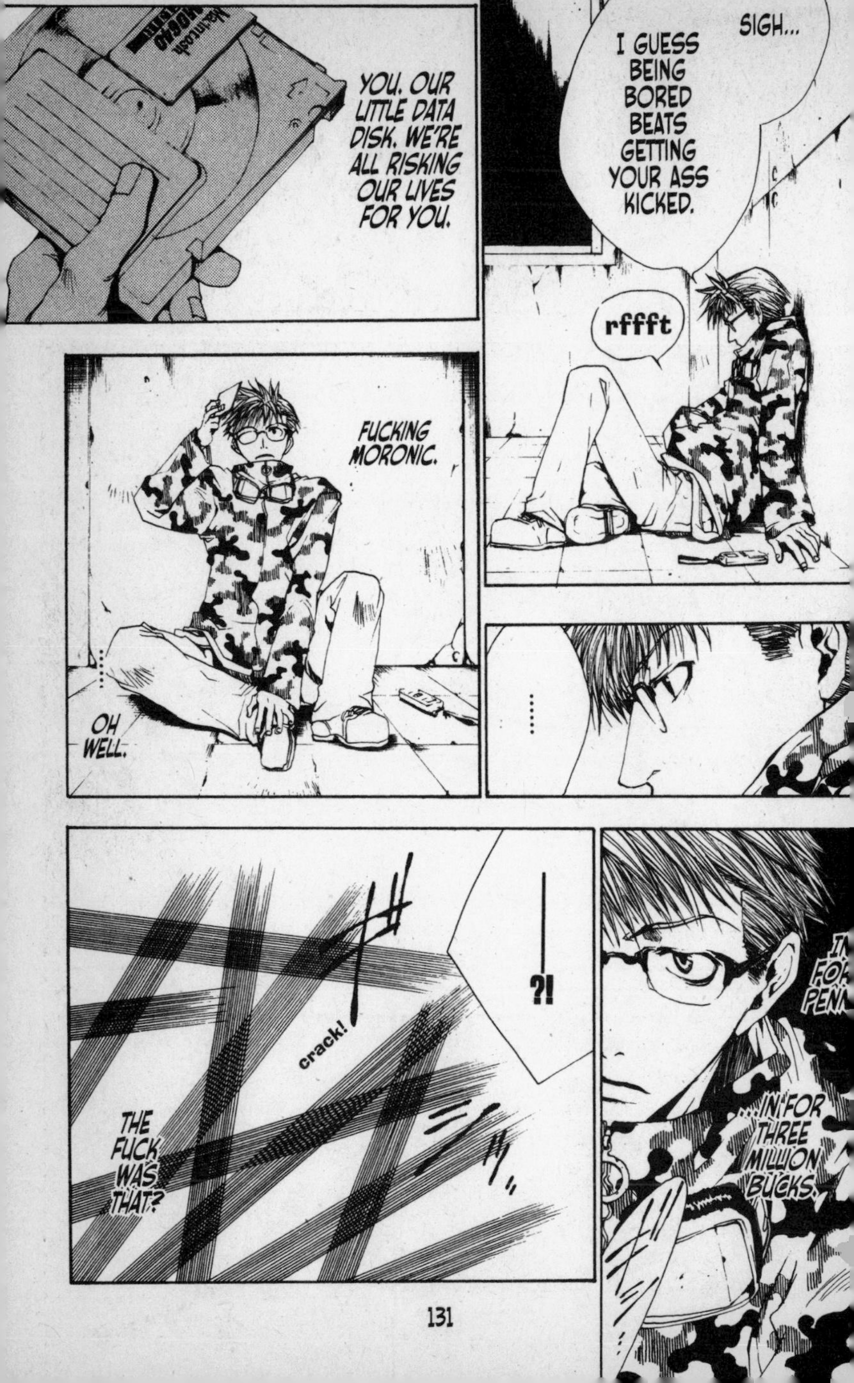
SIGH...
I GUESS BEING BORED BEATS GETTING YOUR ASS KICKED.
rffft
YOU. OUR LITTLE DATA DISK. WE'RE ALL RISKING OUR LIVES FOR YOU.
FUCKING MORONIC.
......
OH WELL.
......
...IN FOR THREE MILLION BUCKS.
?!
crack!
THE FUCK WAS THAT?

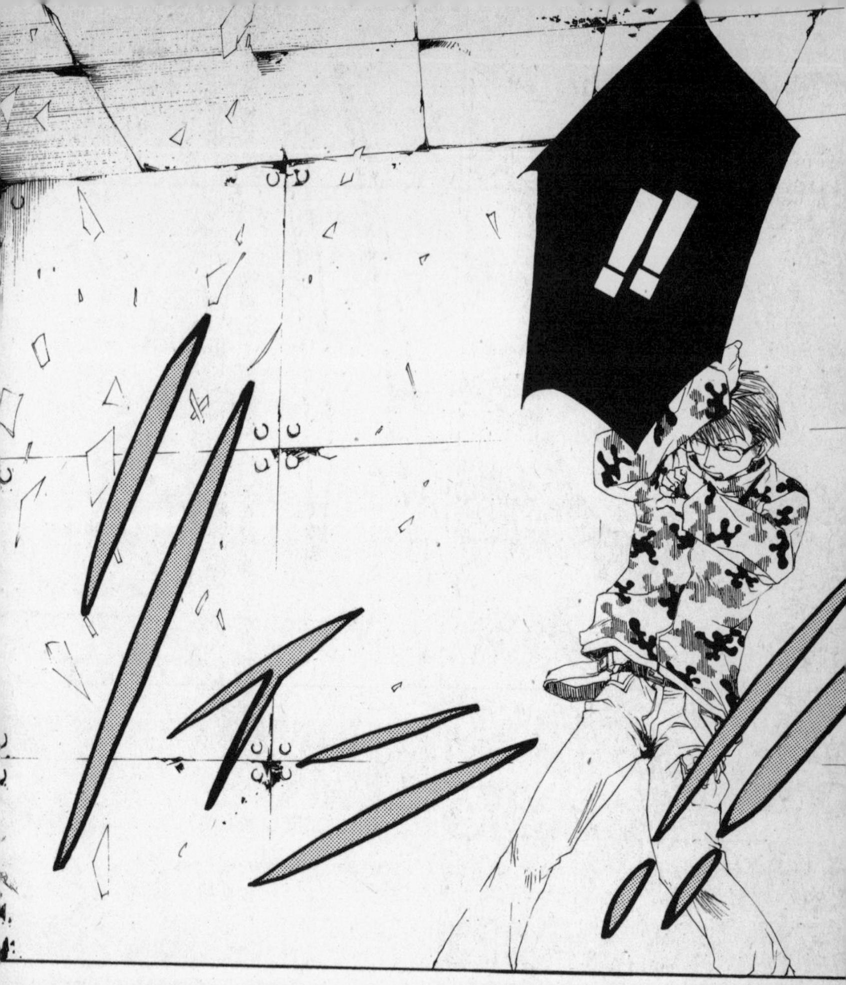
!!
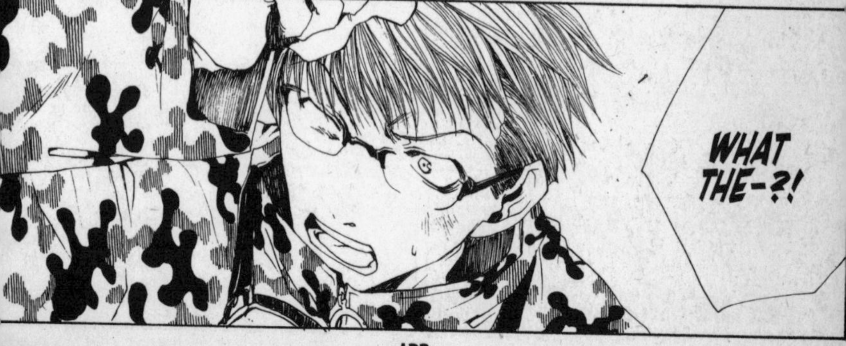
WHAT THE-?!

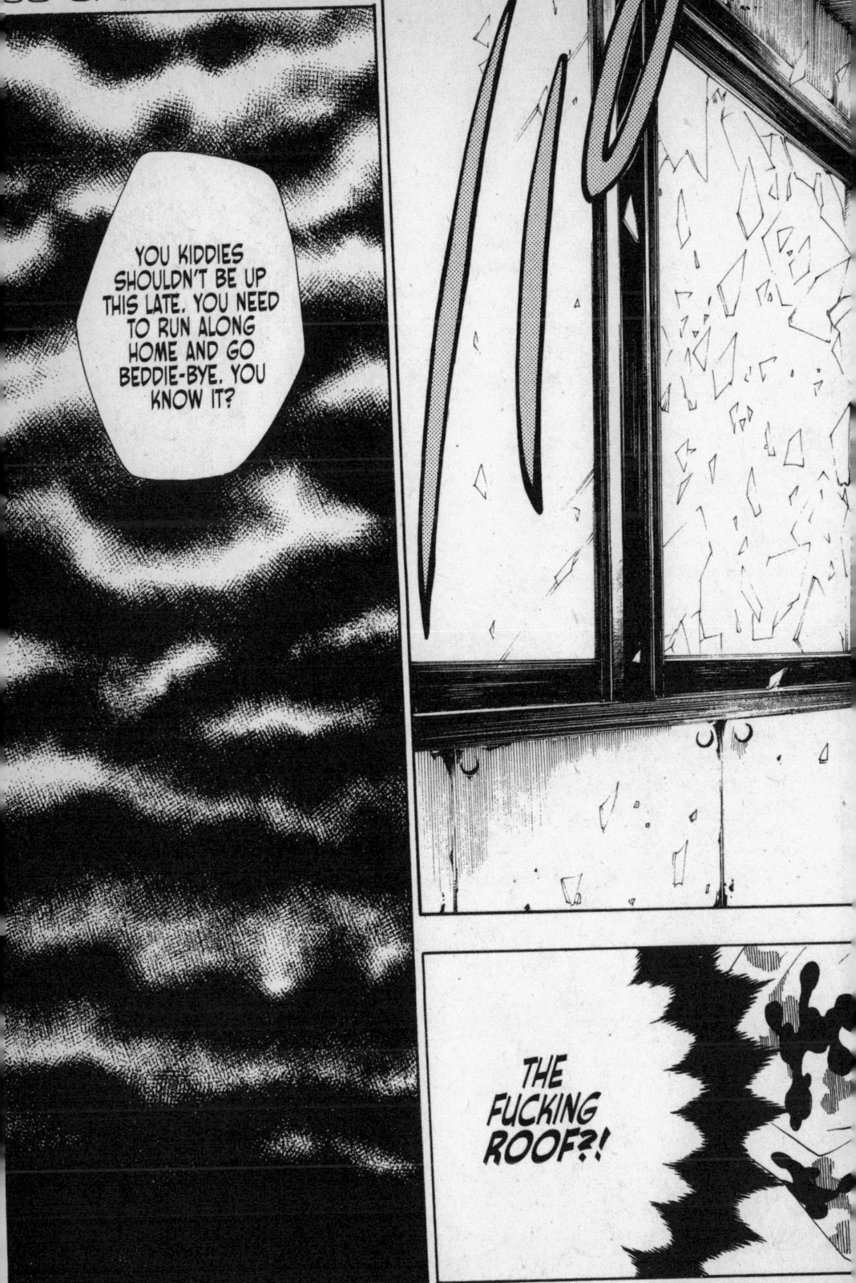
THE FUCKING ROOF?!
YOU KIDDIES SHOULDN'T BE UP THIS LATE. YOU NEED TO RUN ALONG HOME AND GO BEDDIE-BYE. YOU KNOW IT?

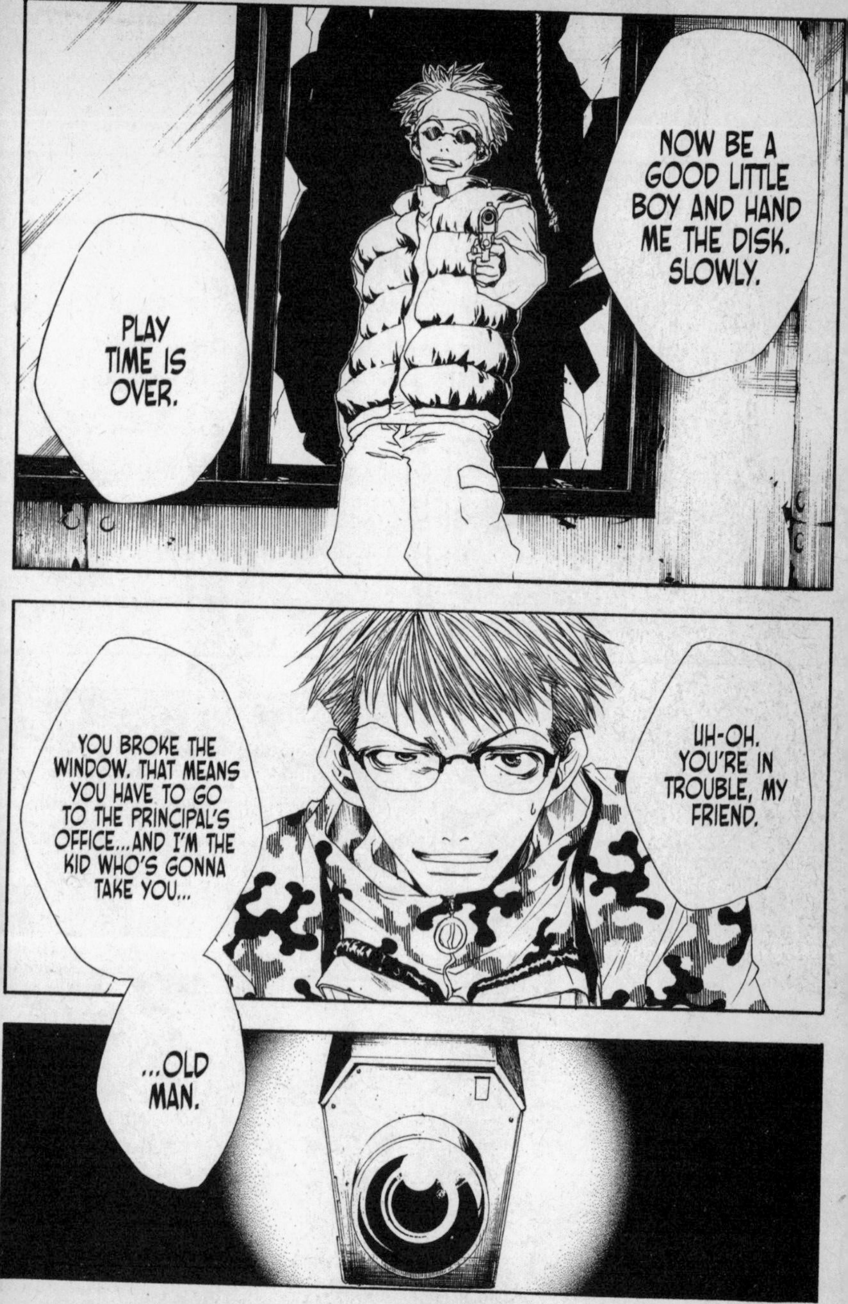
NOW BE A GOOD LITTLE BOY AND HAND ME THE DISK. SLOWLY.
PLAY TIME IS OVER.
UH-OH. YOU'RE IN TROUBLE, MY FRIEND.
YOU BROKE THE WINDOW. THAT MEANS YOU HAVE TO GO TO THE PRINCIPAL'S OFFICE...AND I'M THE KID WHO'S GONNA TAKE YOU...
...OLD MAN.

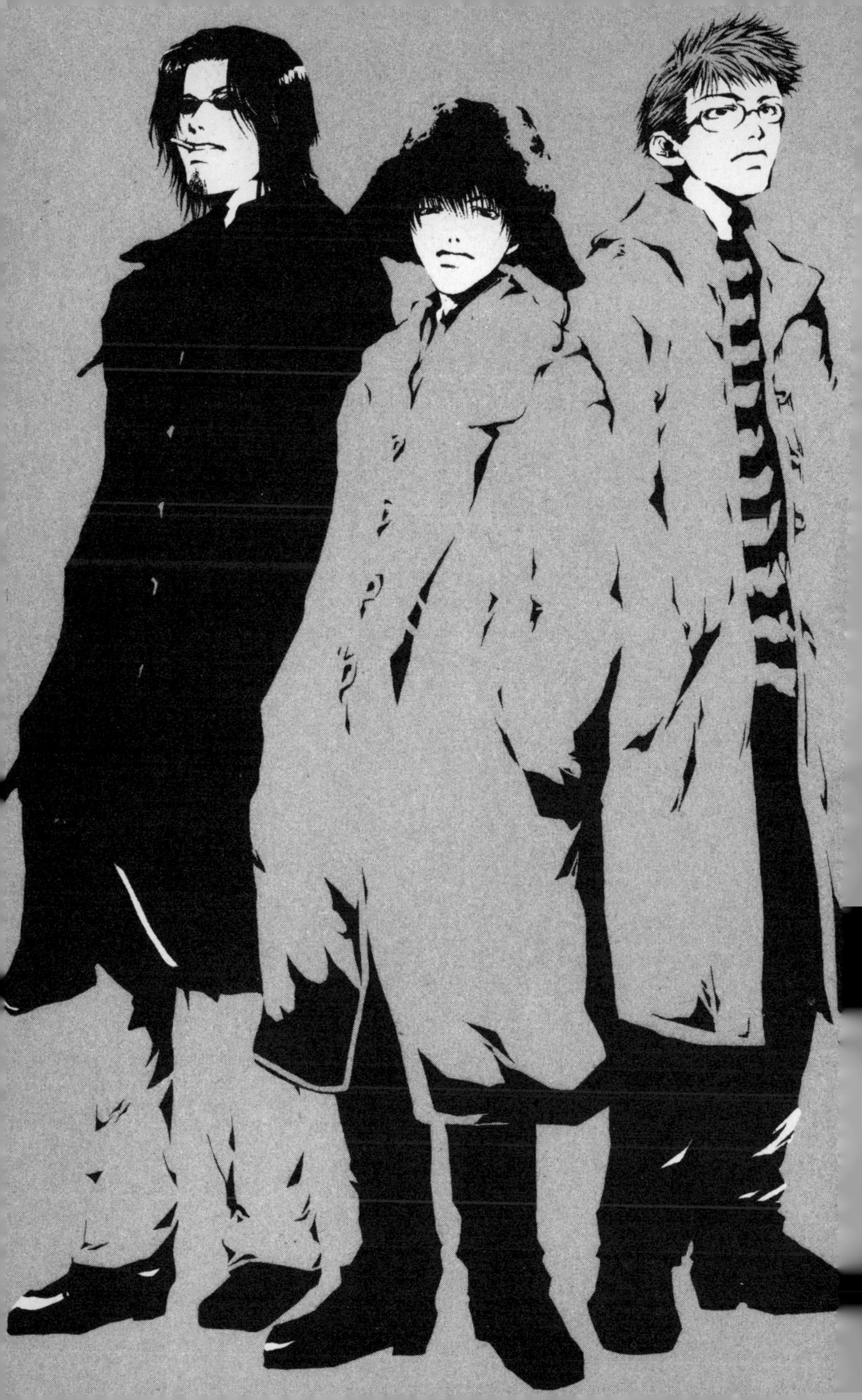

Nobuto Nakajyo

Birthday: March 23rd
Age: 22
Occupation: College student
Blood-type: B
Height: 6 ft.
Weight: 159 lbs.
Hobby: Cooking
Special Skills: Strategy games, theft, street
fighting (recieved training during his gang
tenure)
Favorite food: Beer, ankimo
Notes: Smokes "Cabin" brand cigarettes.
Lectures at a shogi center on his days off.

He's the member of Team AAA with the
greatest moral flexibility. He seems to keep
an emotionally safe distance. Although he
has accepted equal responsibility as an
active team member for the time being, there
remains the possibility that at some crucial
moment he might abandon AAA if it was to
his personal advantage. In that regard, he
is the greatest threat to the team. To put it
nicely, he maintains his neutrality. To put it
another way, he's heartless. Also, the way
he goofs with Saitoh makes him come off
as a very young 22. What circumstances
chiseled his personality down to this cold and
immature nonchalance?

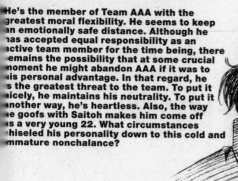

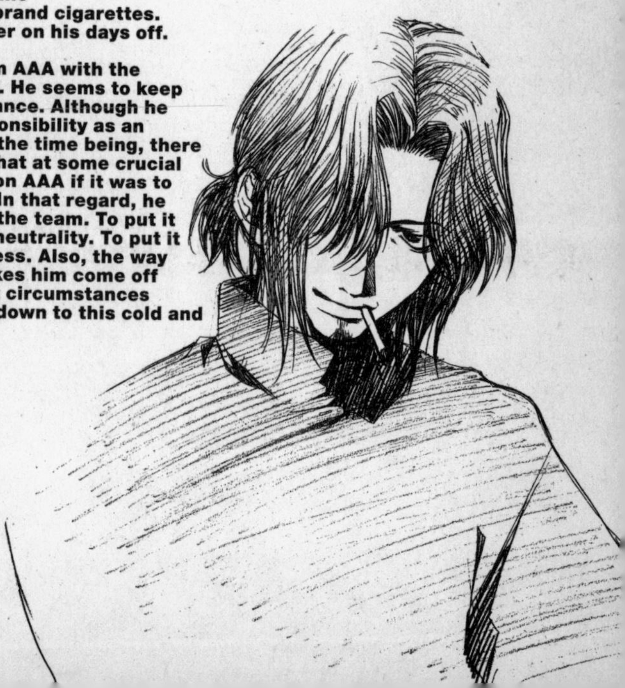

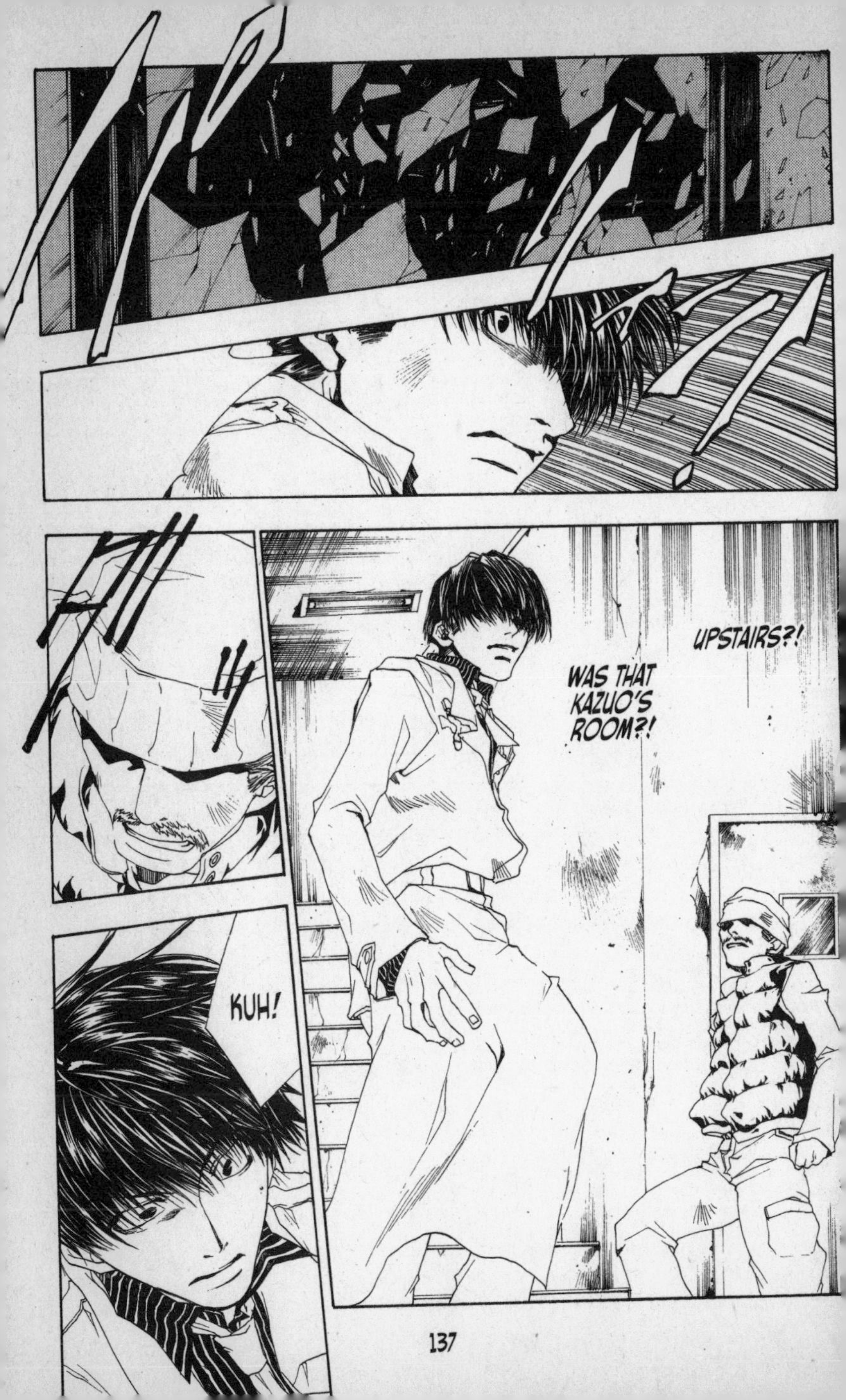

UPSTAIRS?!
WAS THAT KAZUO'S ROOM?!
KUH!

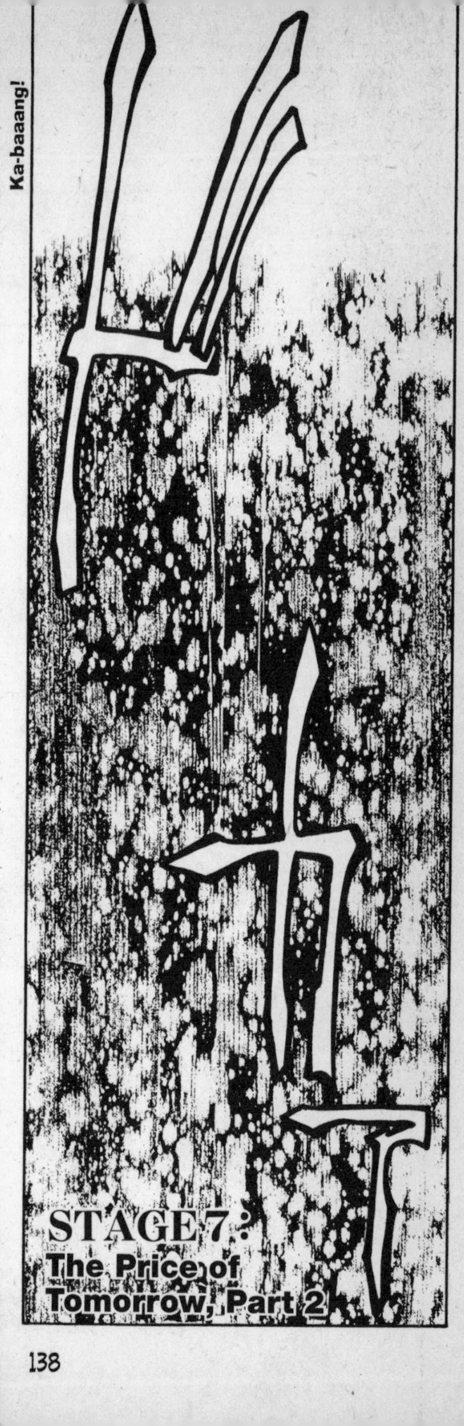
Ka-baaang!
STAGE 7:
The Price of Tomorrow, Part 2

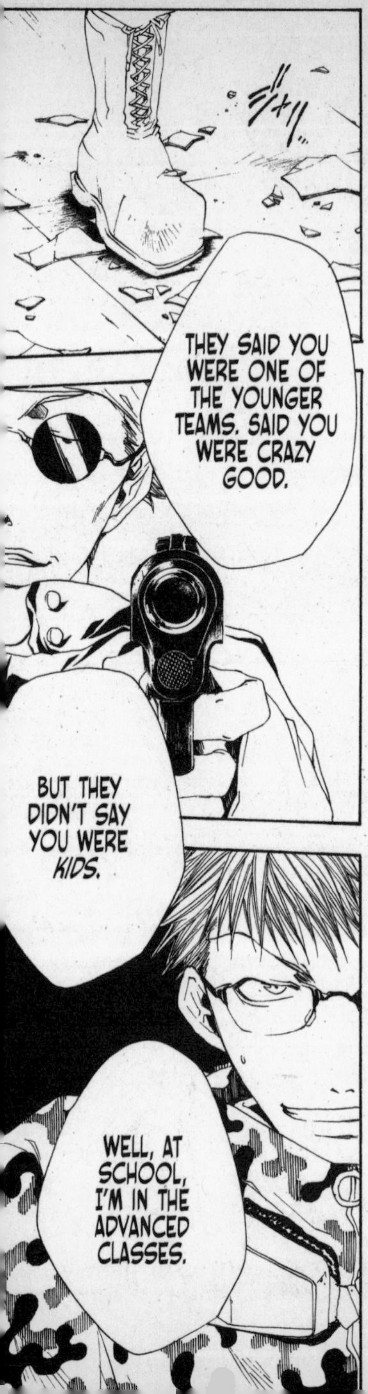
THEY SAID YOU WERE ONE OF THE YOUNGER TEAMS. SAID YOU WERE CRAZY GOOD.
BUT THEY DIDN'T SAY YOU WERE *KIDS.*
WELL, AT SCHOOL, I'M IN THE ADVANCED CLASSES.

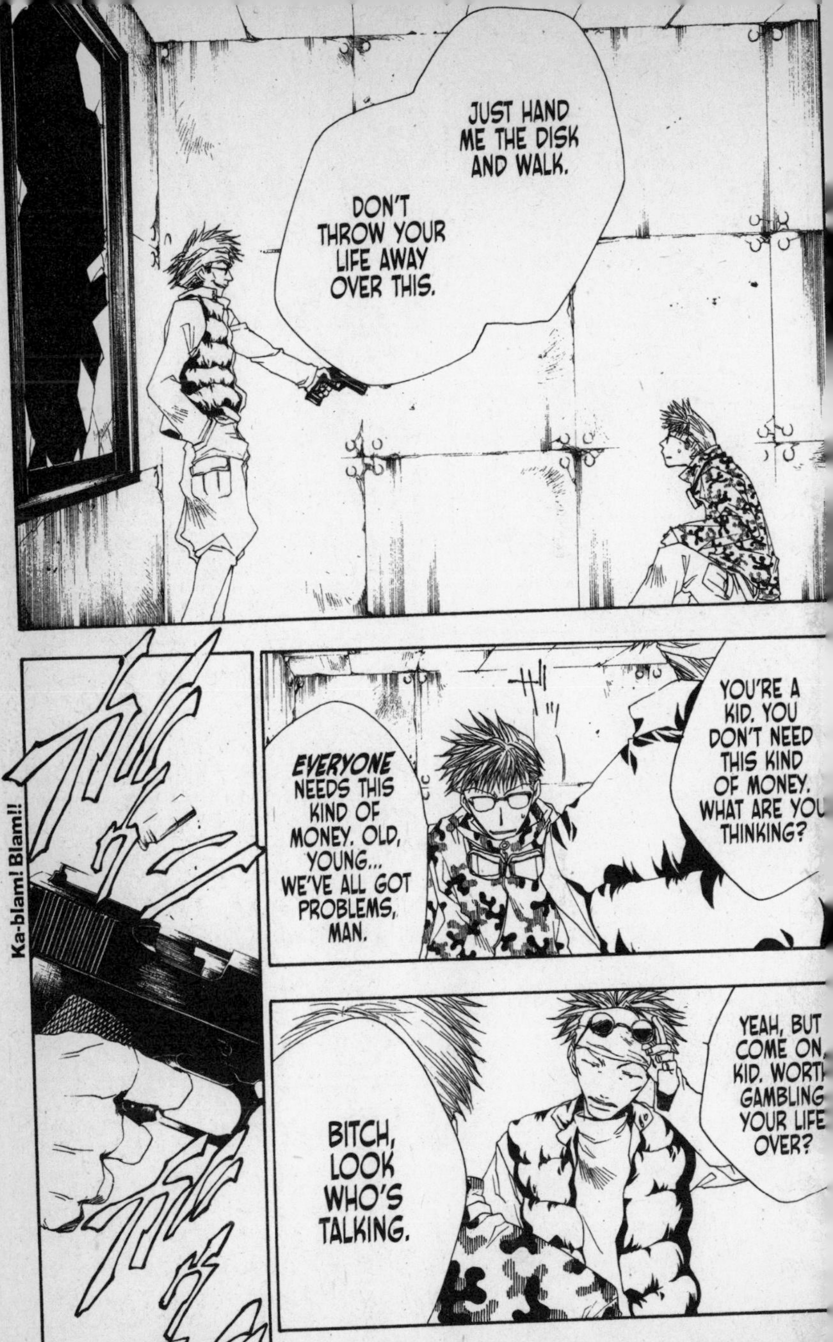
JUST HAND ME THE DISK AND WALK.
DON'T THROW YOUR LIFE AWAY OVER THIS.
YOU'RE A KID. YOU DON'T NEED THIS KIND OF MONEY. WHAT ARE YOU THINKING?
EVERYONE NEEDS THIS KIND OF MONEY. OLD, YOUNG... WE'VE ALL GOT PROBLEMS, MAN.
YEAH, BUT COME ON, KID. WORTH GAMBLING YOUR LIFE OVER?
BITCH, LOOK WHO'S TALKING.
Ka-blam! Blam!!

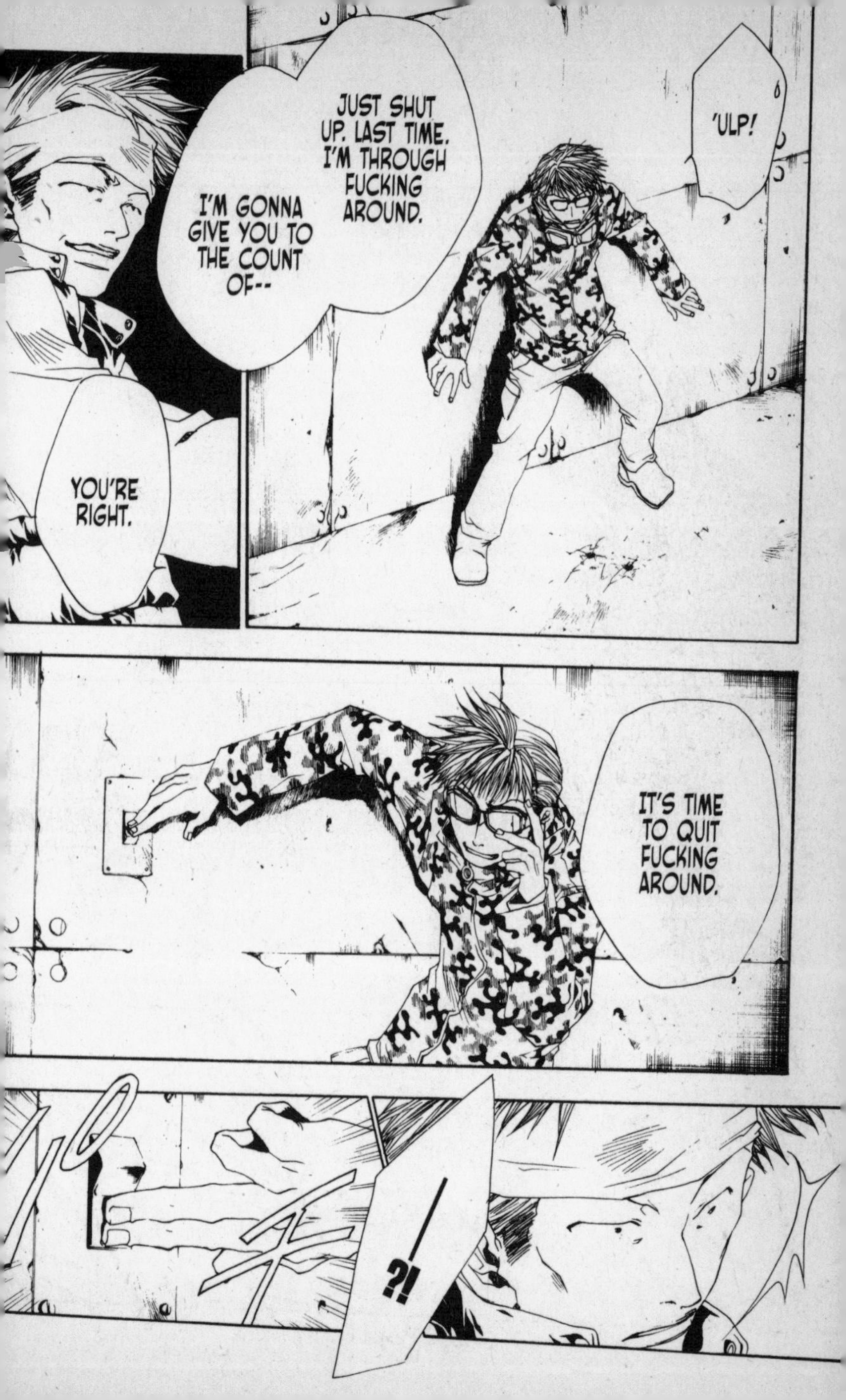
'ULP!
JUST SHUT UP. LAST TIME. I'M THROUGH FUCKING AROUND.
I'M GONNA GIVE YOU TO THE COUNT OF--
YOU'RE RIGHT.
IT'S TIME TO QUIT FUCKING AROUND.
?!

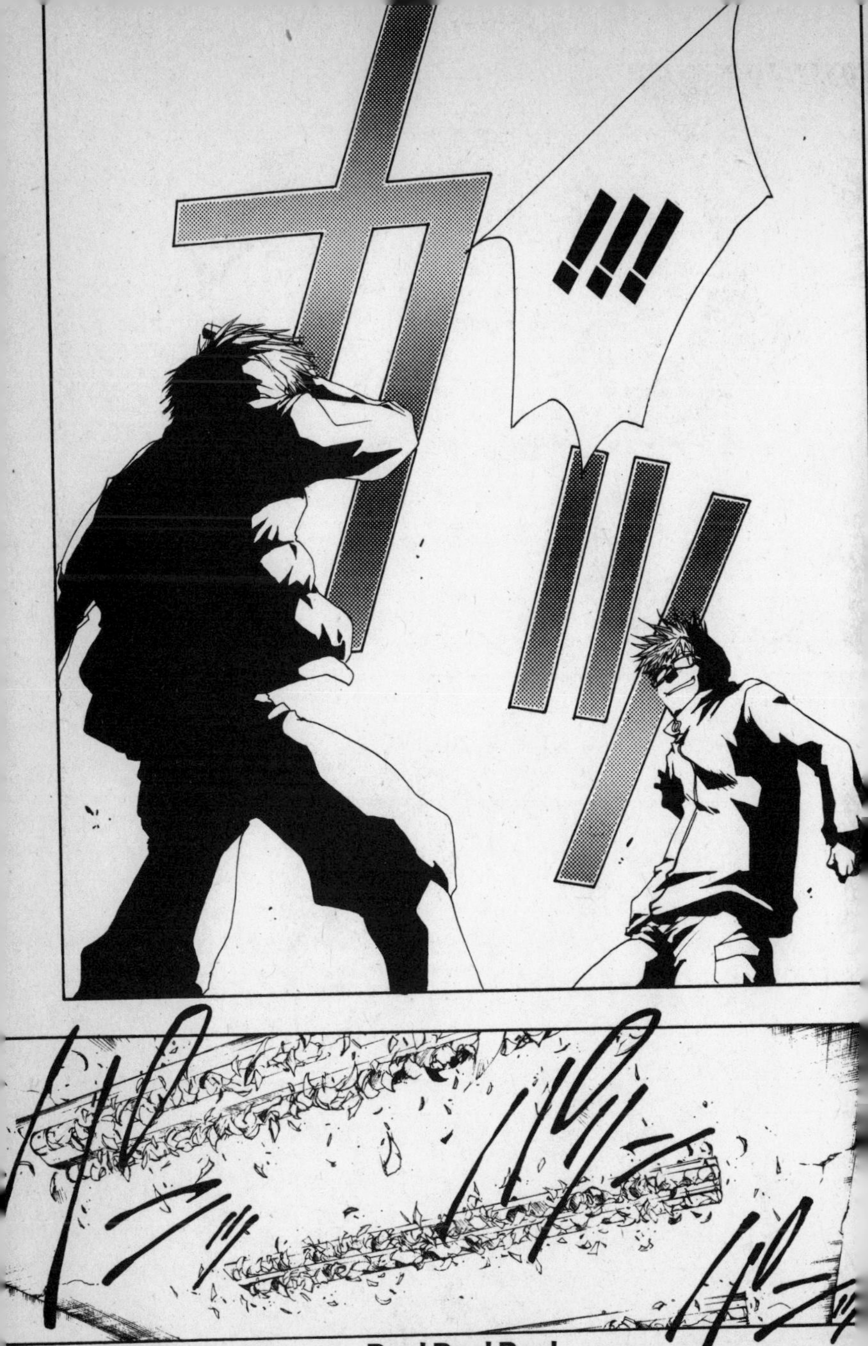
カッ!!!

Pop! Pop! Pop!

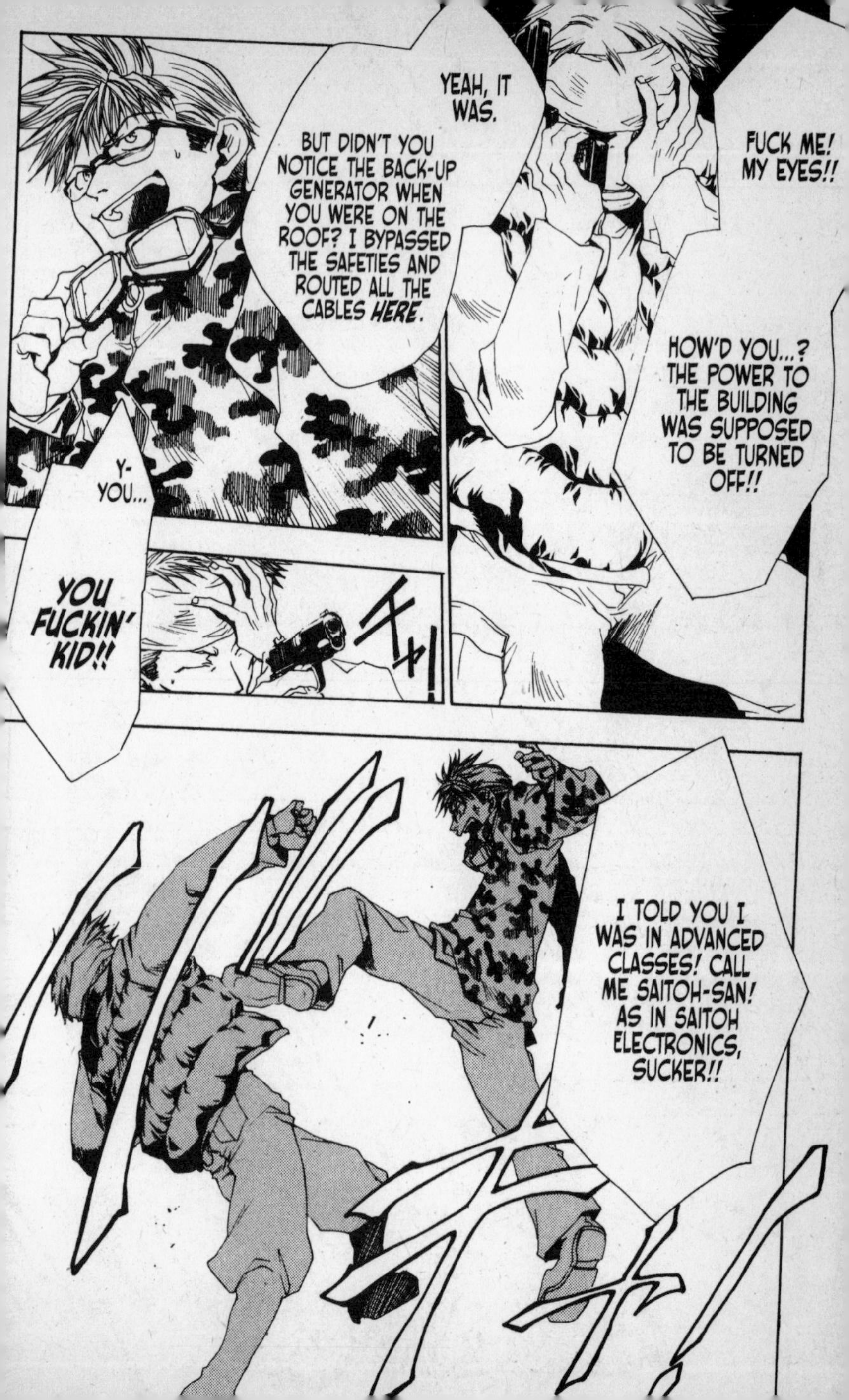
FUCK ME! MY EYES!!
HOW'D YOU...? THE POWER TO THE BUILDING WAS SUPPOSED TO BE TURNED OFF!!
YEAH, IT WAS.
BUT DIDN'T YOU NOTICE THE BACK-UP GENERATOR WHEN YOU WERE ON THE ROOF? I BYPASSED THE SAFETIES AND ROUTED ALL THE CABLES *HERE*.
Y- YOU...
YOU FUCKIN' KID!!
I TOLD YOU I WAS IN ADVANCED CLASSES! CALL ME SAITOH-SAN! AS IN SAITOH ELECTRONICS, SUCKER!!

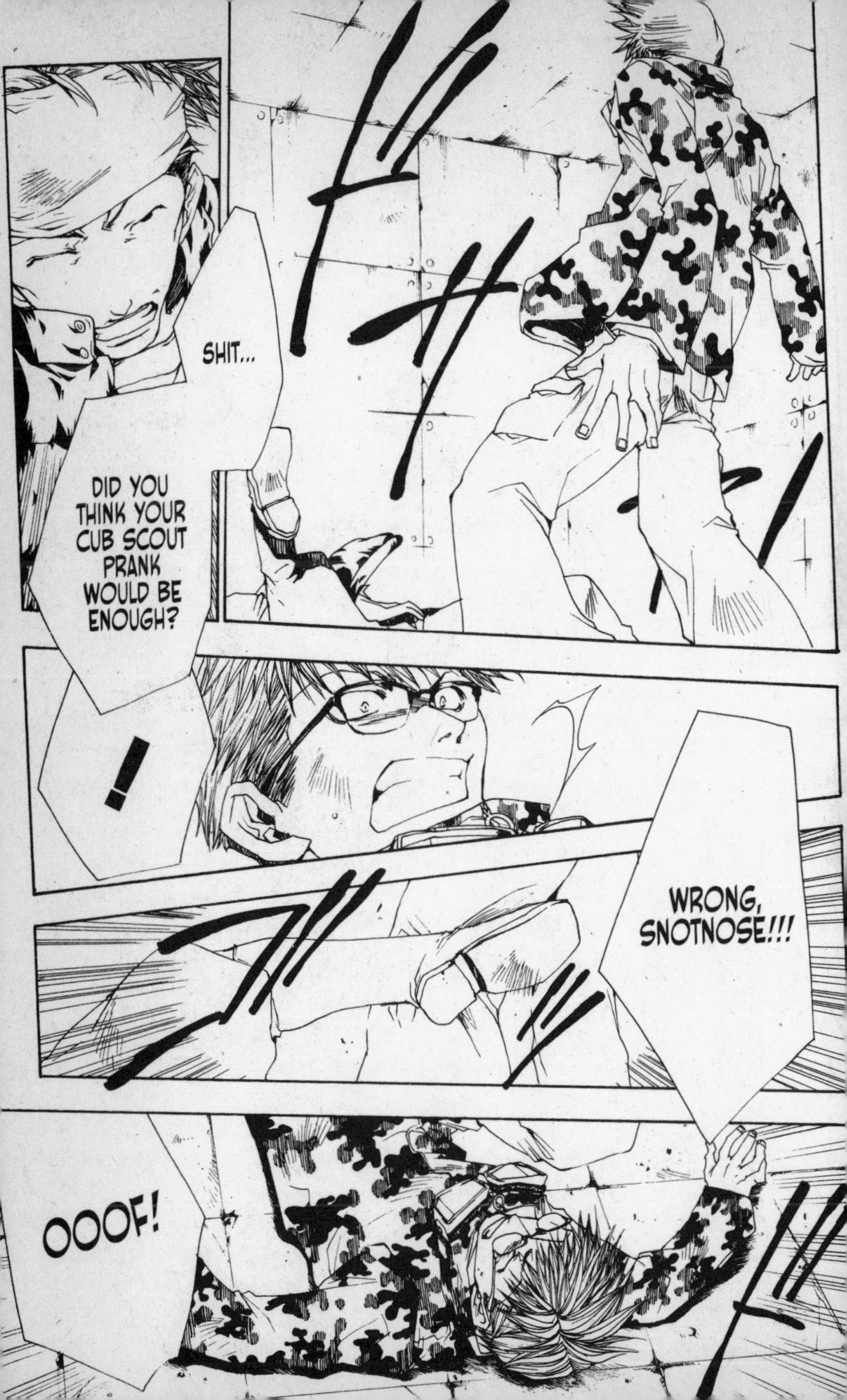
SHIT...
DID YOU THINK YOUR CUB SCOUT PRANK WOULD BE ENOUGH?
!
WRONG, SNOTNOSE!!!
OOOF!

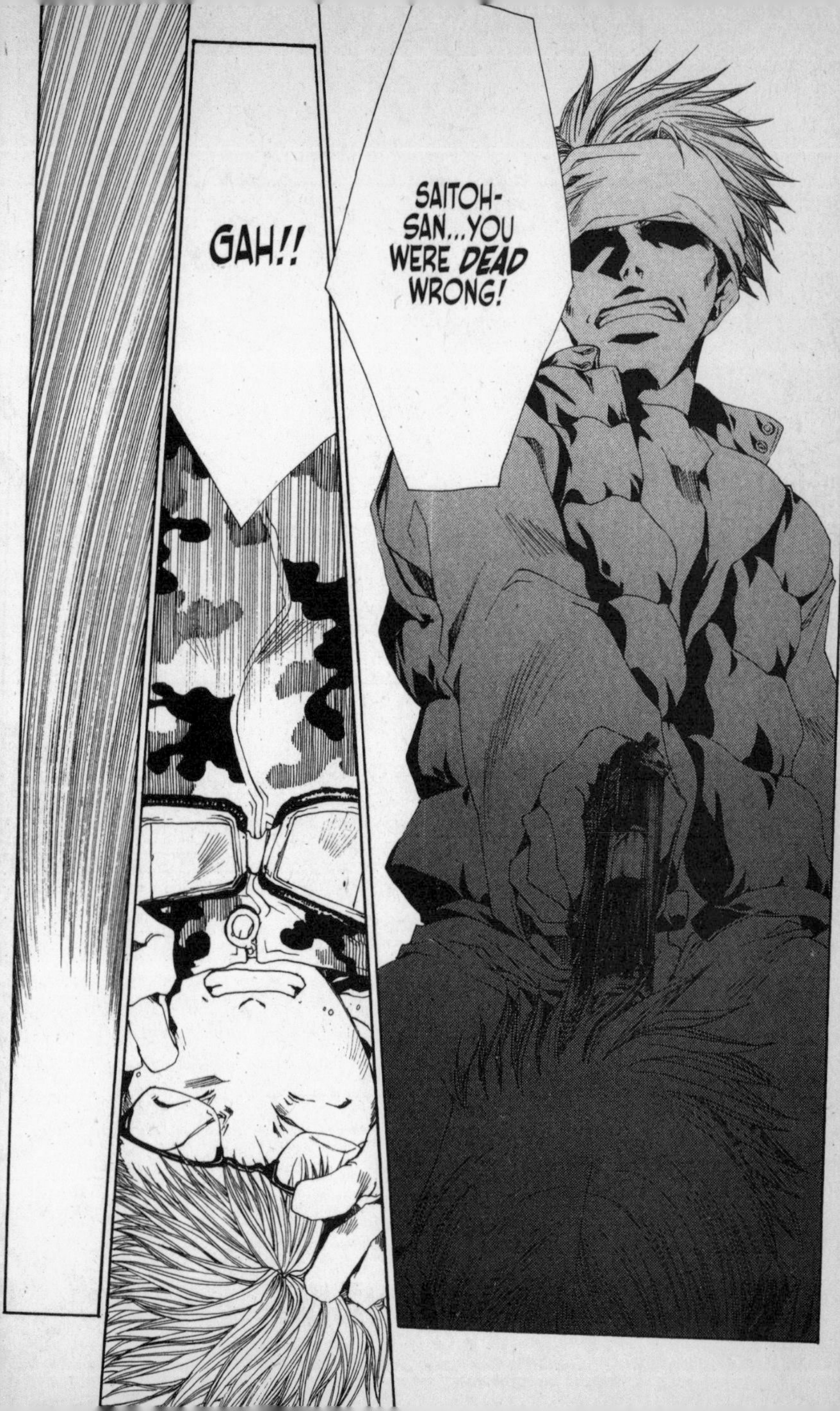
SAITOH-SAN...YOU WERE *DEAD* WRONG!
GAH!!

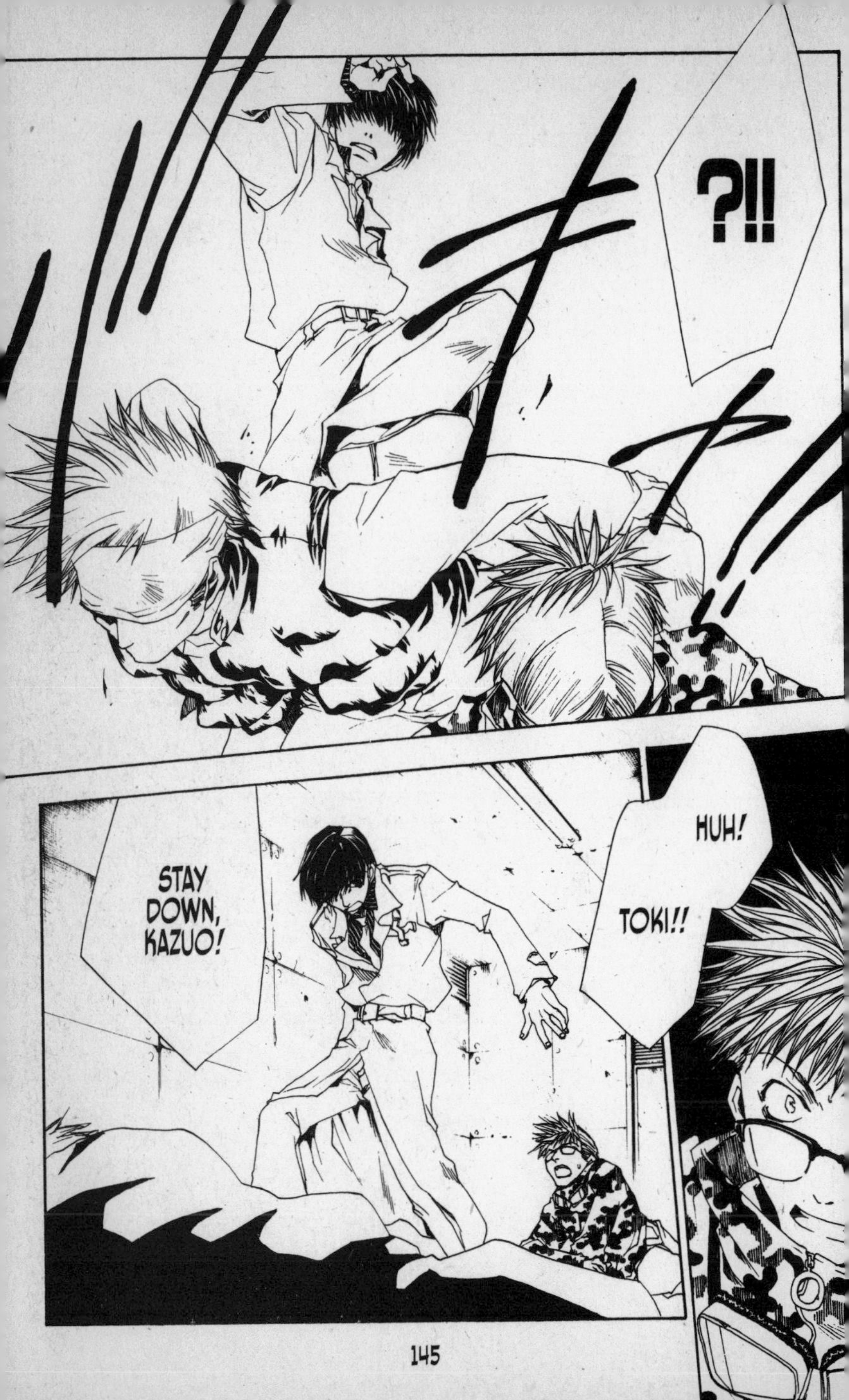
?!!
HUH!
TOKI!!
STAY DOWN, KAZUO!

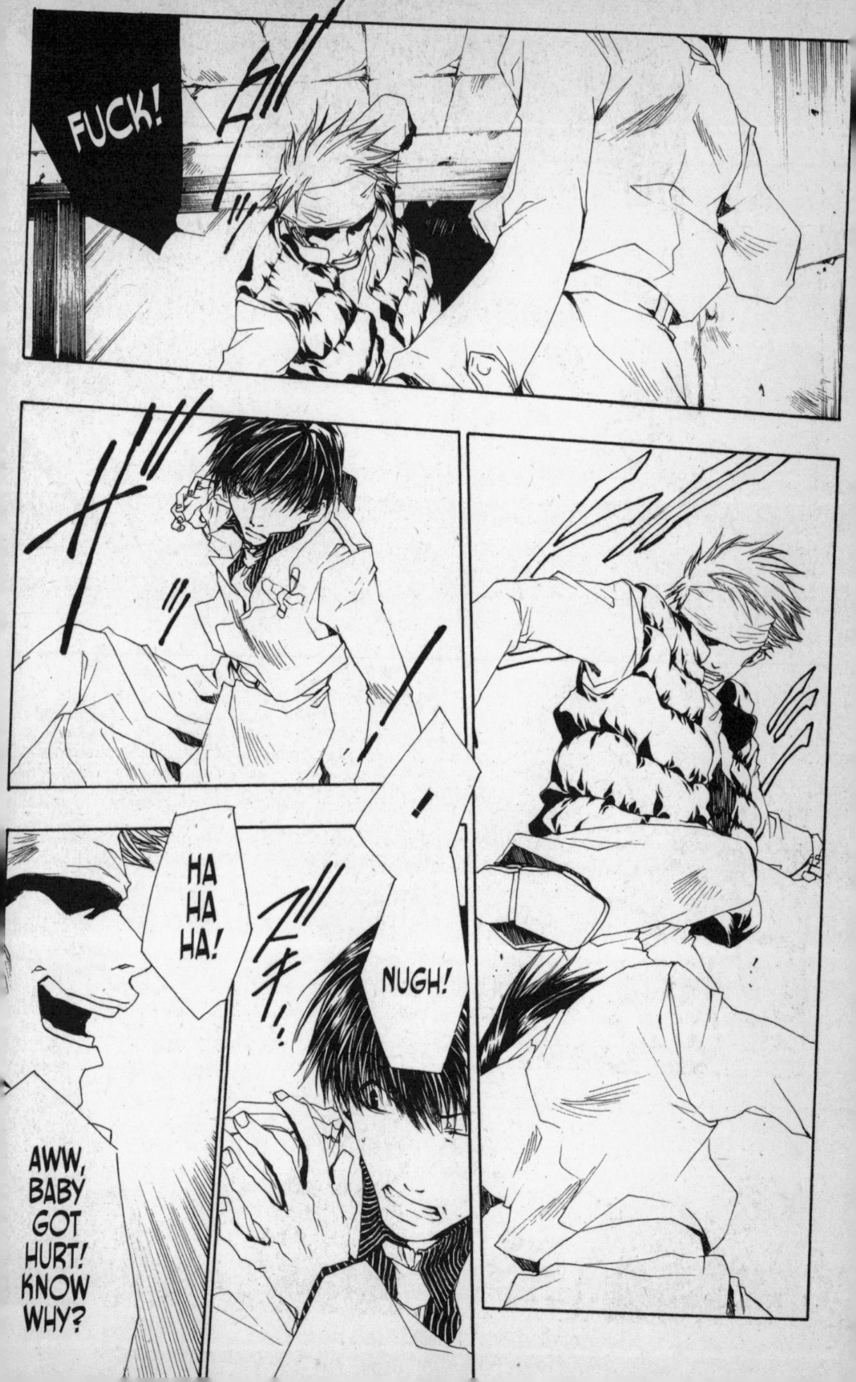
FUCK!
!
NUGH!
HA HA HA!
AWW, BABY GOT HURT! KNOW WHY?

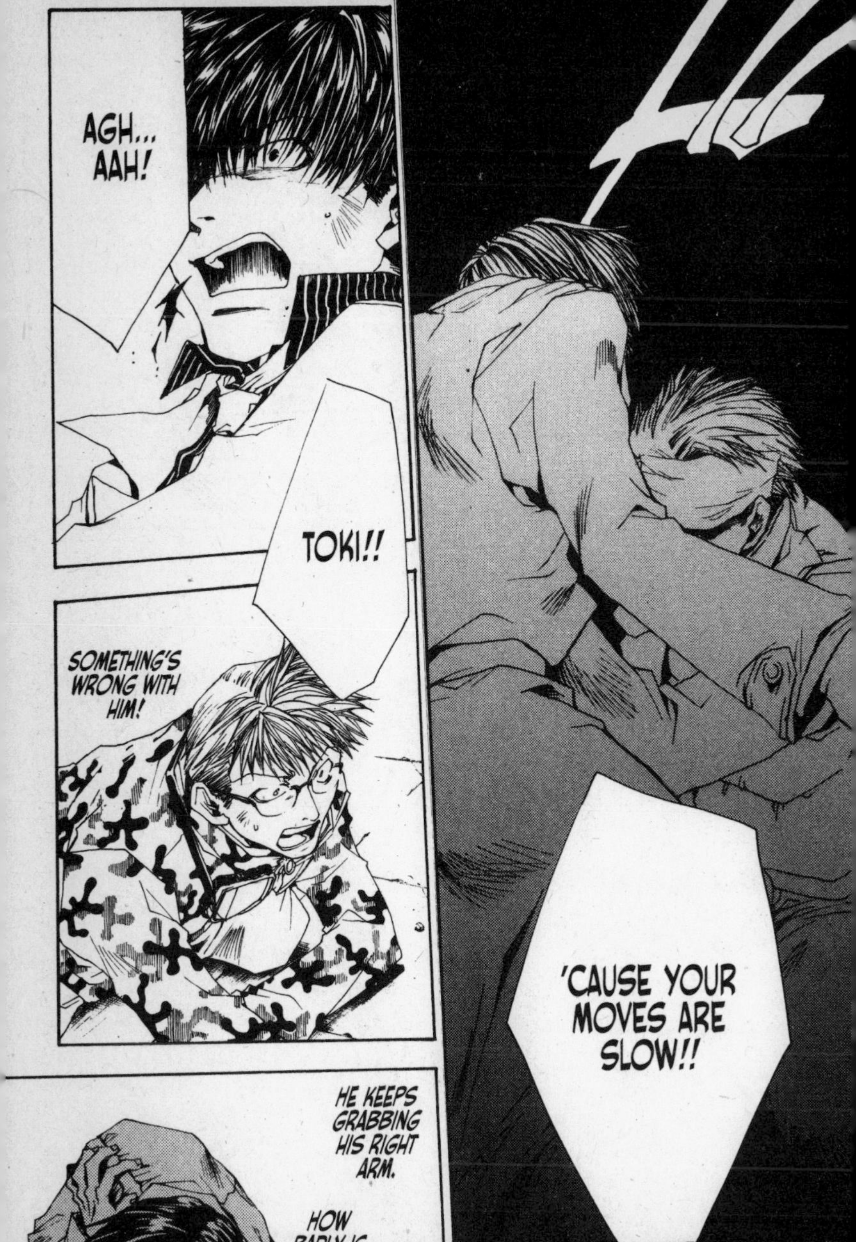
'CAUSE YOUR MOVES ARE SLOW!!
AGH... AAH!
TOKI!!
SOMETHING'S WRONG WITH HIM!
HE KEEPS GRABBING HIS RIGHT ARM.
HOW BADLY IS HE HURT?

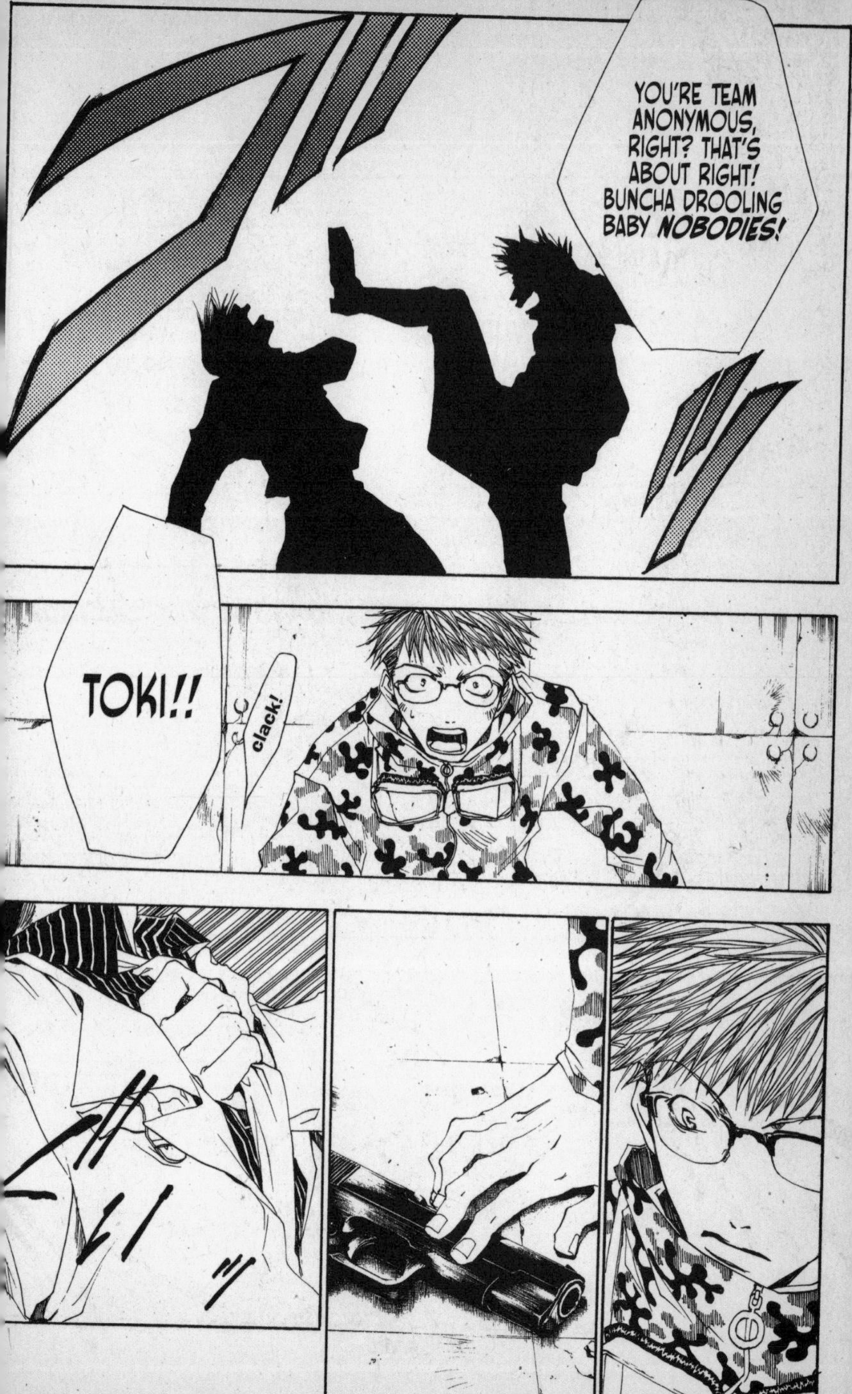
YOU'RE TEAM ANONYMOUS, RIGHT? THAT'S ABOUT RIGHT! BUNCHA DROOLING BABY NOBODIES!
TOKI!!
clack!

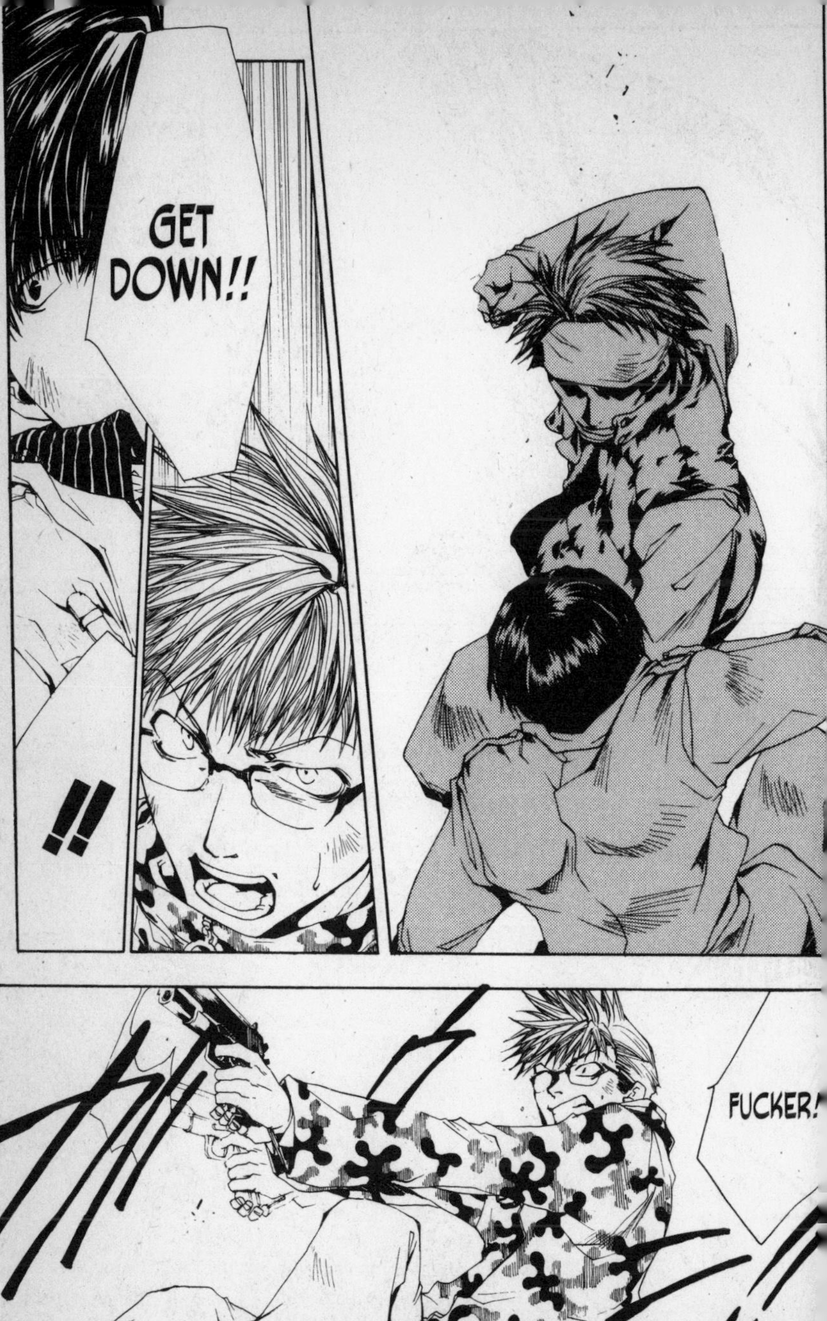
GET DOWN!!
!!
FUCKER!
BLAM!!

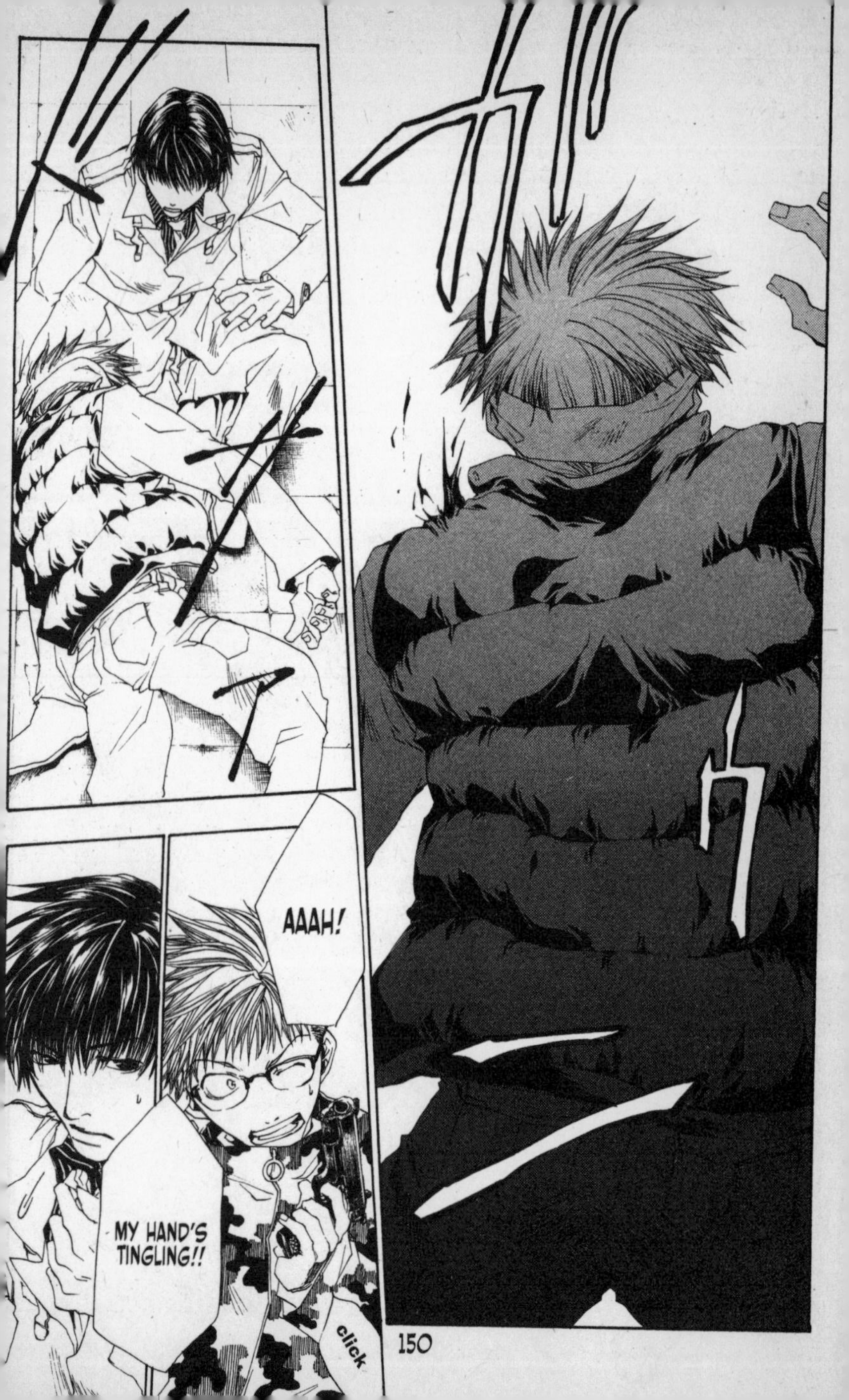
AAAH!
MY HAND'S TINGLING!!
click

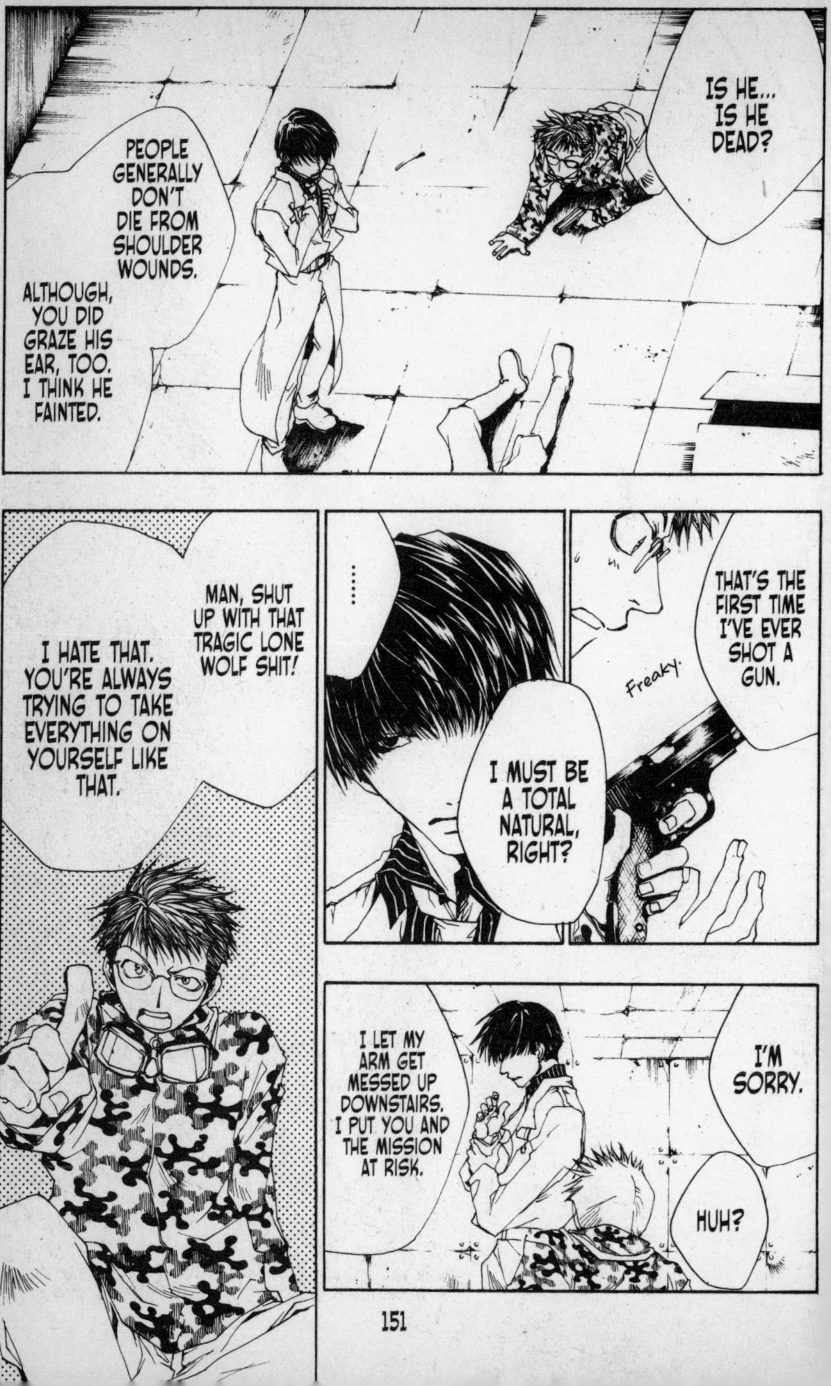
IS HE... IS HE DEAD?
PEOPLE GENERALLY DON'T DIE FROM SHOULDER WOUNDS.
ALTHOUGH, YOU DID GRAZE HIS EAR, TOO. I THINK HE FAINTED.
THAT'S THE FIRST TIME I'VE EVER SHOT A GUN.
Freaky.
I MUST BE A TOTAL NATURAL, RIGHT?
......
I'M SORRY.
HUH?
I LET MY ARM GET MESSED UP DOWNSTAIRS. I PUT YOU AND THE MISSION AT RISK.
MAN, SHUT UP WITH THAT TRAGIC LONE WOLF SHIT!
I HATE THAT. YOU'RE ALWAYS TRYING TO TAKE EVERYTHING ON YOURSELF LIKE THAT.

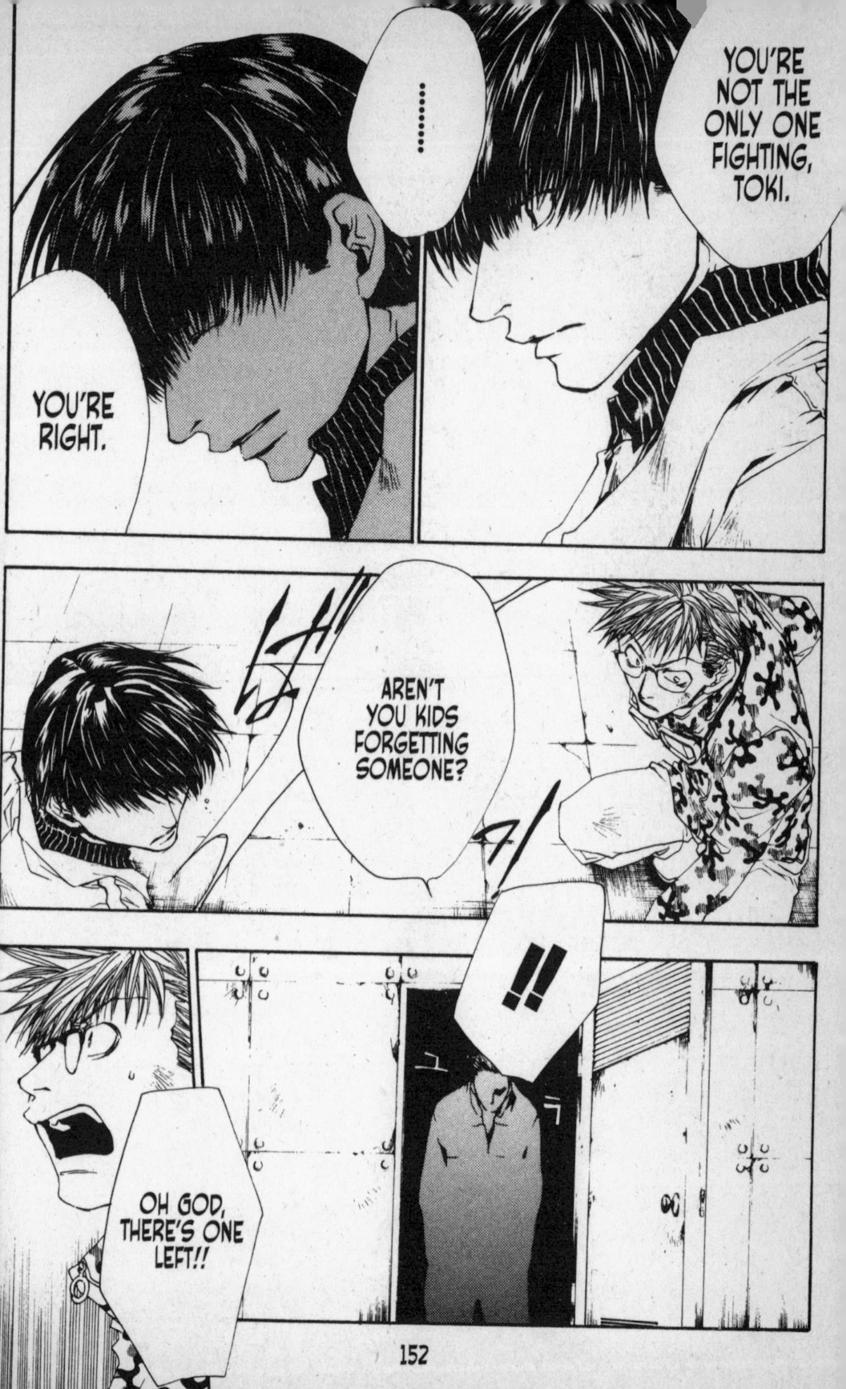
YOU'RE NOT THE ONLY ONE FIGHTING, TOKI.
....
YOU'RE RIGHT.
AREN'T YOU KIDS FORGETTING SOMEONE?
!!
OH GOD, THERE'S ONE LEFT!!

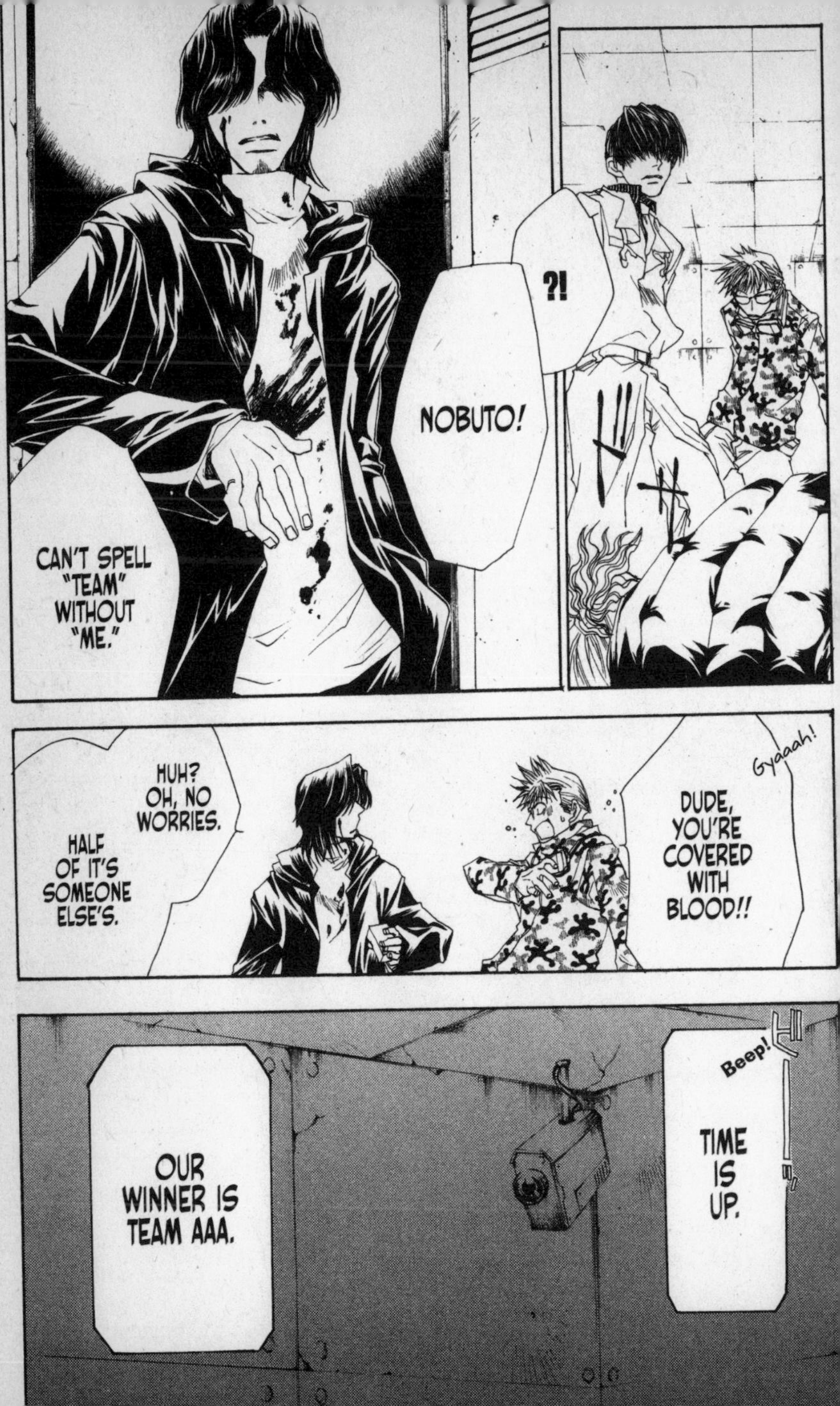
?!
NOBUTO!
CAN'T SPELL "TEAM" WITHOUT "ME."
Gyaaah!
DUDE, YOU'RE COVERED WITH BLOOD!!
HUH? OH, NO WORRIES.
HALF OF IT'S SOMEONE ELSE'S.
Beep!
TIME IS UP.
OUR WINNER IS TEAM AAA.

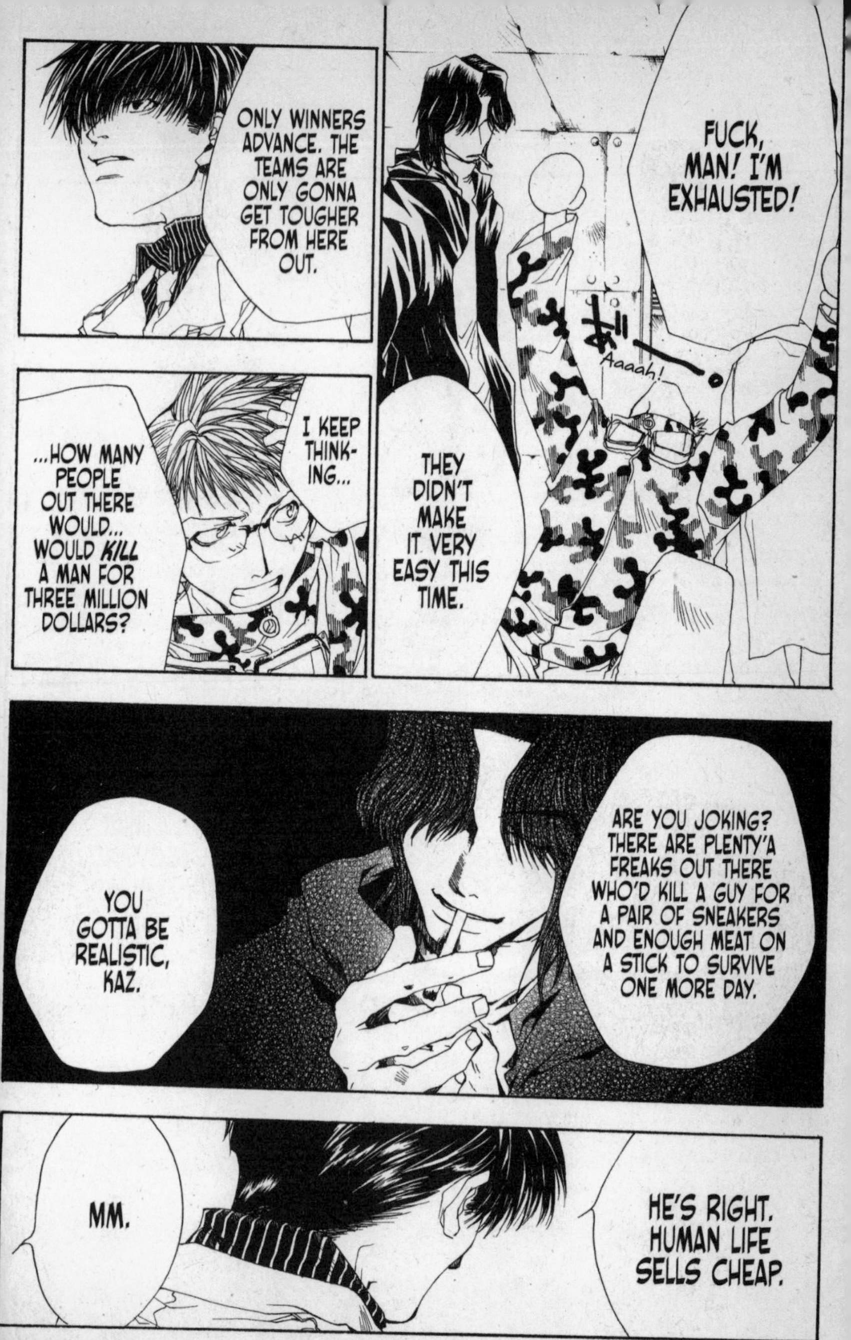
FUCK, MAN! I'M EXHAUSTED!
Aaaah!
THEY DIDN'T MAKE IT VERY EASY THIS TIME.
ONLY WINNERS ADVANCE. THE TEAMS ARE ONLY GONNA GET TOUGHER FROM HERE OUT.
I KEEP THINK-ING...
...HOW MANY PEOPLE OUT THERE WOULD... WOULD *KILL* A MAN FOR THREE MILLION DOLLARS?
ARE YOU JOKING? THERE ARE PLENTY'A FREAKS OUT THERE WHO'D KILL A GUY FOR A PAIR OF SNEAKERS AND ENOUGH MEAT ON A STICK TO SURVIVE ONE MORE DAY.
YOU GOTTA BE REALISTIC, KAZ.
HE'S RIGHT. HUMAN LIFE SELLS CHEAP.
MM.

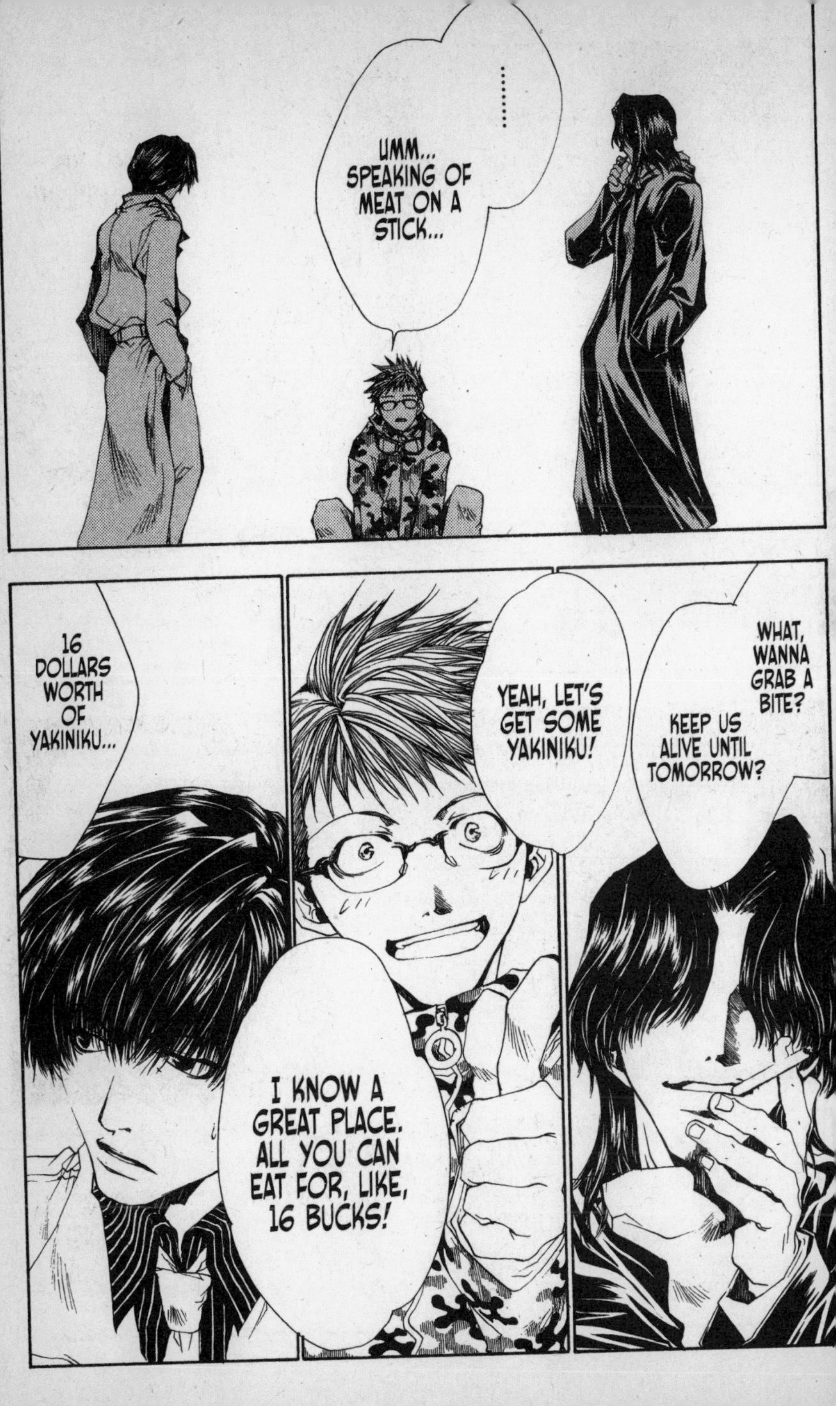
......
UMM... SPEAKING OF MEAT ON A STICK...
WHAT, WANNA GRAB A BITE?
KEEP US ALIVE UNTIL TOMORROW?
YEAH, LET'S GET SOME YAKINIKU!
I KNOW A GREAT PLACE. ALL YOU CAN EAT FOR, LIKE, 16 BUCKS!
16 DOLLARS WORTH OF YAKINIKU...

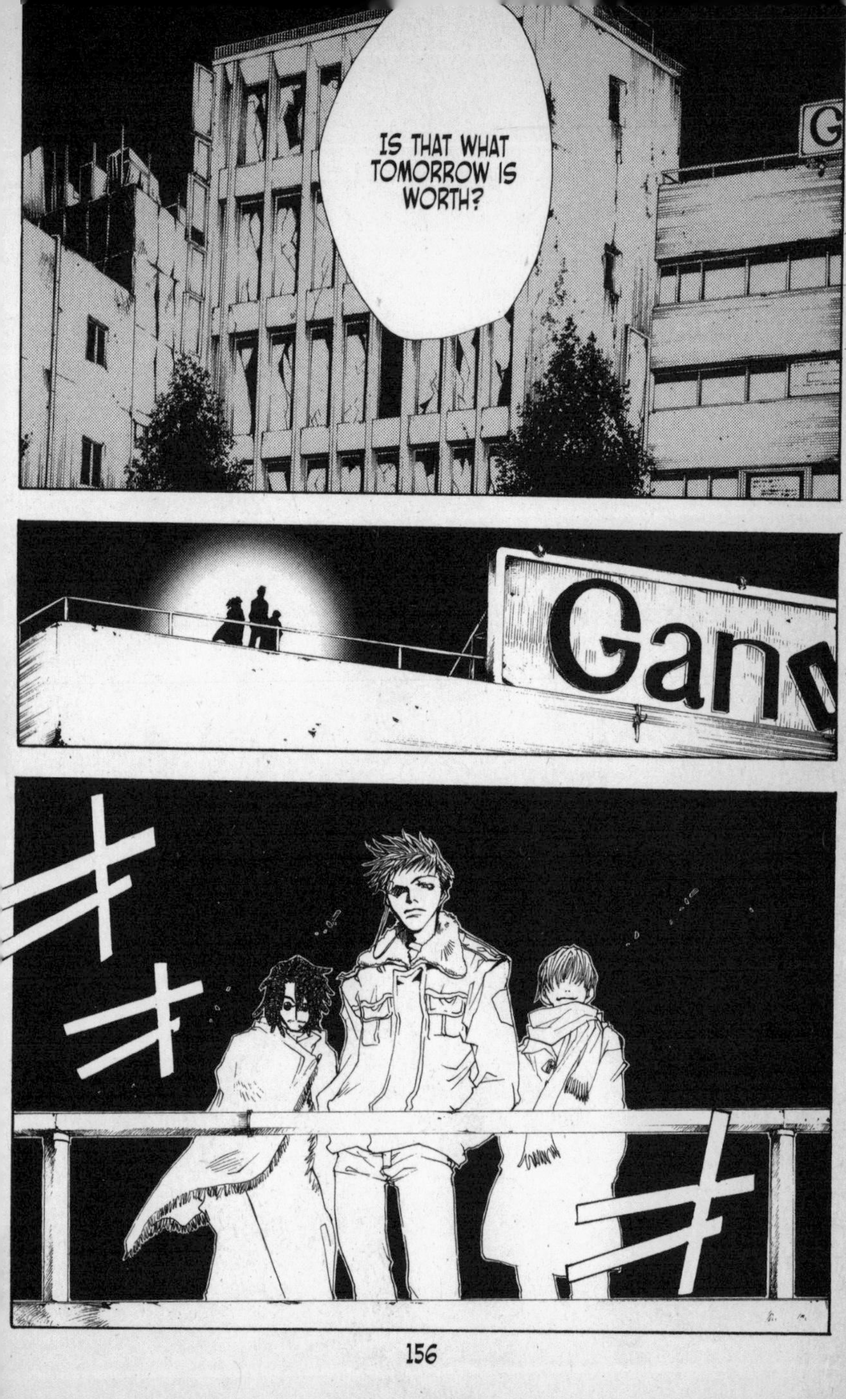
IS THAT WHAT TOMORROW IS WORTH?

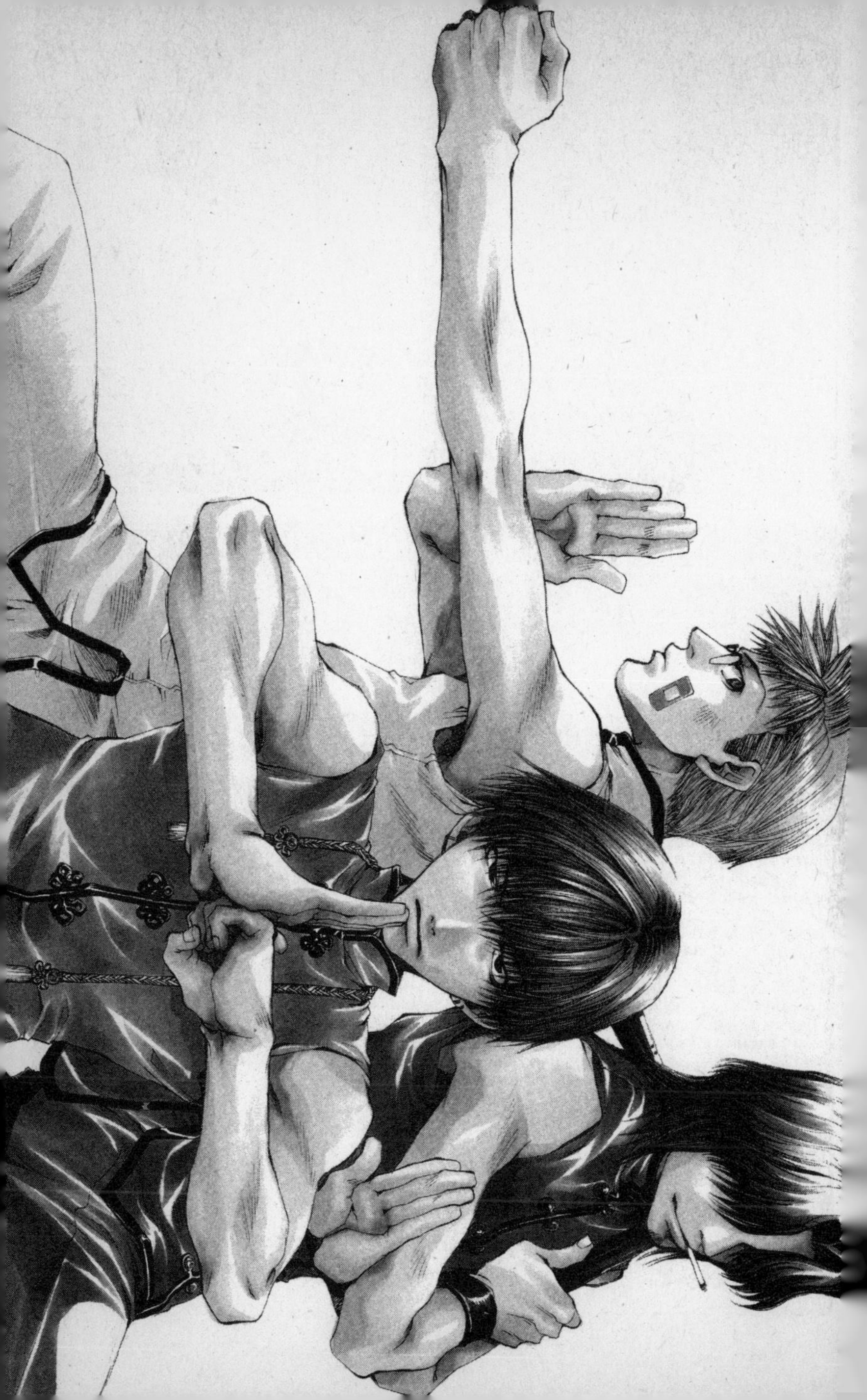

Kazuo Saitoh

Birthday: July 18th
Age: 18
Occupation: High school student
Blood-type: O
Height: 5 ft. 11 in.
Weight: 159 lbs.
Hobbies: Manga, plastic models, video games
Special Skill: Electronics expert
Favorite food: Pretz, yakisoba with peyang sauce, pie fruit
Notes: Recently was forced to head his high school's cultural festival committee.

The de facto conscience of Team AAA and moral critic of Business Gaming. Carries with him a surplus of curiosity (i.e. nosiness) and emotion. He has a tendency to fall on his face (especially when he's showing off), but just when you start to worry about him, he stands back up. He has a yapping case of diarrhea of the mouth, sometimes as if he's begging to be poked fun at. Nevertheless, it would be hard to overstate his importance to AAA. He may come off as young and naïve, but this pup has bite.

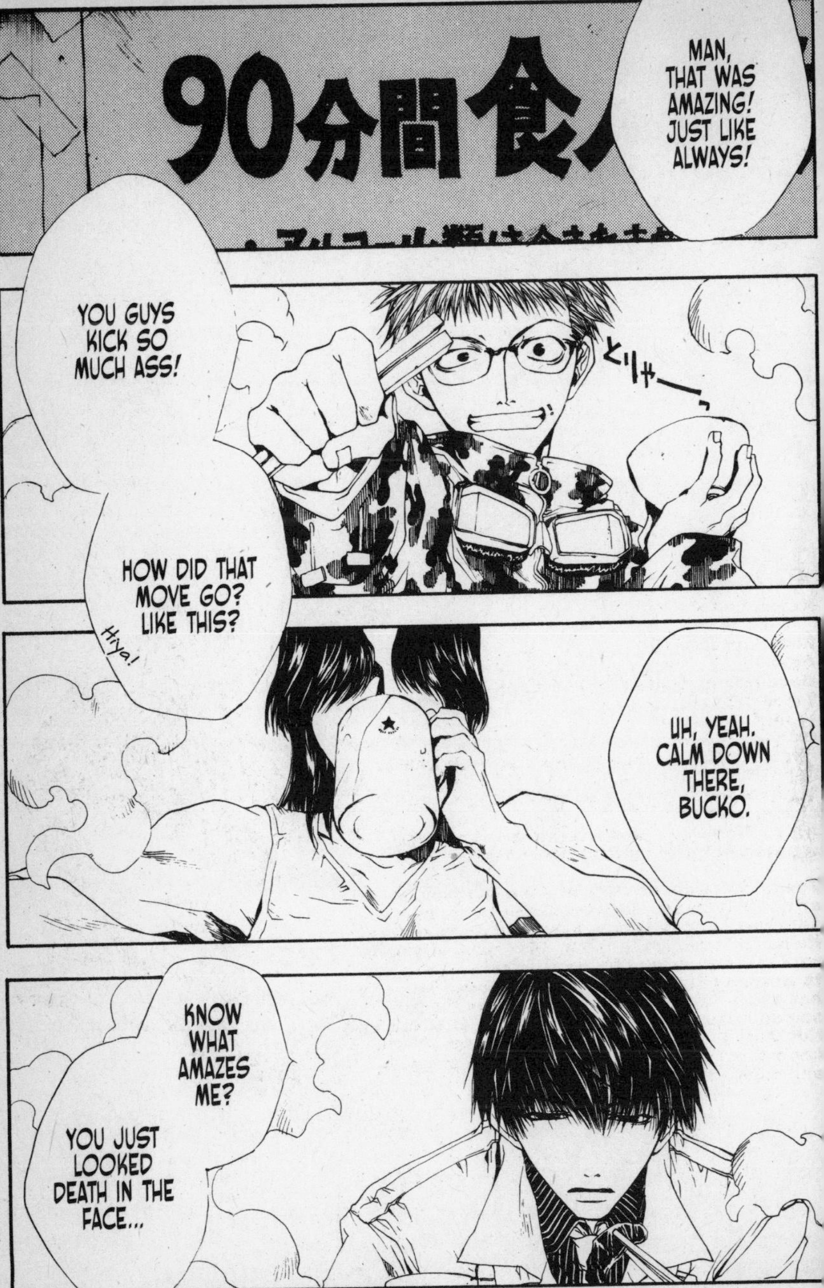
90分間食
MAN, THAT WAS AMAZING! JUST LIKE ALWAYS!
YOU GUYS KICK SO MUCH ASS!
とりゃー
HOW DID THAT MOVE GO? LIKE THIS?
Hiya!
UH, YEAH. CALM DOWN THERE, BUCKO.
KNOW WHAT AMAZES ME?
YOU JUST LOOKED DEATH IN THE FACE...

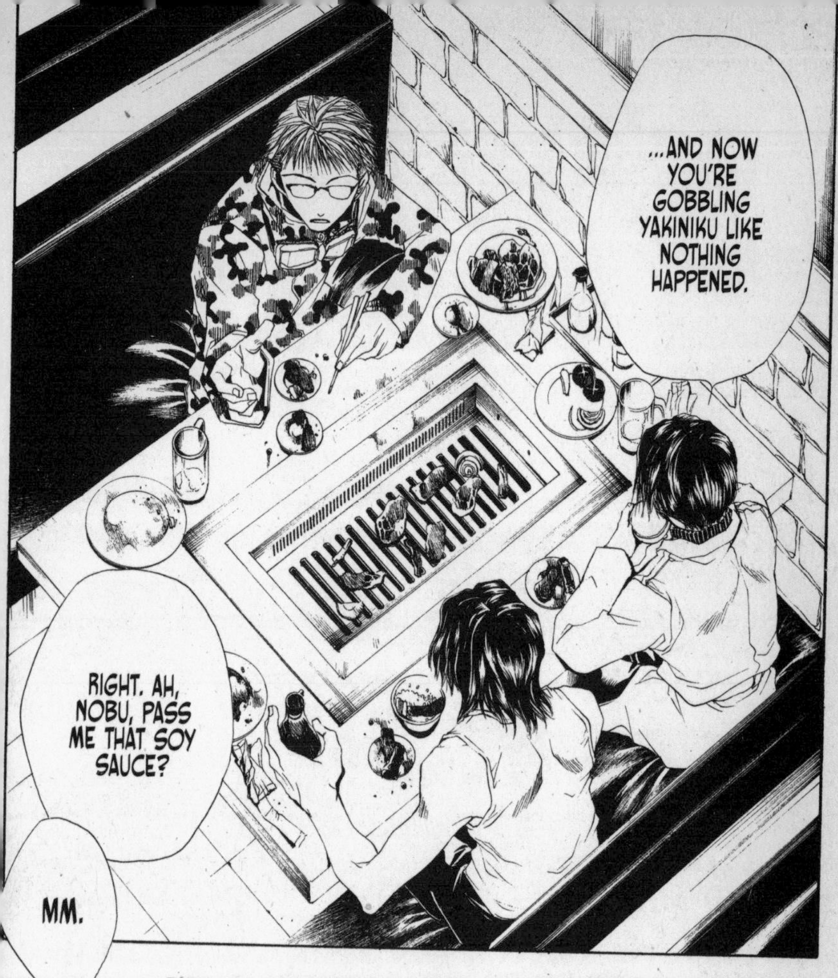
...AND NOW YOU'RE GOBBLING YAKINIKU LIKE NOTHING HAPPENED.
RIGHT. AH, NOBU, PASS ME THAT SOY SAUCE?
MM.

STAGE 8: Professional Courtesy

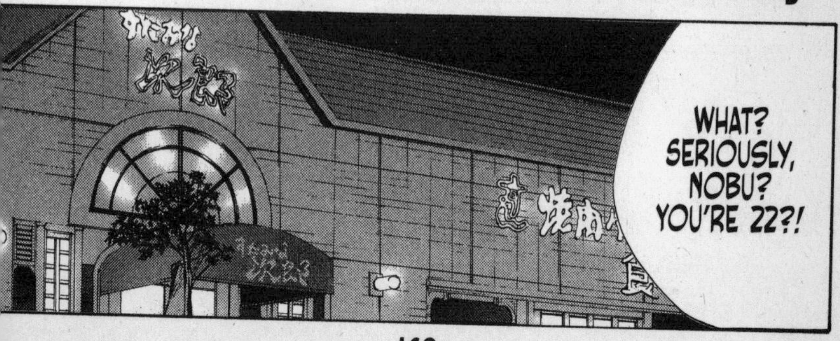
WHAT? SERIOUSLY, NOBU? YOU'RE 22?!

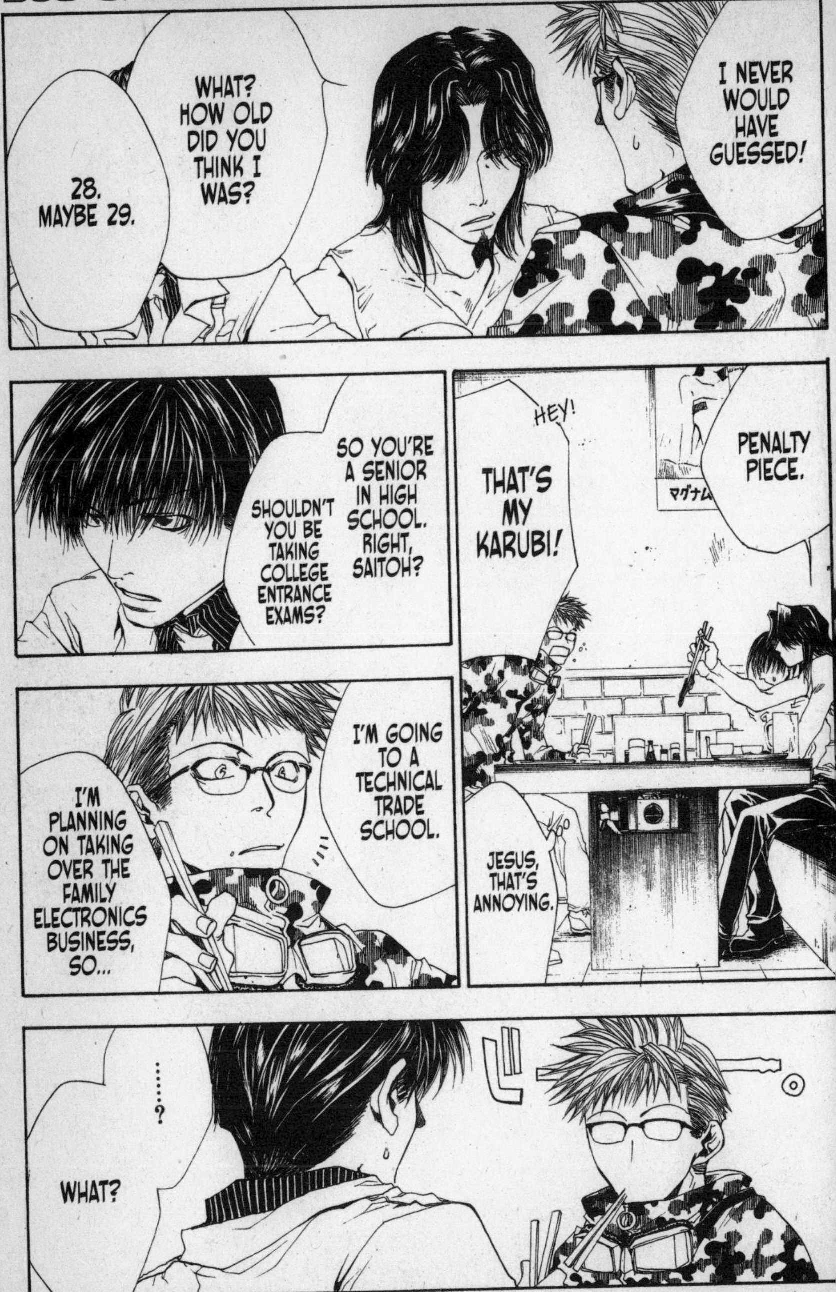
I NEVER WOULD HAVE GUESSED!
WHAT? HOW OLD DID YOU THINK I WAS?
28. MAYBE 29.
PENALTY PIECE.
HEY!
THAT'S MY KARUBI!
JESUS, THAT'S ANNOYING.
SO YOU'RE A SENIOR IN HIGH SCHOOL. RIGHT, SAITOH?
SHOULDN'T YOU BE TAKING COLLEGE ENTRANCE EXAMS?
I'M GOING TO A TECHNICAL TRADE SCHOOL.
I'M PLANNING ON TAKING OVER THE FAMILY ELECTRONICS BUSINESS, SO...
......?
WHAT?

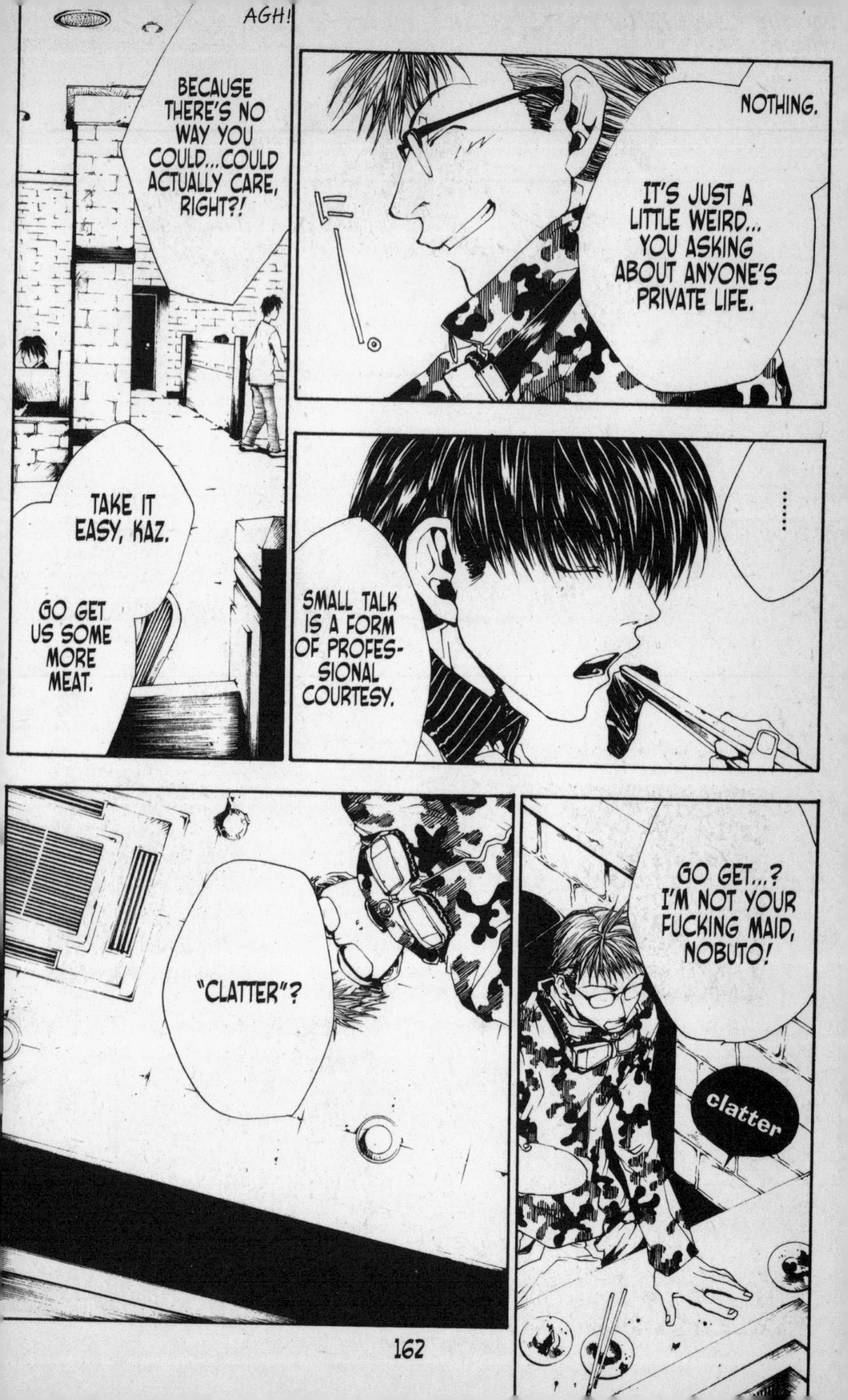
NOTHING.
IT'S JUST A LITTLE WEIRD... YOU ASKING ABOUT ANYONE'S PRIVATE LIFE.
......
SMALL TALK IS A FORM OF PROFES-SIONAL COURTESY.
AGH!
BECAUSE THERE'S NO WAY YOU COULD...COULD ACTUALLY CARE, RIGHT?!
TAKE IT EASY, KAZ.
GO GET US SOME MORE MEAT.
GO GET...? I'M NOT YOUR FUCKING MAID, NOBUTO!
clatter
"CLATTER"?

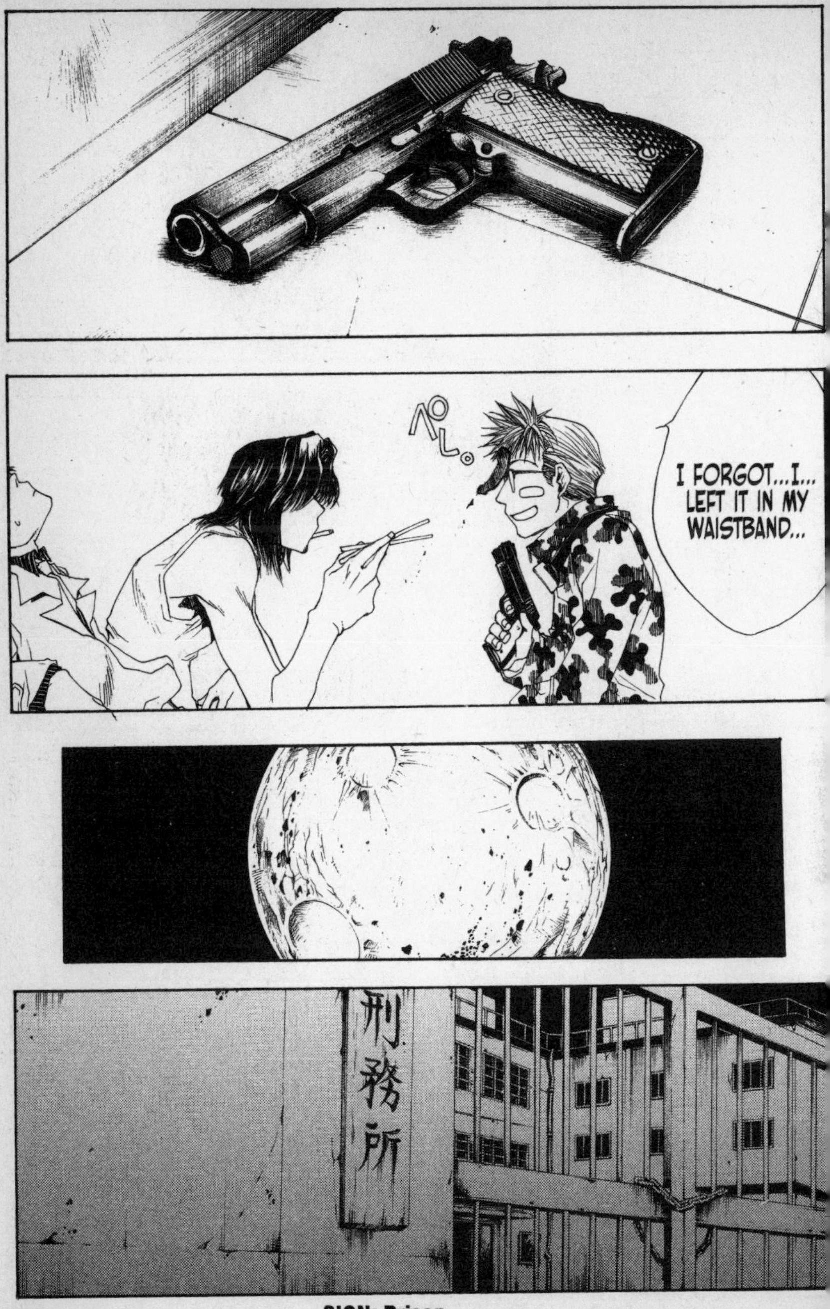
I FORGOT...I... LEFT IT IN MY WAISTBAND...
刑務所

SIGN: Prison

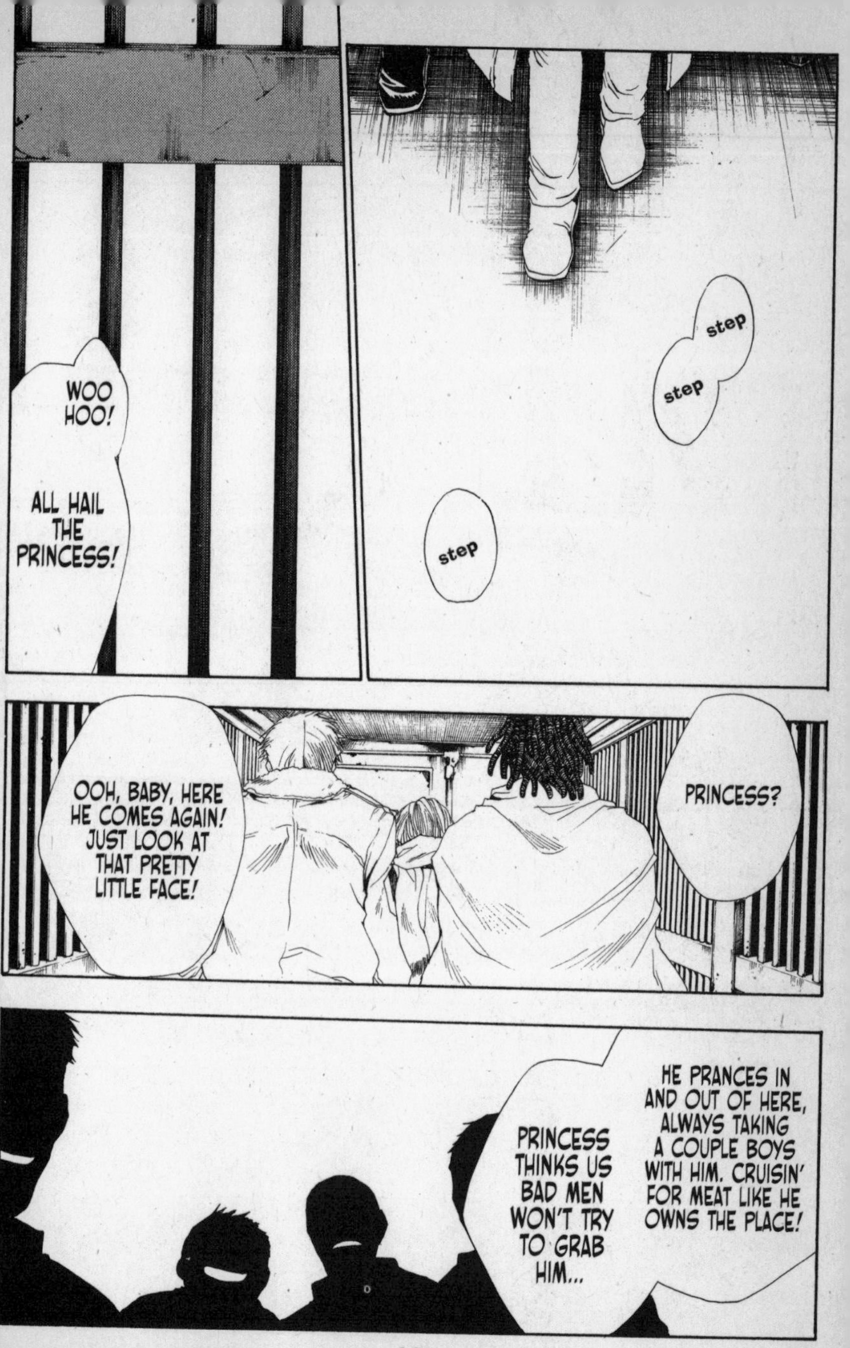
step
step
step
WOO HOO!
ALL HAIL THE PRINCESS!
PRINCESS?
OOH, BABY, HERE HE COMES AGAIN! JUST LOOK AT THAT PRETTY LITTLE FACE!
HE PRANCES IN AND OUT OF HERE, ALWAYS TAKING A COUPLE BOYS WITH HIM. CRUISIN' FOR MEAT LIKE HE OWNS THE PLACE!
PRINCESS THINKS US BAD MEN WON'T TRY TO GRAB HIM...

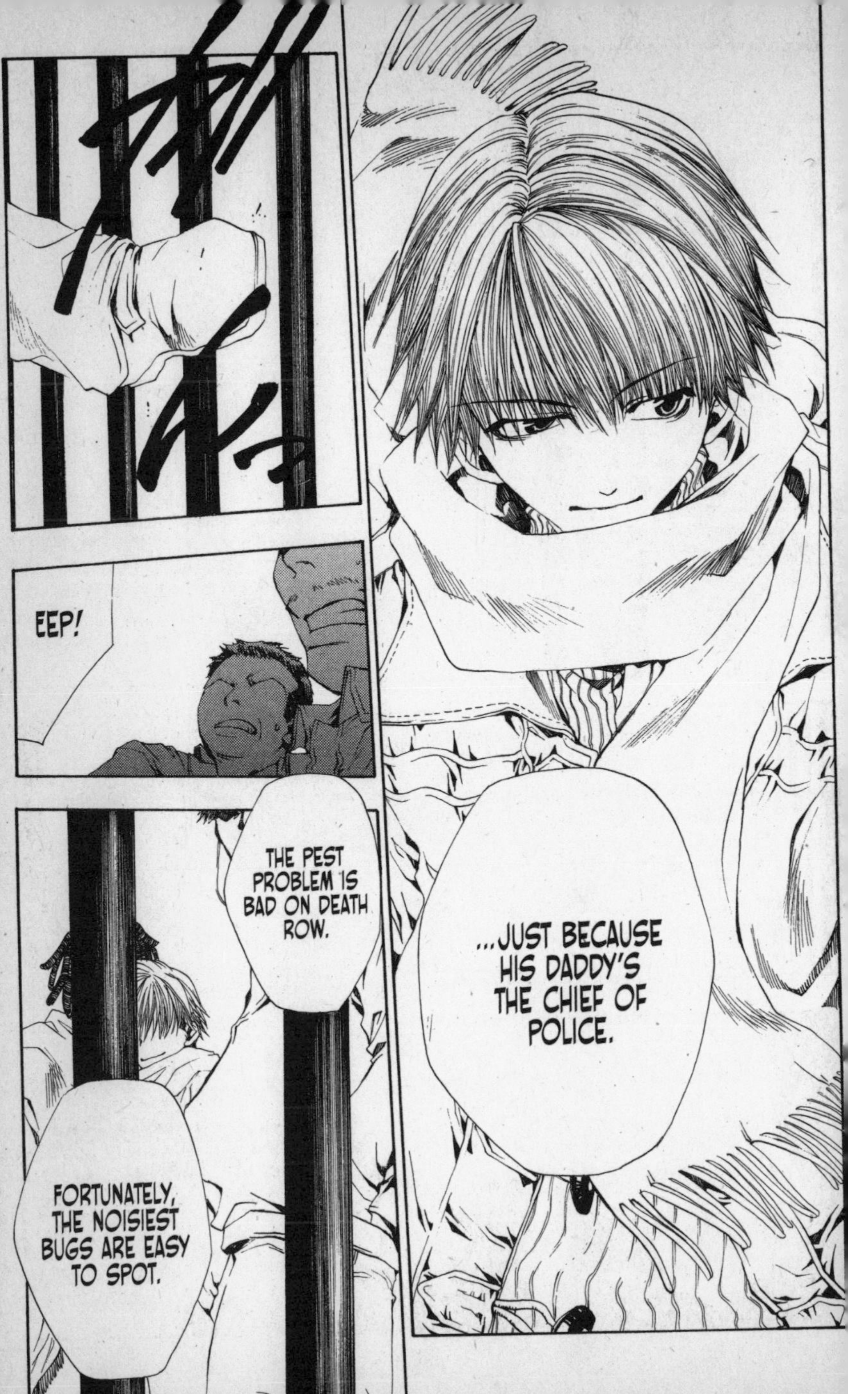
...JUST BECAUSE HIS DADDY'S THE CHIEF OF POLICE.
EEP!
THE PEST PROBLEM IS BAD ON DEATH ROW.
FORTUNATELY, THE NOISIEST BUGS ARE EASY TO SPOT.

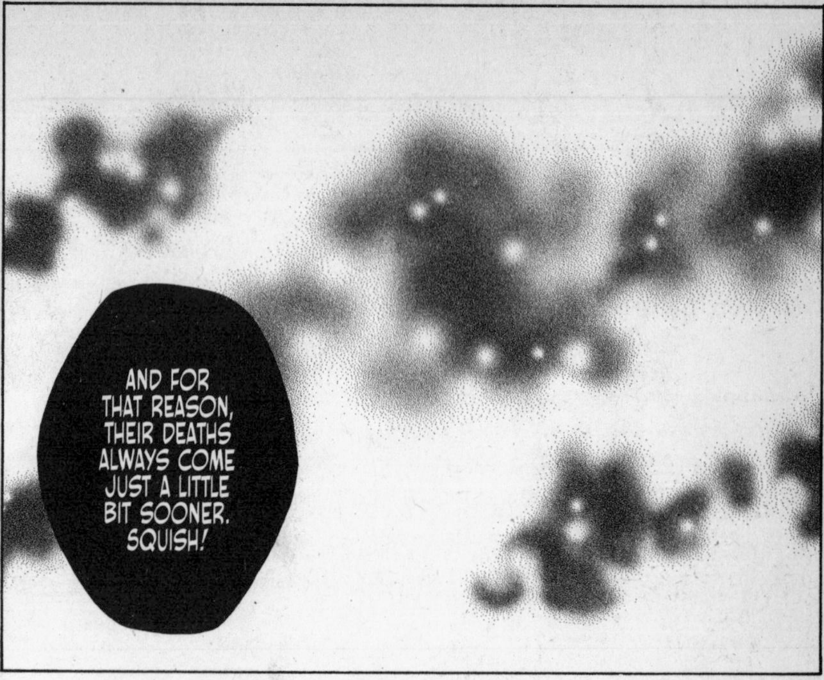
AND FOR THAT REASON, THEIR DEATHS ALWAYS COME JUST A LITTLE BIT SOONER. SQUISH!

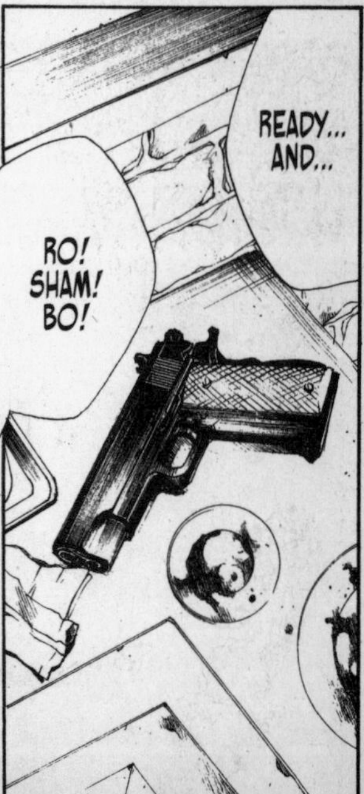
READY... AND...
RO! SHAM! BO!

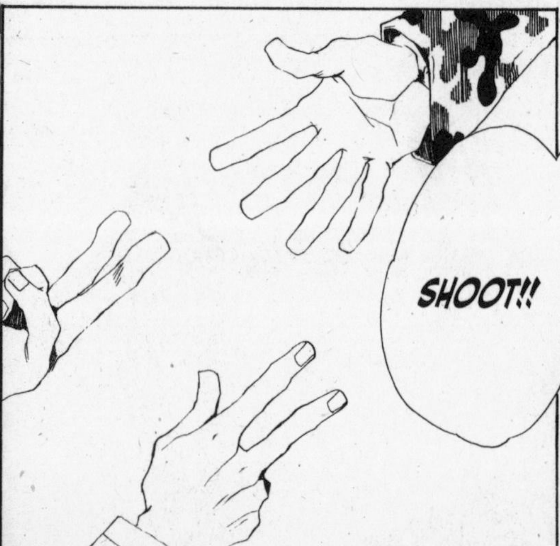
SHOOT!!

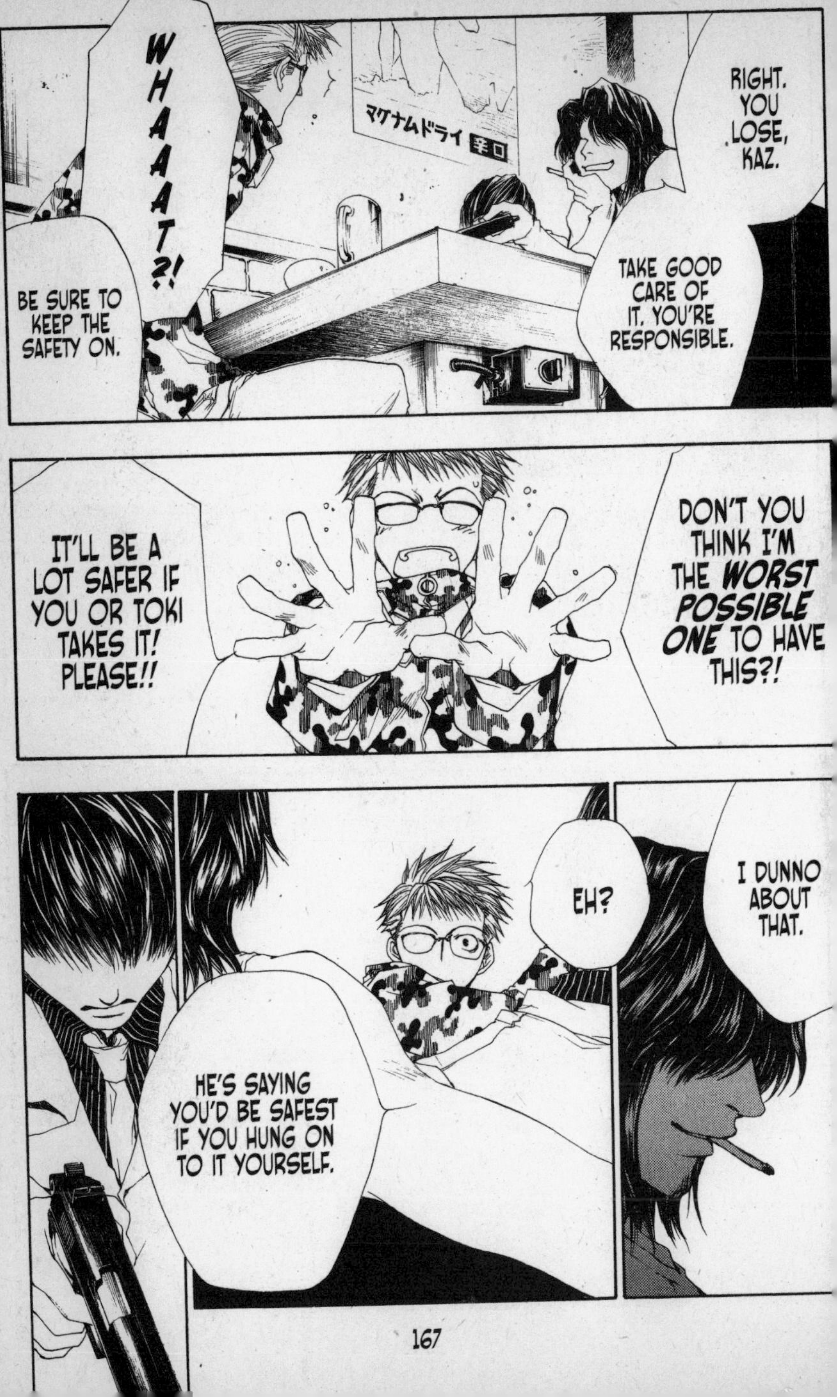
RIGHT. YOU LOSE, KAZ.
TAKE GOOD CARE OF IT. YOU'RE RESPONSIBLE.
マグナムドライ 辛口
WHAAAAT?!
BE SURE TO KEEP THE SAFETY ON.
DON'T YOU THINK I'M THE ***WORST POSSIBLE ONE*** TO HAVE THIS?!
IT'LL BE A LOT SAFER IF YOU OR TOKI TAKES IT! PLEASE!!
I DUNNO ABOUT THAT.
EH?
HE'S SAYING YOU'D BE SAFEST IF YOU HUNG ON TO IT YOURSELF.

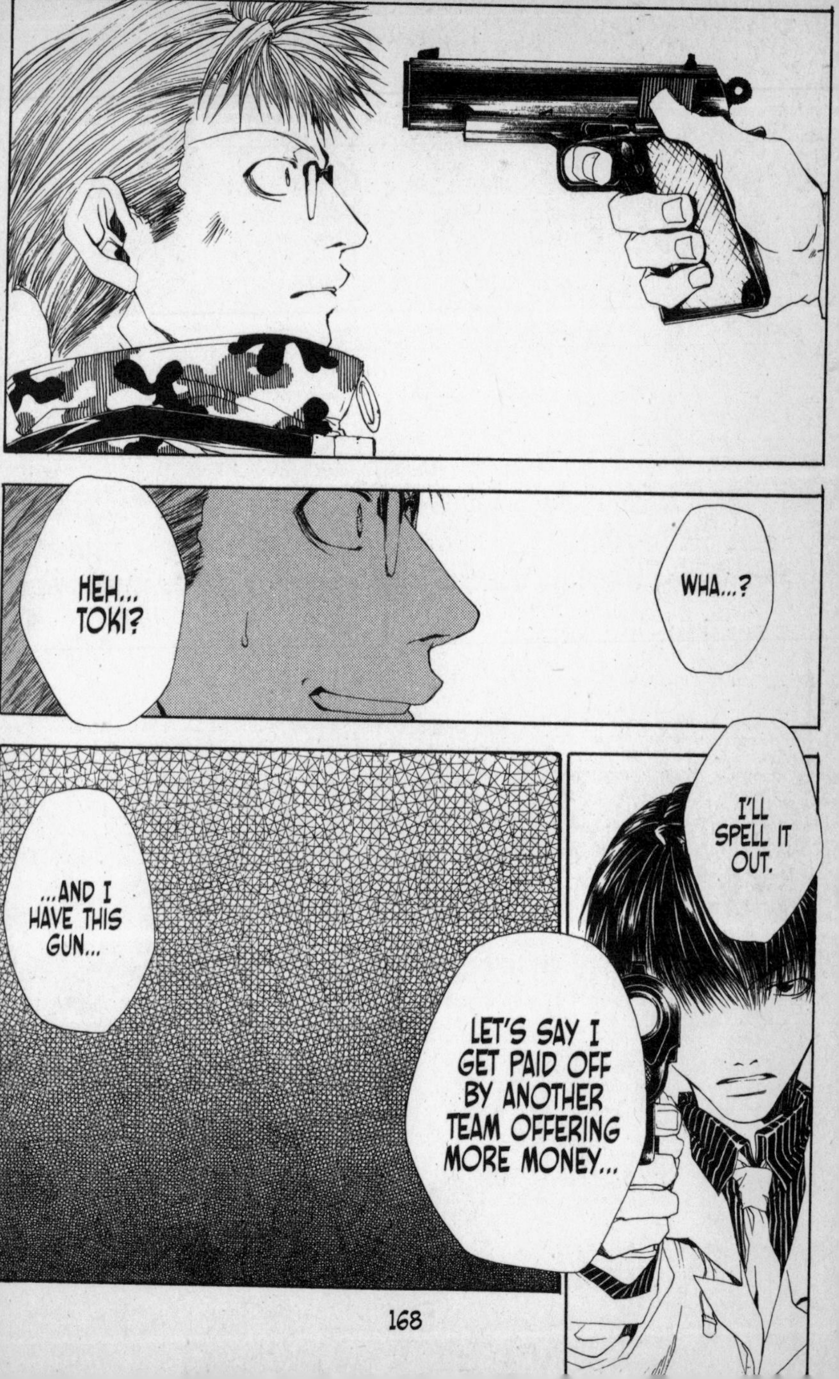
WHA...?
HEH... TOKI?
I'LL SPELL IT OUT.
LET'S SAY I GET PAID OFF BY ANOTHER TEAM OFFERING MORE MONEY...
...AND I HAVE THIS GUN...

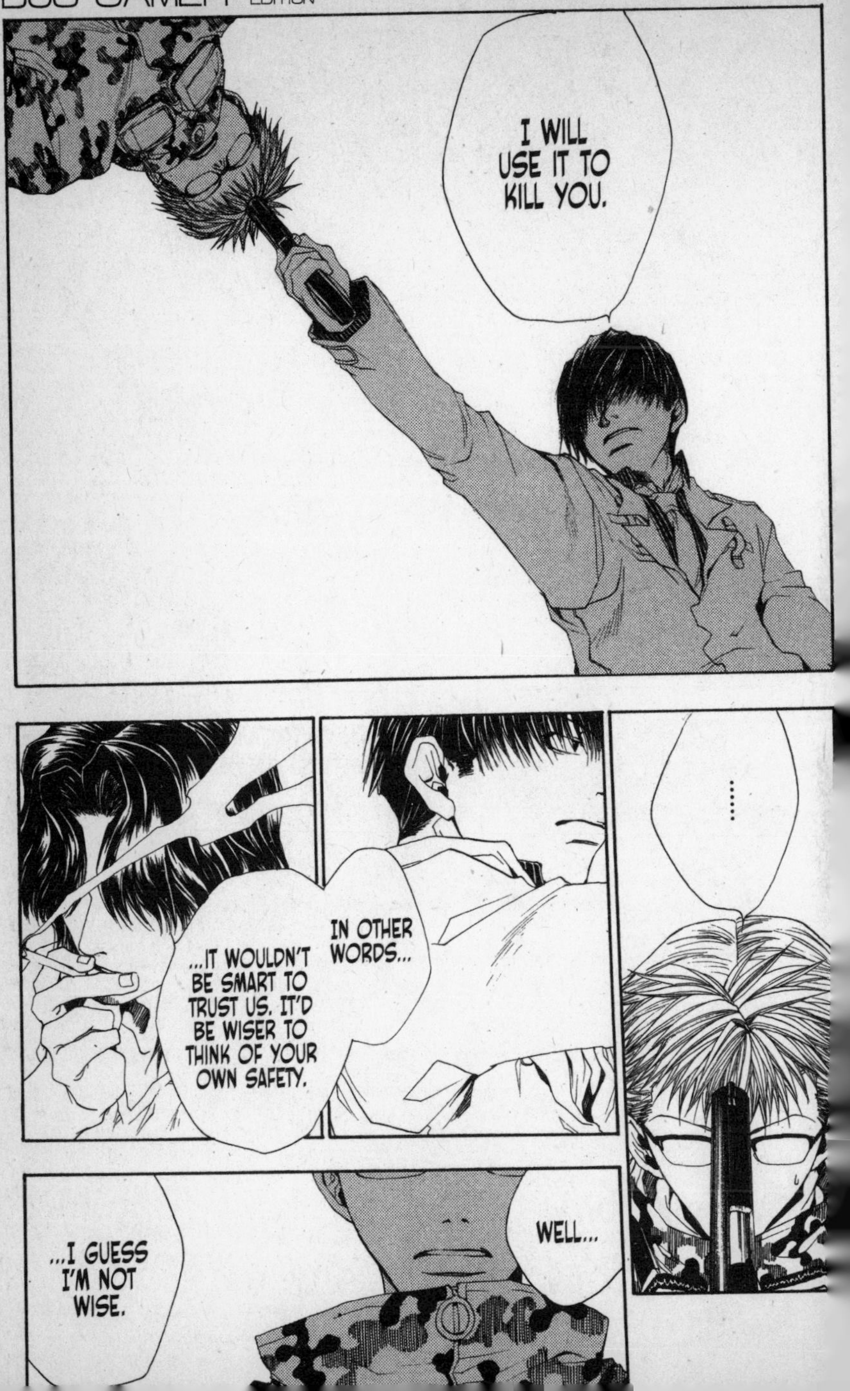
I WILL USE IT TO KILL YOU.
......
IN OTHER WORDS...
...IT WOULDN'T BE SMART TO TRUST US. IT'D BE WISER TO THINK OF YOUR OWN SAFETY.
WELL...
...I GUESS I'M NOT WISE.

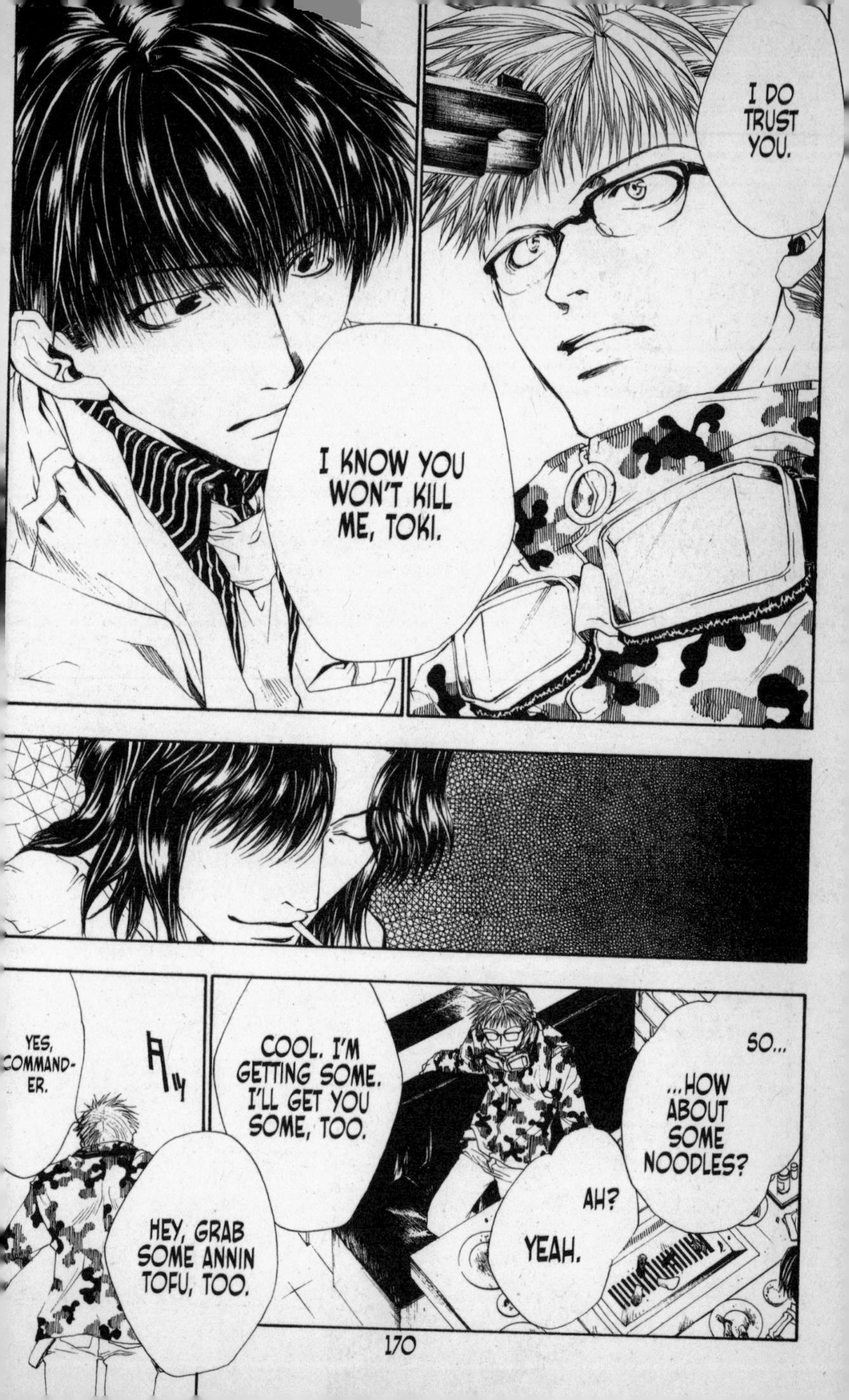
I DO TRUST YOU.
I KNOW YOU WON'T KILL ME, TOKI.
SO...
...HOW ABOUT SOME NOODLES?
AH?
YEAH.
COOL. I'M GETTING SOME. I'LL GET YOU SOME, TOO.
HEY, GRAB SOME ANNIN TOFU, TOO.
YES, COMMAND-ER.

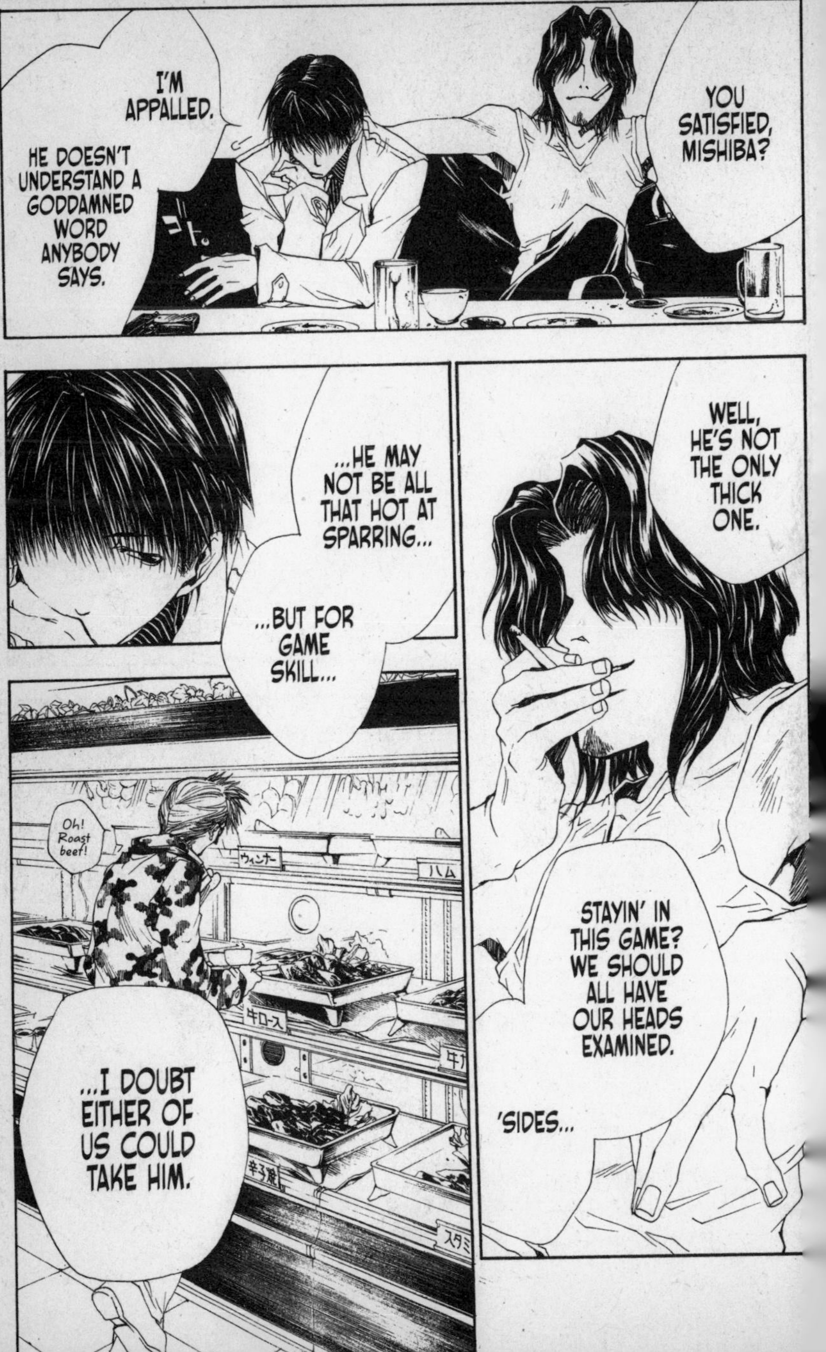
YOU SATISFIED, MISHIBA?
I'M APPALLED.
HE DOESN'T UNDERSTAND A GODDAMNED WORD ANYBODY SAYS.
WELL, HE'S NOT THE ONLY THICK ONE.
STAYIN' IN THIS GAME? WE SHOULD ALL HAVE OUR HEADS EXAMINED.
'SIDES...
...HE MAY NOT BE ALL THAT HOT AT SPARRING...
...BUT FOR GAME SKILL...
Oh! Roast beef!
...I DOUBT EITHER OF US COULD TAKE HIM.

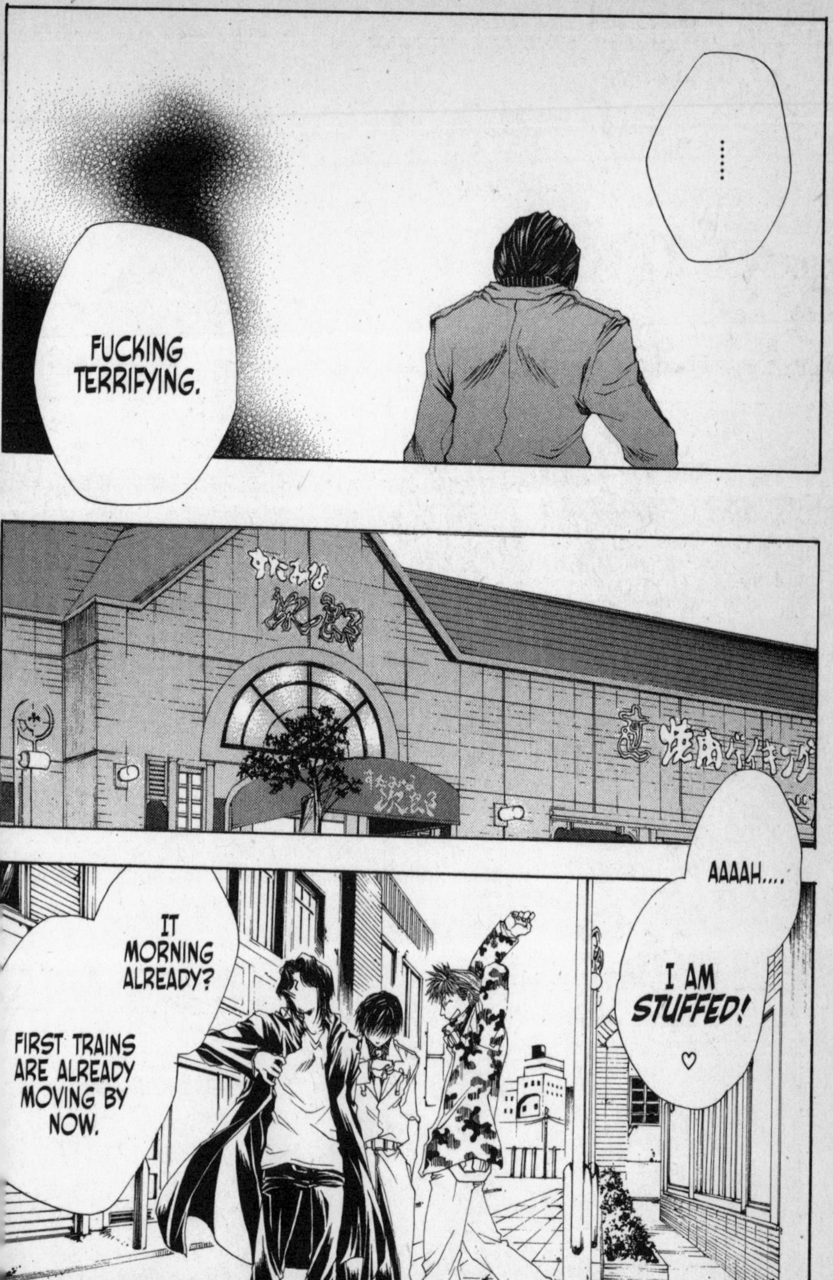
......
FUCKING TERRIFYING.
AAAAH....
I AM STUFFED! ♡
IT MORNING ALREADY?
FIRST TRAINS ARE ALREADY MOVING BY NOW.

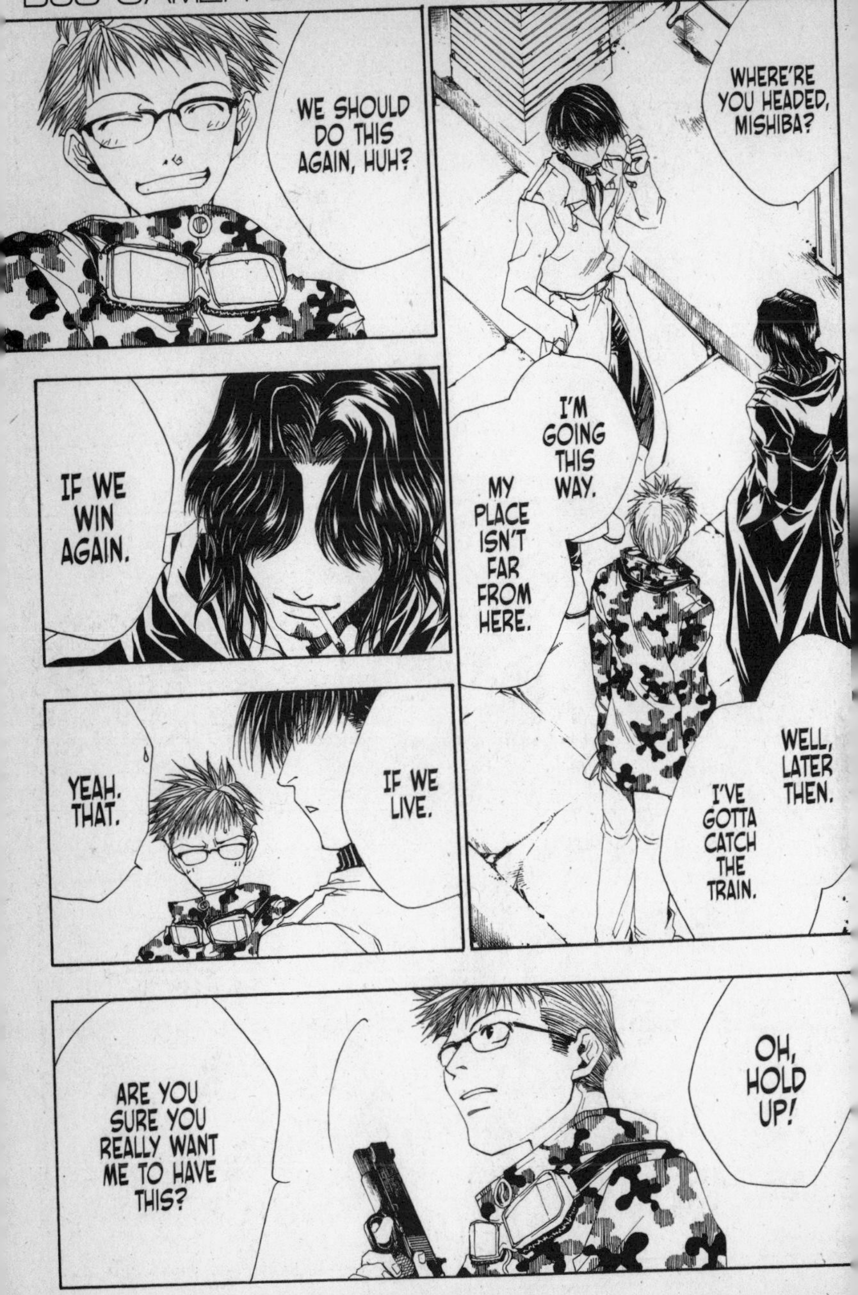
WHERE'RE YOU HEADED, MISHIBA?
I'M GOING THIS WAY.
MY PLACE ISN'T FAR FROM HERE.
WELL, LATER THEN.
I'VE GOTTA CATCH THE TRAIN.
WE SHOULD DO THIS AGAIN, HUH?
IF WE WIN AGAIN.
IF WE LIVE.
YEAH. THAT.
OH, HOLD UP!
ARE YOU SURE YOU REALLY WANT ME TO HAVE THIS?

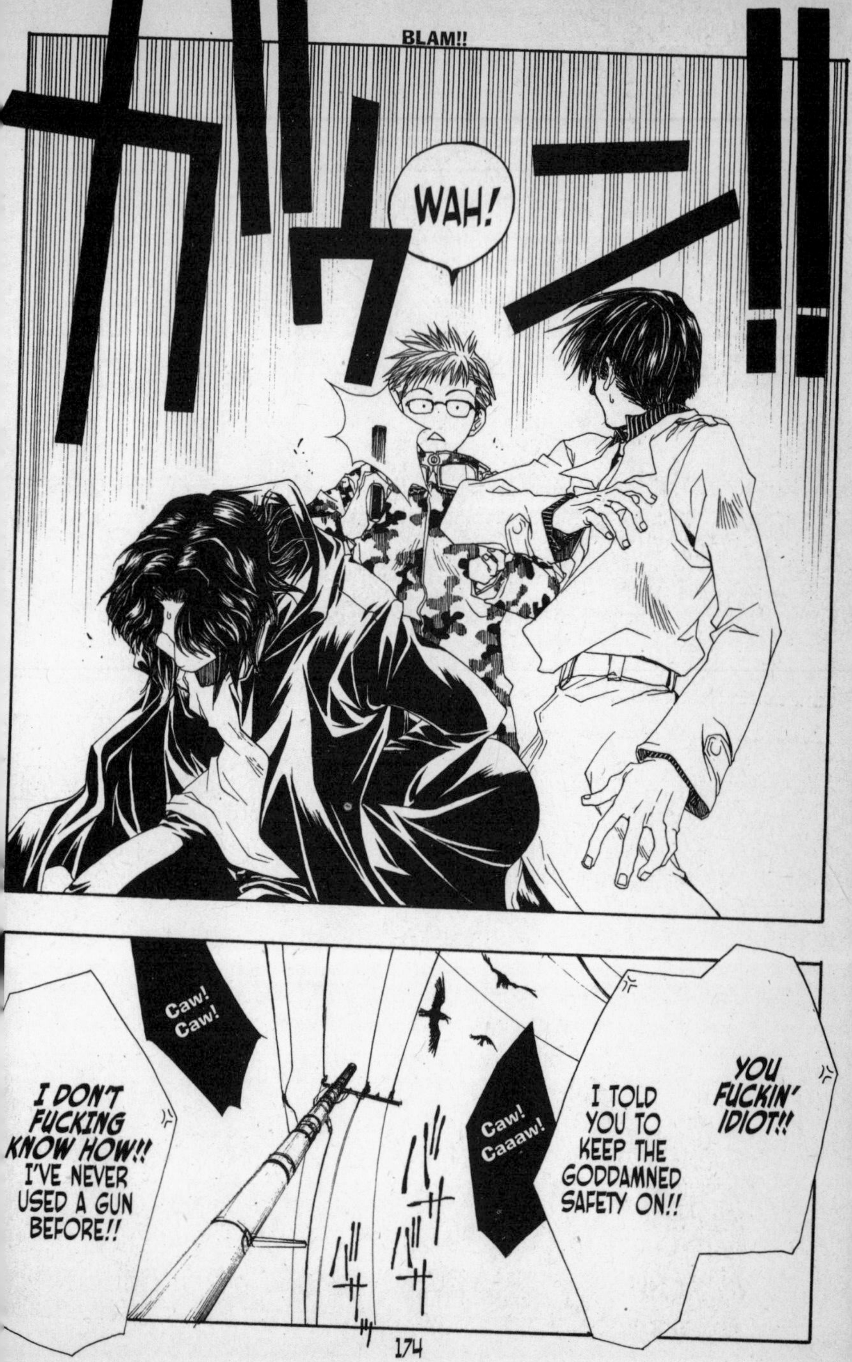
BLAM!!
ガウーン!!
WAH!
YOU FUCKIN' IDIOT!!
I TOLD YOU TO KEEP THE GODDAMNED SAFETY ON!!
Caw! Caaaw!
バサ バサ
Caw! Caw!
I DON'T FUCKING KNOW HOW!! I'VE NEVER USED A GUN BEFORE!!

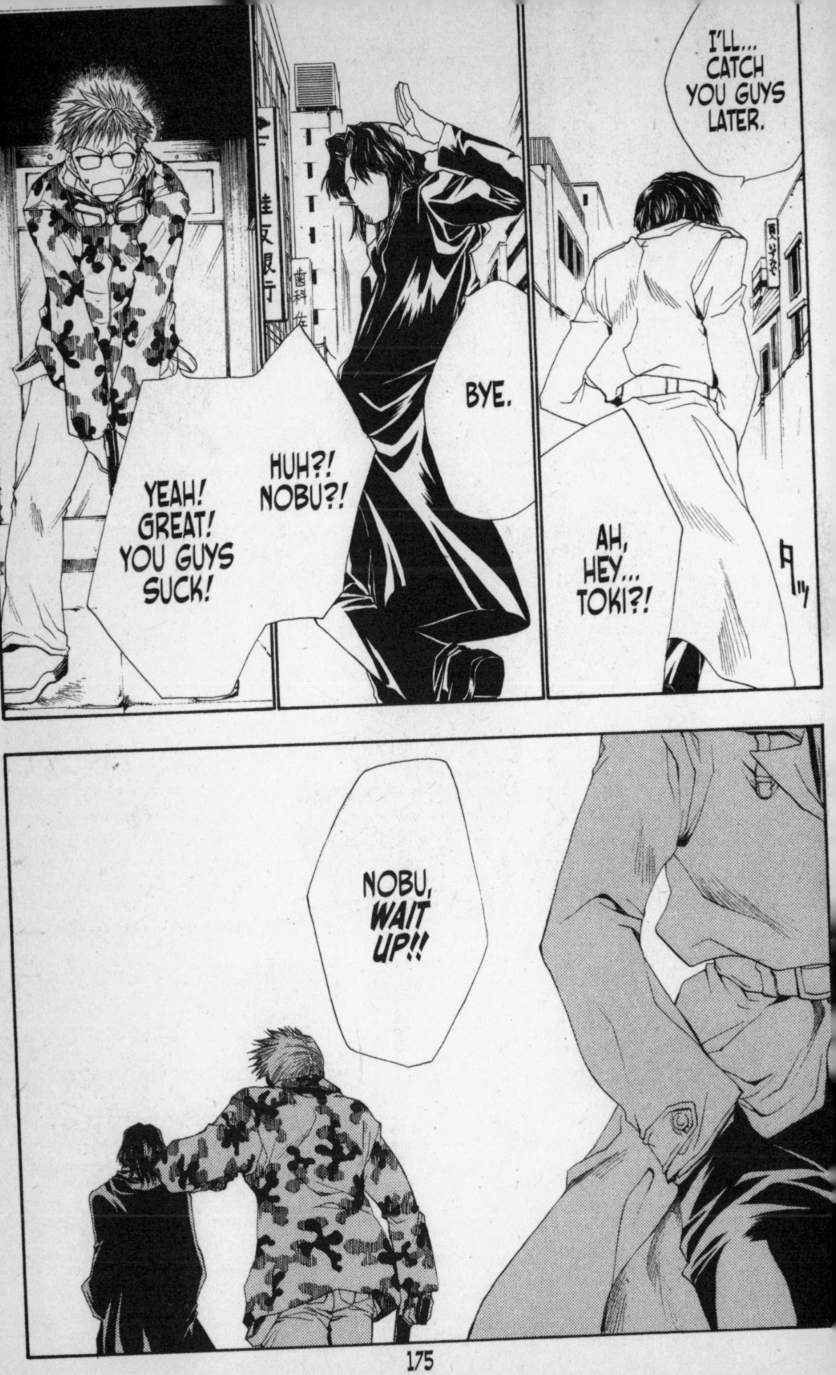
I'LL... CATCH YOU GUYS LATER.
AH, HEY... TOKI?!
BYE.
HUH?! NOBU?!
YEAH! GREAT! YOU GUYS SUCK!
NOBU, WAIT UP!!

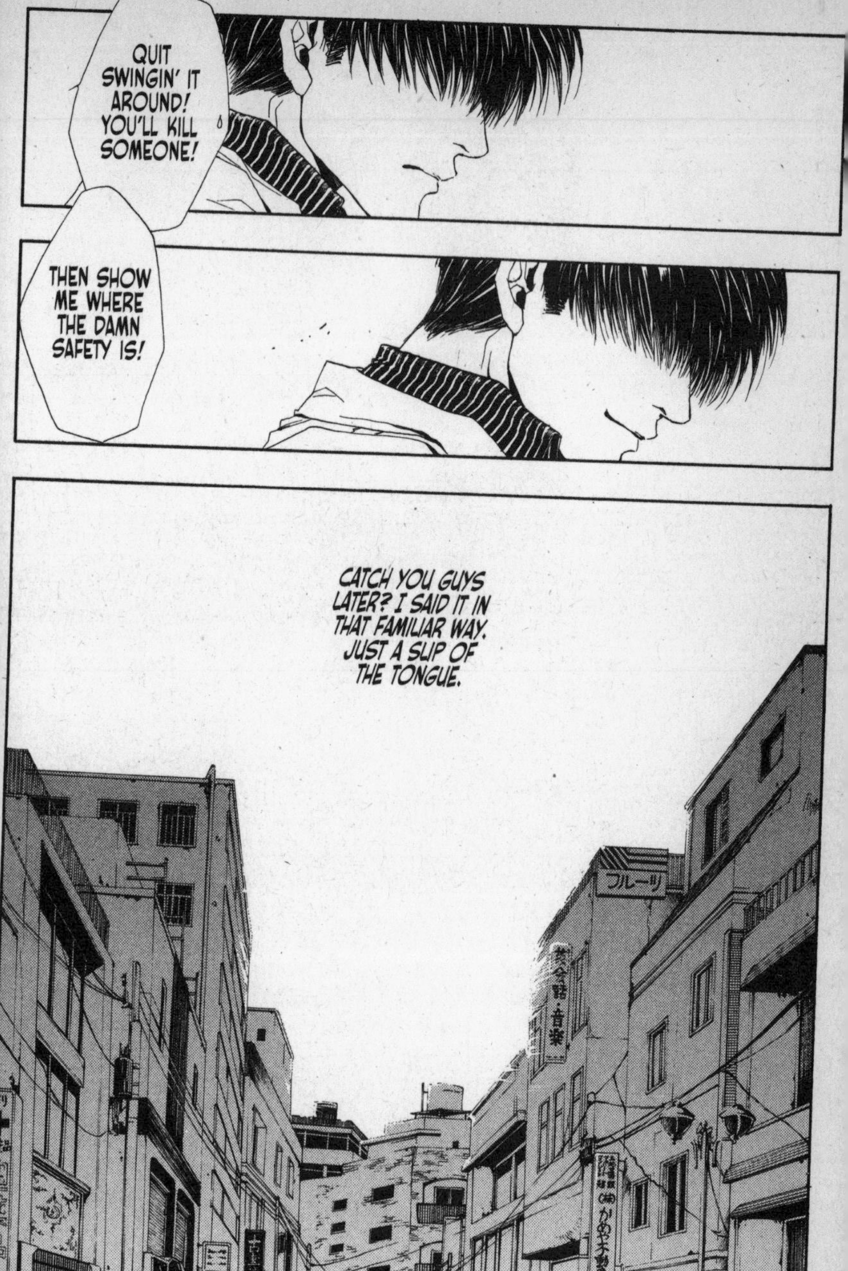
QUIT SWINGIN' IT AROUND! YOU'LL KILL SOMEONE!
THEN SHOW ME WHERE THE DAMN SAFETY IS!
CATCH YOU GUYS LATER? I SAID IT IN THAT FAMILIAR WAY. JUST A SLIP OF THE TONGUE.
フルーツ

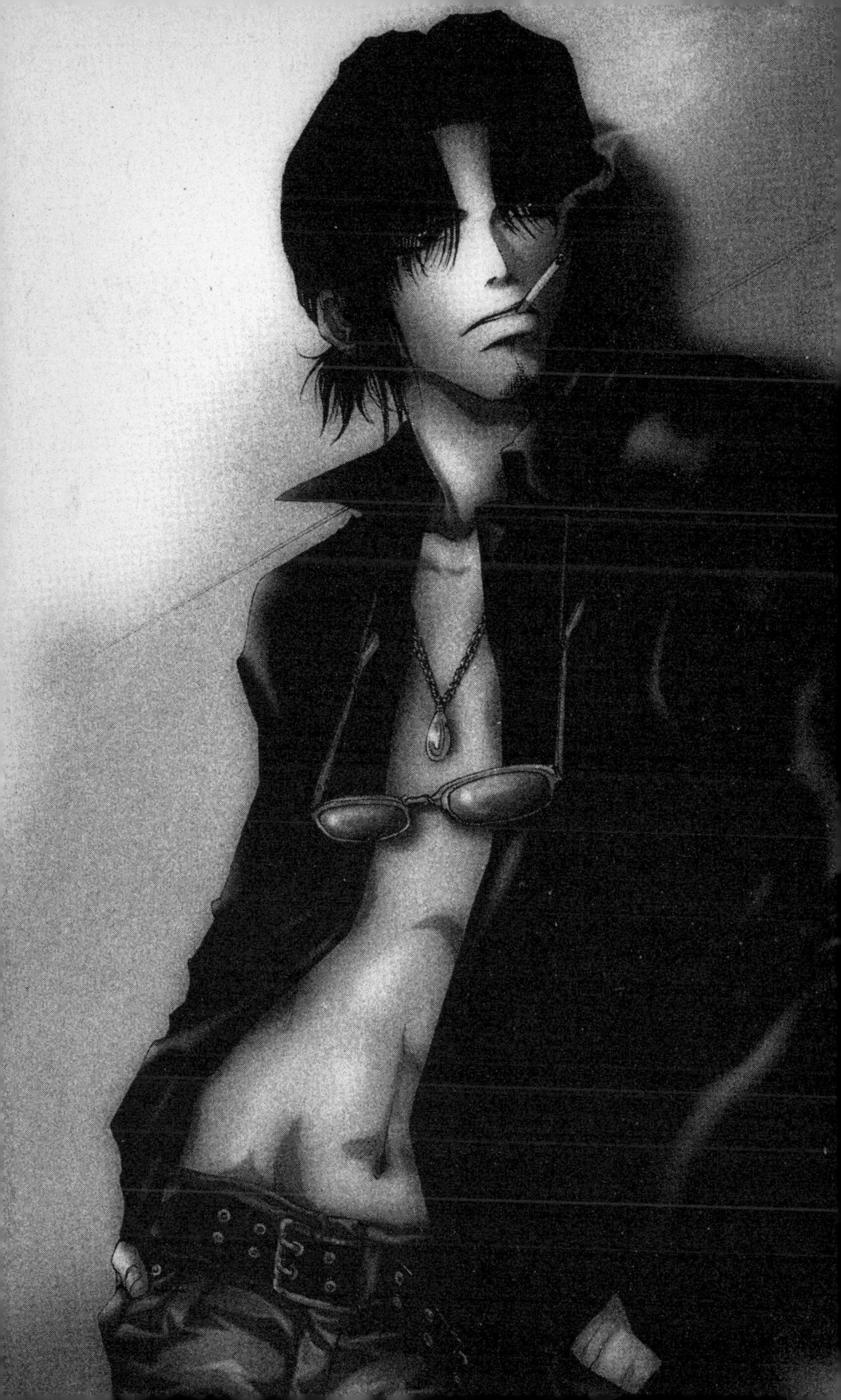

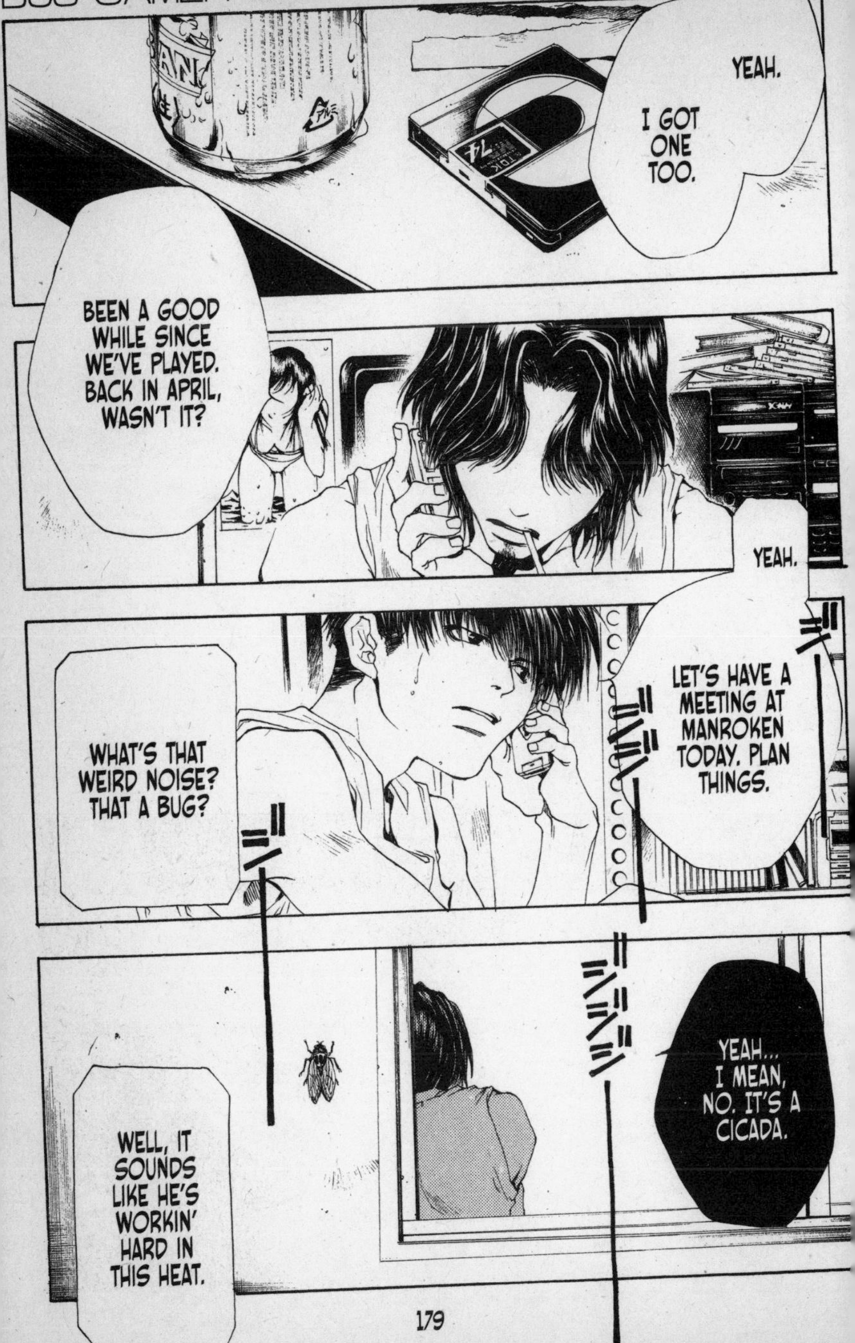
YEAH.
I GOT ONE TOO.
BEEN A GOOD WHILE SINCE WE'VE PLAYED. BACK IN APRIL, WASN'T IT?
YEAH.
LET'S HAVE A MEETING AT MANROKEN TODAY. PLAN THINGS.
WHAT'S THAT WEIRD NOISE? THAT A BUG?
YEAH... I MEAN, NO. IT'S A CICADA.
WELL, IT SOUNDS LIKE HE'S WORKIN' HARD IN THIS HEAT.

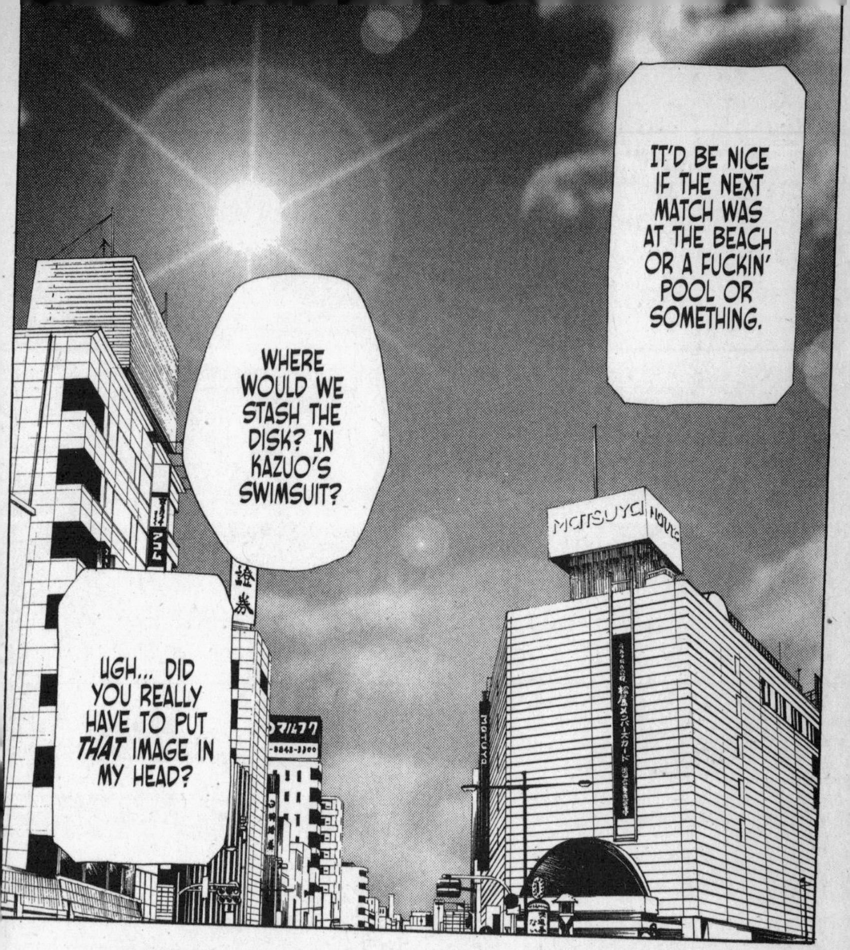
IT'D BE NICE IF THE NEXT MATCH WAS AT THE BEACH OR A FUCKIN' POOL OR SOMETHING.
WHERE WOULD WE STASH THE DISK? IN KAZUO'S SWIMSUIT?
UGH... DID YOU REALLY HAVE TO PUT *THAT* IMAGE IN MY HEAD?

STAGE 9: A New Challenger

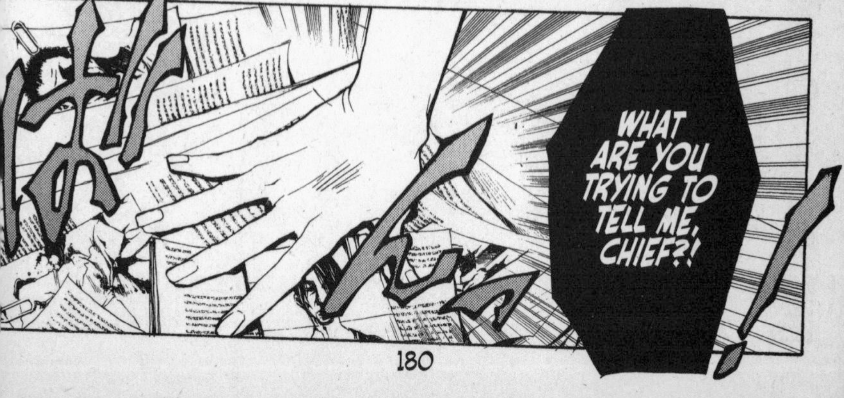
WHAT ARE YOU TRYING TO TELL ME, CHIEF?!

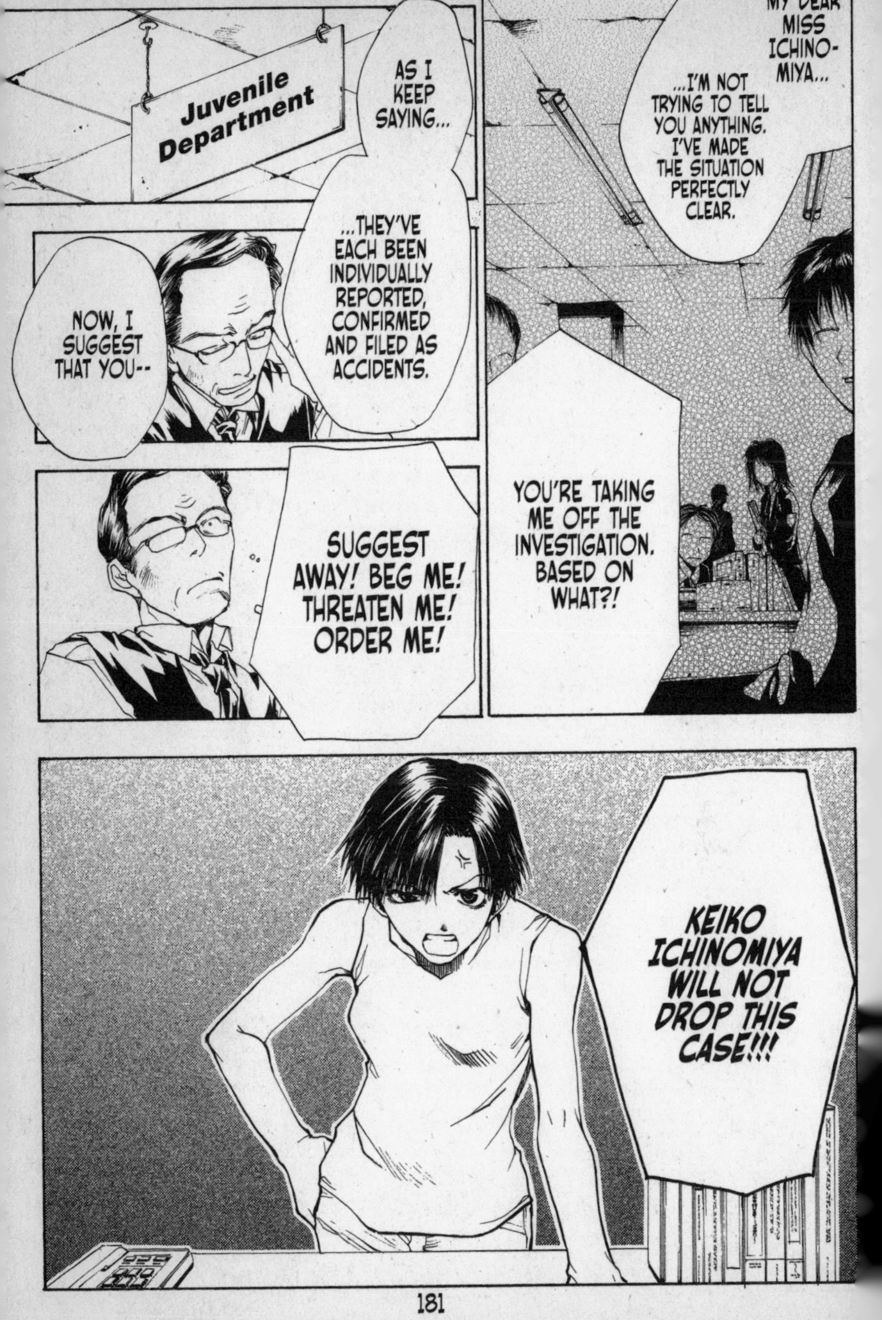
MY DEAR MISS ICHINO-MIYA...
...I'M NOT TRYING TO TELL YOU ANYTHING. I'VE MADE THE SITUATION PERFECTLY CLEAR.
YOU'RE TAKING ME OFF THE INVESTIGATION. BASED ON WHAT?!
Juvenile Department
AS I KEEP SAYING...
...THEY'VE EACH BEEN INDIVIDUALLY REPORTED, CONFIRMED AND FILED AS ACCIDENTS.
NOW, I SUGGEST THAT YOU--
SUGGEST AWAY! BEG ME! THREATEN ME! ORDER ME!
KEIKO ICHINOMIYA WILL NOT DROP THIS CASE!!!

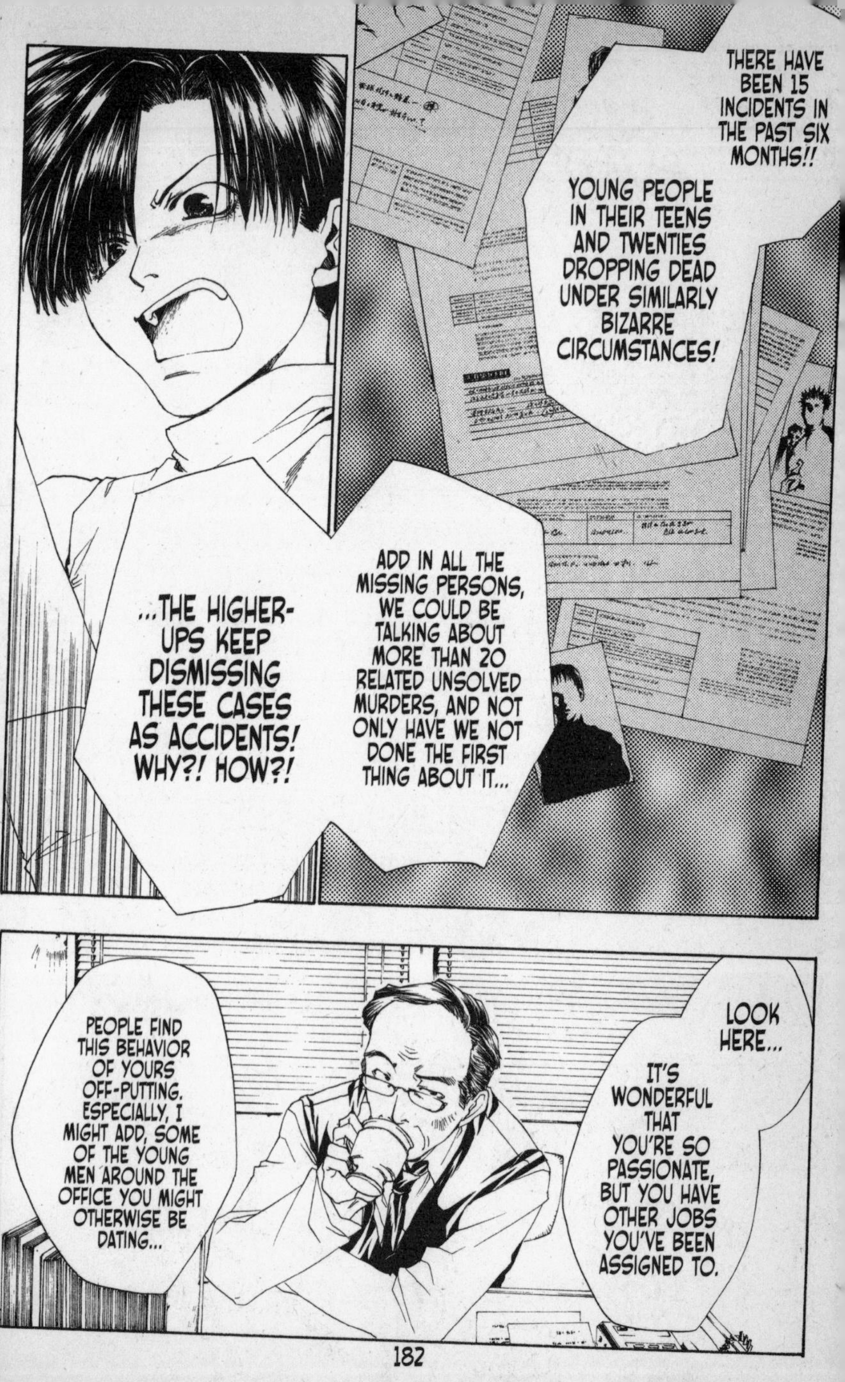
THERE HAVE BEEN 15 INCIDENTS IN THE PAST SIX MONTHS!!
YOUNG PEOPLE IN THEIR TEENS AND TWENTIES DROPPING DEAD UNDER SIMILARLY BIZARRE CIRCUMSTANCES!
ADD IN ALL THE MISSING PERSONS, WE COULD BE TALKING ABOUT MORE THAN 20 RELATED UNSOLVED MURDERS, AND NOT ONLY HAVE WE NOT DONE THE FIRST THING ABOUT IT...
...THE HIGHER-UPS KEEP DISMISSING THESE CASES AS ACCIDENTS! WHY?! HOW?!
LOOK HERE...
IT'S WONDERFUL THAT YOU'RE SO PASSIONATE, BUT YOU HAVE OTHER JOBS YOU'VE BEEN ASSIGNED TO.
PEOPLE FIND THIS BEHAVIOR OF YOURS OFF-PUTTING. ESPECIALLY, I MIGHT ADD, SOME OF THE YOUNG MEN AROUND THE OFFICE YOU MIGHT OTHERWISE BE DATING...

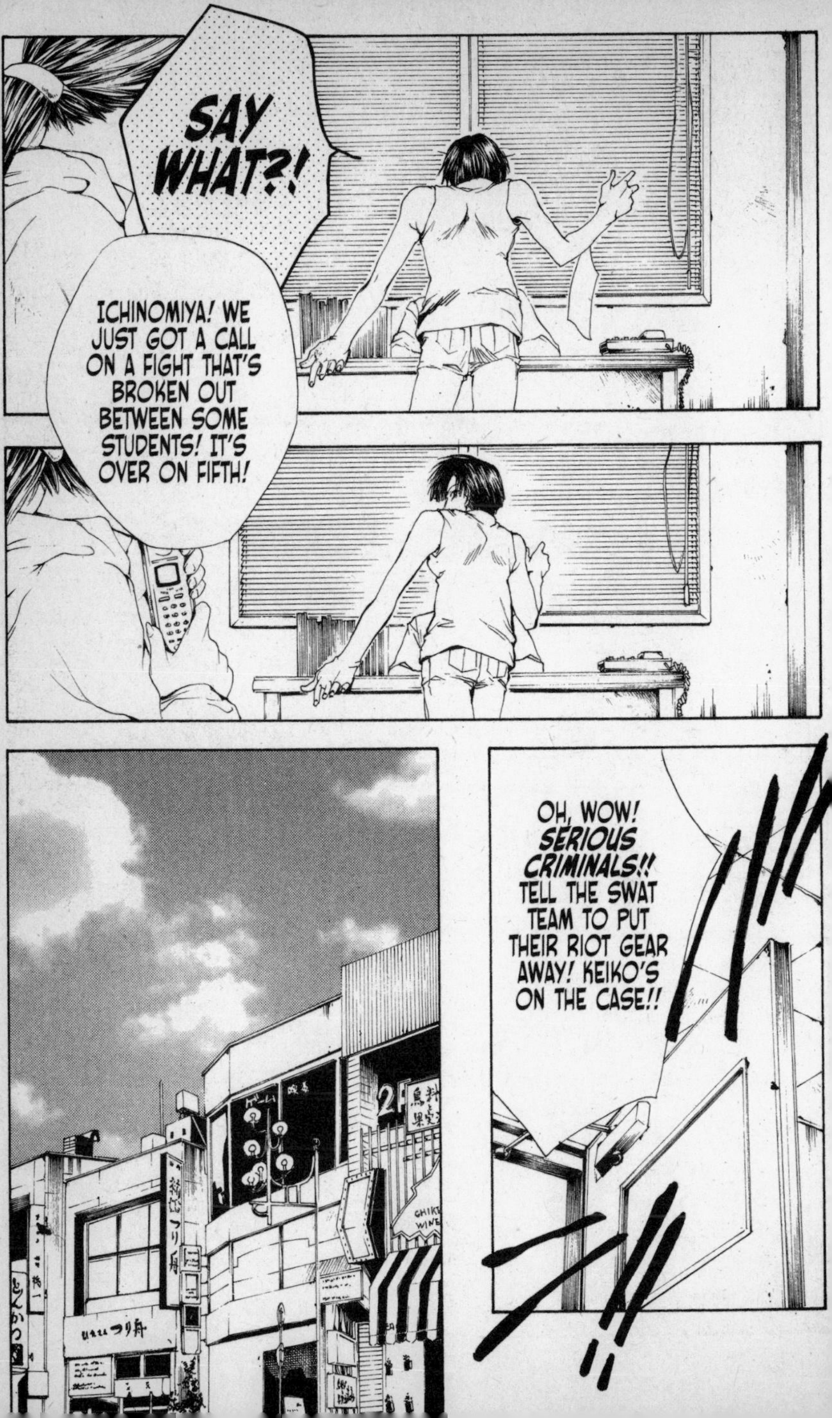
SAY WHAT?!
ICHINOMIYA! WE JUST GOT A CALL ON A FIGHT THAT'S BROKEN OUT BETWEEN SOME STUDENTS! IT'S OVER ON FIFTH!
OH, WOW! SERIOUS CRIMINALS!! TELL THE SWAT TEAM TO PUT THEIR RIOT GEAR AWAY! KEIKO'S ON THE CASE!!

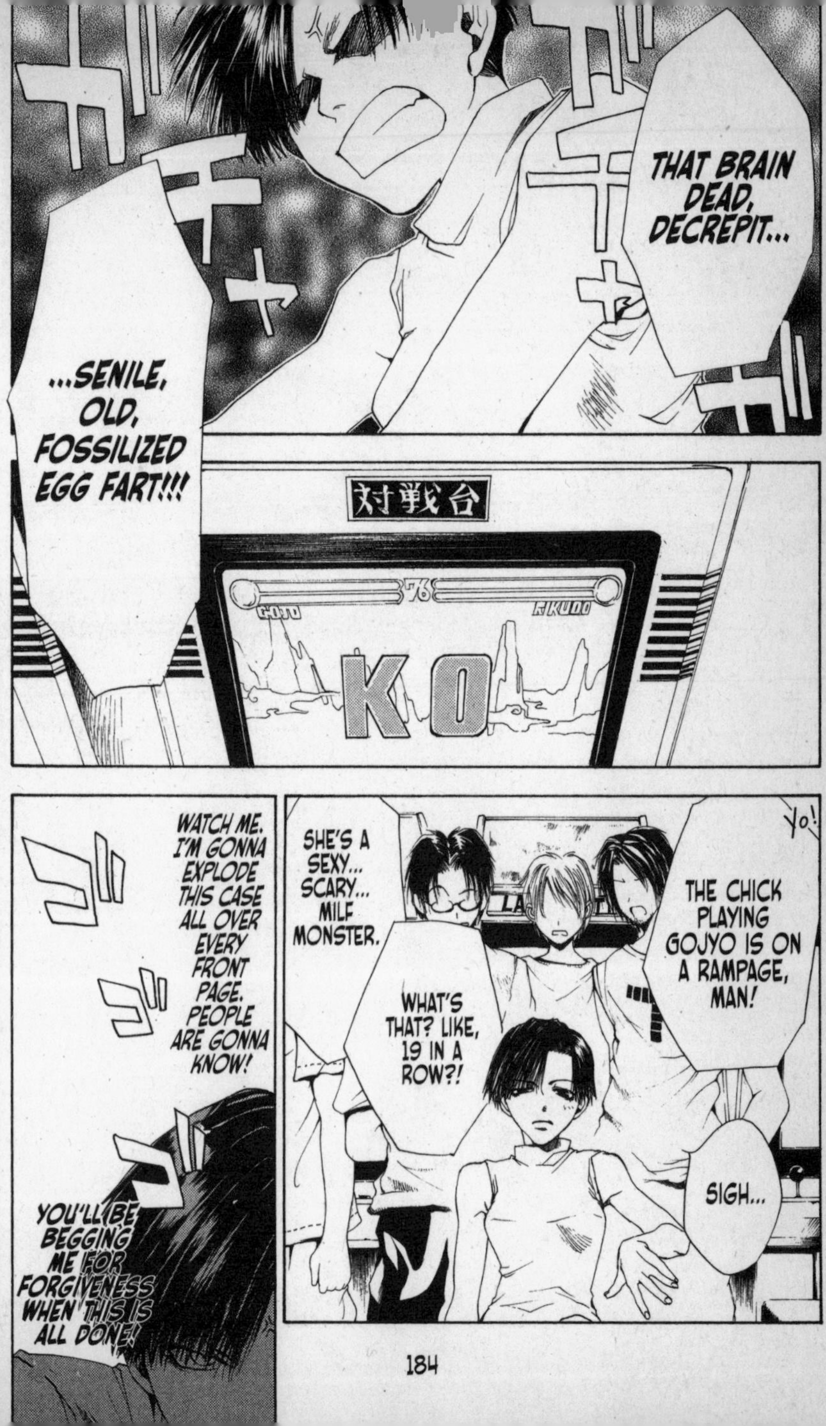
THAT BRAIN DEAD, DECREPIT...
...SENILE, OLD, FOSSILIZED EGG FART!!!
対戦台
KO
Yo!
THE CHICK PLAYING GOJYO IS ON A RAMPAGE, MAN!
SHE'S A SEXY... SCARY... MILF MONSTER.
WHAT'S THAT? LIKE, 19 IN A ROW?!
SIGH...
WATCH ME. I'M GONNA EXPLODE THIS CASE ALL OVER EVERY FRONT PAGE. PEOPLE ARE GONNA KNOW!
YOU'LL BE BEGGING ME FOR FORGIVENESS WHEN THIS IS ALL DONE!

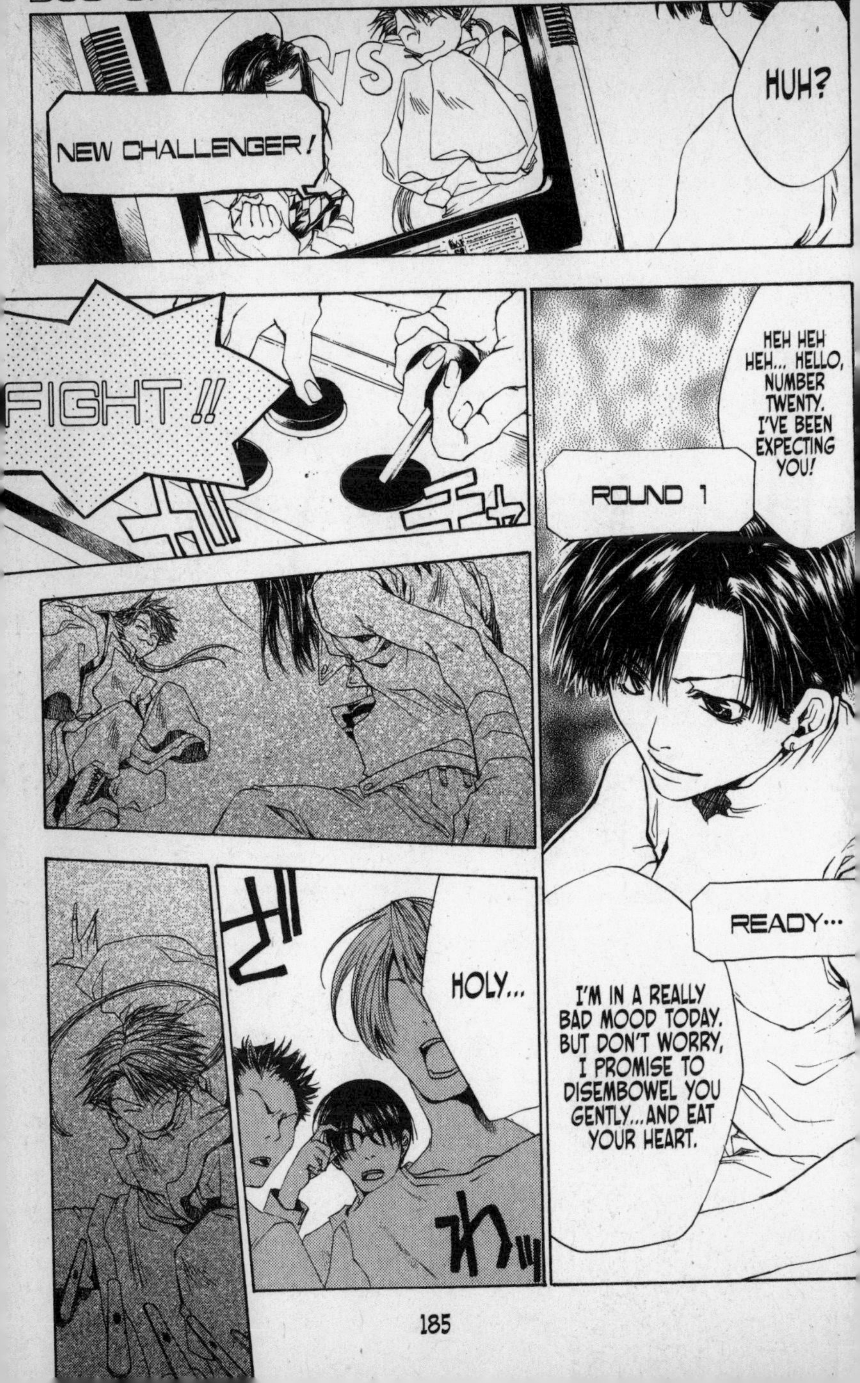
HUH?
NEW CHALLENGER!
HEH HEH HEH... HELLO, NUMBER TWENTY. I'VE BEEN EXPECTING YOU!
ROUND 1
READY...
I'M IN A REALLY BAD MOOD TODAY. BUT DON'T WORRY, I PROMISE TO DISEMBOWEL YOU GENTLY...AND EAT YOUR HEART.
FIGHT!!
HOLY...

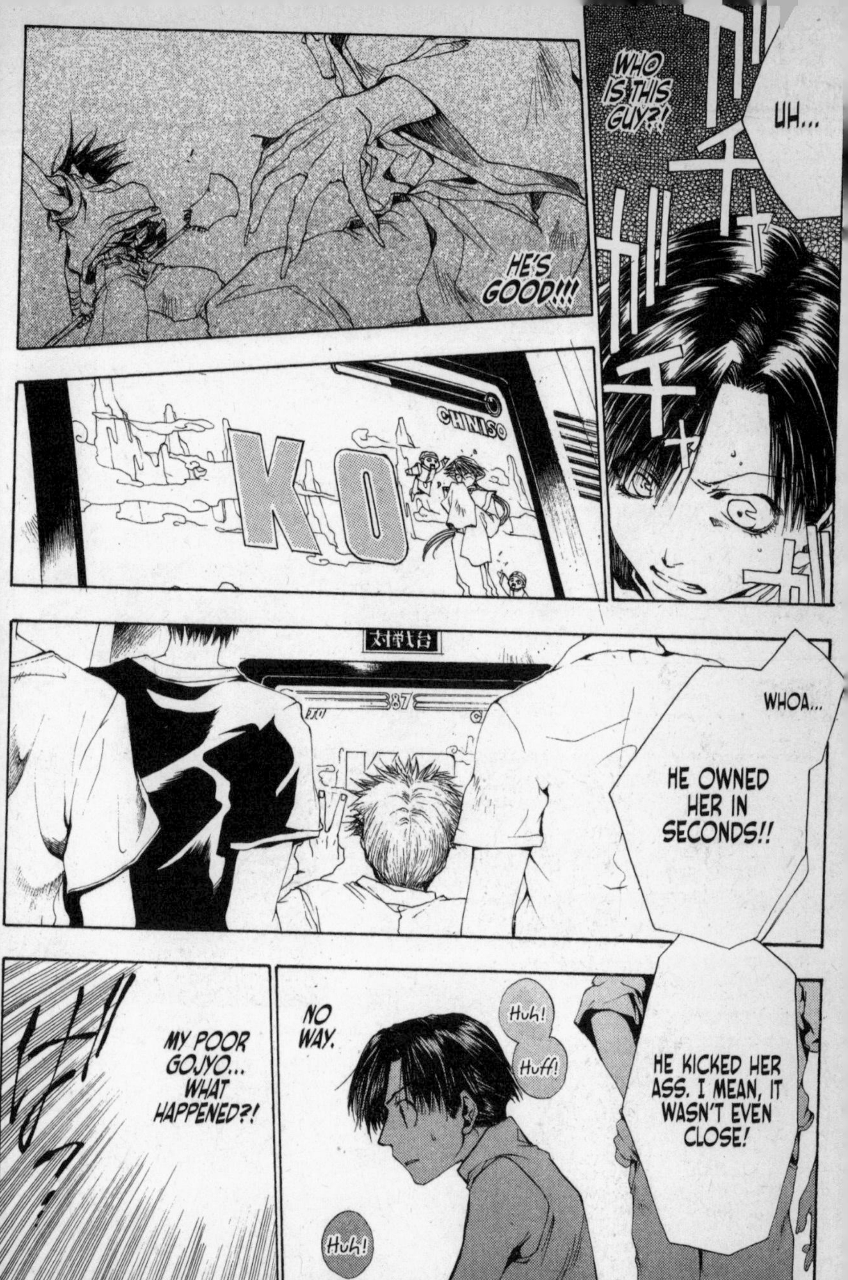
WHO IS THIS GUY?!
UH...
HE'S GOOD!!!
CHINISO
KO
対戦台
87
WHOA...
HE OWNED HER IN SECONDS!!
HE KICKED HER ASS. I MEAN, IT WASN'T EVEN CLOSE!
Huh!
Huff!
NO WAY.
Huh!
MY POOR GOJYO... WHAT HAPPENED?!

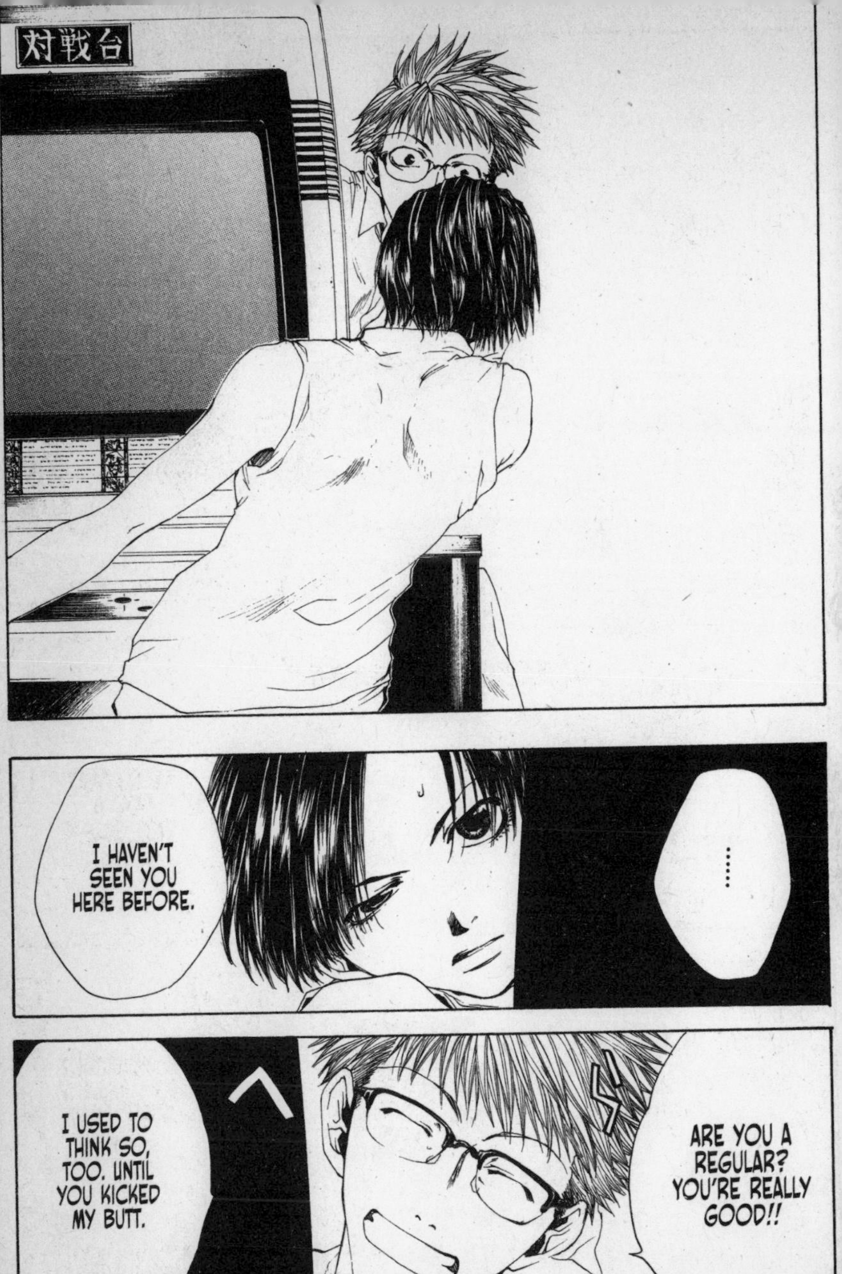
対戦台
……
I HAVEN'T SEEN YOU HERE BEFORE.
ARE YOU A REGULAR? YOU'RE REALLY GOOD!!
へ
I USED TO THINK SO, TOO. UNTIL YOU KICKED MY BUTT.

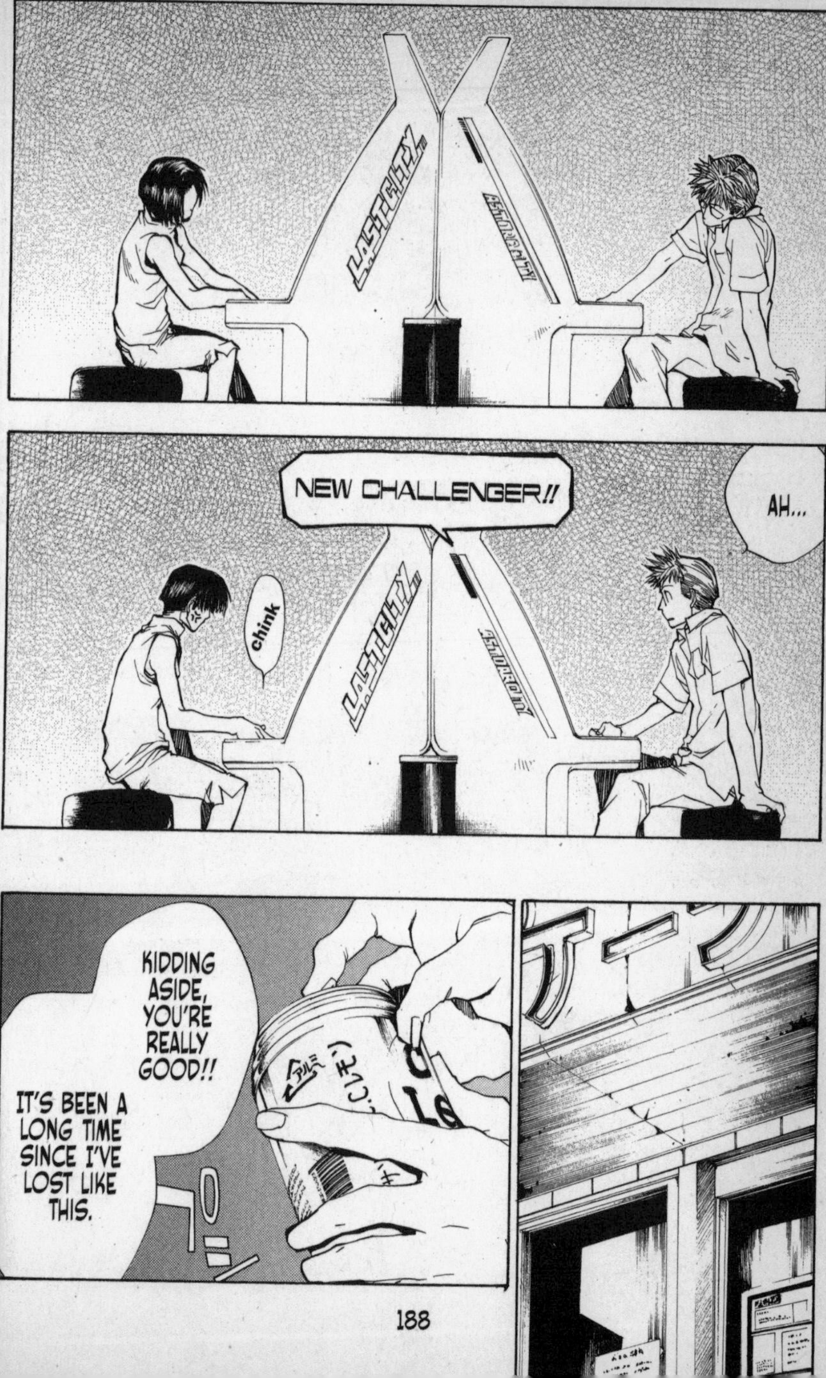
AH...
NEW CHALLENGER!!
chink
KIDDING ASIDE, YOU'RE REALLY GOOD!!
IT'S BEEN A LONG TIME SINCE I'VE LOST LIKE THIS.

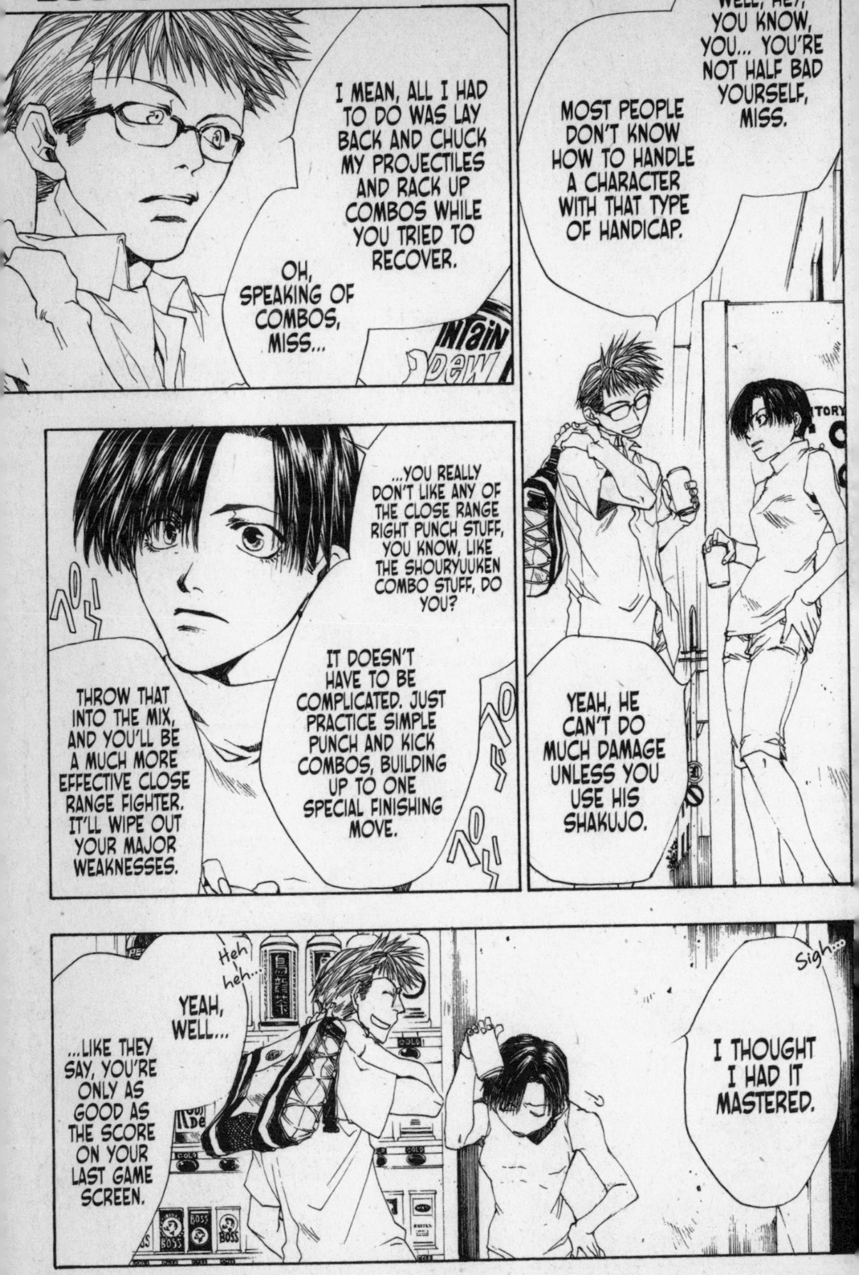
WELL, HEY, YOU KNOW, YOU... YOU'RE NOT HALF BAD YOURSELF, MISS.
MOST PEOPLE DON'T KNOW HOW TO HANDLE A CHARACTER WITH THAT TYPE OF HANDICAP.
YEAH, HE CAN'T DO MUCH DAMAGE UNLESS YOU USE HIS SHAKUJO.
I MEAN, ALL I HAD TO DO WAS LAY BACK AND CHUCK MY PROJECTILES AND RACK UP COMBOS WHILE YOU TRIED TO RECOVER.
OH, SPEAKING OF COMBOS, MISS...
...YOU REALLY DON'T LIKE ANY OF THE CLOSE RANGE RIGHT PUNCH STUFF, YOU KNOW, LIKE THE SHOURYUUKEN COMBO STUFF, DO YOU?
IT DOESN'T HAVE TO BE COMPLICATED. JUST PRACTICE SIMPLE PUNCH AND KICK COMBOS, BUILDING UP TO ONE SPECIAL FINISHING MOVE.
THROW THAT INTO THE MIX, AND YOU'LL BE A MUCH MORE EFFECTIVE CLOSE RANGE FIGHTER. IT'LL WIPE OUT YOUR MAJOR WEAKNESSES.
Sigh...
I THOUGHT I HAD IT MASTERED.
Heh heh...
YEAH, WELL...
...LIKE THEY SAY, YOU'RE ONLY AS GOOD AS THE SCORE ON YOUR LAST GAME SCREEN.

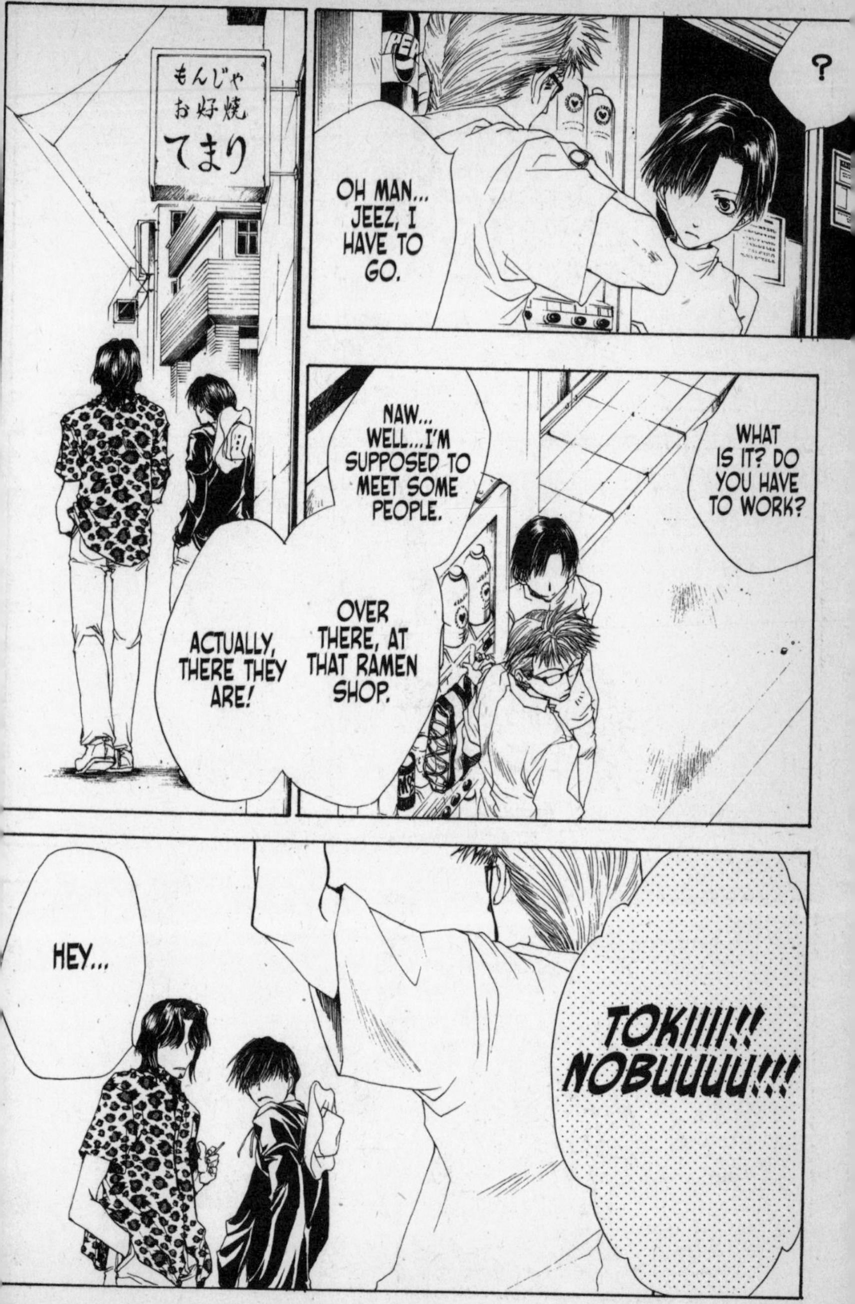
?
OH MAN... JEEZ, I HAVE TO GO.
WHAT IS IT? DO YOU HAVE TO WORK?
NAW... WELL...I'M SUPPOSED TO MEET SOME PEOPLE.
OVER THERE, AT THAT RAMEN SHOP.
もんじゃ
お好焼
てまり
ACTUALLY, THERE THEY ARE!
TOKIIII!! NOBUUUU!!!
HEY...

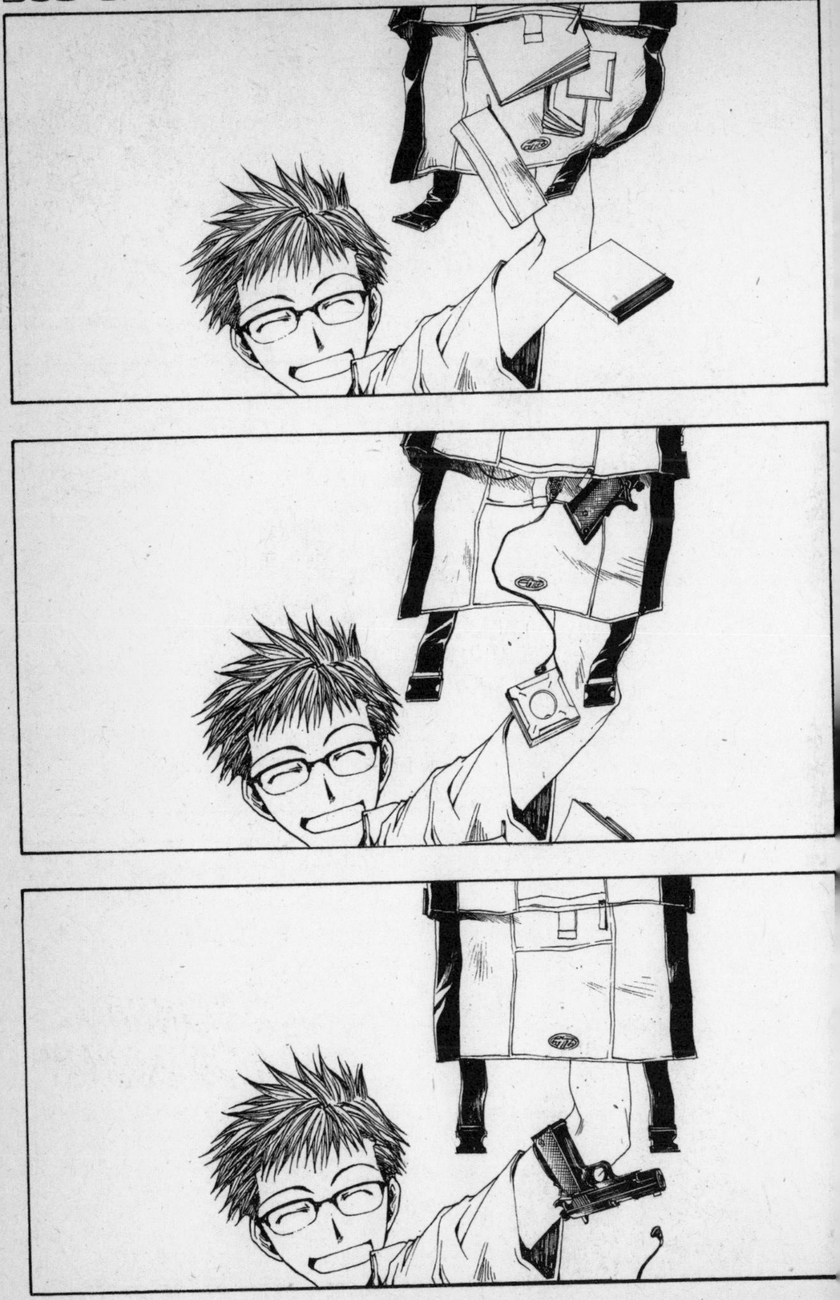

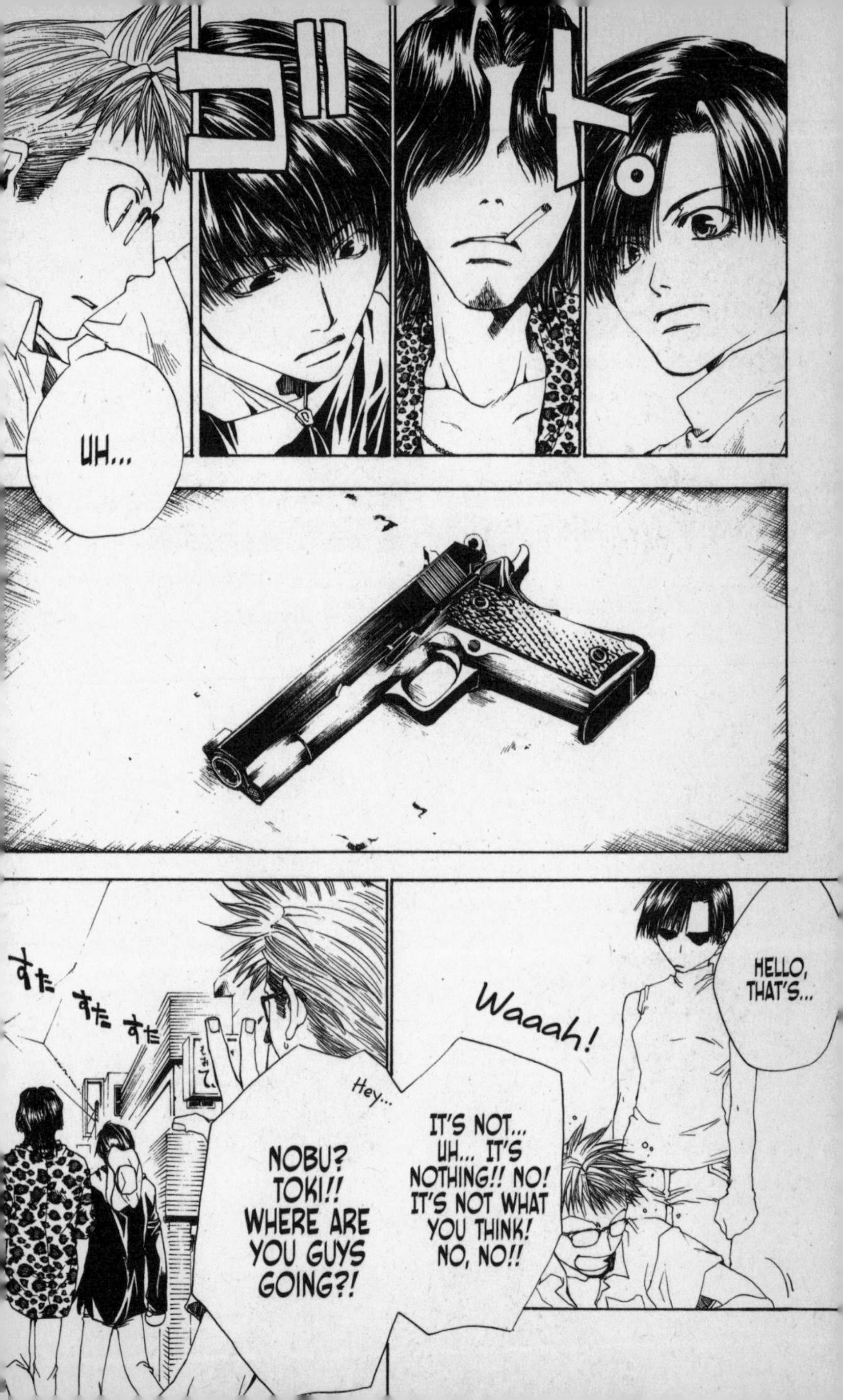
ゴト
UH...
HELLO, THAT'S...
Waaah!
IT'S NOT... UH... IT'S NOTHING!! NO! IT'S NOT WHAT YOU THINK! NO, NO!!
Hey...
NOBU? TOKI!! WHERE ARE YOU GUYS GOING?!
すた すた すた

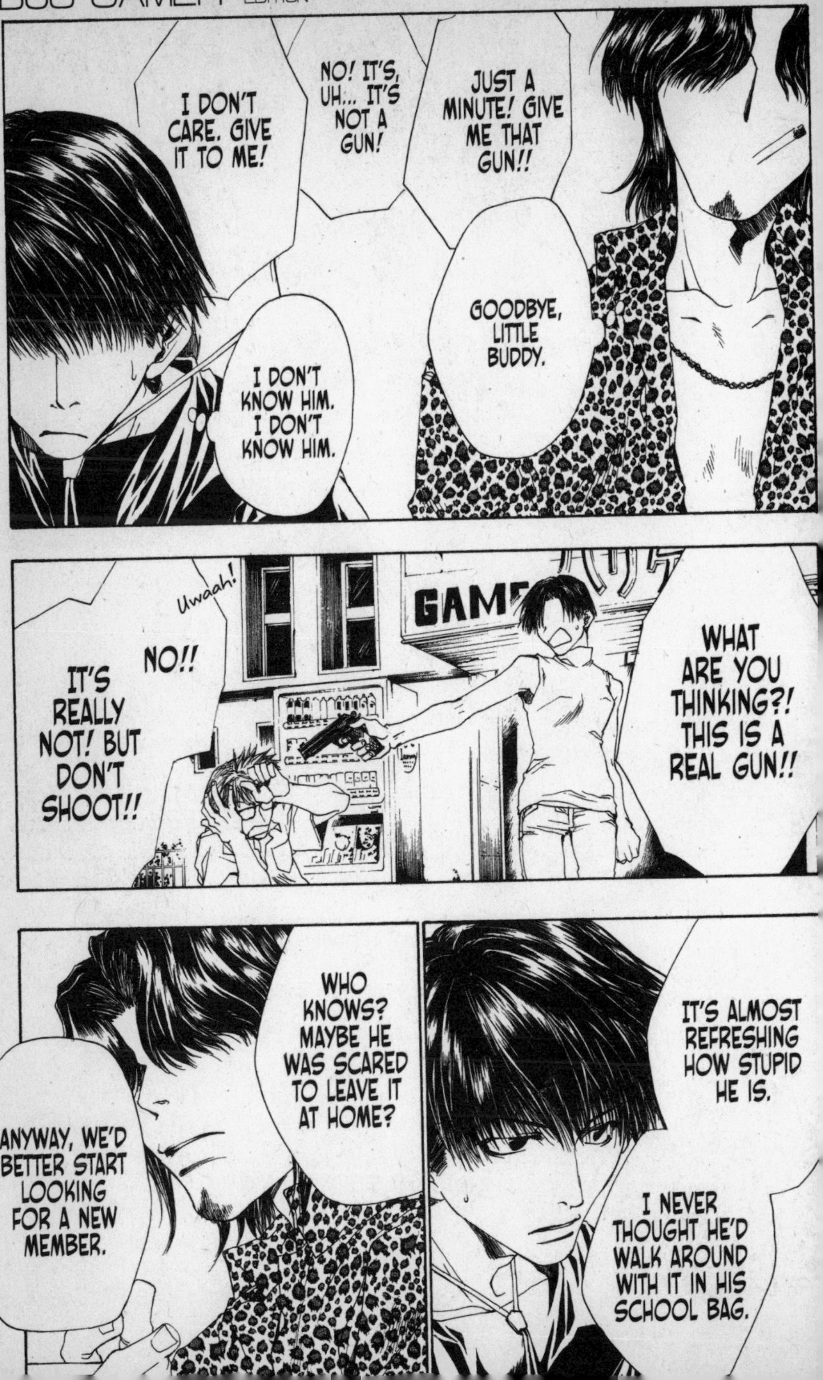
JUST A MINUTE! GIVE ME THAT GUN!!
NO! IT'S, UH... IT'S NOT A GUN!
I DON'T CARE. GIVE IT TO ME!
GOODBYE, LITTLE BUDDY.
I DON'T KNOW HIM. I DON'T KNOW HIM.
WHAT ARE YOU THINKING?! THIS IS A REAL GUN!!
Uwaah!
NO!!
IT'S REALLY NOT! BUT DON'T SHOOT!!
IT'S ALMOST REFRESHING HOW STUPID HE IS.
I NEVER THOUGHT HE'D WALK AROUND WITH IT IN HIS SCHOOL BAG.
WHO KNOWS? MAYBE HE WAS SCARED TO LEAVE IT AT HOME?
ANYWAY, WE'D BETTER START LOOKING FOR A NEW MEMBER.

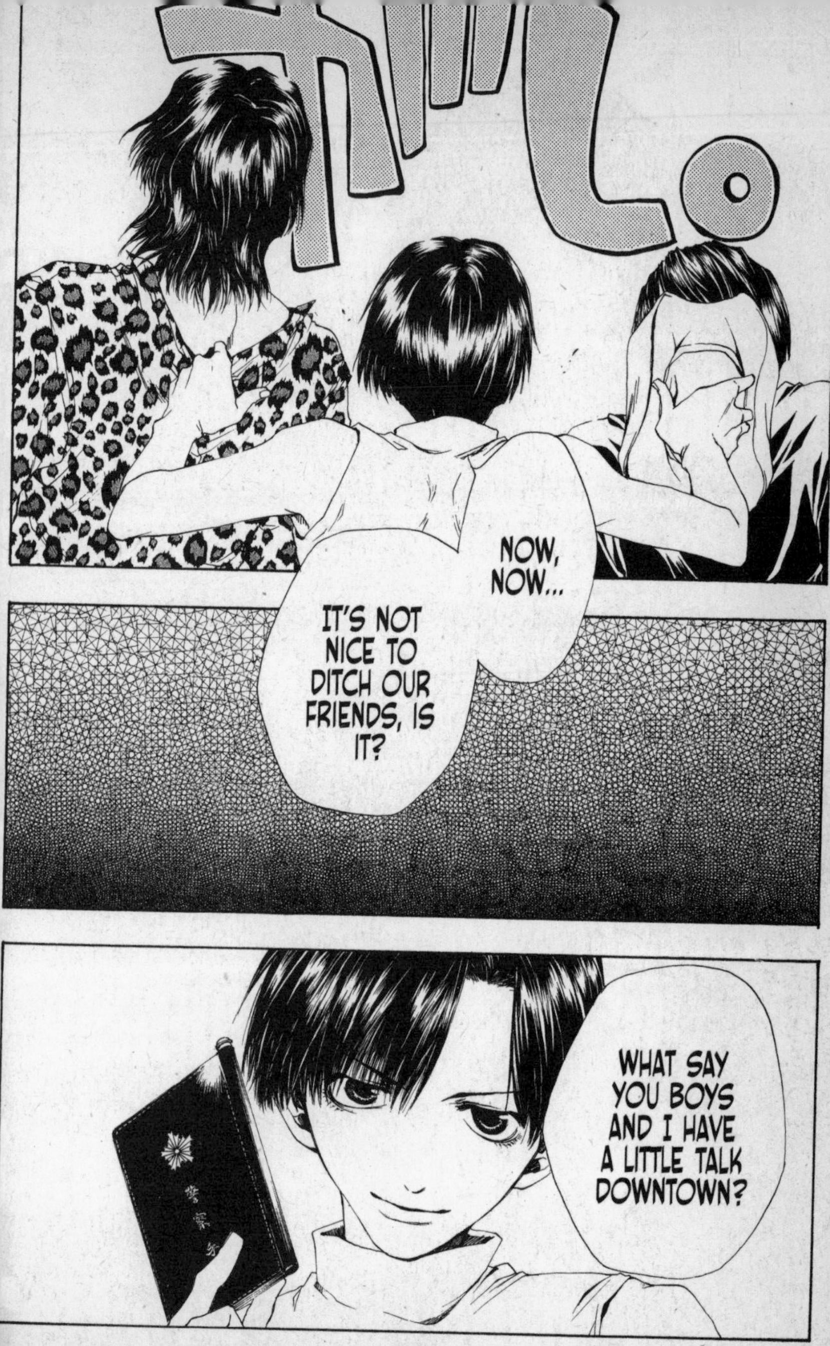
NOW, NOW...
IT'S NOT NICE TO DITCH OUR FRIENDS, IS IT?
WHAT SAY YOU BOYS AND I HAVE A LITTLE TALK DOWNTOWN?

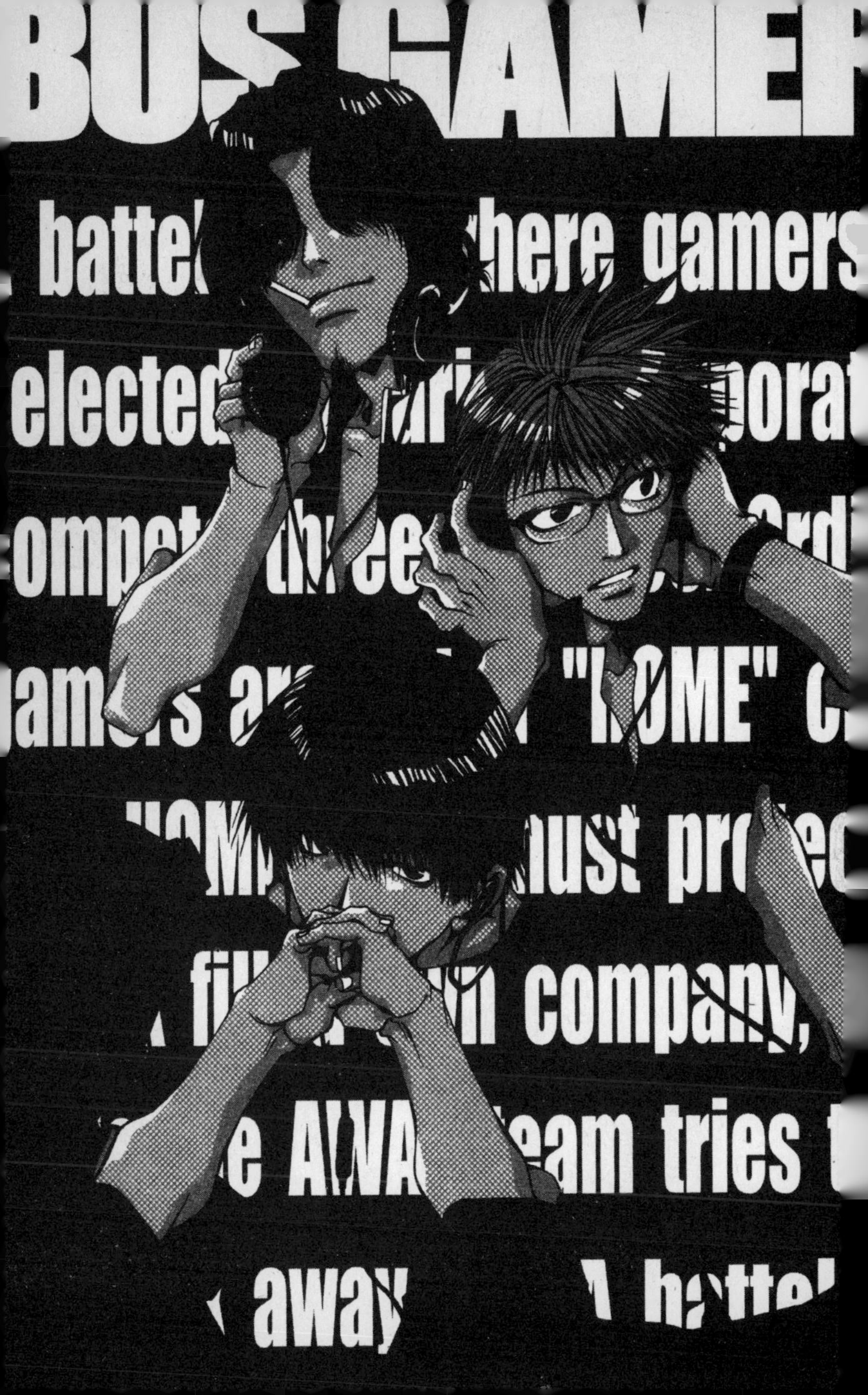
BUS GAMER
battel here gamers
elected
HOME
company,
team tries
away

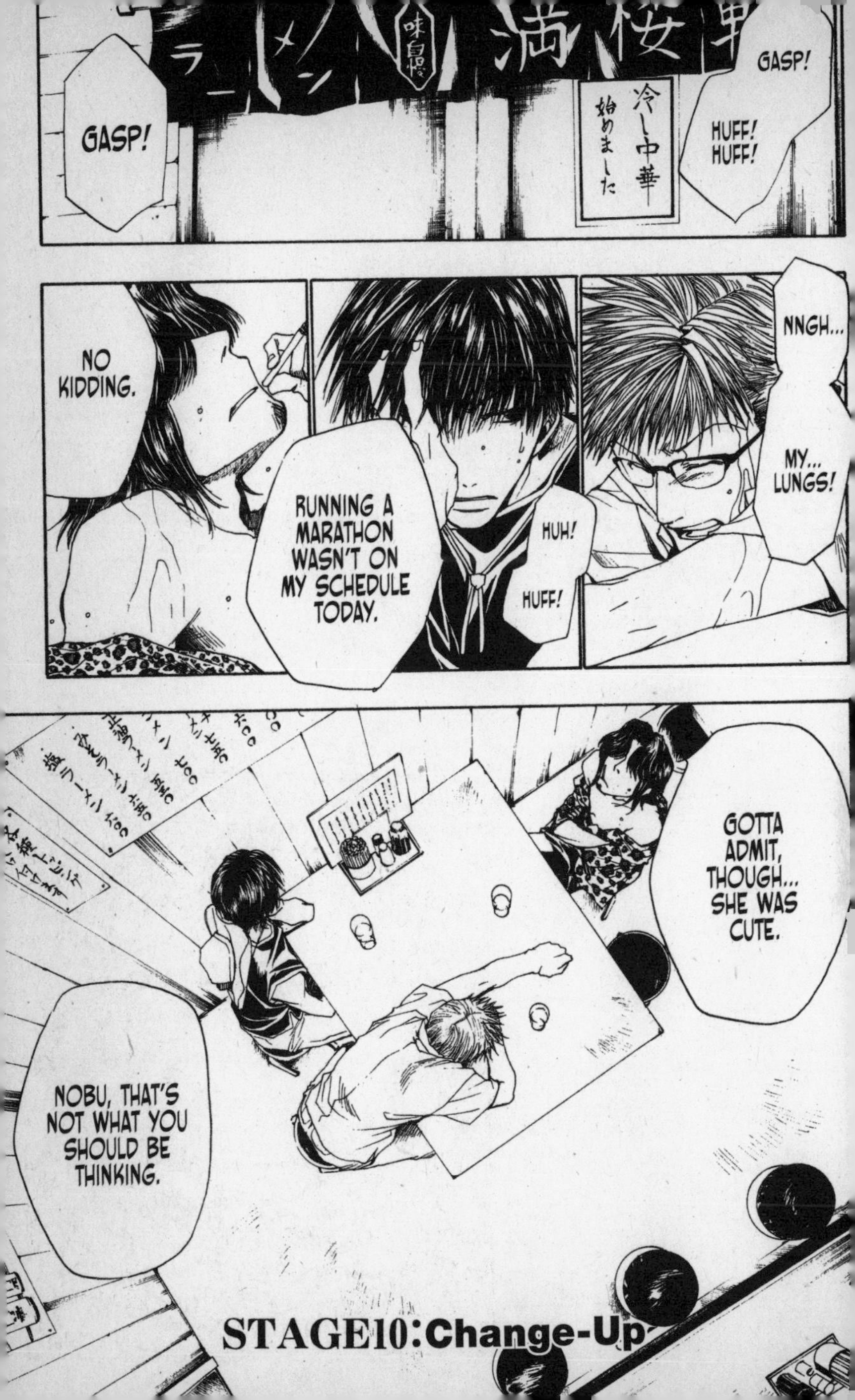
GASP!
HUFF! HUFF!
冷し中華始めました
GASP!
NNGH...
MY... LUNGS!
HUH!
HUFF!
RUNNING A MARATHON WASN'T ON MY SCHEDULE TODAY.
NO KIDDING.
GOTTA ADMIT, THOUGH... SHE WAS CUTE.
NOBU, THAT'S NOT WHAT YOU SHOULD BE THINKING.
STAGE10: Change-Up

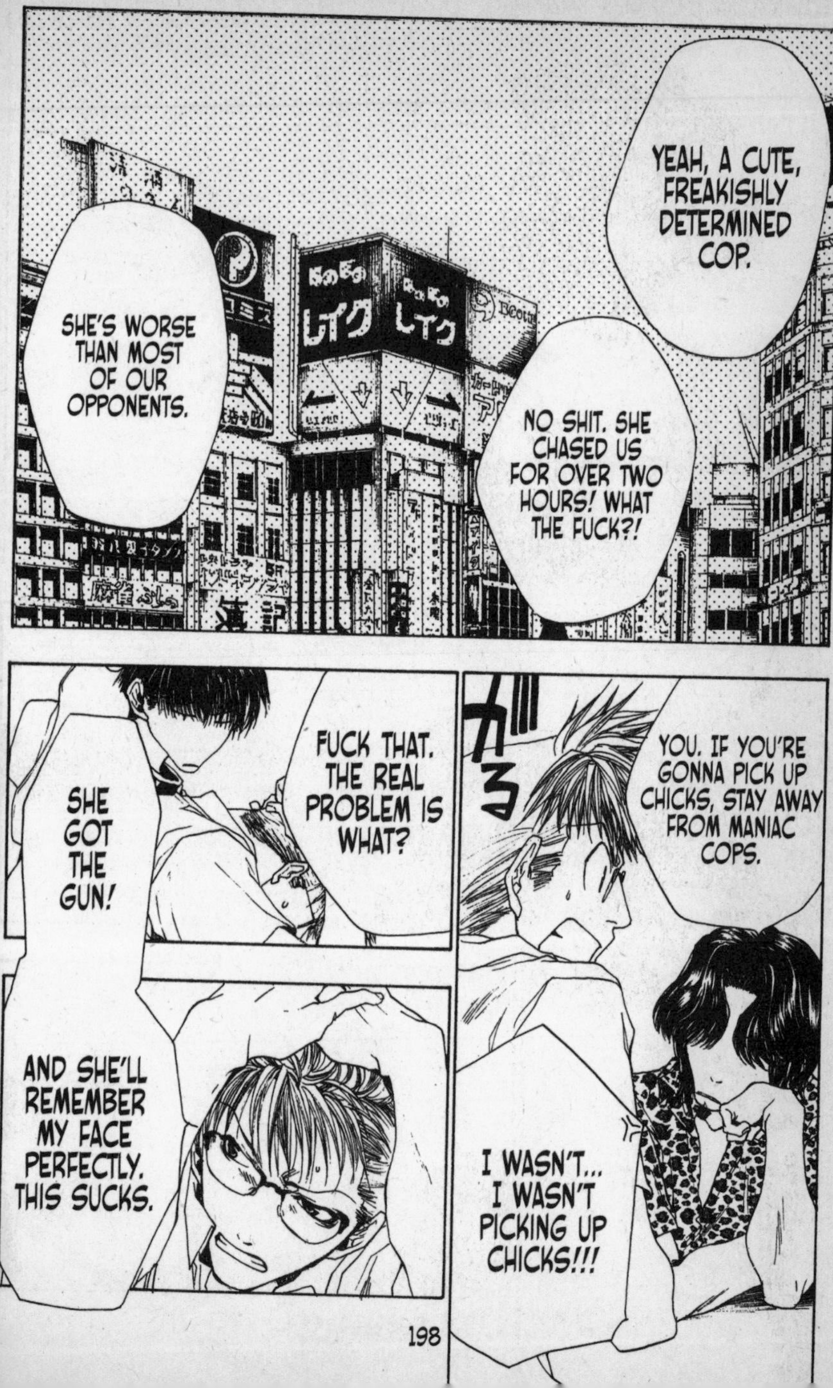

YEAH, A CUTE, FREAKISHLY DETERMINED COP.
NO SHIT. SHE CHASED US FOR OVER TWO HOURS! WHAT THE FUCK?!
SHE'S WORSE THAN MOST OF OUR OPPONENTS.
YOU. IF YOU'RE GONNA PICK UP CHICKS, STAY AWAY FROM MANIAC COPS.
I WASN'T... I WASN'T PICKING UP CHICKS!!!
FUCK THAT. THE REAL PROBLEM IS WHAT?
SHE GOT THE GUN!
AND SHE'LL REMEMBER MY FACE PERFECTLY. THIS SUCKS.

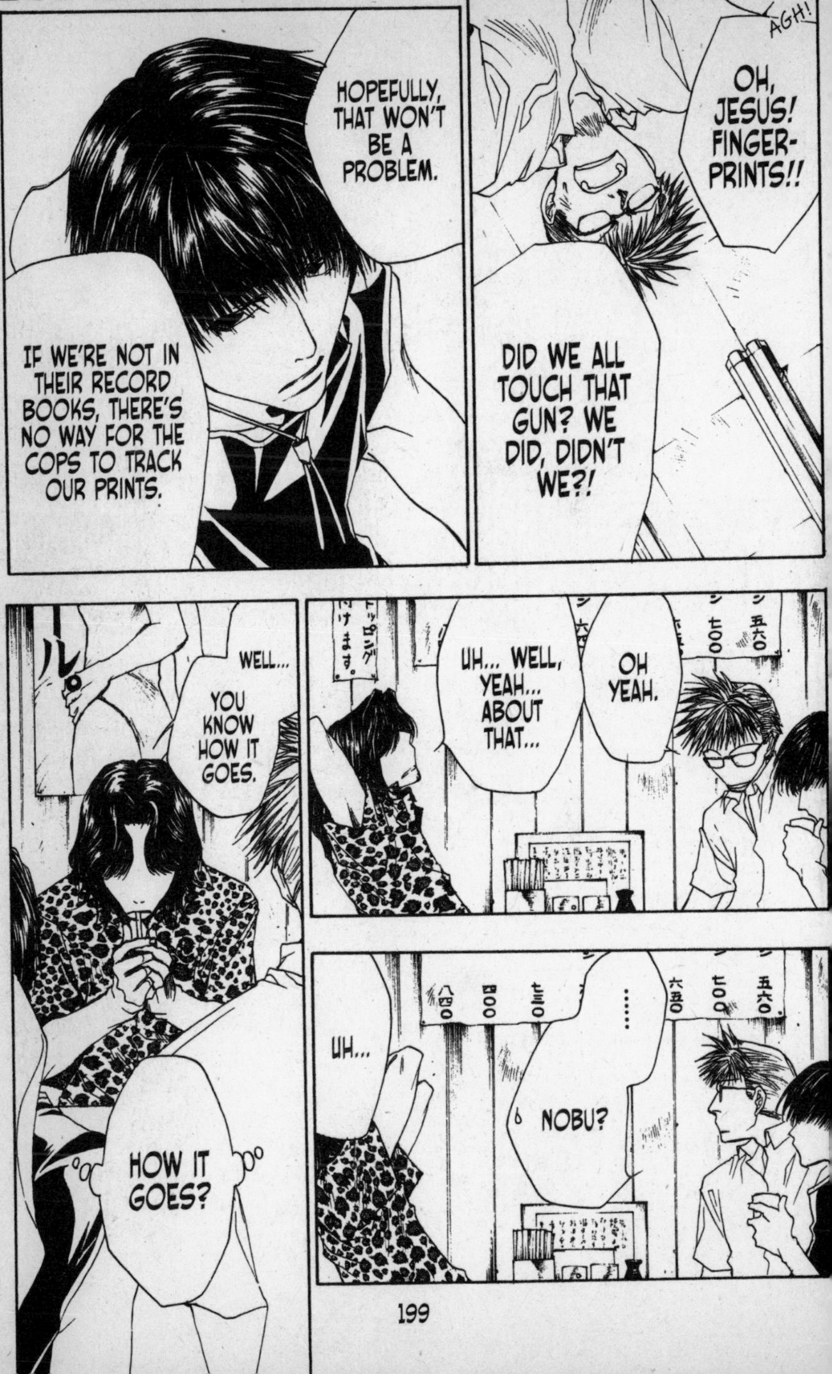
AGH!
OH, JESUS! FINGER-PRINTS!!
DID WE ALL TOUCH THAT GUN? WE DID, DIDN'T WE?!
HOPEFULLY, THAT WON'T BE A PROBLEM.
IF WE'RE NOT IN THEIR RECORD BOOKS, THERE'S NO WAY FOR THE COPS TO TRACK OUR PRINTS.
OH YEAH.
UH... WELL, YEAH... ABOUT THAT...
......
NOBU?
UH...
WELL...
YOU KNOW HOW IT GOES.
HOW IT GOES?

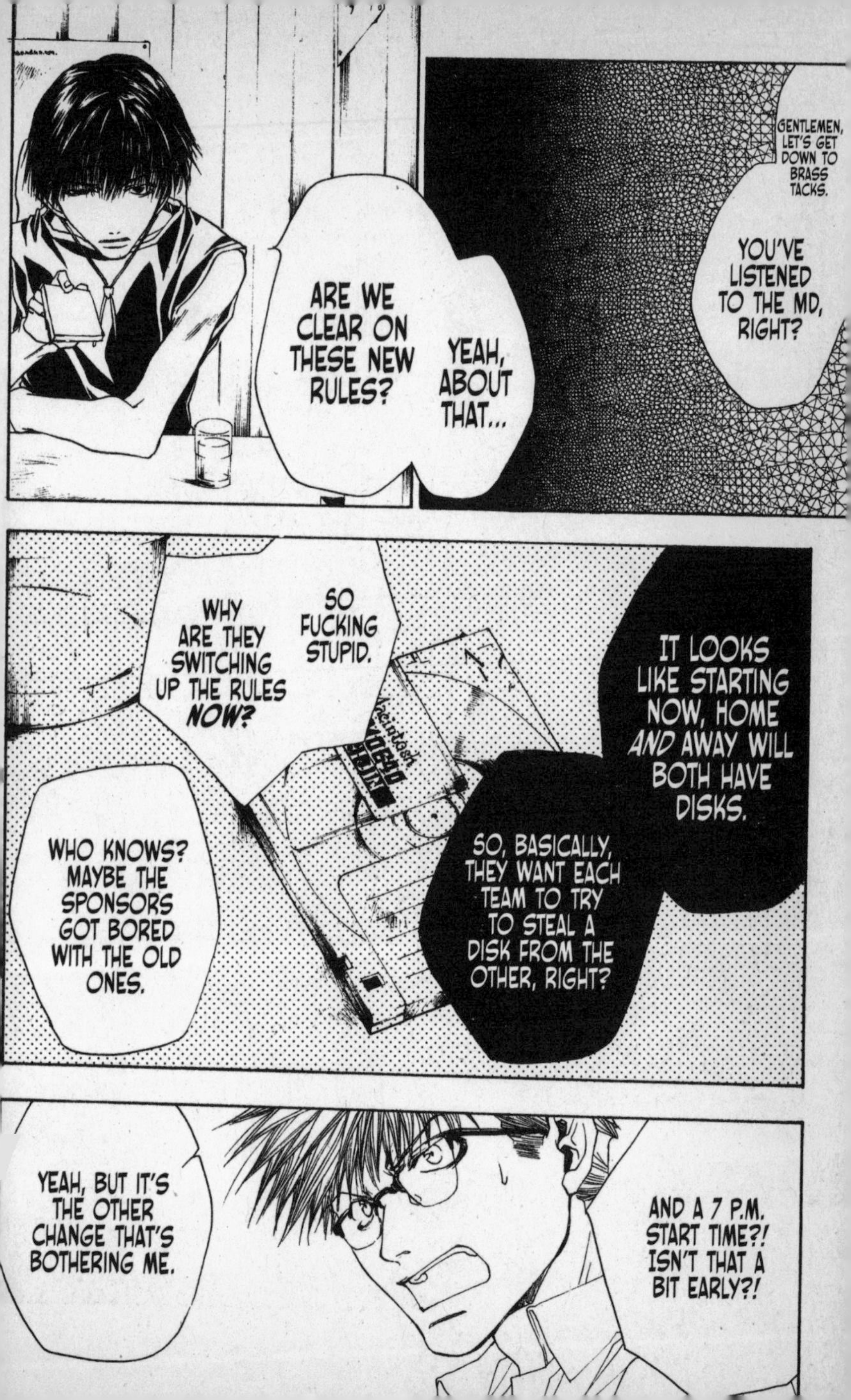
GENTLEMEN, LET'S GET DOWN TO BRASS TACKS.
YOU'VE LISTENED TO THE MD, RIGHT?
YEAH, ABOUT THAT...
ARE WE CLEAR ON THESE NEW RULES?
IT LOOKS LIKE STARTING NOW, HOME *AND* AWAY WILL BOTH HAVE DISKS.
SO, BASICALLY, THEY WANT EACH TEAM TO TRY TO STEAL A DISK FROM THE OTHER, RIGHT?
SO FUCKING STUPID.
WHY ARE THEY SWITCHING UP THE RULES *NOW?*
WHO KNOWS? MAYBE THE SPONSORS GOT BORED WITH THE OLD ONES.
AND A 7 P.M. START TIME?! ISN'T THAT A BIT EARLY?!
YEAH, BUT IT'S THE OTHER CHANGE THAT'S BOTHERING ME.

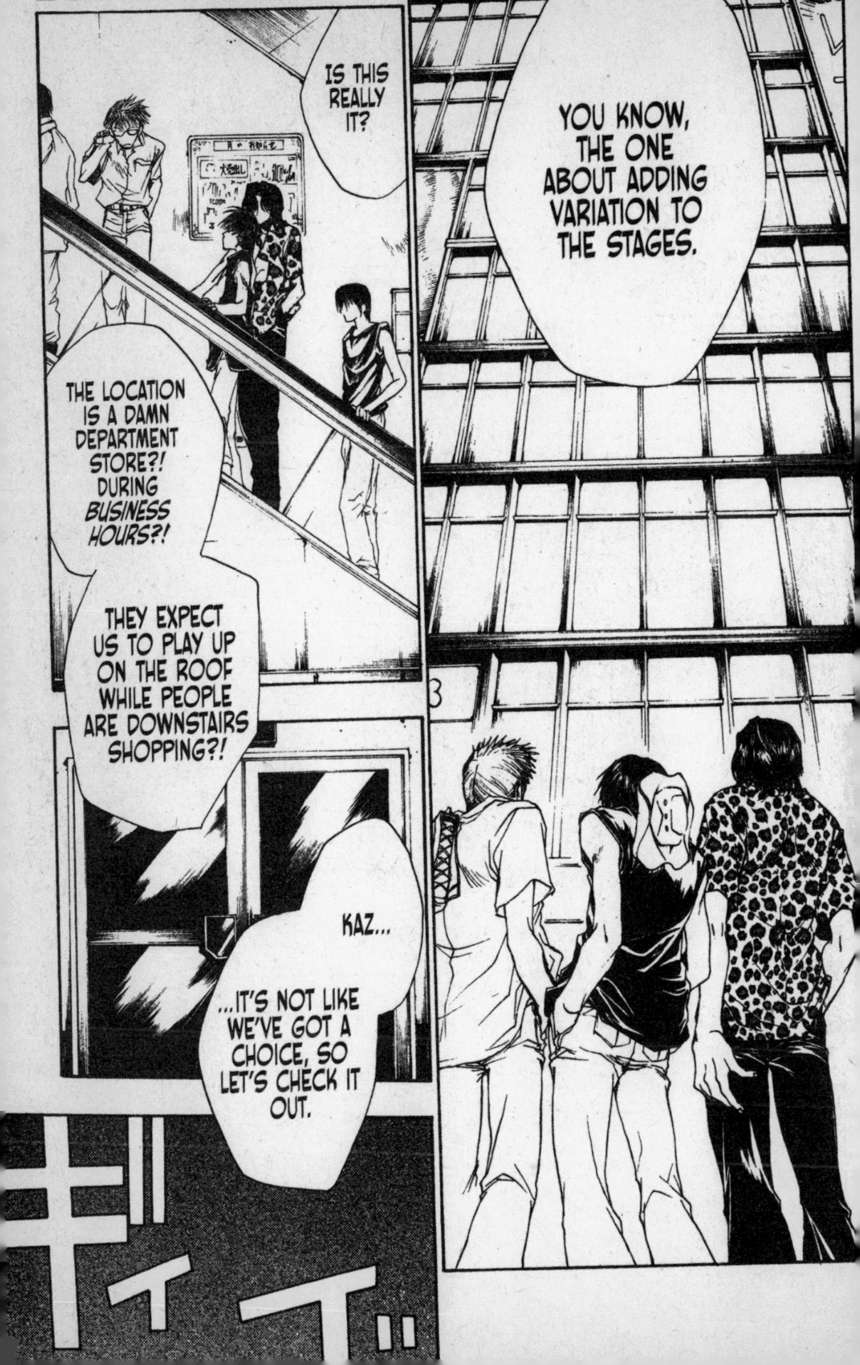
YOU KNOW, THE ONE ABOUT ADDING VARIATION TO THE STAGES.
IS THIS REALLY IT?
THE LOCATION IS A DAMN DEPARTMENT STORE?! DURING *BUSINESS HOURS?!*
THEY EXPECT US TO PLAY UP ON THE ROOF WHILE PEOPLE ARE DOWNSTAIRS SHOPPING?!
KAZ...
...IT'S NOT LIKE WE'VE GOT A CHOICE, SO LET'S CHECK IT OUT.
ギィイ

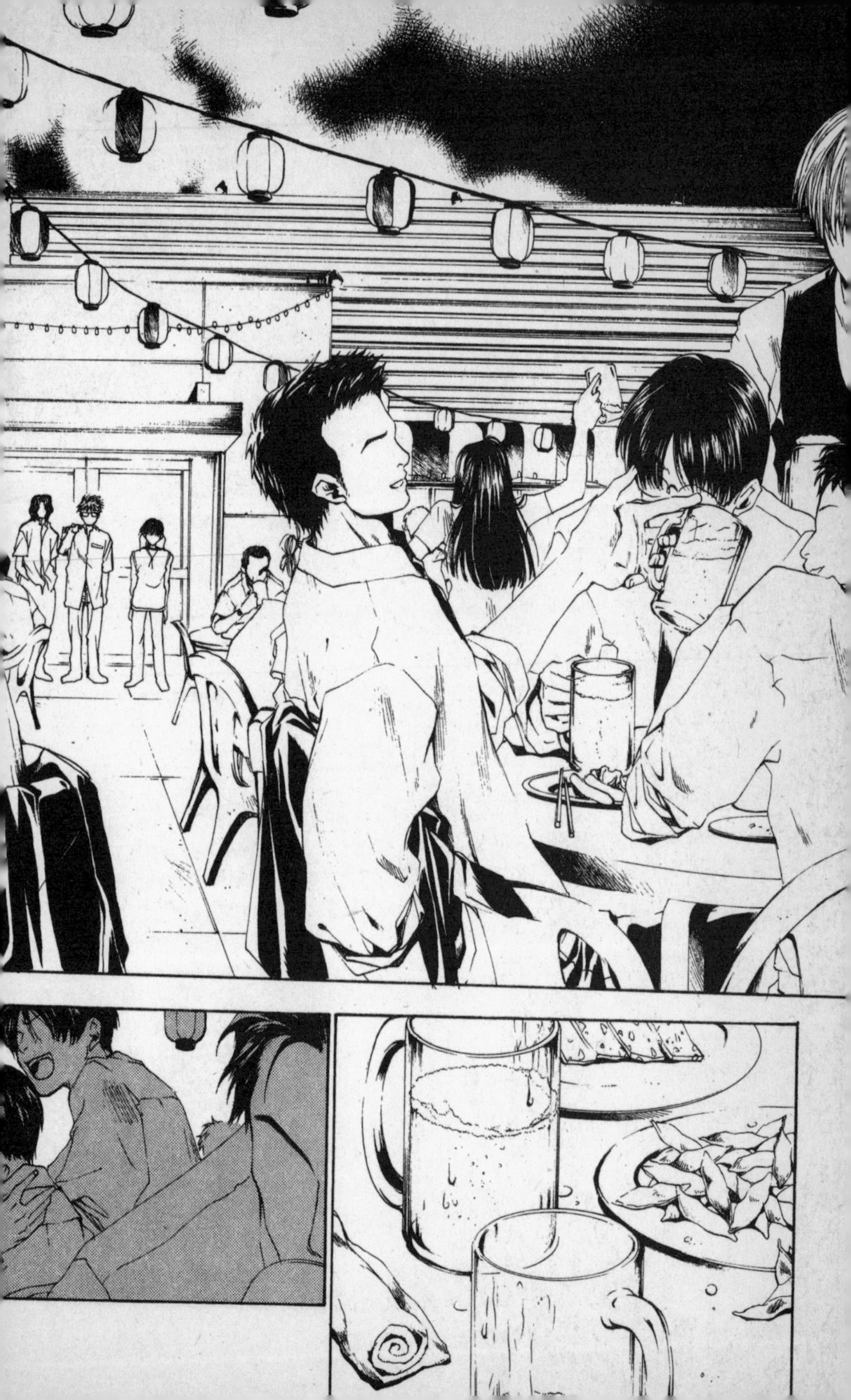

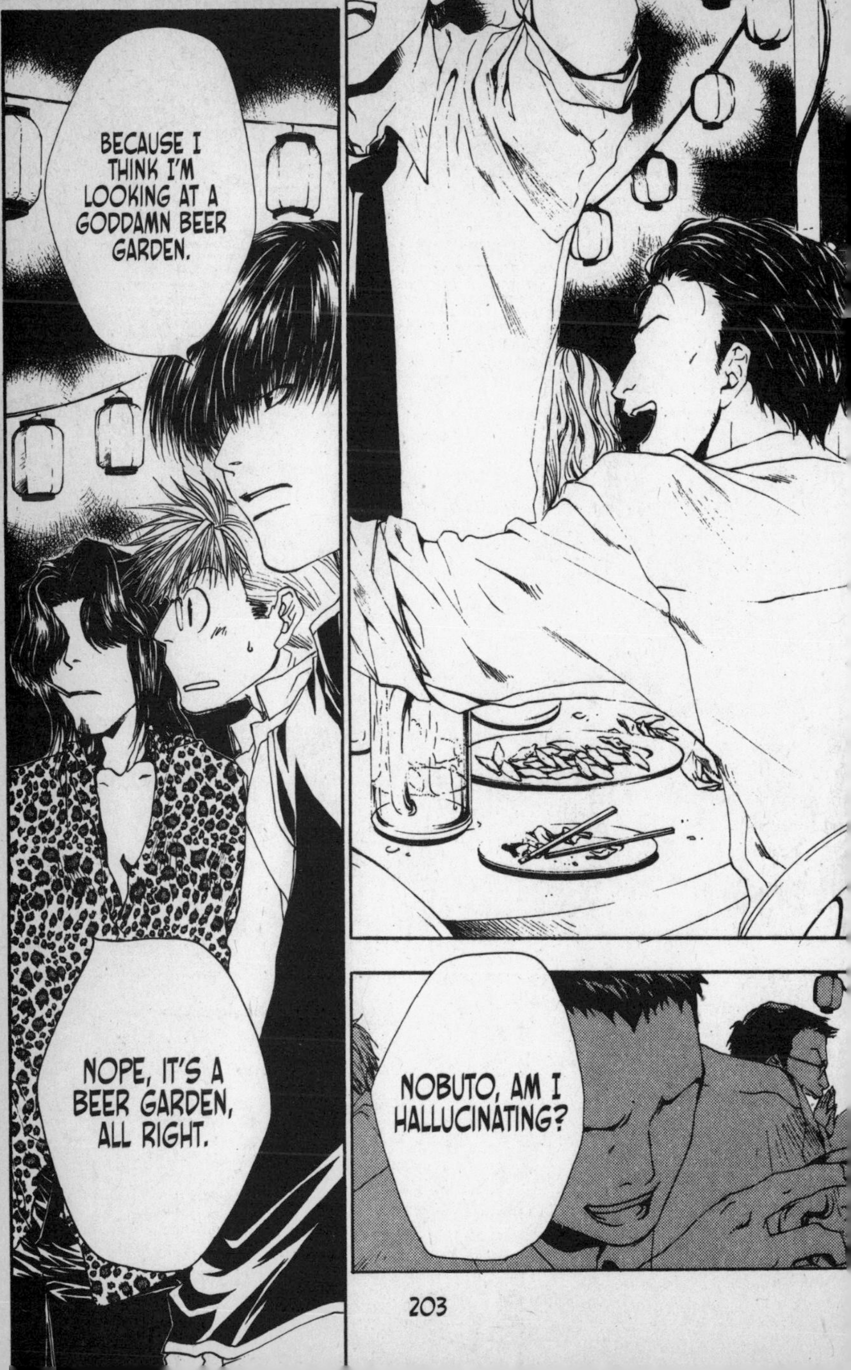
NOBUTO, AM I HALLUCINATING?
BECAUSE I THINK I'M LOOKING AT A GODDAMN BEER GARDEN.
NOPE, IT'S A BEER GARDEN, ALL RIGHT.

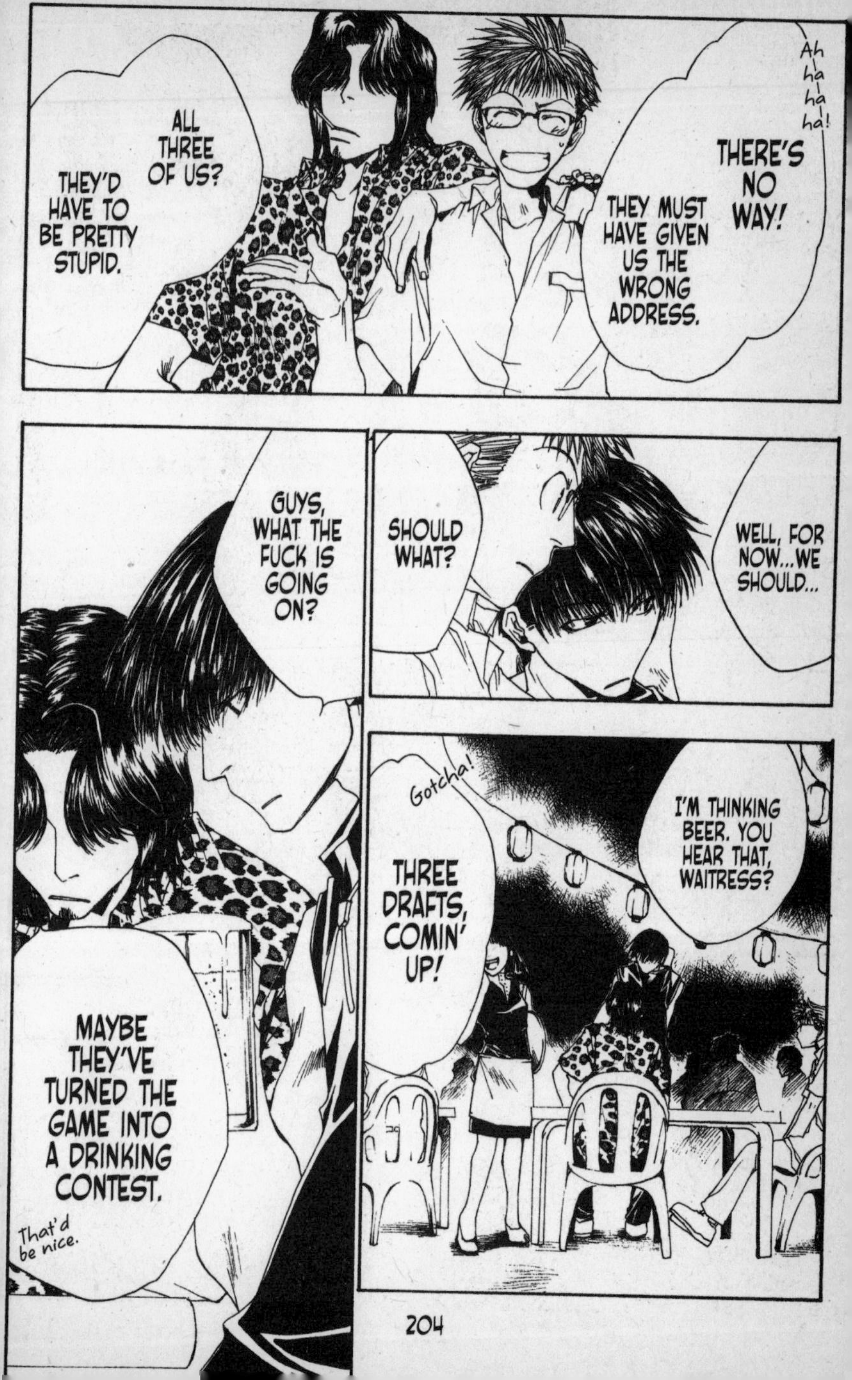
Ah ha ha ha!
THERE'S NO WAY!
THEY MUST HAVE GIVEN US THE WRONG ADDRESS.
ALL THREE OF US?
THEY'D HAVE TO BE PRETTY STUPID.
WELL, FOR NOW...WE SHOULD...
SHOULD WHAT?
I'M THINKING BEER. YOU HEAR THAT, WAITRESS?
Gotcha!
THREE DRAFTS, COMIN' UP!
GUYS, WHAT THE FUCK IS GOING ON?
MAYBE THEY'VE TURNED THE GAME INTO A DRINKING CONTEST.
That'd be nice.

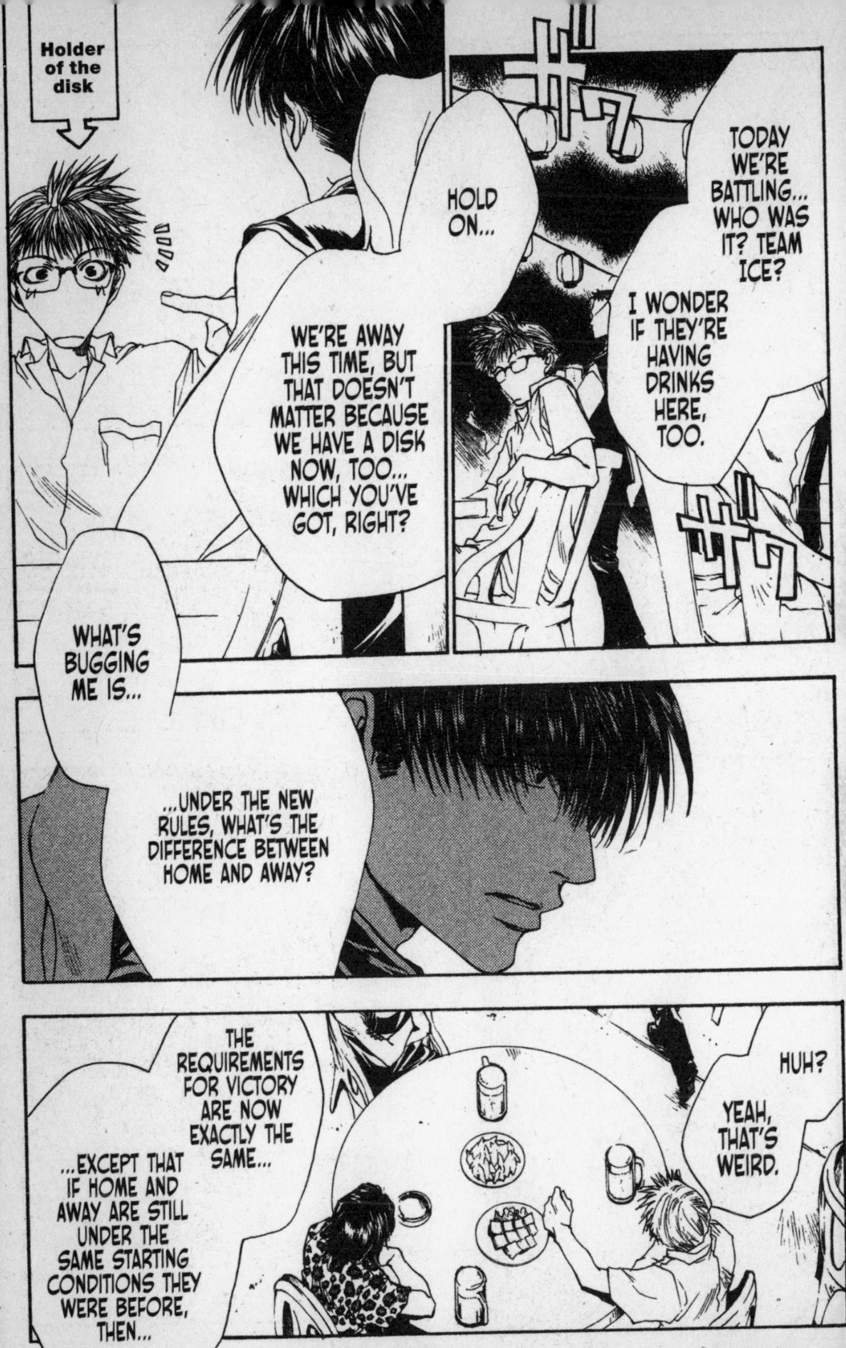
ギク
TODAY WE'RE BATTLING... WHO WAS IT? TEAM ICE?
I WONDER IF THEY'RE HAVING DRINKS HERE, TOO.
ギク
HOLD ON...
WE'RE AWAY THIS TIME, BUT THAT DOESN'T MATTER BECAUSE WE HAVE A DISK NOW, TOO... WHICH YOU'VE GOT, RIGHT?
Holder of the disk
WHAT'S BUGGING ME IS...
...UNDER THE NEW RULES, WHAT'S THE DIFFERENCE BETWEEN HOME AND AWAY?
HUH?
YEAH, THAT'S WEIRD.
THE REQUIREMENTS FOR VICTORY ARE NOW EXACTLY THE SAME...
...EXCEPT THAT IF HOME AND AWAY ARE STILL UNDER THE SAME STARTING CONDITIONS THEY WERE BEFORE, THEN...

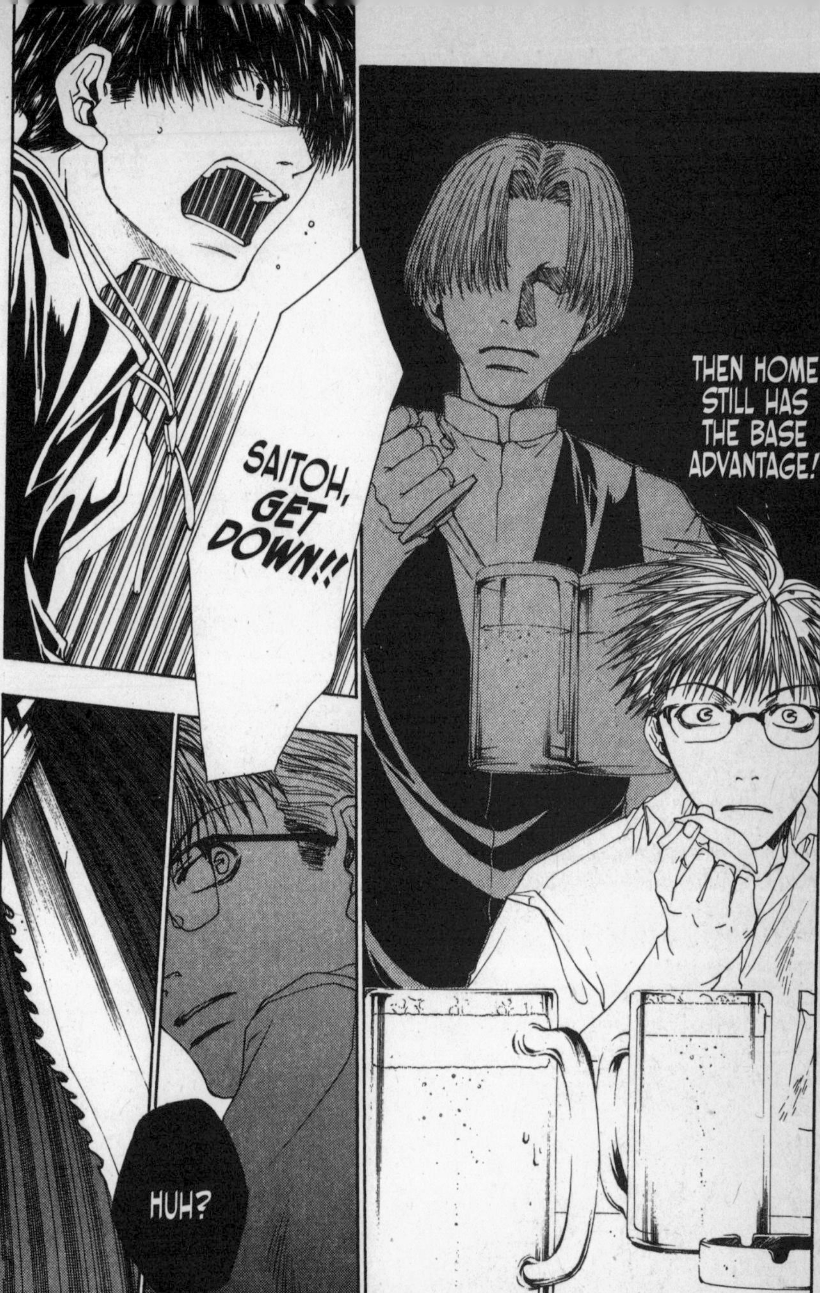
THEN HOME STILL HAS THE BASE ADVANTAGE!
SAITOH, GET DOWN!!
HUH?

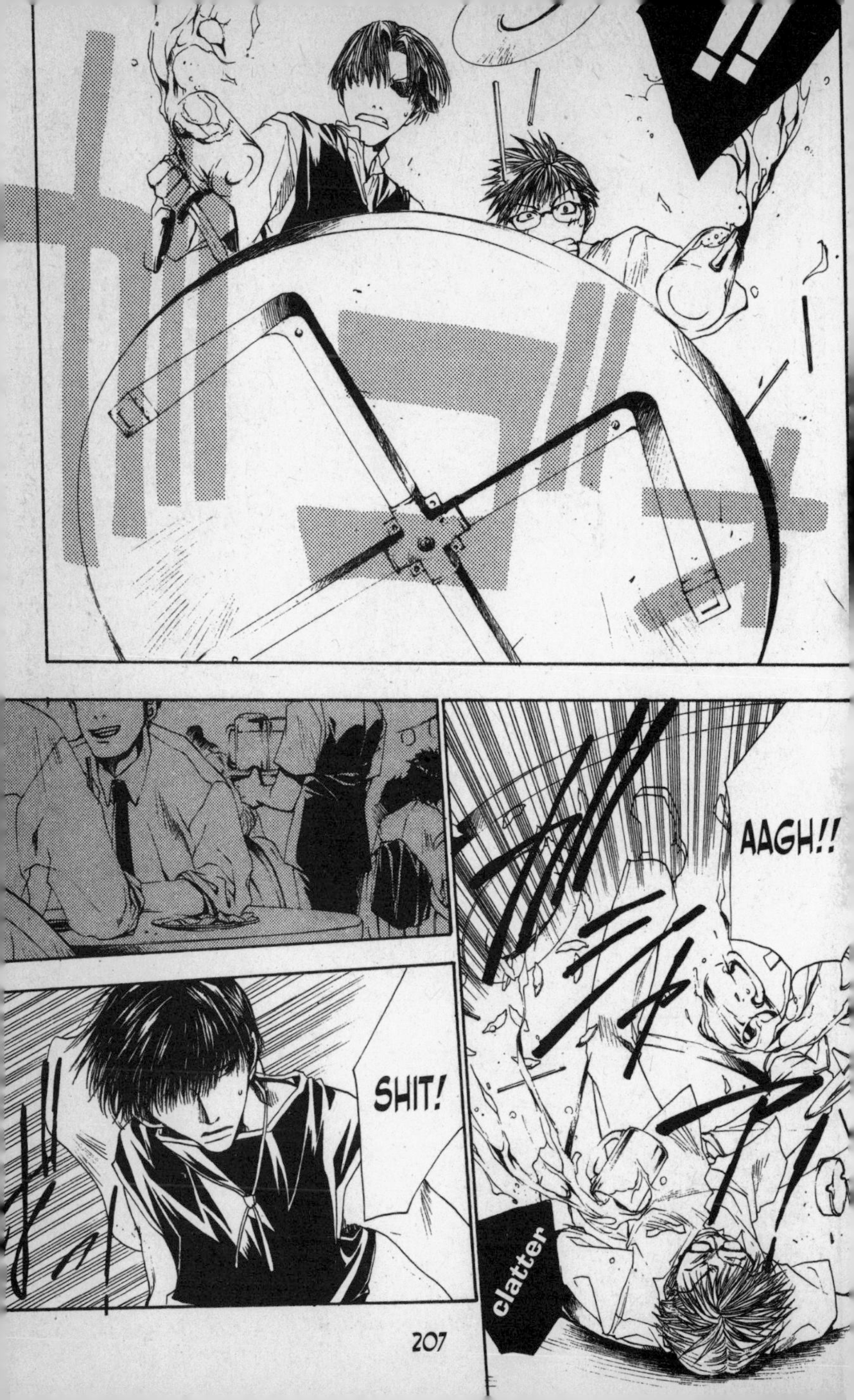
AAGH!!
clatter
SHIT!

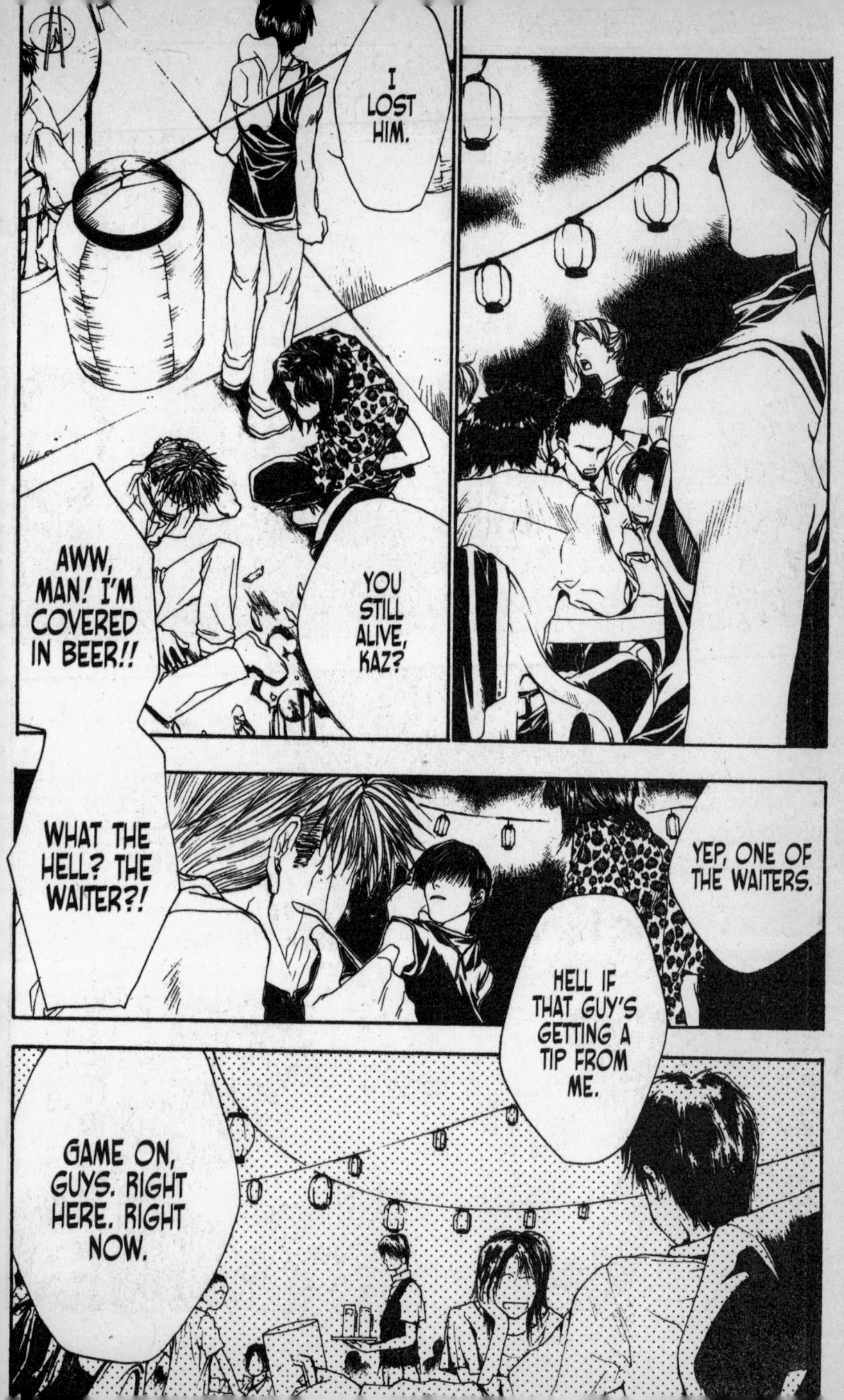

I LOST HIM.
YOU STILL ALIVE, KAZ?
AWW, MAN! I'M COVERED IN BEER!!
WHAT THE HELL? THE WAITER?!
YEP, ONE OF THE WAITERS.
HELL IF THAT GUY'S GETTING A TIP FROM ME.
GAME ON, GUYS. RIGHT HERE. RIGHT NOW.

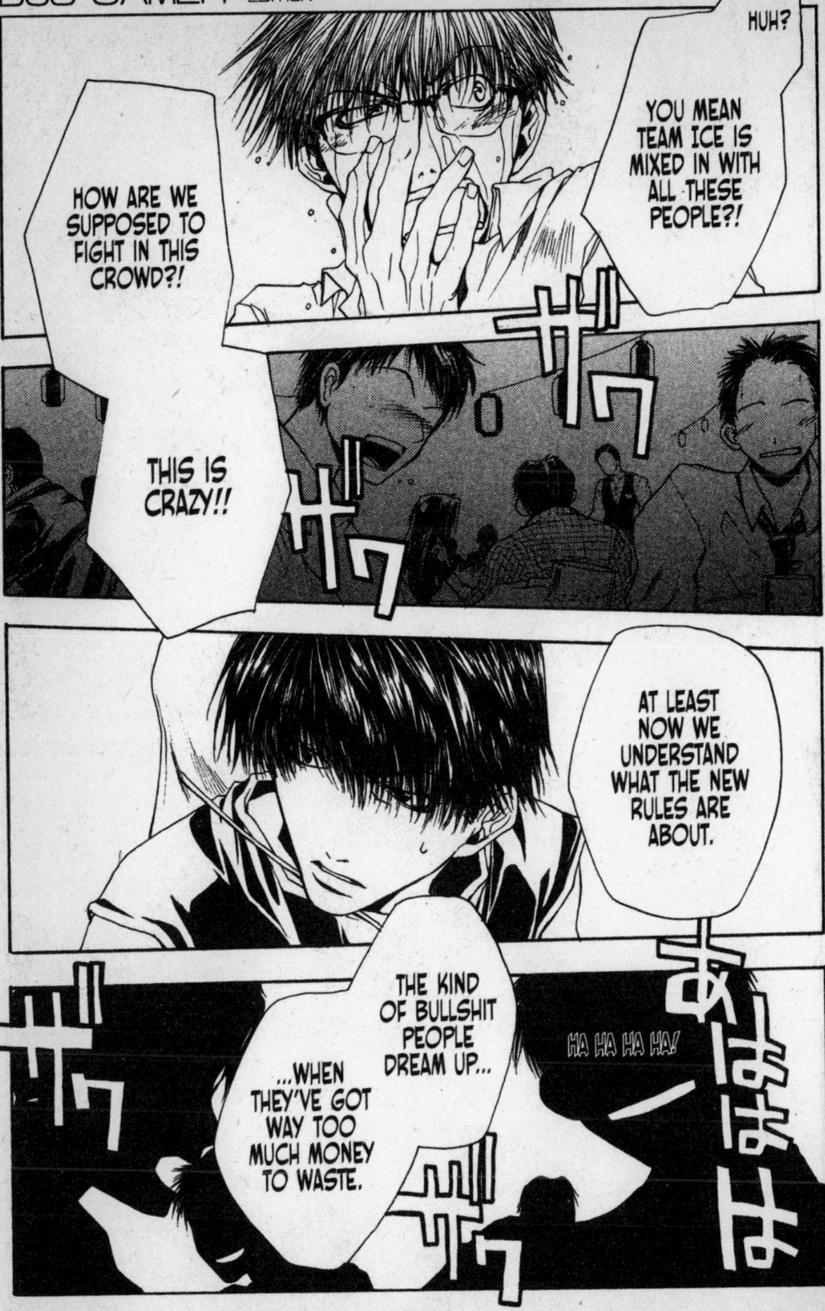
HUH?
YOU MEAN TEAM ICE IS MIXED IN WITH ALL THESE PEOPLE?!
HOW ARE WE SUPPOSED TO FIGHT IN THIS CROWD?!
ザワ
ザワ
THIS IS CRAZY!!
AT LEAST NOW WE UNDERSTAND WHAT THE NEW RULES ARE ABOUT.
HA HA HA HA!
THE KIND OF BULLSHIT PEOPLE DREAM UP...
...WHEN THEY'VE GOT WAY TOO MUCH MONEY TO WASTE.
ザワ
ザワ

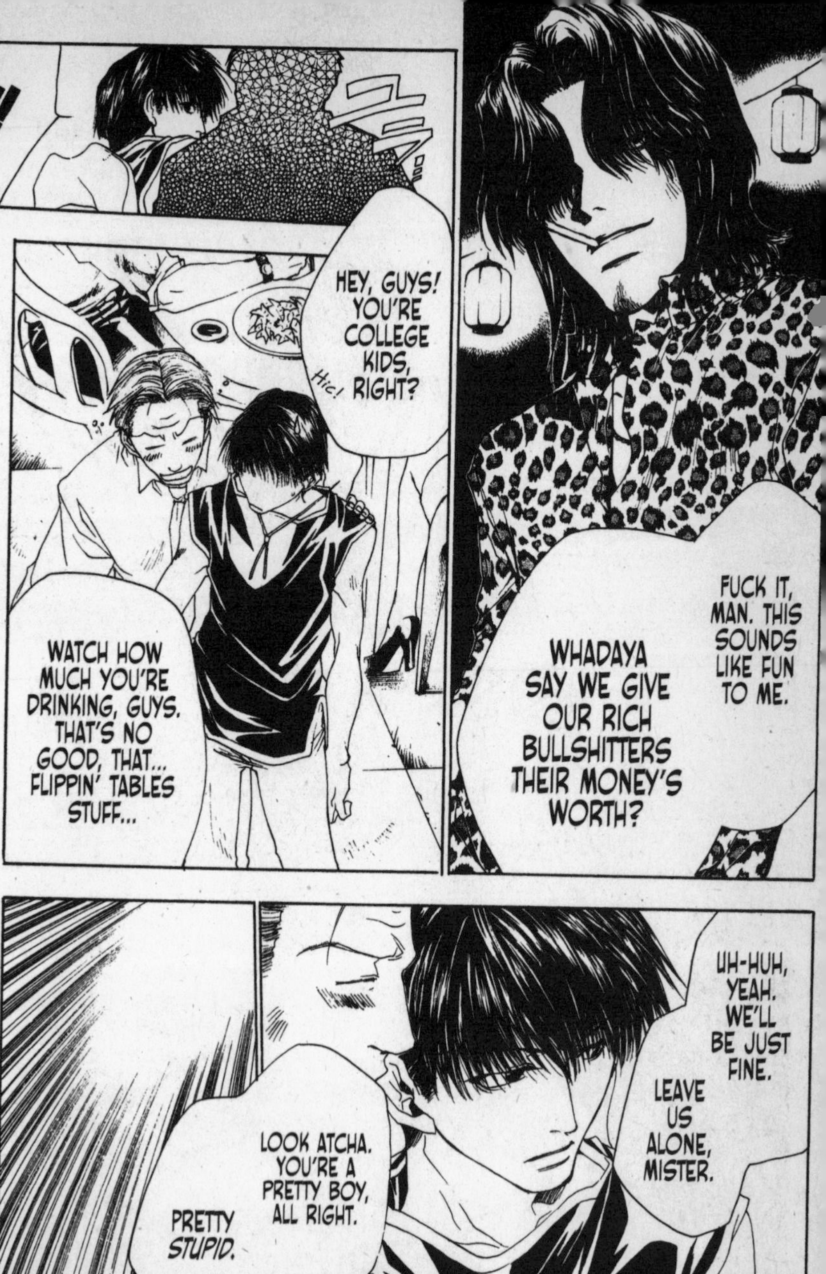
FUCK IT, MAN. THIS SOUNDS LIKE FUN TO ME.
WHADAYA SAY WE GIVE OUR RICH BULLSHITTERS THEIR MONEY'S WORTH?
!!
HEY, GUYS! YOU'RE COLLEGE KIDS, RIGHT?
Hic!
WATCH HOW MUCH YOU'RE DRINKING, GUYS. THAT'S NO GOOD, THAT... FLIPPIN' TABLES STUFF...
UH-HUH, YEAH. WE'LL BE JUST FINE.
LEAVE US ALONE, MISTER.
LOOK ATCHA. YOU'RE A PRETTY BOY, ALL RIGHT.
PRETTY *STUPID.*

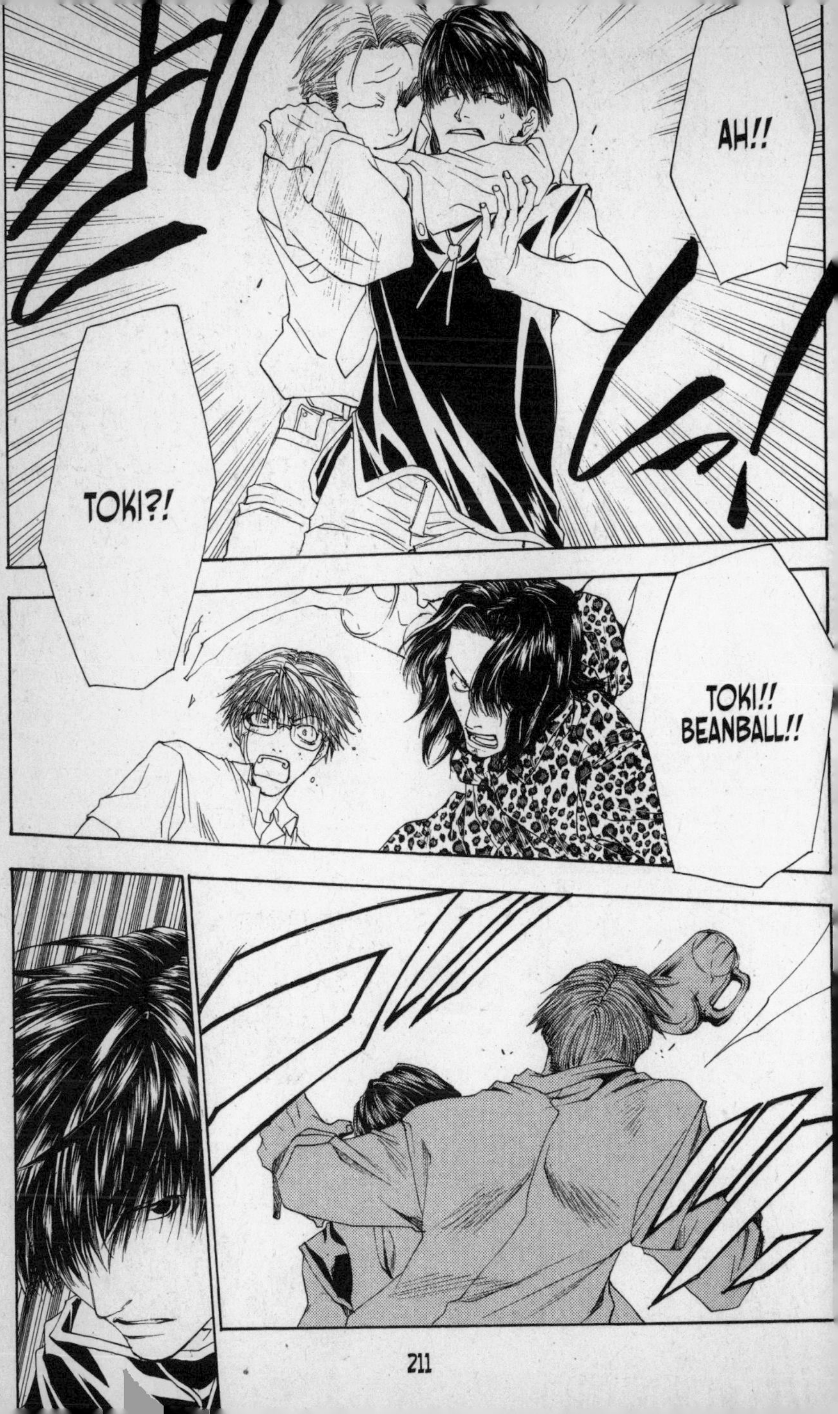
AH!!
TOKI?!
TOKI!! BEANBALL!!

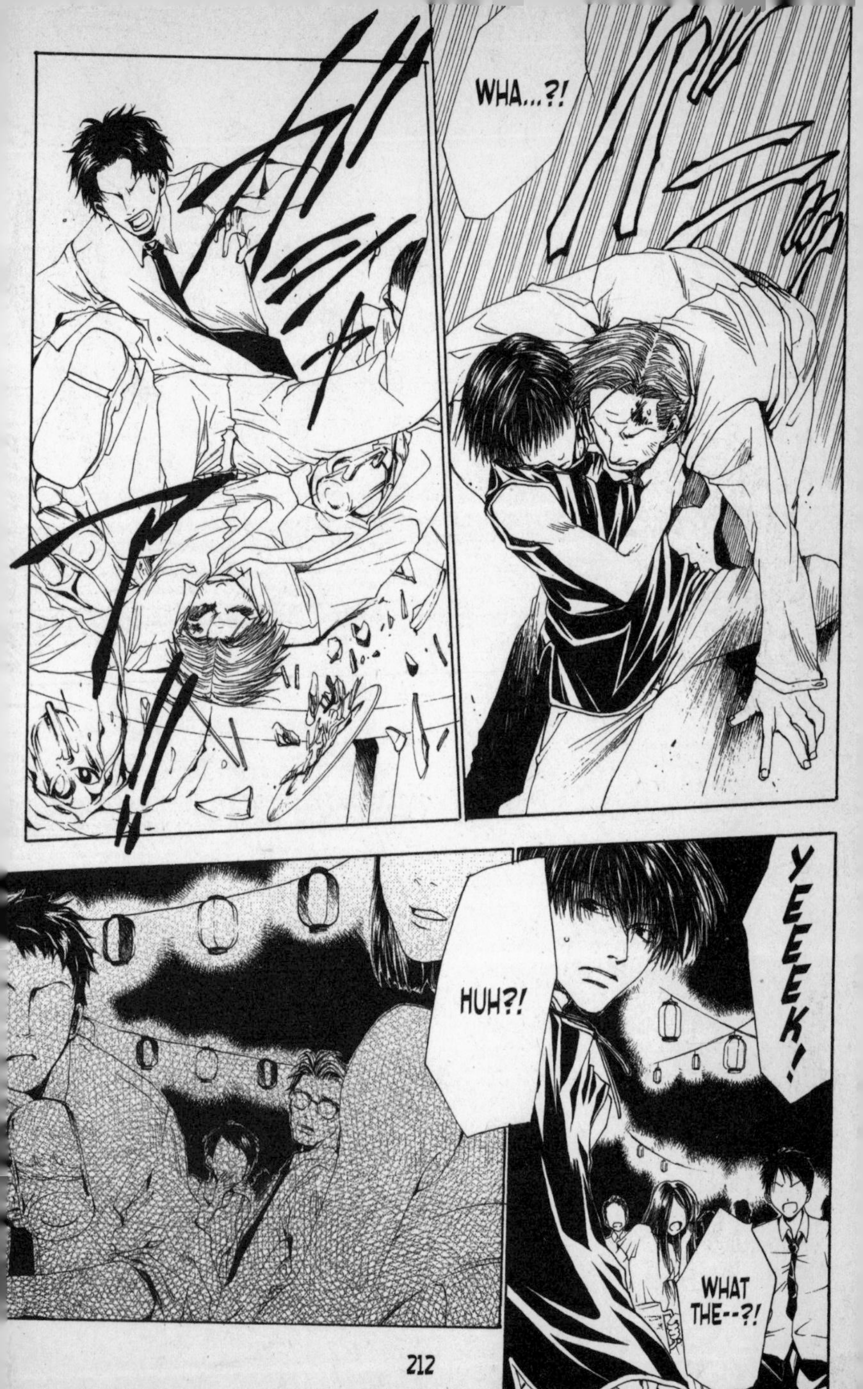
WHA...?!
YEEEK!
HUH?!
WHAT THE--?!

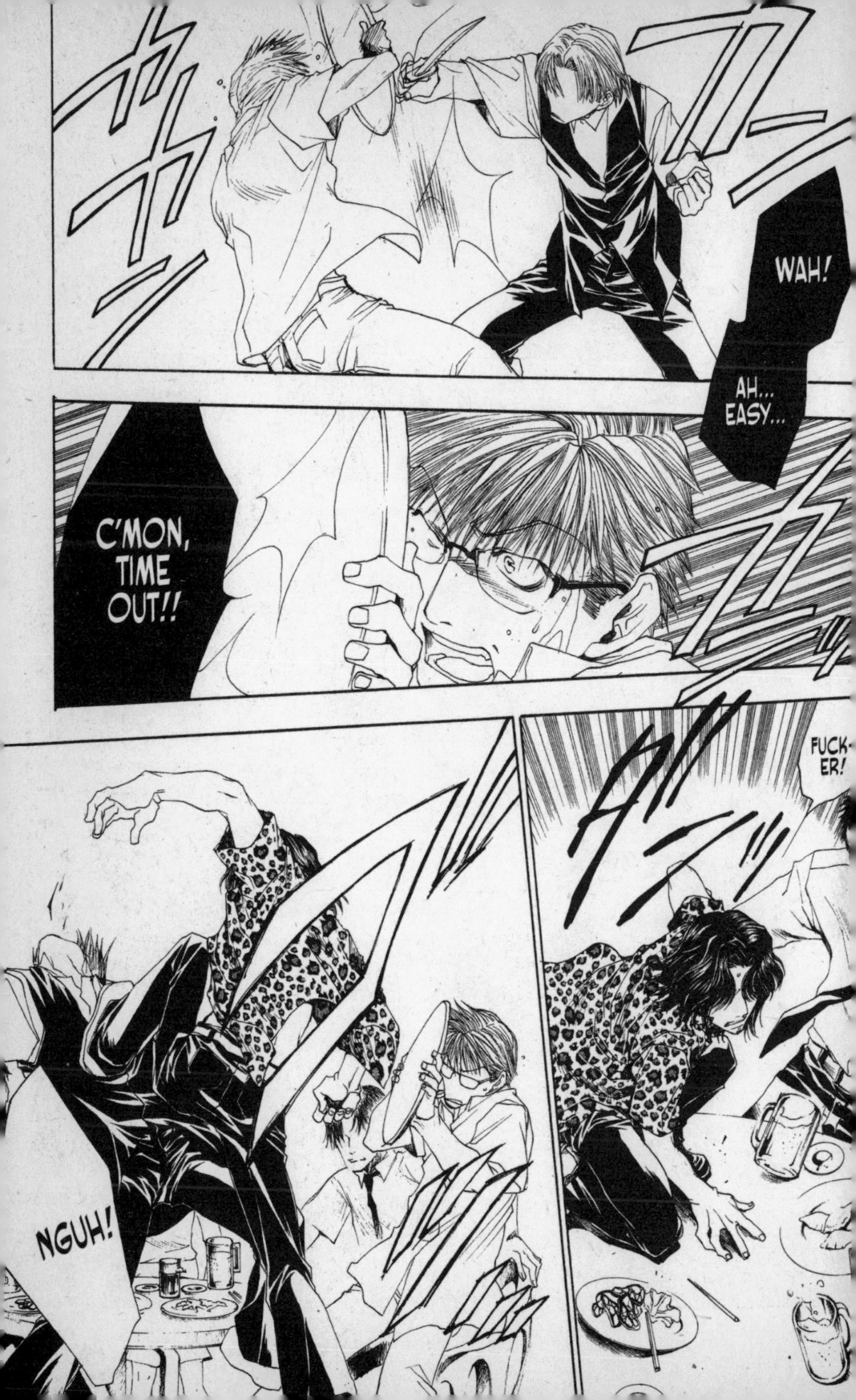
WAH!
AH... EASY...
C'MON, TIME OUT!!
FUCK-ER!
NGUH!

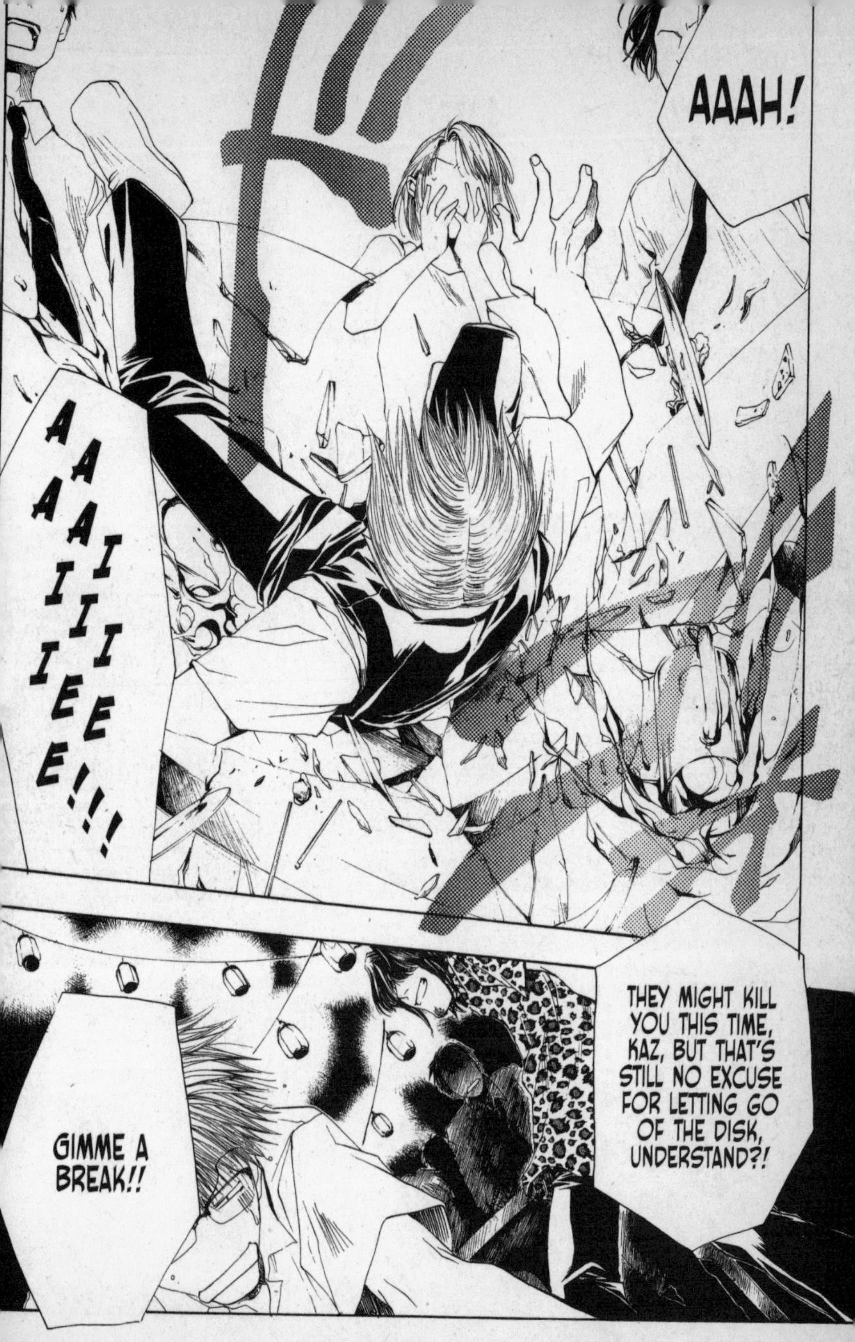
AAAH!
AAAAIIIIIEEE!!!
THEY MIGHT KILL YOU THIS TIME, KAZ, BUT THAT'S STILL NO EXCUSE FOR LETTING GO OF THE DISK, UNDERSTAND?!
GIMME A BREAK!!

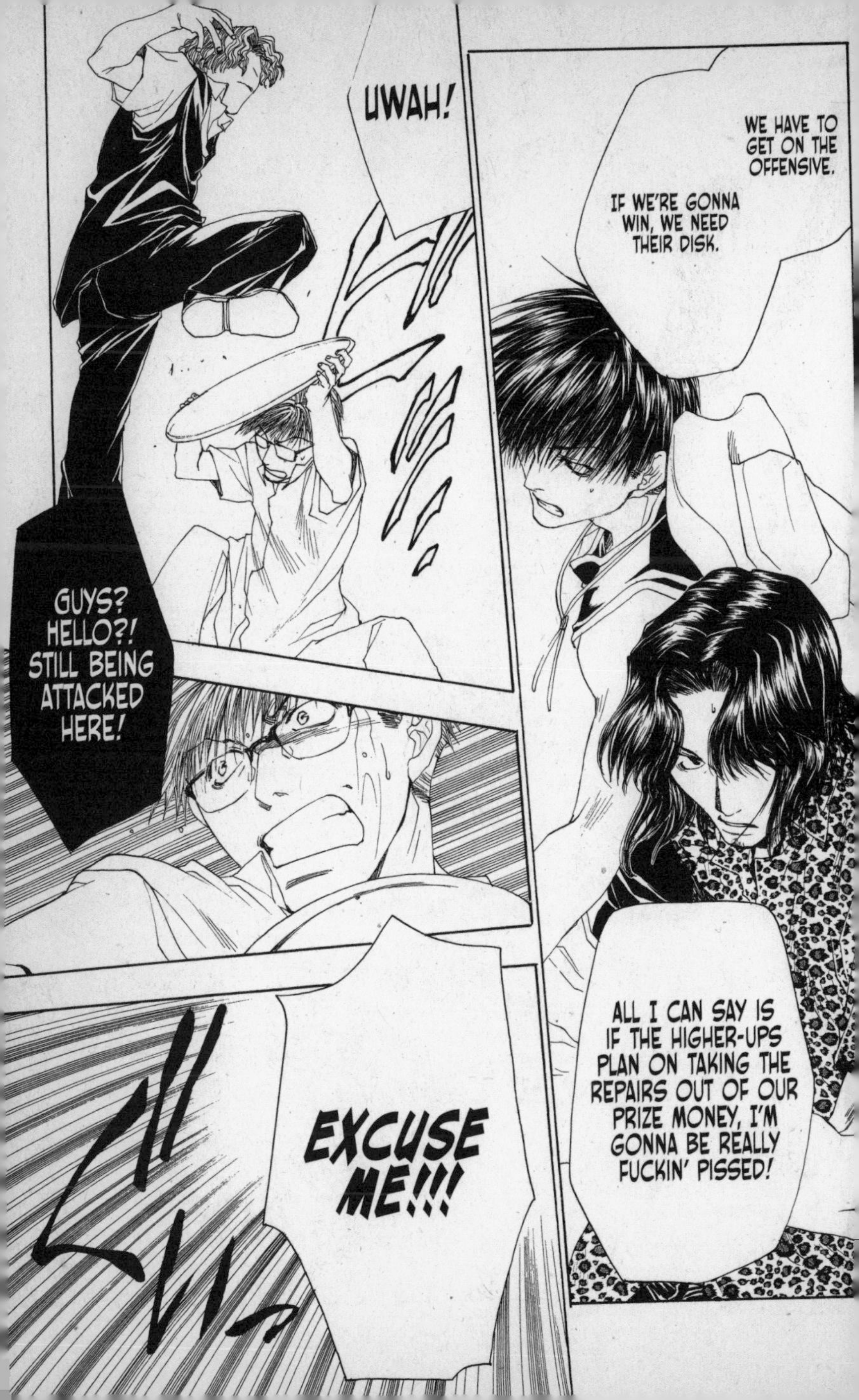
WE HAVE TO GET ON THE OFFENSIVE.
IF WE'RE GONNA WIN, WE NEED THEIR DISK.
ALL I CAN SAY IS IF THE HIGHER-UPS PLAN ON TAKING THE REPAIRS OUT OF OUR PRIZE MONEY, I'M GONNA BE REALLY FUCKIN' PISSED!
UWAH!
GUYS? HELLO?! STILL BEING ATTACKED HERE!
EXCUSE ME!!!

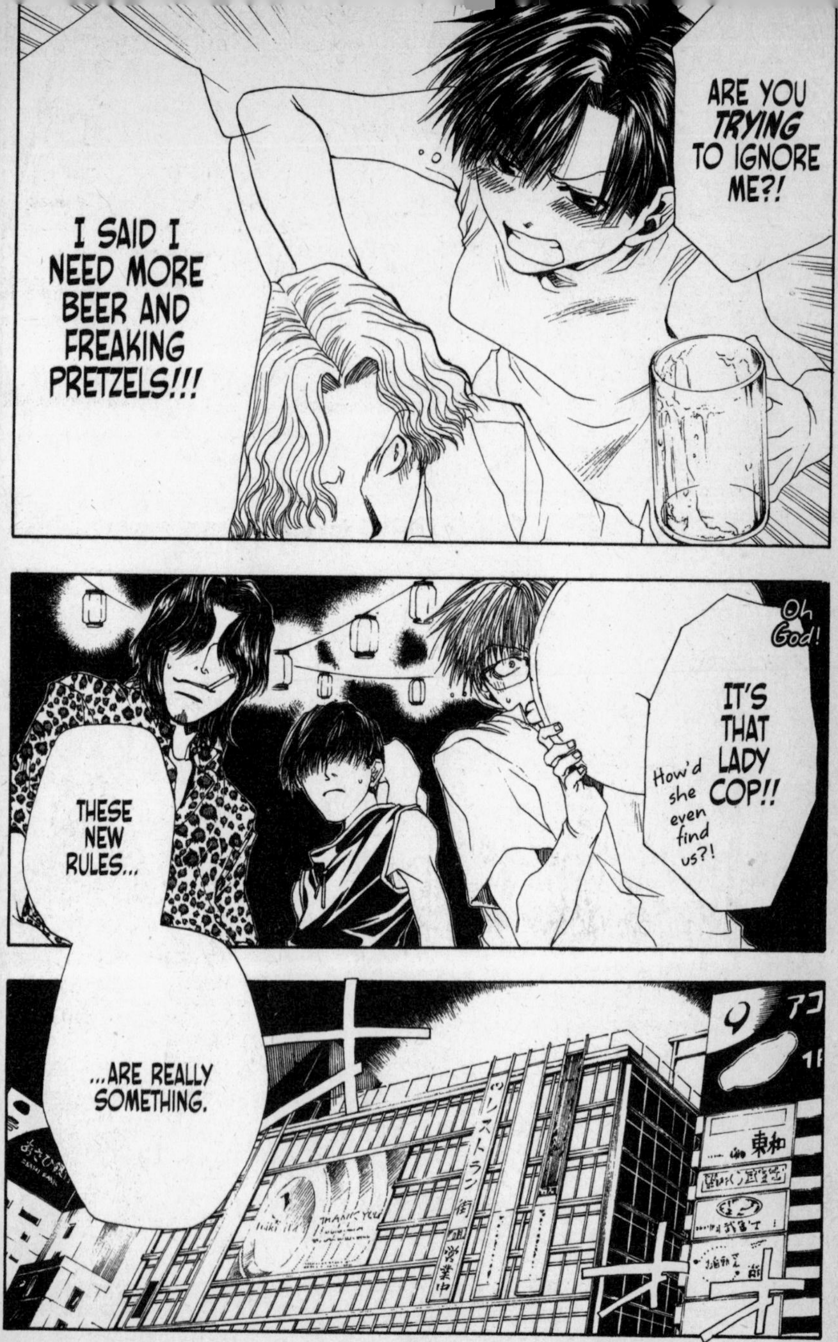
ARE YOU *TRYING* TO IGNORE ME?!
I SAID I NEED MORE BEER AND FREAKING PRETZELS!!!
Oh God!
IT'S THAT LADY COP!!
How'd she even find us?!
THESE NEW RULES...
...ARE REALLY SOMETHING.
レストラン街
営業中
東和

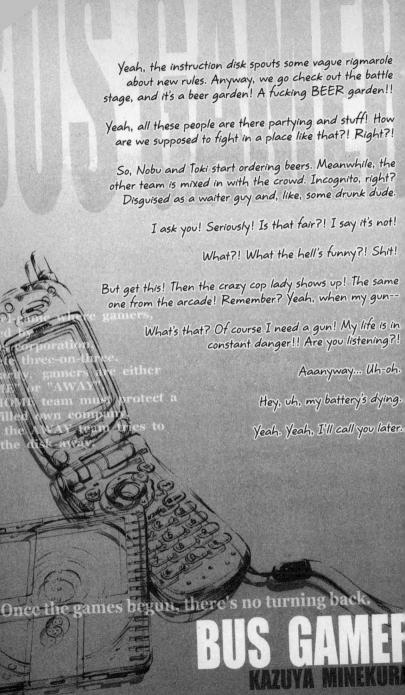

Yeah, the instruction disk spouts some vague rigmarole about new rules. Anyway, we go check out the battle stage, and it's a beer garden! A fucking BEER garden!!

Yeah, all these people are there partying and stuff! How are we supposed to fight in a place like that?! Right?!

So, Nobu and Toki start ordering beers. Meanwhile, the other team is mixed in with the crowd. Incognito, right? Disguised as a waiter guy and, like, some drunk dude.

I ask you! Seriously! Is that fair?! I say it's not!

What?! What the hell's funny?! Shit!

But get this! Then the crazy cop lady shows up! The same one from the arcade! Remember? Yeah, when my gun--

What's that? Of course I need a gun! My life is in constant danger!! Are you listening?!

Aaanyway... Uh-oh.

Hey, uh, my battery's dying.

Yeah. Yeah, I'll call you later.

ball-game where gamers,
lected by
rious corporation,
mpete three-on-three.
rdinarily, gamers are either
HOME or "AWAY"
he HOME team must protect a
sk filled own company,
hile the AWAY team tries to
eal the disk away

Once the games begun, there's no turning back.

BUS GAMER

KAZUYA MINEKUR

T.MISHI

A battle simulation where gamers, selected by various corporations, compete three-on-three. Typically, gamers are designated as either HOME or AWAY. The HOME team must protect a disk filled with its company's secrets, while the AWAY team attempts to steal the disk away.

BUS GAMER

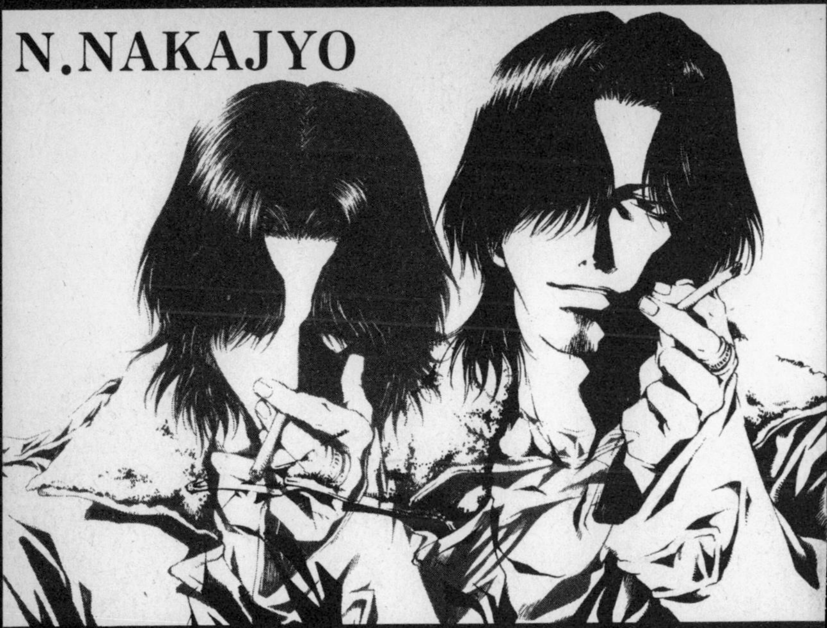
N.NAKAJYO

Once the game's begun, there's no turning back.

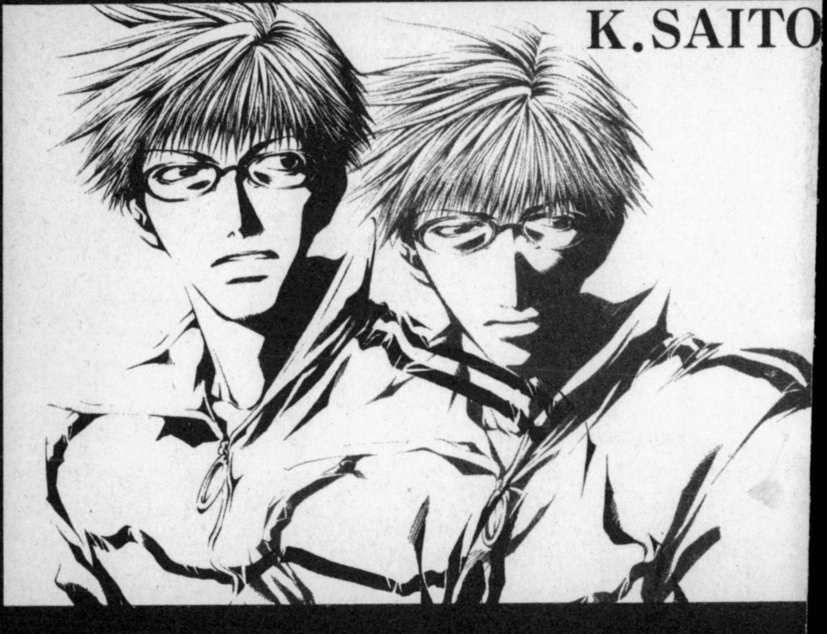
K.SAITO

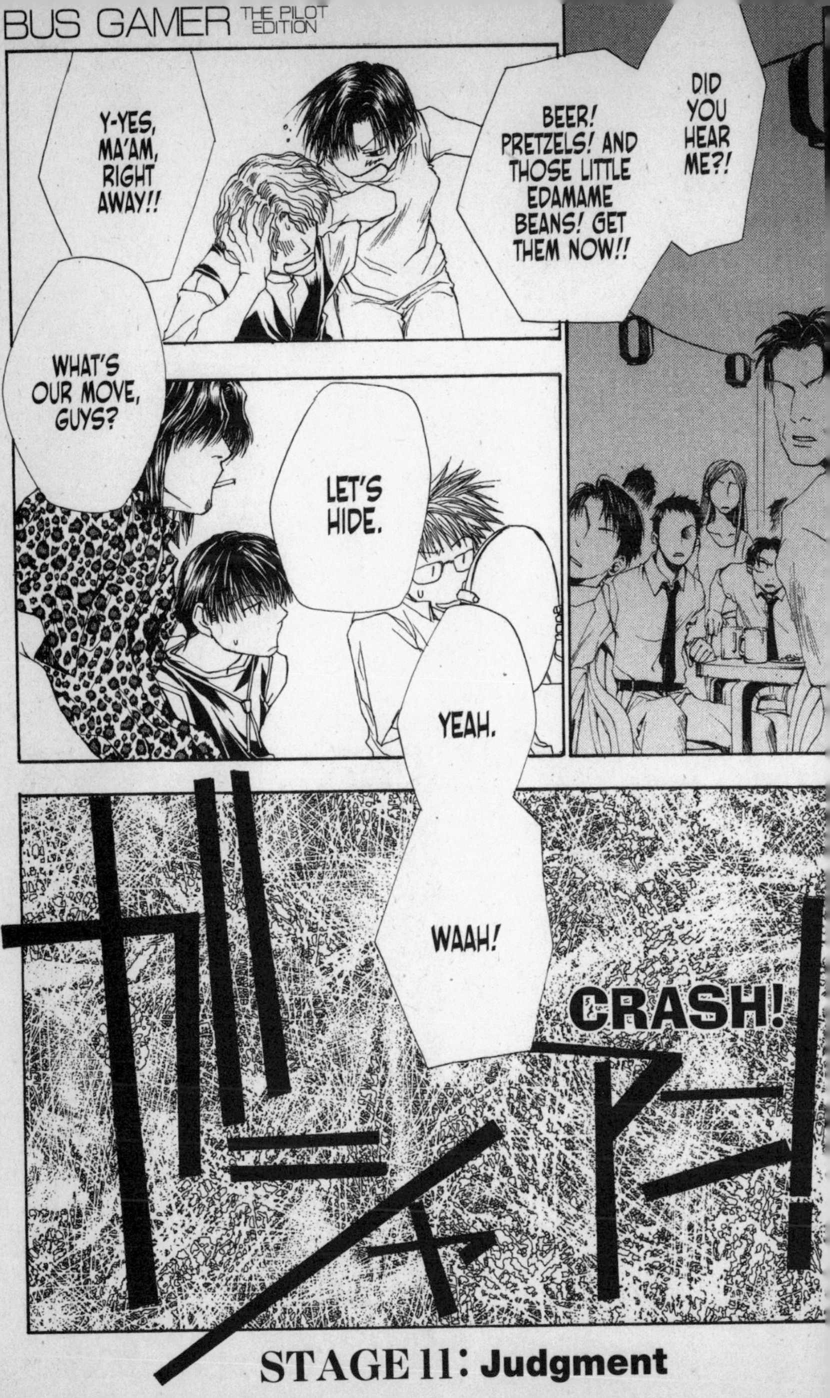
DID YOU HEAR ME?!
BEER! PRETZELS! AND THOSE LITTLE EDAMAME BEANS! GET THEM NOW!!
Y-YES, MA'AM, RIGHT AWAY!!
WHAT'S OUR MOVE, GUYS?
LET'S HIDE.
YEAH.
WAAH!
CRASH!

STAGE 11: Judgment

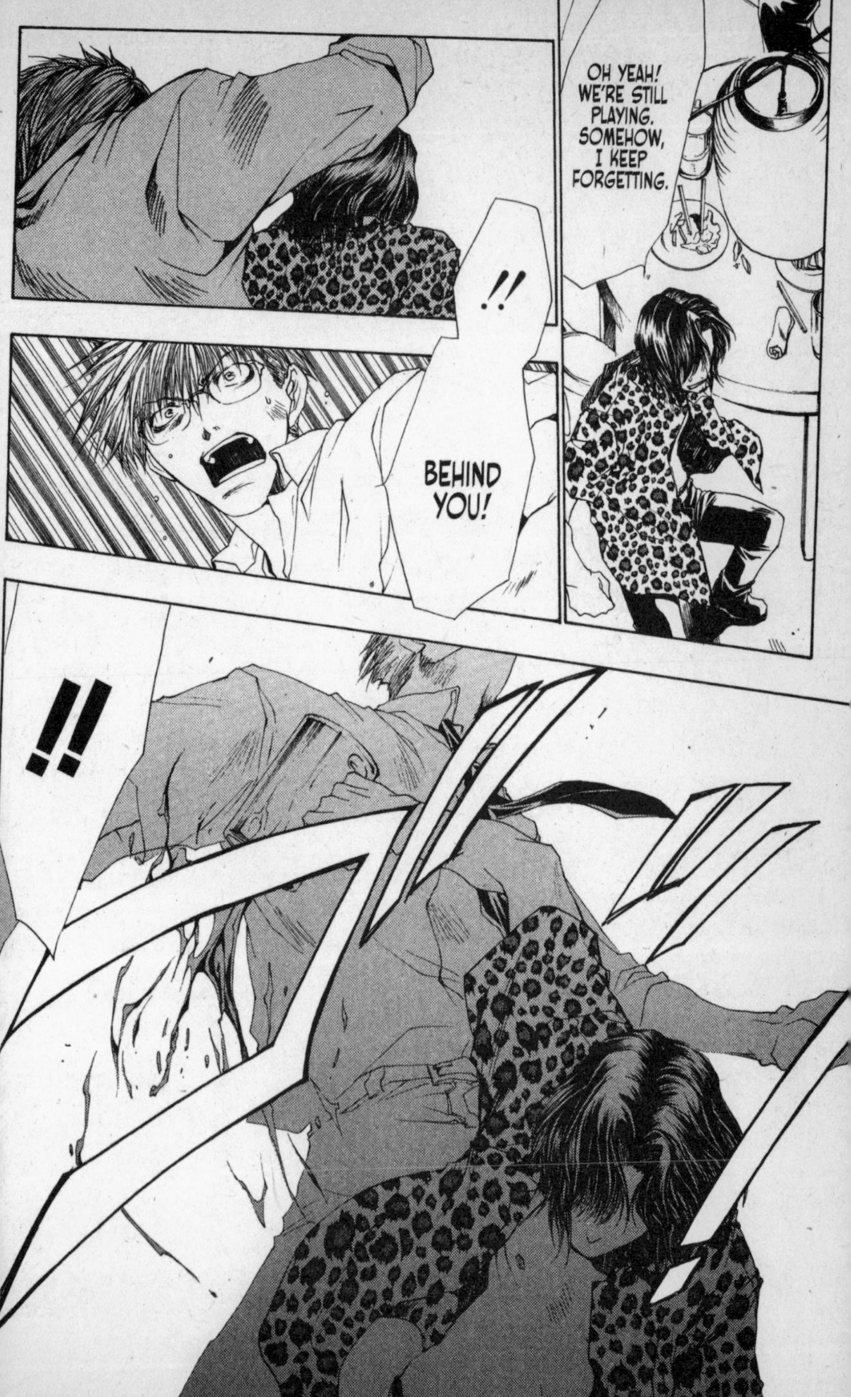
OH YEAH! WE'RE STILL PLAYING. SOMEHOW, I KEEP FORGETTING.
!!
BEHIND YOU!
!!

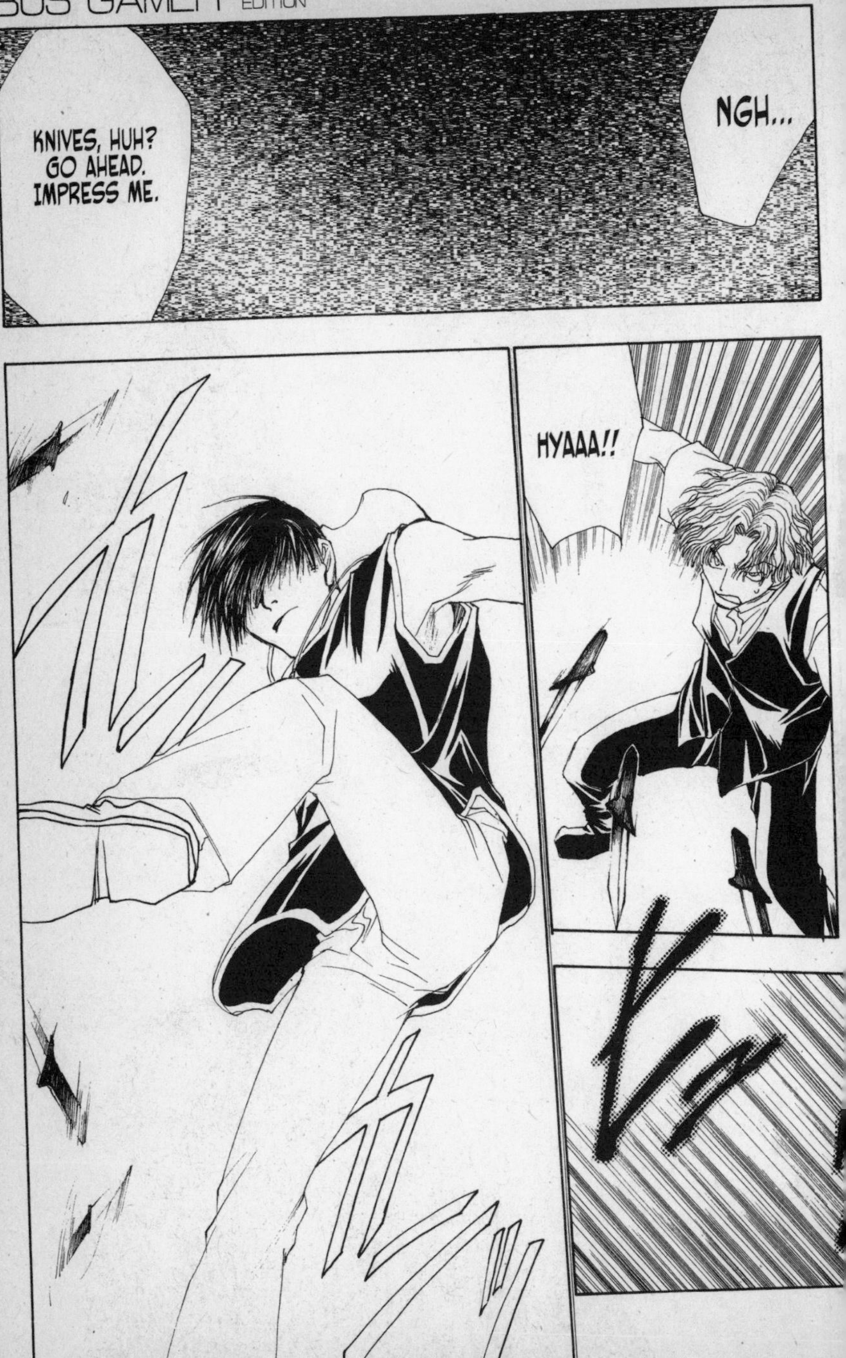
NGH...
KNIVES, HUH? GO AHEAD. IMPRESS ME.
HYAAA!!

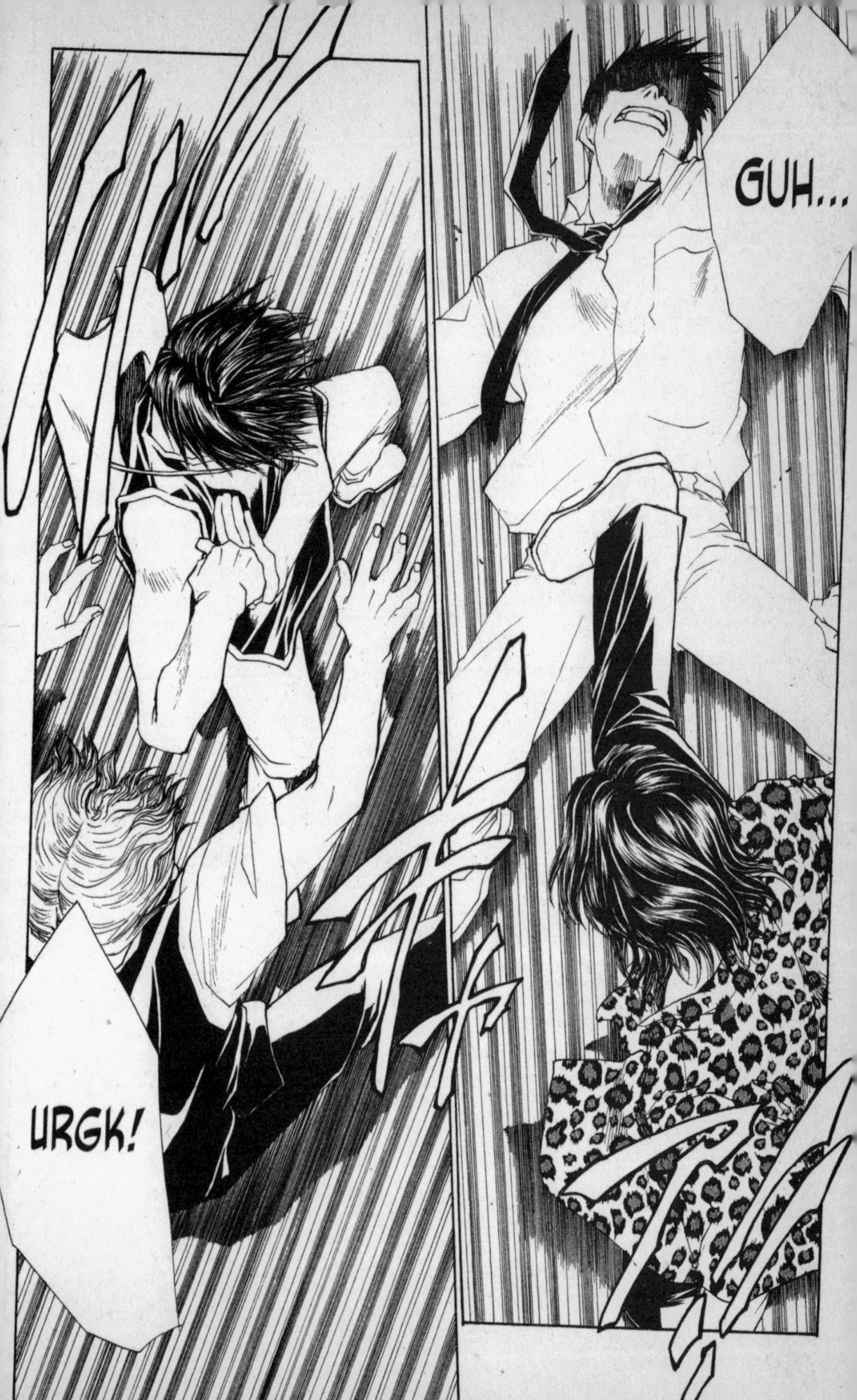
GUH...
URGK!

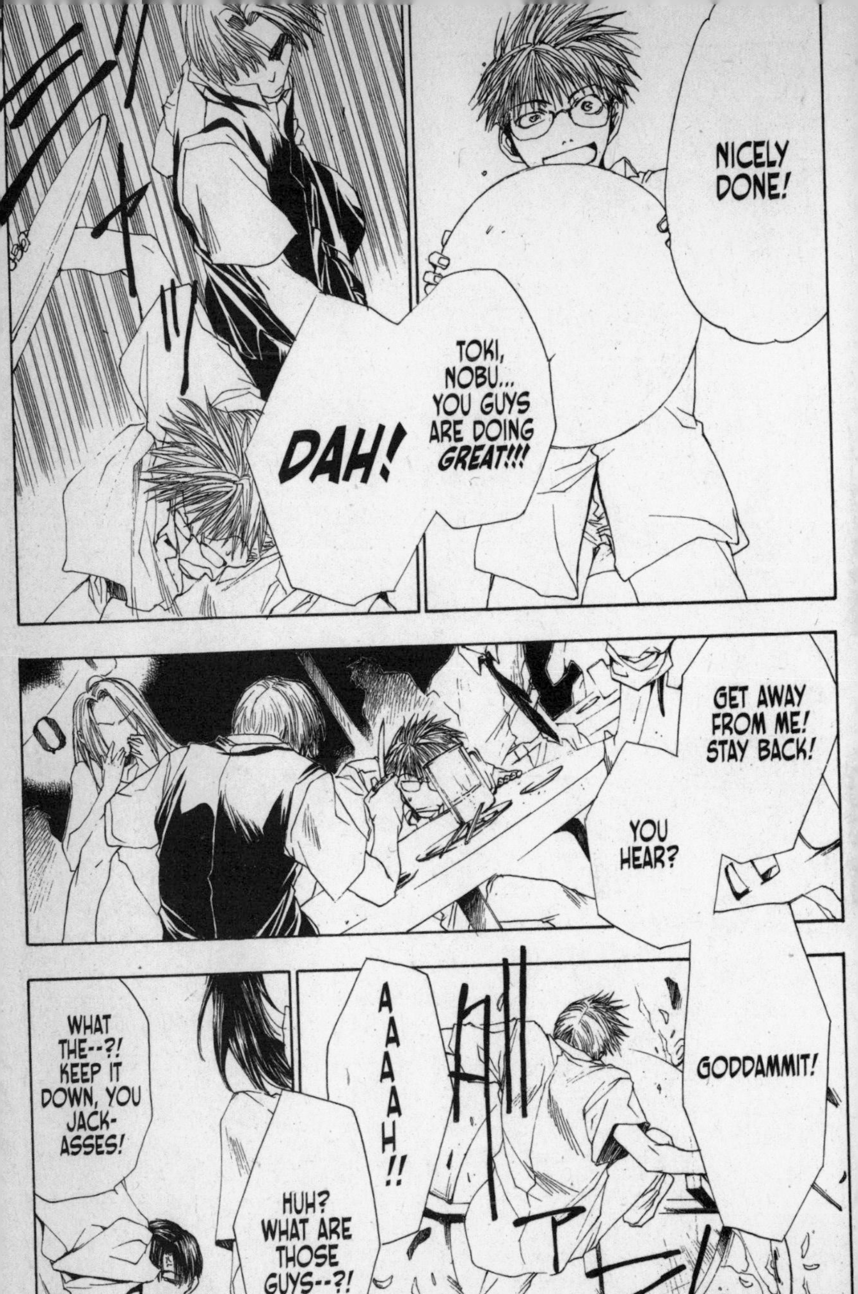
NICELY DONE!
TOKI, NOBU... YOU GUYS ARE DOING GREAT!!!
DAH!
GET AWAY FROM ME! STAY BACK!
YOU HEAR?
GODDAMMIT!
AAAAAH!!
HUH? WHAT ARE THOSE GUYS--?!
WHAT THE--?! KEEP IT DOWN, YOU JACK-ASSES!

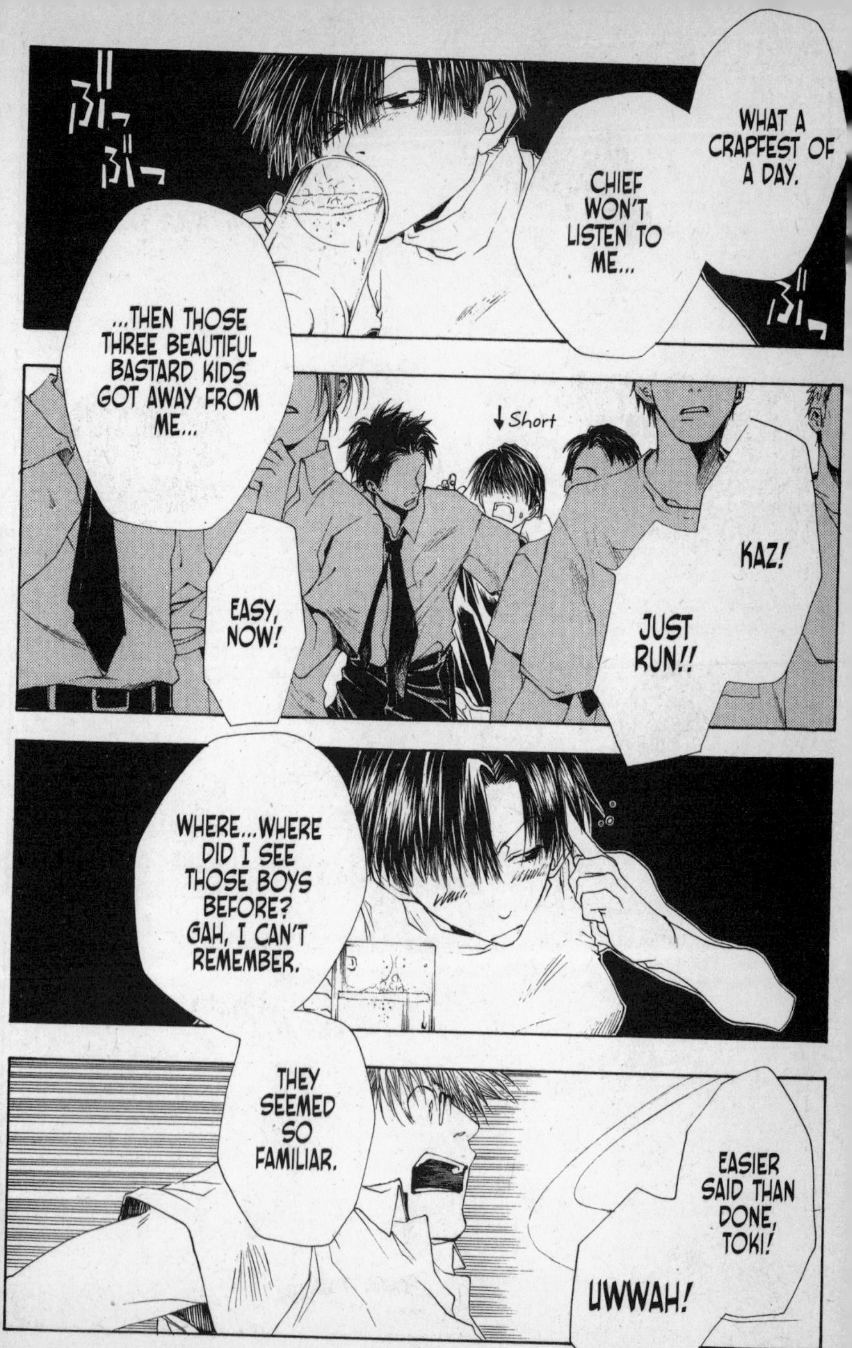

WHAT A CRAPFEST OF A DAY.
ぶーっ
CHIEF WON'T LISTEN TO ME...
ぶーっ ぶーっ
...THEN THOSE THREE BEAUTIFUL BASTARD KIDS GOT AWAY FROM ME...
KAZ!
JUST RUN!!
↓Short
EASY, NOW!
WHERE...WHERE DID I SEE THOSE BOYS BEFORE? GAH, I CAN'T REMEMBER.
THEY SEEMED SO FAMILIAR.
EASIER SAID THAN DONE, TOKI!
UWWAH!

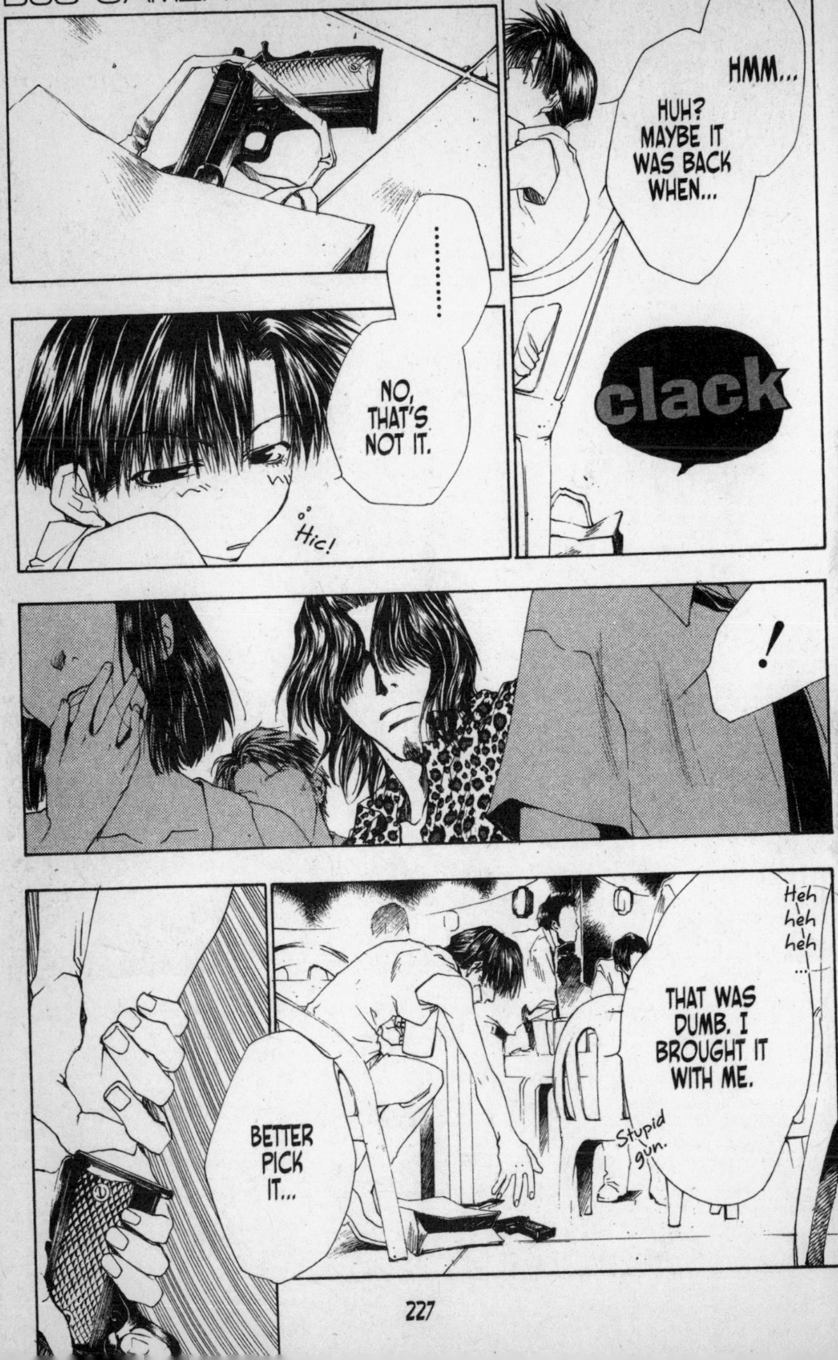
HMM...
HUH? MAYBE IT WAS BACK WHEN...
clack
......
NO, THAT'S NOT IT.
Hic!
!
Heh heh heh...
THAT WAS DUMB. I BROUGHT IT WITH ME.
Stupid gun.
BETTER PICK IT...

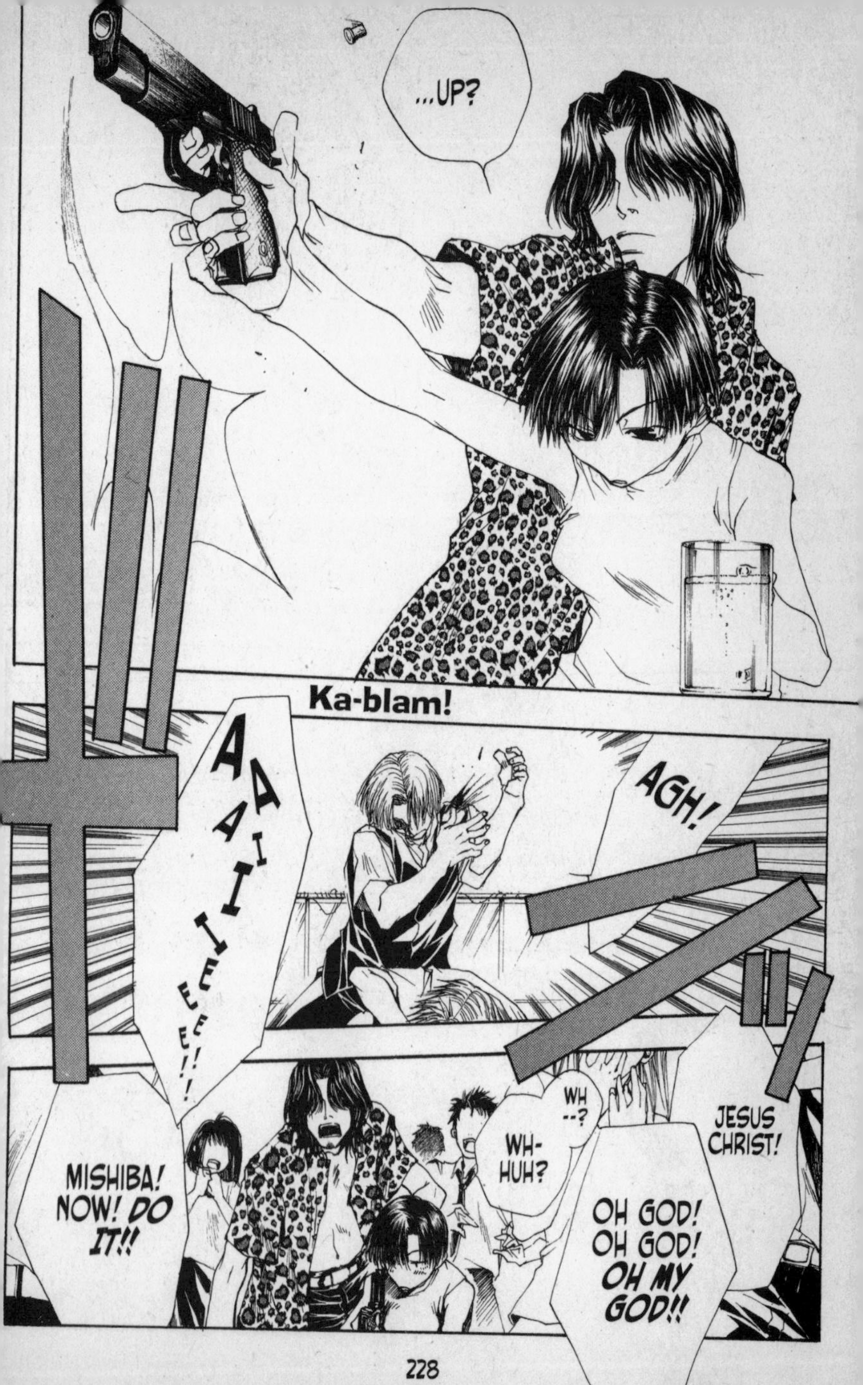
...UP?
Ka-blam!
AGH!
AAAIIIEEEE!!
JESUS CHRIST!
OH GOD! OH GOD! OH MY GOD!!
WH--?
WH-HUH?
MISHIBA! NOW! DO IT!!

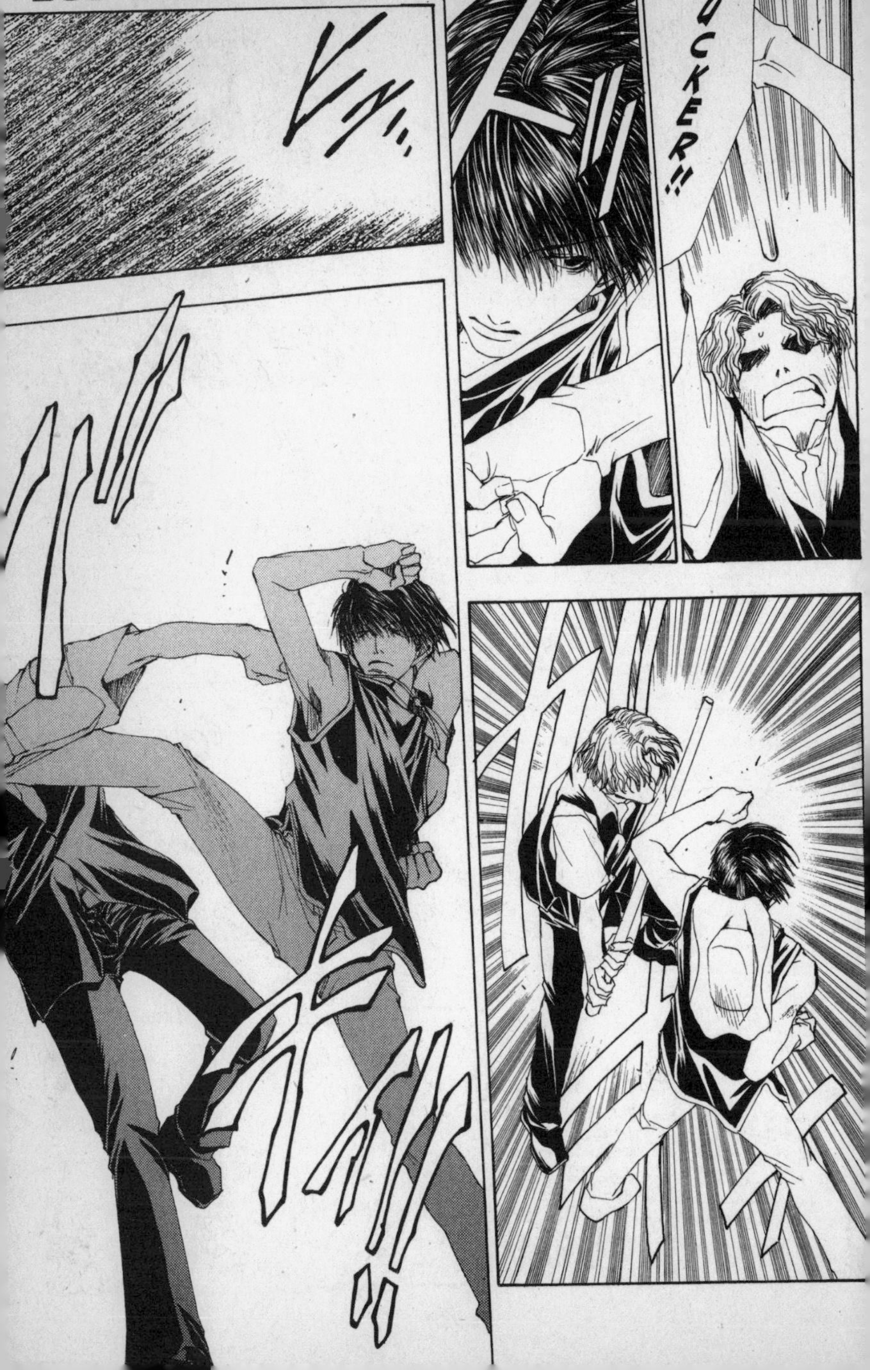
FUCKER!!

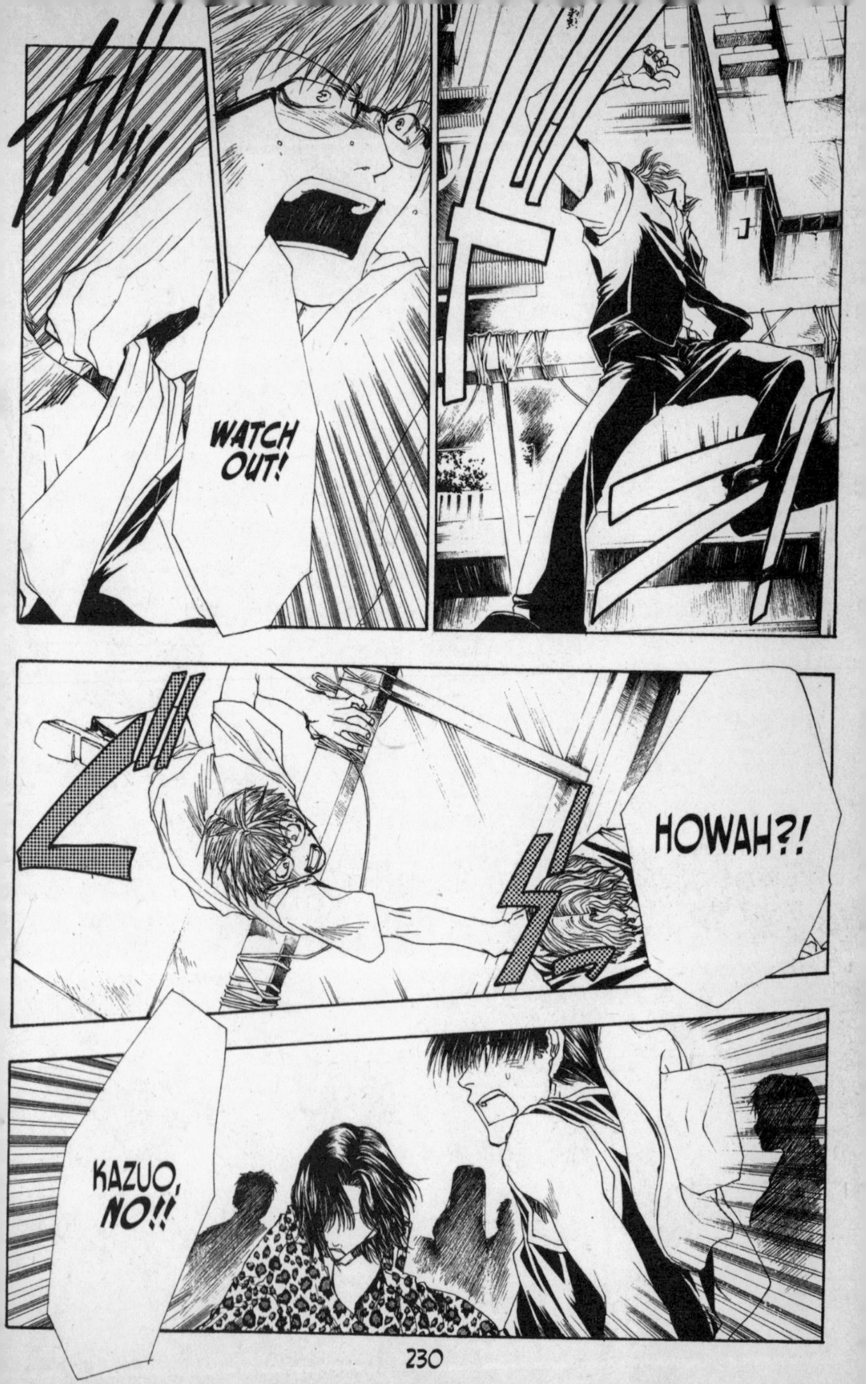
WATCH OUT!
HOWAH?!
KAZUO, NO!!

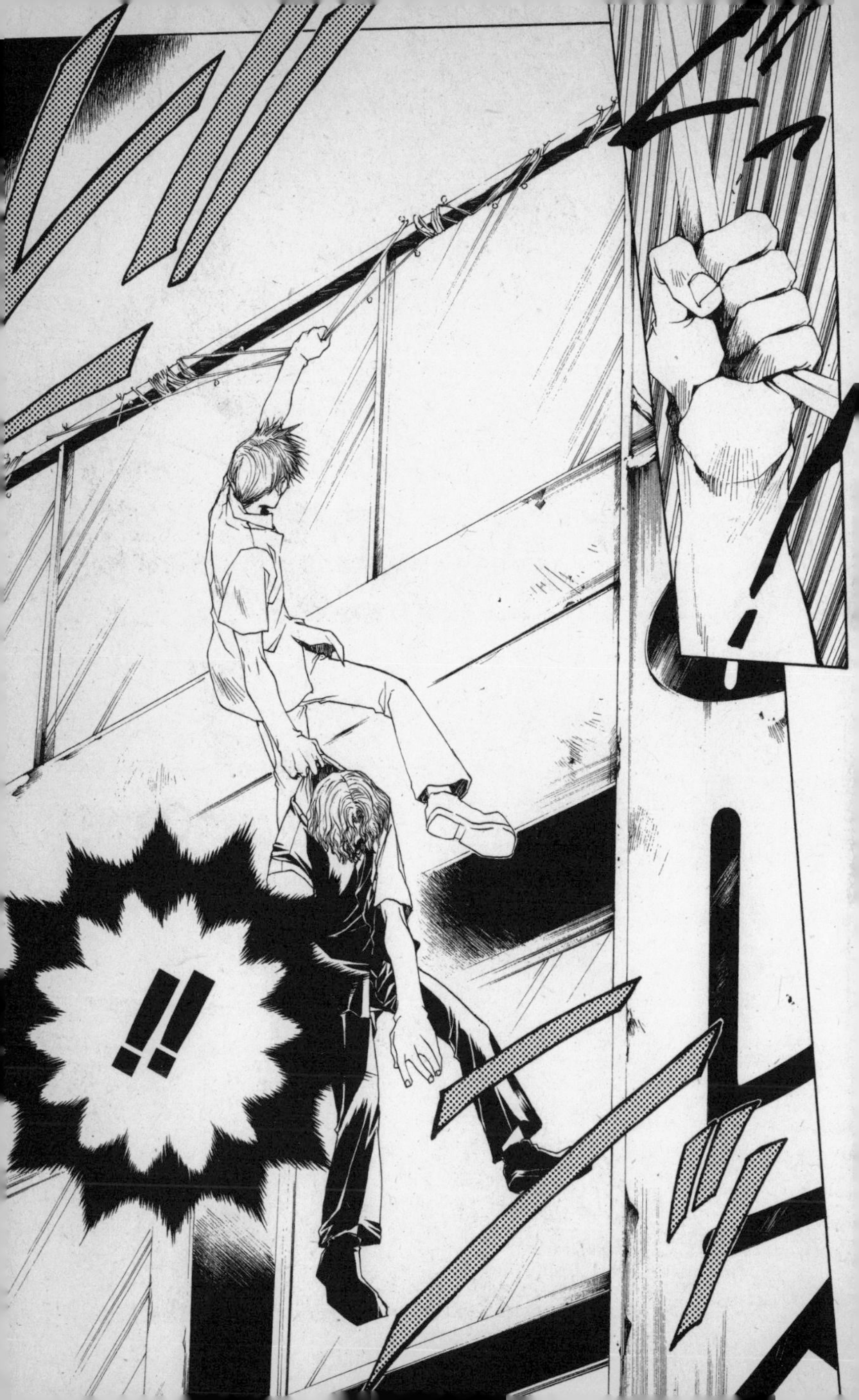
!!

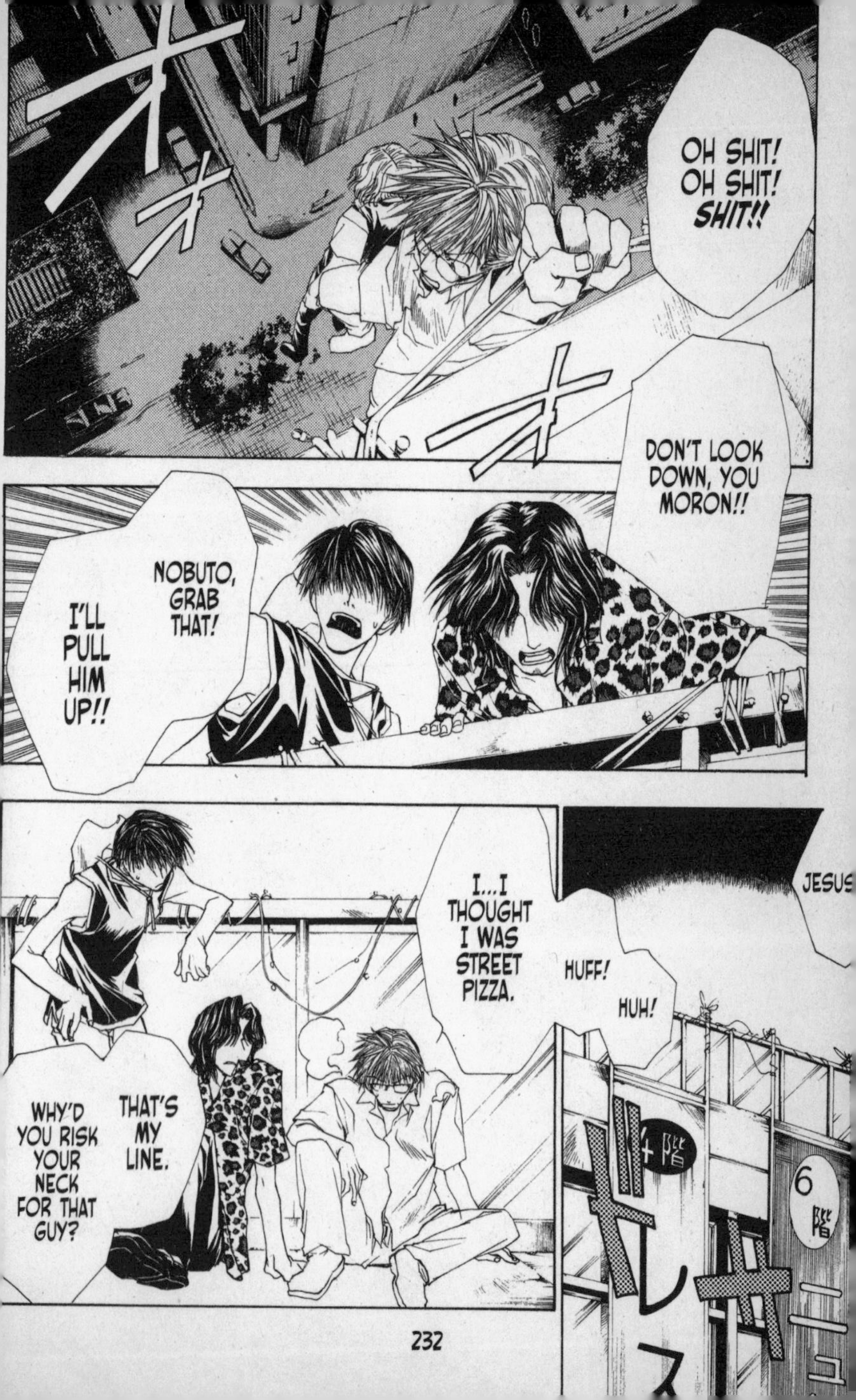
OH SHIT! OH SHIT! SHIT!!
DON'T LOOK DOWN, YOU MORON!!
NOBUTO, GRAB THAT!
I'LL PULL HIM UP!!
JESUS
HUFF!
HUH!
I...I THOUGHT I WAS STREET PIZZA.
THAT'S MY LINE.
WHY'D YOU RISK YOUR NECK FOR THAT GUY?

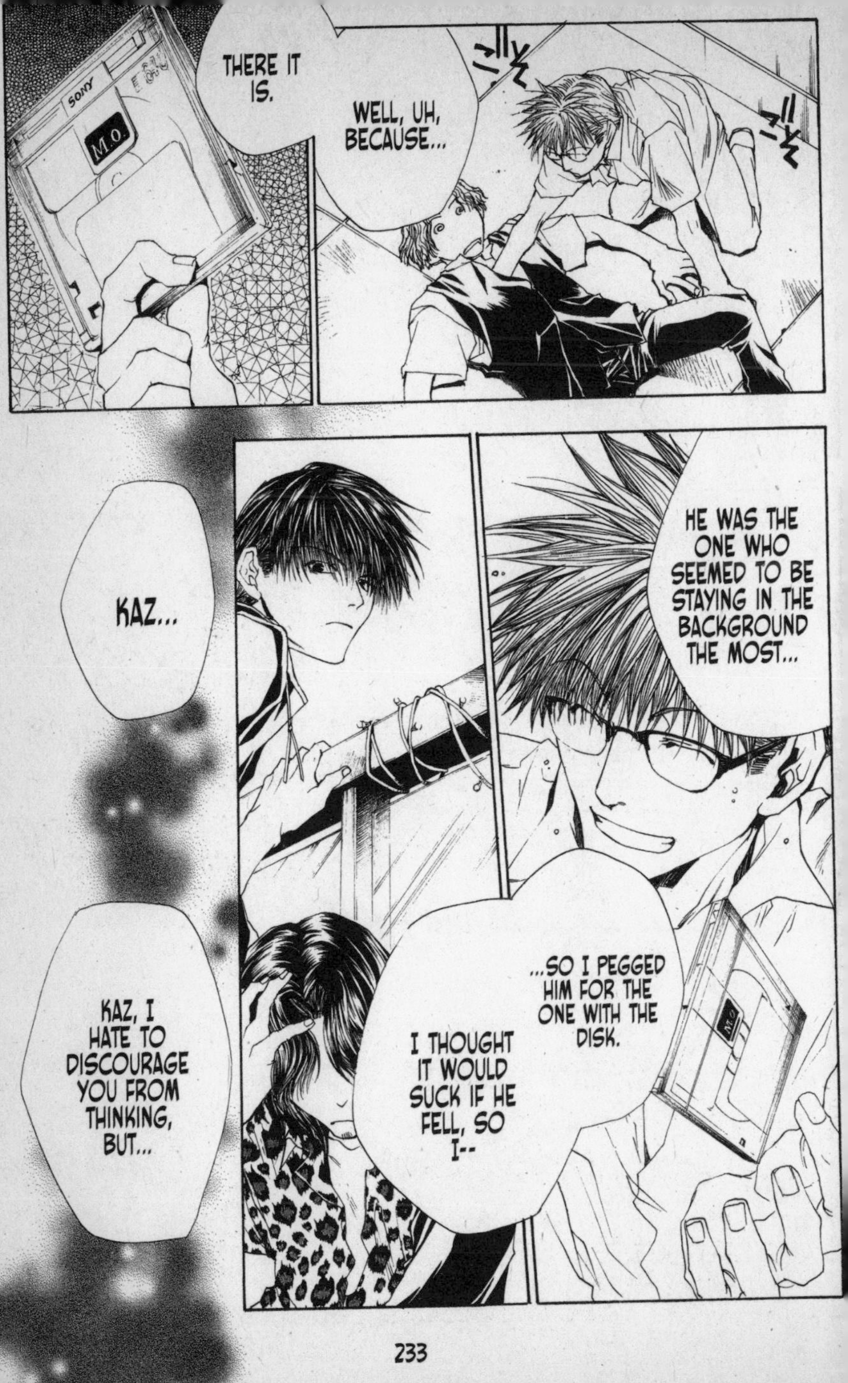
SONY
M.O.
THERE IT IS.
WELL, UH, BECAUSE...
HE WAS THE ONE WHO SEEMED TO BE STAYING IN THE BACKGROUND THE MOST...
...SO I PEGGED HIM FOR THE ONE WITH THE DISK.
M.O.
I THOUGHT IT WOULD SUCK IF HE FELL, SO I--
KAZ...
KAZ, I HATE TO DISCOURAGE YOU FROM THINKING, BUT...

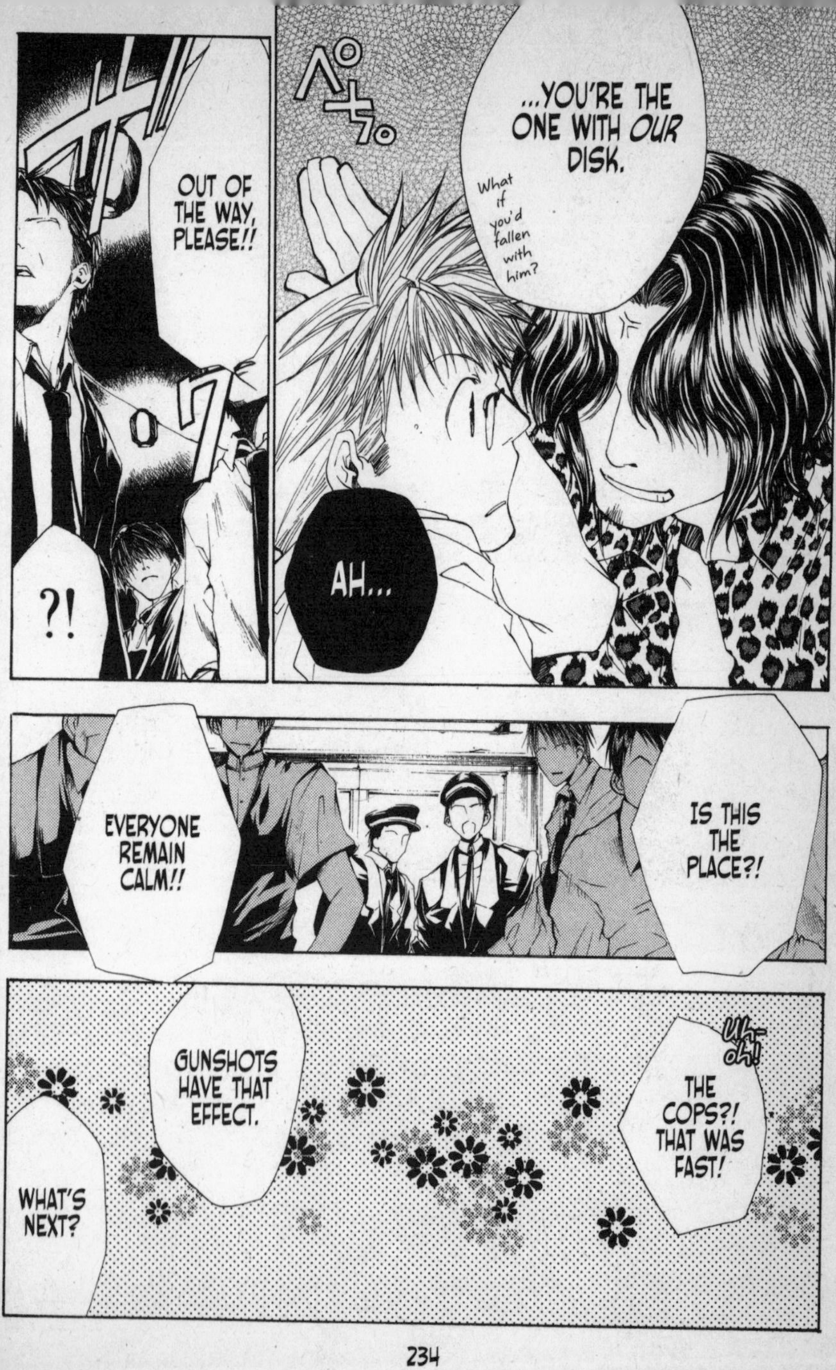
...YOU'RE THE ONE WITH *OUR* DISK.
What if you'd fallen with him?
AH...
OUT OF THE WAY, PLEASE!!
?!
IS THIS THE PLACE?!
EVERYONE REMAIN CALM!!
Uh-oh!
THE COPS?! THAT WAS FAST!
GUNSHOTS HAVE THAT EFFECT.
WHAT'S NEXT?

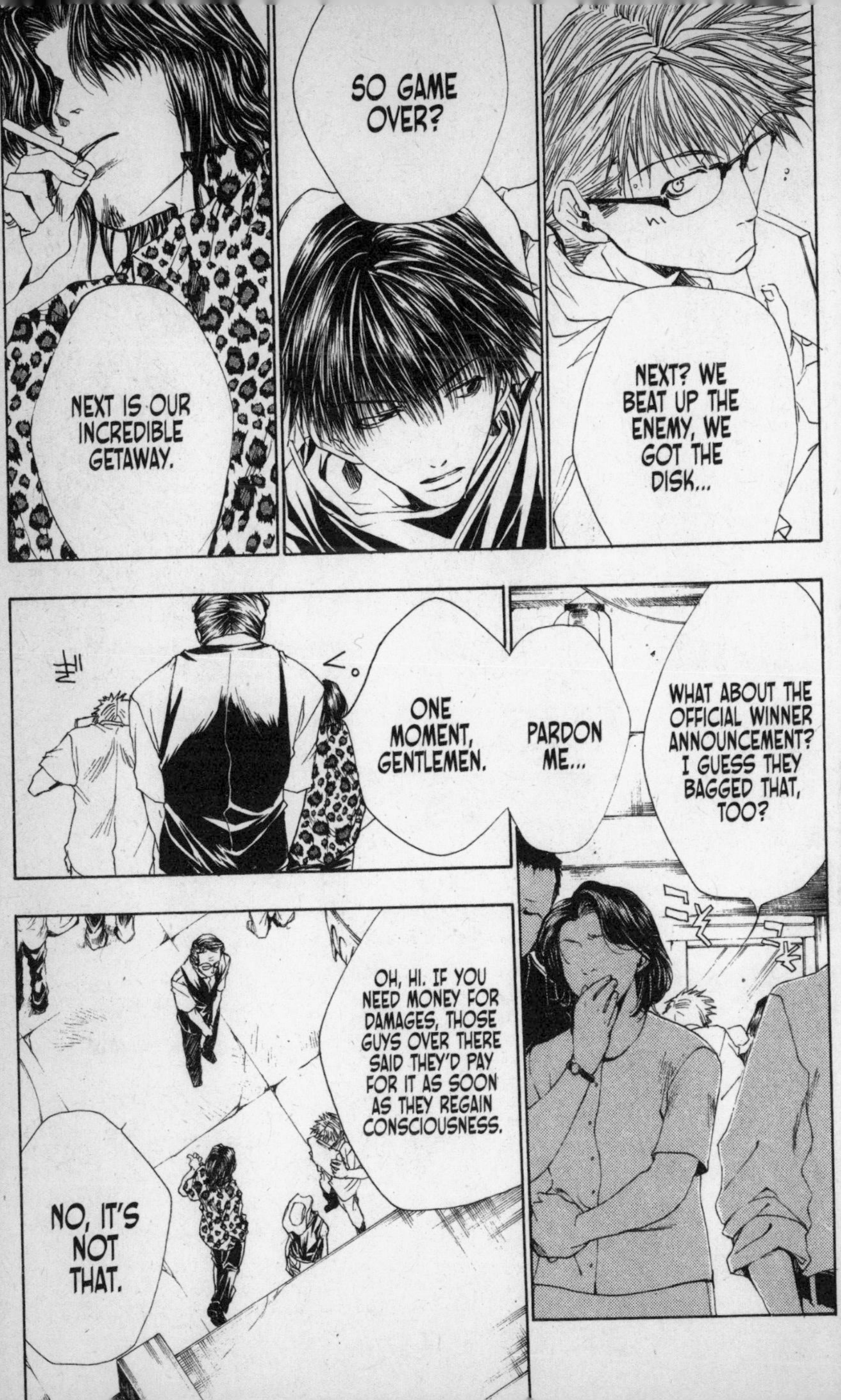
NEXT? WE BEAT UP THE ENEMY, WE GOT THE DISK...
SO GAME OVER?
NEXT IS OUR INCREDIBLE GETAWAY.
WHAT ABOUT THE OFFICIAL WINNER ANNOUNCEMENT? I GUESS THEY BAGGED THAT, TOO?
PARDON ME...
ONE MOMENT, GENTLEMEN.
OH, HI. IF YOU NEED MONEY FOR DAMAGES, THOSE GUYS OVER THERE SAID THEY'D PAY FOR IT AS SOON AS THEY REGAIN CONSCIOUSNESS.
NO, IT'S NOT THAT.

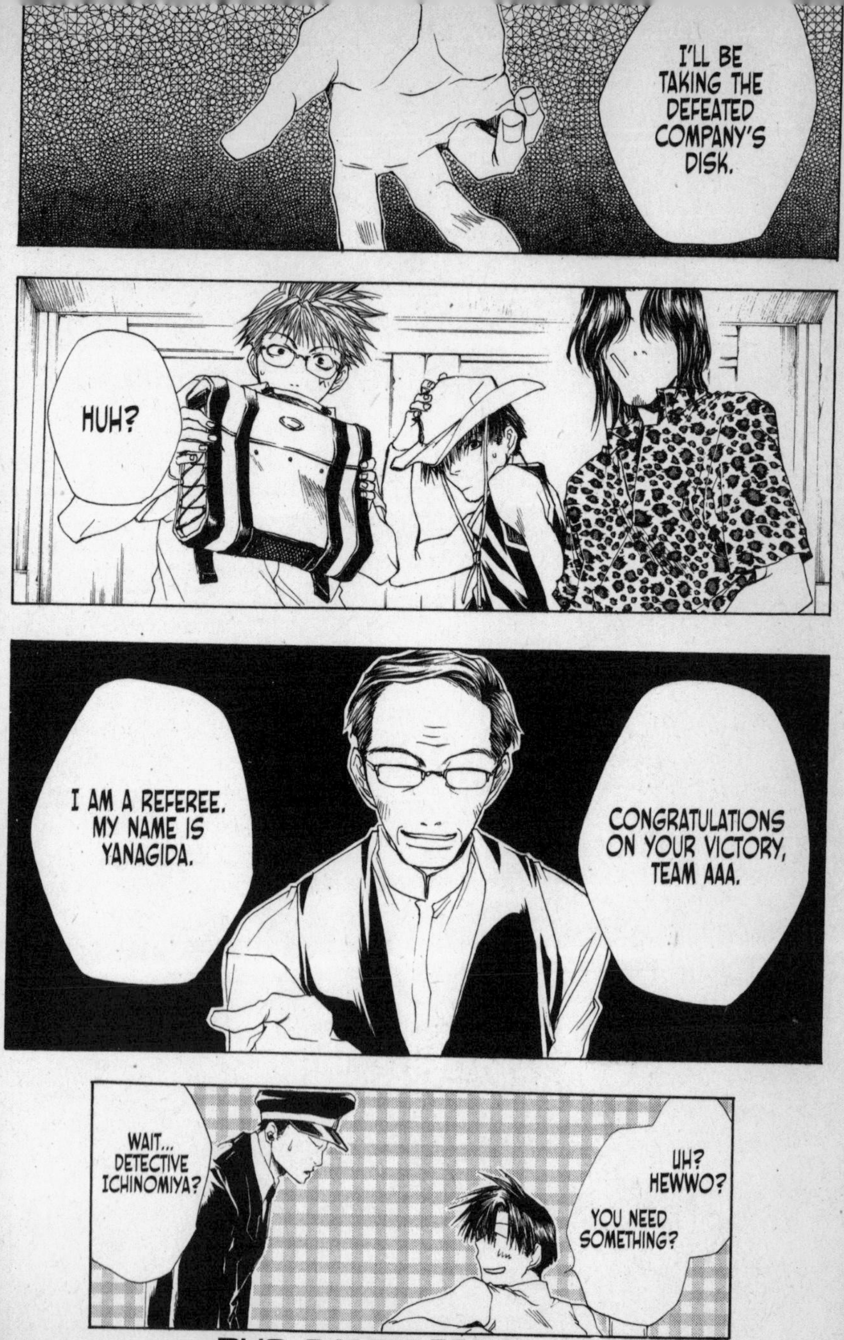
I'LL BE TAKING THE DEFEATED COMPANY'S DISK.
HUH?
CONGRATULATIONS ON YOUR VICTORY, TEAM AAA.
I AM A REFEREE. MY NAME IS YANAGIDA.
UH? HEWWO?
YOU NEED SOMETHING?
WAIT... DETECTIVE ICHINOMIYA?

Afterword

So there you have it. Three chapters that had yet to be compiled into a book have been added to this graphic novel, and the whole thing is being re-released as a new version of Bus Gamer. This is the extent of what I drew for Enix. When Bus Gamer first started, it was serialized in a seasonal publication, then the magazine was put on hiatus and was revived as a bi-monthly publication...until the series was put on hiatus. Certainly, there were a lot of twists and turns for this one volume to come out.

Rest assured that I have no intention of ending Bus Gamer here. No, I've made up my mind. This is merely the prologue. 'Cause I like these three.

And so, we put it all together, and called it "The Pilot Edition."

While waiting to pounce on an opportunity to draw the continuation—that is, the main story—I will keep it warm, like a mother bird, until my next chance to have some fun with these guys.

This has been Minekura.

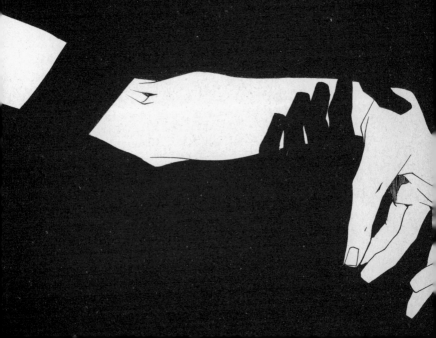

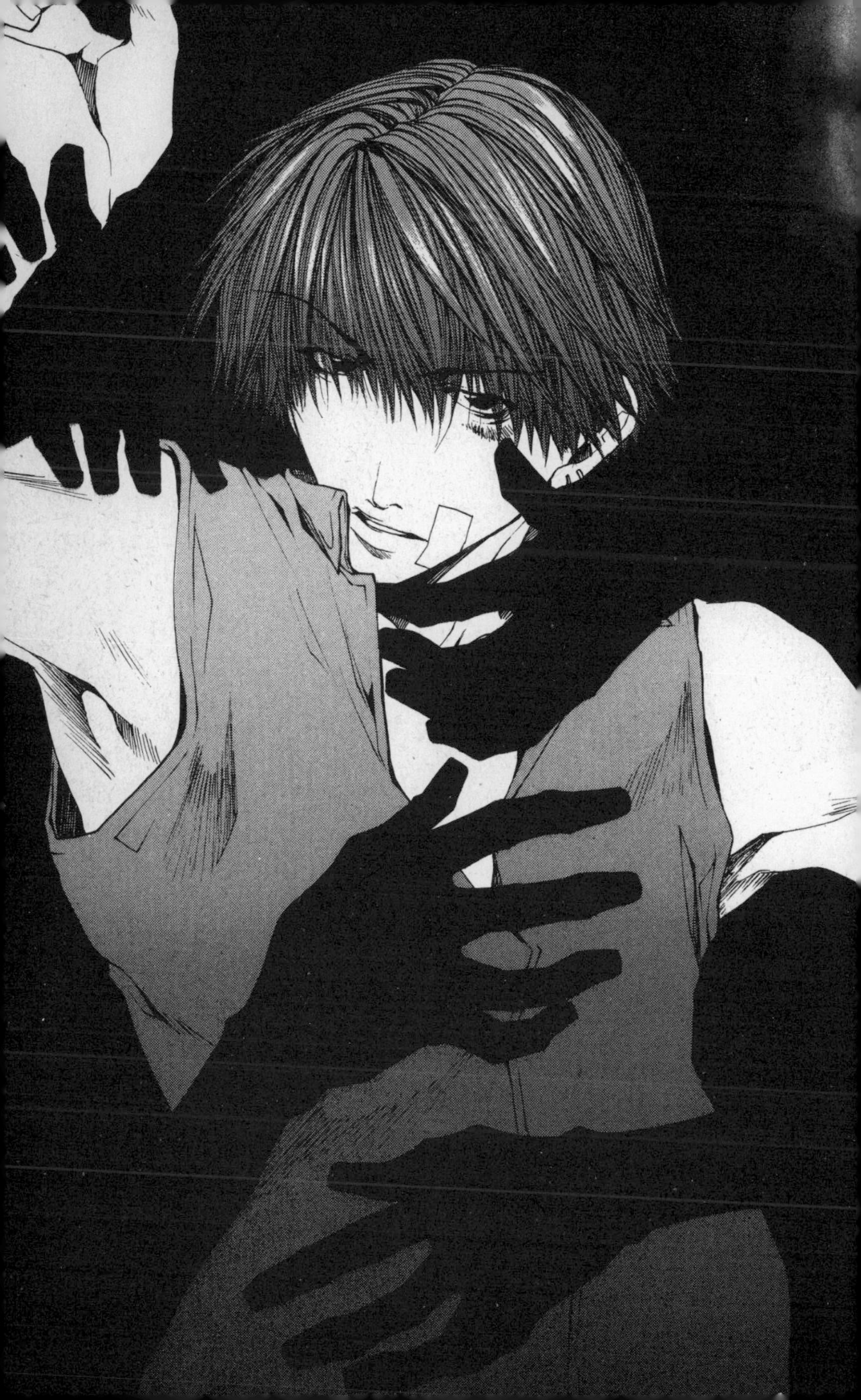

TOKYOPOP.COM

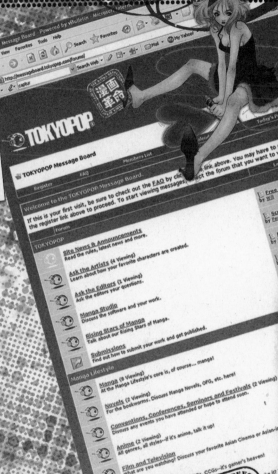

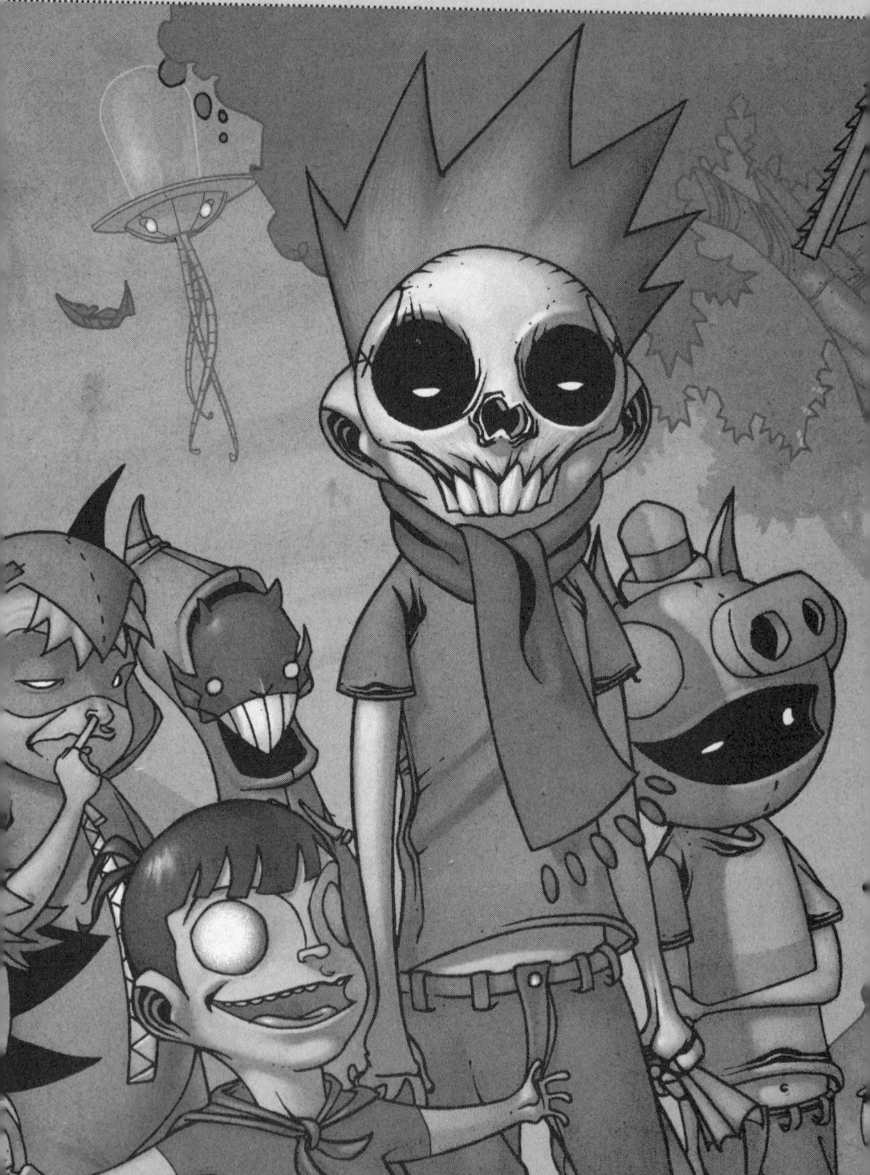

ART BY: **BENJAMIN ROMAN** STORY BY: **KEITH GIFFEN**

FH FAIRVIEW:HOSPITAL

X-RAY REPORT : NOTES
1 bag of Halloween candy; 2 razor blades found in apples, 1 metal die-cast car
found lodged in the bottom of an apple, 1 hatpin found in candy bar.

IT'S LIKE TAKING CANDY FROM A DEAD GUY...

They say bad things come in threes,
and the third round of trick o' treating
is here amidst a close encounter of the
disturbing kind.

"**I Luv Halloween is pure filth.**"
- Robert Sparling, fanboyplanet.com

"**Crass, tasteless, and brilliant.**"
- Newtype USA

HORROR

OT OLDER TEEN
AGE 16+

© Keith Giffen and Benjamin Roman

FOR MORE INFORMATION VISIT:

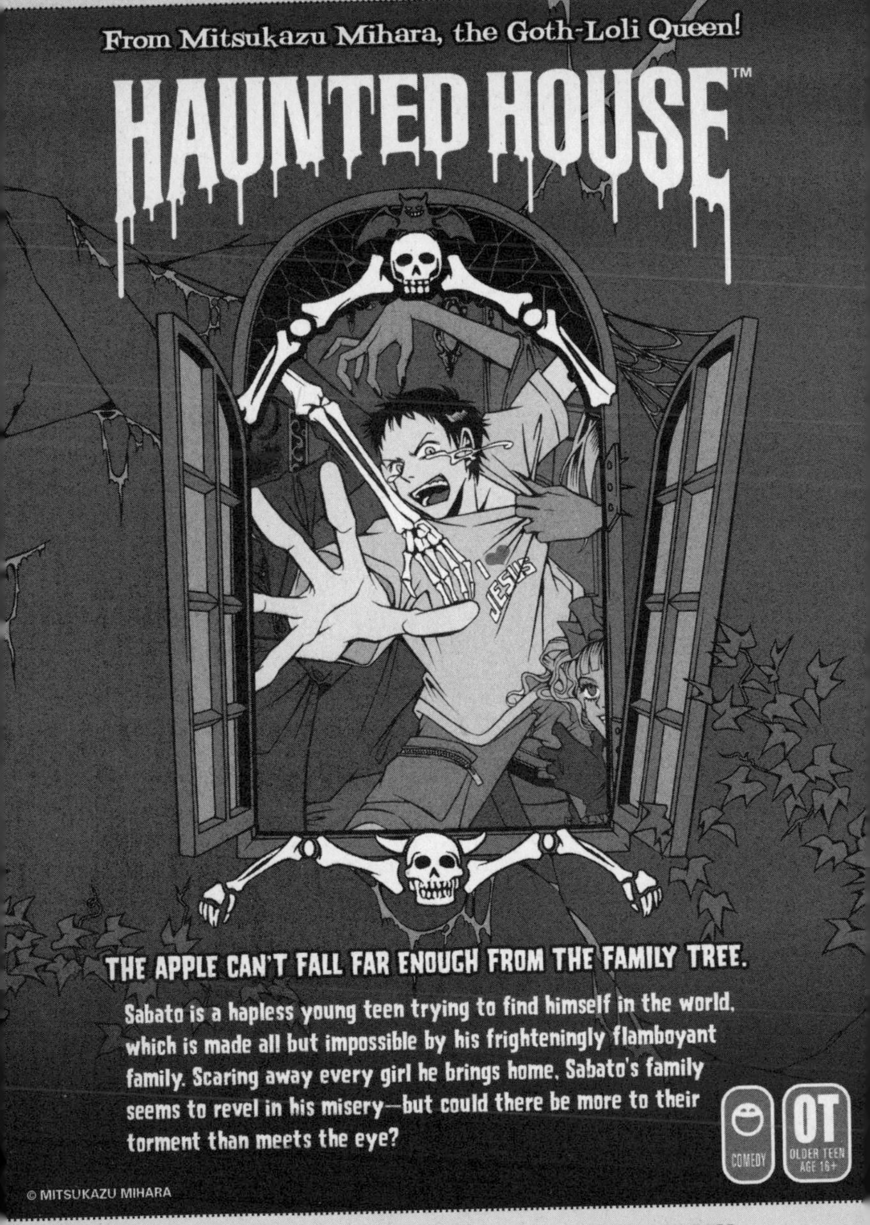
From Mitsukazu Mihara, the Goth-Loli Queen!
HAUNTED HOUSE™
I ♥ JESUS
THE APPLE CAN'T FALL FAR ENOUGH FROM THE FAMILY TREE.
Sabato is a hapless young teen trying to find himself in the world, which is made all but impossible by his frighteningly flamboyant family. Scaring away every girl he brings home, Sabato's family seems to revel in his misery—but could there be more to their torment than meets the eye?
COMEDY
OT
OLDER TEEN AGE 16+
© MITSUKAZU MIHARA

STOP!

This is the back of the book.
You wouldn't want to spoil a great ending!

This book is printed "manga-style," in the authentic Japanese right-to-left format. Since none of the artwork has been flipped or altered, readers get to experience the story just as the creator intended. You've been asking for it, so TOKYOPOP® delivered: authentic, hot-off-the-press, and far more fun!

DIRECTIONS

If this is your first time reading manga-style, here's a quick guide to help you understand how it works.

It's easy... just start in the top right panel and follow the numbers. Have fun, and look for more 100% authentic manga from TOKYOPOP®!